The Dynamic Constitution

The Dynamic Constitution

A Historical Bibliography

Suzanne Robitaille Ontiveros
Editor

Foreword By
Ralph Clark Chandler

ABC-CLIO

Santa Barbara, California
Oxford, England

This book is Smyth sewn and printed on acid-free paper to meet library standards.

Library of Congress Cataloging-in-Publication Data

The Dynamic Constitution.

√ (ABC-Clio research guides ; 19)
   Includes index.
   1. United States—Constitutional history—Bibliography.
I. Ontiveros, Suzanne R.   II. Series.
KF4541.D95   1986   016.34273'029   86-20618
ISBN 0-87436-470-1   016.34730229

ABC-Clio, Inc.
2040 Alameda Padre Serra, Box 4397
Santa Barbara, California 93140-4397

Clio Press Ltd.
55 St. Thomas Street
Oxford, OX1 1JG, England

Manufactured in the United States of America.

ABC-CLIO RESEARCH GUIDES

The ABC-CLIO Research Guides are designed to provide convenient coverage of the recent journal literature on high-interest topics in history and the related social sciences. These annotated bibliographies are prepared by editor/historians and other subject specialists from ABC-CLIO's comprehensive history data bases.

The unique subject profile index (ABC-SPIndex), which carries both generic and specific index terms, presents a profile of the indexed article, allowing precise and rapid access to the entries.

The titles in this series are prepared to save researchers, students, and librarians the considerable time and expense usually associated with accessing materials manually or through online searching. ABC-CLIO's Research Guides offer unmatched reference to significant scholarly articles on the topics of most current interest to historians and social scientists.

ABC-CLIO RESEARCH GUIDES

Pamela R. Byrne, Executive Editor
Suzanne R. Ontiveros, Managing Editor

1. **World War II from an American Perspective** *(1982)*; ISBN 0-87436-035-8

2. **The Jewish Experience in America** *(1982)*; ISBN 0-87436-034-X

3. **Nuclear America** *(1983)*; ISBN 0-87436-360-8

4. **The Great Depression** *(1983)*; ISBN 0-87436-361-6

5. **Corporate America** *(1983)*; ISBN 0-87436-362-4

6. **Crime and Punishment in America** *(1983)*; ISBN 0-87436-363-2

7. **The Democratic and Republican Parties** *(1983)*; ISBN 0-87436-364-0

8. **The American Electorate** *(1983)*; ISBN 0-87436-372-1

9. **The Weimar Republic** *(1984)*; ISBN 0-87436-378-0

10. **The Third Reich, 1933-1939** *(1984)*; ISBN 0-87436-379-9

11. **The Third Reich at War** *(1984)*; ISBN 0-87436-393-4

12. **American Family History** *(1984)*; ISBN 0-87436-380-2

13. **Sino-Soviet Conflict** *(1985)*; ISBN 0-87436-382-0

14. **The United States in East Asia** *(1985)*; ISBN 0-87436-452-3

15. **Women in the Third World** *(1986)*; ISBN 0-87436-459-0

16. **Global Terrorism** *(1986)*; ISBN 0-87436-453-1

17. **American Maritime History** *(1986)*; ISBN 0-87436-471-X

18. **Latinos in the United States** *(1986)*; ISBN 0-87436-458-2

19. **The Dynamic Constitution** *(1986)*; ISBN 0-87436-470-1

RELATED TITLES PUBLISHED BY ABC-CLIO

CONGRESS AND LAW-MAKING: Researching the Legislative Process. Robert U. Goehlert. (ABC-CLIO, 1979.)

THE CONSTITUTIONAL LAW DICTIONARY. Ralph C. Chandler, Richard A. Enslen, and Peter G. Renstrom. (ABC-CLIO, 1984.)

THE DICTIONARY OF POLITICAL ANALYSIS. Second Edition. Jack C. Plano, Robert E. Riggs, and Helenan S. Robin. (ABC-CLIO, 1982.)

THE PRESIDENCY: A Research Guide. Robert U. Goehlert and Fenton S. Martin. (ABC-CLIO, 1984.)

THE PRESIDENTIAL-CONGRESSIONAL POLITICAL DICTIONARY. Jeffrey M. Elliot and Sheikh R. Ali. (ABC-CLIO, 1984.)

CONTENTS

LIST OF ABBREVIATIONS

A.	Author-prepared Abstract	*Illus.*	Illustrated, Illustration
Acad.	Academy, Academie, Academia	*Inst.*	Institute, Institut-.
Agric.	Agriculture, Agricultural	*Int.*	International, Internacional,
AIA	Abstracts in Anthropology		Internationaal, Internationaux,
Akad.	Akademie		Internazionale
Am.	America, American	*J.*	Journal, Journal-prepared Abstract
Ann.	Annals, Annales, Annual, Annali	*Lib.*	Library, Libraries
Anthrop.	Anthropology, Anthropological	*Mag.*	Magazine
Arch.	Archives	*Mus.*	Museum, Musee, Museo
Archaeol.	Archaeology, Archaeological	*Nac.*	Nacional
Art.	Article	*Natl.*	National, Nationale
Assoc.	Association, Associate	*Naz.*	Nazionale
Biblio.	Bibliography, Bibliographical	*Phil.*	Philosophy, Philosophical
Biog.	Biography, Biographical	*Photo.*	Photograph
Bol.	Boletim, Boletin	*Pol.*	Politics, Political, Politique, Politico
Bull.	Bulletin	*Pr.*	Press
c.	century (in index)	*Pres.*	President
ca.	circa	*Pro.*	Proceedings
Can.	Canada, Canadian, Canadien	*Publ.*	Publishing, Publication
Cent.	Century	*Q.*	Quarterly
Coll.	College	*Rev.*	Review, Revue, Revista, Revised
Com.	Committee	*Riv.*	Rivista
Comm.	Commission	*Res.*	Research
Comp.	Compiler	*RSA*	Romanian Scientific Abstracts
DAI	Dissertation Abstracts	*S.*	Staff-prepared Abstract
	International	*Sci.*	Science, Scientific
Dept.	Department	*Secy.*	Secretary
Dir.	Director, Direktor	*Soc.*	Society, Societe, Sociedad,
Econ.	Economy, Econom-.		Societa
Ed.	Editor, Edition	*Sociol.*	Sociology, Sociological
Educ.	Education, Educational	*Tr.*	Transactions
Geneal.	Genealogy, Genealogical,	*Transl.*	Translator, Translation
	Genealogique	*U.*	University, Universi-.
Grad.	Graduate	*US*	United States
Hist.	History, Hist-.	*Vol.*	Volume
IHE	Indice Historico Espanol	*Y.*	Yearbook

FOREWORD

At the birth of societies, the rulers of republics establish institutions; and afterwards, the institutions mould the rulers.

—Montesquieu

When the 55 men we now call the founding fathers gathered in Philadelphia that hot summer of 1787, only a few of them had any intention of writing a new Constitution. The Continental Congress had instructed them to convene "for the sole and express purpose of revising the Articles of Confederation" under which the former colonies were now loosely governed—too loosely according to some. It soon became apparent to all the delegates, however, that the old Articles were just too ramshackle to be fixed. A new document had to be written, a new form of government devised, a new beginning made, if the young nation were to survive against European and internal invitations to disunity. Because the Articles of Confederation deprived the central government of any real power over the individual states, a host of problems had arisen over domestic and foreign commerce, the national debt, and internal and external security.

With the possible exception of Periclean Athens and late Republican Rome, there had never been so much political genius assembled in one generation. The founders were eminently well-qualified for the task they set themselves. They were learned in the law, particularly in the common law of England. They were widely read in political theory, particularly in that of John Locke and the Baron de Montesquieu. They were devotees of the new science of economics, aware that the Declaration of Independence and Adam Smith's *The Wealth of Nations* had been published in the same year. They were men of letters, and they were practical men, many of them having played leading roles in the drafting of their state constitutions. Only the great Jefferson was not among them. He was in France representing American interests, explaining to the Europeans, and buying time for the upstart nation to establish itself.

The framers faced formidable problems of consensus building among themselves. The Connecticut Compromise attempted to balance the interests of small and large states. Another agreement guaranteed to the commercial North the federal protection of all trade, while to the agrarian South it guaranteed freedom from export taxes and the right to continue the slave trade until at least the year 1808. The memory of the excessive power of the royal governors assured concord on a clear separation of the powers of government in the new Constitution. In yet another compromise between direct popular election, considered dangerously populist, and election by state legislatures, considered too great a concession to state sovereignty, the Convention approved the election of the President by an electoral college. The states' rights group in Philadelphia successfully insisted on the powers of Congress being enumerated rather than broad and unspecified. To win this concession, however, they had to support the Necessary and Proper Clause of Article I, Section 8, which did in fact give Congress wide discretionary powers. And so on. The Constitution was and is a document of compromise.

The fact that the framers chose to reconcile their differences and provide for continuing dialogue about the development of American government has given Americans of all subsequent generations the legacy of a living Constitution. The words of our fundamental law take on different meaning and are interpreted in different ways as social needs change. The authoritative interpreter of the Constitution, and the umpire of the federal system, is the Supreme Court of the United States. Its pathfinding Chief Justice, John Marshall, summarized the Court's function in *McCulloch v. Maryland* (1819): "It is a Constitution we are expounding, intended to endure for ages to come and consequently to be adapted to the various crises of human affairs."

The Constitutional Convention and its work product have enormous psychological importance in American life. The Convention is to us what the story of Aeneas was to Athens and the legend of Romulus was to Rome: a normative founding event. The Constitution is the symbol of the authority of the state. It is our sacred text. Those who exegete it wear the black robes of the secular priesthood. American statesmen habitually invoke its spirit to support the policies of the day. Increasingly, however, such invocations take place in a context that is hostile to the consensus which emerged in Philadelphia. "Getting back to the spirit of the founding fathers" is usually an easily deciphered code for reducing the scope of government. The assumption is that the framers of the Constitution would disapprove of the power of the federal government today. In allowing government to become so powerful, we have somehow betrayed our heritage.

There is no doubt the framers would be amazed at what the government they created has become, but it is not clear they would disapprove. The framers were unalterably committed to the preservation of individual rights as the purpose of government, but they did not see such rights in competition with governmental power in a zero sum game. In the debates at the Convention and in *The Federalist* papers one of the major arguments in favor of the new Constitution was that a strong government is needed to protect individual rights. Among the advocates of a strong government were George Washington, James Madison, Benjamin Franklin, and Alexander Hamilton. The moderate nationalists included Oliver Ellsworth, Eldridge Gerry, George Mason, and Roger Sherman. The strong state sovereignty representatives included Gunning Bedford, John Lansing, William Peterson, and Robert Yates. All agreed on the social contract, however: that there is a common interest in liberty which brings civilized people together to draft constitutions and form governments. Thirty-nine of the 55 delegates signed the Constitution as a promissory note to which every American has fallen heir.

Madison and Yates kept careful notes of the Convention proceedings. We have newspaper accounts, tracts, and pamphlets detailing the long and furious debate over ratification of the Constitution which took place prior to and during the state ratifying conventions before the requisite ninth state, New Hampshire, said yes on June 21, 1788. By reading these sources we can learn of the striking similarities of the arguments in the late 1780s and the late 1980s over the proper role of government in American society.

The strong and moderate nationalists joined forces in Philadelphia to create a document that today consists of a preamble of purpose, a body of articles, and a series of amendments. The preamble reads as follows:

> *We the people of the United States, in order to form a more perfect union, establish justice, insure domestic tranquility, provide for the common defense, promote the general welfare, and secure the blessings of liberty to ourselves and our posterity, do ordain and establish this Constitution for the United States of America.*

The body of articles regulates the following subjects: (I) the legislative branch; (II) the executive branch; (III) the judicial branch; (IV) the relation of the states to each other and to the central government, the admission of new states, and the regulation of territories; (V) the methods of amending the Constitution; (VI) provisions for the national debt, the oath required of all state and federal officials to support the federal Constitution, laws, and treaties as ''the supreme law of the land,'' and the prohibition of religious tests for officeholders; and (VII) provisions for ratification of the Constitution.

In the 200 years since the Constitution was written, 26 amendments have been ratified. They may be classified by historical period: (1) early amendments (Amendments 1-12), 1791-1804, dealing with the elaboration of individual rights, judicial power, and the electoral process; (2) Reconstruction Era amendments (Amendments 13-15), 1865-1870, dealing with slavery, the definition and prerogatives of citizenship, and voting rights; (3) Progressive Era amendments (Amendments 16-19 and Amendment 21), 1913-1933, dealing with the personal income tax, popular election of United States Senators, prohibition, the right of women to vote, and the repeal of prohibition; (4) procedural amendments (Amendment 20 and Amendments 22-25), 1933-1967, dealing with the terms of the President and Vice President, the electoral representation of the District of Columbia, the outlawing of the poll tax, and the succession to the presidency; and (5) social reform amendments (Amendment 26), 1971-present, dealing with the right of eighteen-year-old citizens to vote. (Two amendments currently under consideration for adoption also fall into this category: the Equal Rights Amendment and the Right to Life Amendment.)

In terms of the Constitution's historical development, the student of constitutional history is aware that the federal Constitution of 1787-1789 is really the second Constitution of the United States. The first was the Articles of Confederation drafted in 1777, ratified in 1781, and in place until the current Constitution was put into effect on March 4, 1789. The development of the Constitution since that time is marked by various phases of interpretation. The most critical phase was the first one.

Thomas Jefferson returned from France in 1789 eventually to lead the antifederalist cause and gain election to the presidency. The Federalists realized by the waning days of John Adams' term that they could no longer command the electoral strength necessary to continue their nationalizing policies. Jefferson's dictum, "that government governs best which governs least" was the wave of the future. This opinion would in fact describe constitutional interpretation for a long time with the crucial exception of the years 1801-1835.

On January 20, 1801, six weeks before Jefferson's inauguration, President Adams sent to the Federalist Senate for its approval the name of his 45-year-old Secretary of State, John Marshall, to be Chief Justice of the Supreme Court. Marshall was Jefferson's cousin and avowed political enemy, referred to by Jefferson as "that gloomy malignity." That gloomy malignity served as Chief Justice for over 34 years and imprinted Federalist policies on the Constitution and the nation with a distinction that can only be categorized as *sui generis*. Twenty-five years after he appointed Marshall, Adams said, "My gift of John Marshall to the people of the United States was the proudest act of my life."

Marshall handed down four of the most momentous decisions in the nation's history: (1) *Marbury* v. *Madison* (1803), which established the doctrine of judicial review of all legislative acts and the supremacy of the Constitution; (2) *McCulloch* v. *Maryland* (1819), which reaffirmed the supremacy of the Constitution and said the federal government derived its power directly from the people rather than from the states; (3) *Dartmouth College* v. *Woodward* (1819), which upheld the inviolability of contracts; and (4) *Gibbons* v. *Ogden* (1824), which established plenary federal authority over interstate and foreign commerce. In these and other opinions the Federalist dreams of a powerful nation found articulation and sanction. Lord Bryce, Britain's Ambassador to the United States from 1907 to 1913 and a close student of American democracy, spoke of Marshall's decisions as "never having been surpassed and rarely equaled by the most famous jurists of modern Europe or of ancient Rome."

In the next phase of American constitutional history, Marshall's defense of federal supremacy and of inviolate rights yielded to Chief Justice Roger B. Taney's emphasis on community rights as a limitation on property rights. Then came Salmon P. Chase's defense of local sovereignty against federal legislation. Then there was a return to Marshall's constitutional interpretations by Stephen J. Field, Joseph P. Bradley, and Melville W. Fuller. Permission for broad federal regulation was generally granted by the Court in the Progressive Era. Then came a new Court's staunch property-oriented opposition to New Deal legislation that lasted until 1937, when it began to concentrate on guarantees of personal rights. The eras and the emphases of judicial policymaking change, while the process of change itself continues to be the chief characteristics of the constitutional system.

Always the Supreme Court is dealing with case law, not with theoretical constructs, and it is studying the evolution of the political, economic, and moral climate of the nation as these factors must influence the interpretation and enforcement of constitutional law. Any citizen at any time can enter the adjudication process and defeat the entire administrative state. The world marvels at that, as well as the remarkable stability of a government that gets challenged so often. The Constitution of the United

States is the oldest documentary constitution in force in the modern world. It endures because it is still an unfinished work. Each generation of Americans provides new framers to devise ways to secure the blessings of libery to ourselves and our posterity.

Ralph Clark Chandler
Western Michigan University
June 1986

PREFACE

To honor the upcoming bicentennial of the Constitution of the United States, this 19th title in the ABC-CLIO Research Guides series brings together in a single bibliographic sourcebook the scholarship in history on the Constitution.

The first of the series to offer coverage of books and dissertations, *THE DYNAMIC CONSTITUTION* contains 1370 citations drawn from ABC-CLIO's comprehensive history database, which covers over 2,000 periodicals published in some 90 countries. In creating this annotated bibliography, the editors reviewed thousands of article, book, and dissertation citations and selected only those relevant to the subject. Within chronological chapters, entries are arranged by document type and then alphabetically by author. Chapter 1 includes historiography, bibliography, and overviews of constitutional history too broad to fall into any one chronological section. Chapter 2 covers constitutionalism from 1777 to 1787; Chapter 3 the Constitutional Convention and the ratification of the Constitution, 1787 to 1790. Chapters 4 and 5 include the development of the Constitution from 1790 to 1900 and 1900 to 1985, respectively.

Additional access to the abstracts and citations in *THE DYNAMIC CONSTITUTION* is provided through ABC-SPIndex (Subject Profile Index), a highly specific subject index. Key subject terms are linked with the historical dates to form a complete profile of the articles, books, and dissertations. Each set of index terms is rotated alphabetically so the complete profile appears under each of the subject terms. Thus, the accuracy and specificity of subject access is enhanced as compared to conventional, hierarchical indexes. Care has been taken to eliminate inconsistencies that might have appeared in the subject index as a result of merging many years of database material. The explanatory note at the beginning of the subject index provides further information for using ABC-SPIndex.

To the worldwide community of scholars who wrote the citations that comprise *THE DYNAMIC CONSTITUTION: A HISTORICAL BIBLIOGRAPHY,* we extend our sincere appreciation.

1

HISTORIOGRAPHY, BIBLIOGRAPHY, AND AN OVERVIEW

Article Abstracts

1. Adams, Willi Paul. "THE SPIRIT OF COMMERCE REQUIRES THAT PROPERTY BE SACRED": GOUVERNEUR MORRIS AND THE AMERICAN REVOLUTION. *Amerikastudien/Am. Studies [West Germany] 1976 21(2): 309-334.* The New York lawyer, businessman and politician Gouverneur Morris (1752-1816) was an active force in the movement for American independence and for the subsequent establishment of a strong central government. The following article consists of an edition of four Morris documents and an interpretation. In his letter of May 20, 1774, (document 1) Morris still hoped for reunion. In his speech before New York's Provincial Congress in May or June 1776 (document 2) he argued that "independence is absolutely necessary." In his essay "Political Enquiries" of 1776 or 1777 (document 3) he gives us an example of how Lockean and other political theory had filtered down to the level of an active politician's convictions. In an address of circa 1800 (document 4) Morris provides further evidence for the astonishing vision of national greatness that motivated a considerable number of the men who had fought for the constitution of 1787/88. The introduction concludes that just as the American Revolution was not a political process firmly under the control of any one tightly organized group, so the political theory and the values espoused were not of a monolithic nature. From its beginning, the consensus upon which the American nation state was founded contained within itself a plebiscitarian as well as an elitist element, localist agrarian values as well as cosmopolitan commercial values, and a great distrust of powerful men and institutions as well as the desire to see powerful agencies protect the nation's interests. Gouverneur Morris was an articulate representative of the more elitist and more commercially and more nationally minded political leaders of 1776 and 1787.   J

2. Agria, John J. CONSTITUTIONAL BASIS OF EXECUTIVE IMPOUNDMENT. *Michigan Acadmician 1974 7(2): 157-165.*

3.   Anderson, Alexis J. THE FORMATIVE PERIOD OF FIRST AMEND-
MENT HISTORY, 1870-1915. *Am. J. of Legal Hist. 1980 24(1): 56-75.* An
assessment of the historiography of free speech from the First Amendment,
1791, through 1915, centering on the transition era of 1870-1915, when "a new
concept of freedom of speech developed which freed it from the mainstream of
democratic principles." Lawsuits from municipal and state institutions arising
from the Bill of Rights or state constitutions show how test cases of minority
groups and individuals against alleged repression of their First Amendment
rights at the municipal and state level laid the groundwork for the protection
of free speech in the modern era. The use of police power in theory and
practice is a recurrent theme. 98 notes.   L. A. Knafla

4.   Angermann, Erich. DER DEUTSCHE FRÜHKONSTITUTIONALIS-
MUS UND DAS AMERIKANISCHE VORBILD [The early stages of
constitutionalism in Germany and the American example]. *Hist. Zeitschrift
[West Germany] 1974 219(1): 1-32.* Although much has been written about
the American model as a guide for German liberals of the *Vormärz* period,
they probably did not understand the complicated American constitution. They
attempted to adapt part of it to a monarchical system but the principles were
incompatible. The American constitution grew out of a long period of tumult
and revolt. The men of the *Vormärz* feared that such violence would only
strengthen the reactionaries. 56 notes.   G. H. Davis

5.   Aron, Raymond. THE AMERICAN EXPERIENCE: UNIQUE OR
UNIVERSAL? *Atlantic Community Q. 1976 14(3): 306-313.* Raymond Aron,
author, journalist and professor at the European Center of Historical Sociology
(Paris) looks again at De Tocqueville's America. Whether America was "a
unique adventure" or the wave of the future, Aron concludes that "the free
world, more than ever, needs leadership from the last great western power."
                                                                              J

6.   Bedau, Hugo Adam. THE PROBLEM OF CAPITAL PUNISHMENT.
Current Hist. 1976 71(418): 14-18, 34. Touches on the history of the controversy over the death penalty since the initial organized protests to it in the
1780's, the legal status of capital punishment in the states 1846-1972, the
Supreme Court decision *Furman* v. *Georgia* (US, 1972) which called it cruel
and unusual punishment, and alternatives to it.

7.   Berger, Andrew. ALIEN VENUE: NEITHER NECESSARY NOR
CONSTITUTIONAL. *New York U. J. of Int. Law and Pol. 1976 9(2):
155-176.* "Alien venue was born to fill a gap in venue caused by an alien's
inability to satisfy the general venue statutes. That inability is now over in most
cases. Aliens who are resident here... should be deemed residents for venue
purposes. ... The alien venue statute should now be amended to provide that
it be the last grasp. Only where an alien's contacts with this country are
insufficient to satisfy the other provisions of the venue statue should a plaintiff
be permitted to rest venue anywhere under the alien venue statute. Ideally,
Congress should now modify that statute to so provide. In the absence of
congressional action, there is ample support for a court to reach the same
result."   E. P. Stickney

8.   Berger, Raoul. EXECUTIVE PRIVILEGE IN LIGHT OF UNITED STATES V. NIXON. *Maryland Historian 1975 6(2): 67-78.* Traces the history of executive privilege which was recognized in *United States* v. *Nixon* (US, 1974). Contends that no basis for executive privilege exists in the constitution nor is intent to establish executive privilege evidenced in the commentary of the framers of the constitution. Based on primary and secondary constitutional law sources; 70 notes.   G. O. Gagnon

9.   Bergold, Laurel R. THE CHANGING LEGAL STATUS OF AMERICAN WOMEN. *Current Hist. 1976 70(416): 206-210, 230-231.* Discusses reforms in law regarding the legal status of women from the 19th century to the 1970's, emphasizing marriage, Supreme Court rulings regarding sex discrimination, and the proposed Equal Rights Amendment.

10.   Bickel, Alexander M. NOTES ON THE CONSTITUTION. *Commentary 1975 60(2): 53-57.* Examines the traditions of conservatism and liberalism that go into the interpretation of the Constitution by the Supreme Court.   S

11.   Bickel, Alexander M. THE "UNINHIBITED, ROBUST, AND WIDE OPEN" FIRST AMENDMENT. *Commentary 1972 54(5): 60-67.* Discusses court decisions concerning freedom of speech.   S

12.   Blaustein, Albert P. and Mersky, Roy M. RATING SUPREME COURT JUSTICES. *Am. Bar Assoc. J. 1972 58(11): 1183-1189.* Sixty-five school deans and professors of law, history and political science have attempted to evaluate the Supreme Court Justices with service on the high court from its establishment until just prior to the appointment of Chief Justice Burger in 1969. Perhaps their conclusions will be of help in future selection of Justices.   J

13.   Brigham, John. PROPERTY & THE SUPREME COURT: DO THE JUSTICES MAKE SENSE? *Polity 1983 16(2): 242-262.* Examines the Supreme Court's tradition with reference to property claims and how it has settled them. The basic understanding of the concept of property would seem to have remained stable over time, but new forms to which it applies have appeared in response to changing socioeconomic and political conditions. Property rights in titles, offices, grants, and franchises—among others—have been asserted and sustained. Since the idea of settled expectations is central to such assertions and determinations, it makes sense to regard statutory entitlements as property under the Constitution.   J

14.   Burnham, James. AND THE SWORD. *Marine Corps Gazette 1960 44(10): 10-14.* Examines how the war powers of Congress and the President have changed since the promulgation of the Constitution of the United States, with particular reference to the ability of contemporary presidents to wage war without Congress's expressed consent by dubbing war a "police action."

15.   Burns, James MacGregor and Morris, Richard B. THE CONSTITUTION: THIRTEEN CRUCIAL QUESTIONS. *This Constitution 1983 (1): 4-8.* Surveys 13 issues of constitutional law, such as the balance of power

between the branches of the federal government, and the extent of individual civil rights.

16.   Cannon, Mark W. ADMINISTRATIVE CHANGE AND THE SU-PREME COURT. *Judicature 1974 57(8): 334-341.*

17.   Carey, George W. and McClellan, James. TOWARDS THE RESTORA-TION OF THE AMERICAN POLITICAL TRADITION. *J. of Pol. 1976 38(3): 110-127.* A study of the history and relation of the liberal and conservative traditions in American political life beginning with the Declaration of Independence and the Constitution which according to much current thought reflect these two traditions respectively. Current liberal efforts at reinterpreting the tradition to give support to their case should help us to realize more clearly the enduring elements in our tradition relating to the values, assumptions, and goals of those structuring our form of government. These include "an hostility toward direct.. . plebiscitary democracy" to offset the possible evils of faction, the maintenance of the division of powers because of their "distrust of government." 56 notes.   R. V. Ritter

18.   Carson, Clarence B. THE FOUNDING OF THE AMERICAN RE-PUBLIC. *Freeman 1972 22(5): 273-283, (6): 341-354, (7): 419-433, (8): 471-485, (9): 550-561, (10): 616-627, (11): 684-699, (12): 734-736, 1973 23(1): 31-44, (2): 85-98, (3): 165-182, (4): 195-206.* Continued from a previous article. Part X. A unique document, the American Declaration of Independence from Great Britain was a carefully rationalized justification of majority revolution; but its most enduring and essential message was its affirmation of what constitutes a good and proper government. 3 notes. Part XI. Traces civilian and military difficulties encountered by Americans in their struggle for independence, from the declaration of war to Valley Forge. 10 notes. Part XII. The most serious obstacle to the patriot war effort of the Revolution was inflation, the product of deficit financing and issuance of fiat money by the American governments. 38 notes. Part XIII. Considers ingredients of victory for the patriot cause: the war in the South which culminated in the glory of Yorktown; the happy, however inadequate, solution to the necessity for federated government, limited by the first written constitution of the United States; the double achievement of victory and empire negotiated at Paris; and the successful disbandment of the Army and the return of George Washington to Virginia without a crown. 14 notes. Part XIV. Changes in America after the Revolutionary War were directed toward freeing the individual citizen. 21 notes. Part XV. The impotence of the state and federal governments contributed to the series of domestic and international crises between 1782 and 1787 that in turn led to the call for a constitutional convention. 19 notes. Part XVI. Reviews the background of the participants and the issues at Philadelphia in 1787 at the Constitutional Convention. 29 notes. Part XVII. Examines the unique applications of political philosophy discussed and adopted by the Constitutional Convention: federal system, republican form of government, separation and balance of powers, limited government, and transformation of empire (state making). 19 notes. Part XVIII. The passage of the Bill of Rights was essential to the ratification of the U.S. Constitution, because without amendment there was no check against a consolidated government and no

guarantee of individual freedom. 6 notes. Part XIX. Discusses the founding fathers' problems in making the federal government a reality in 1789. 15 notes. Part XX. Reviews the Washington administrations with particular emphasis on the unified program of Hamilton, which is defended, and the development of political parties. 15 notes. Part XXI. Concludes series with praise for the American revolutionaries, because they always kept their ideal in sight— "ordered liberty." From the author's *Rebirth of Liberty: The Founding of the American Republic, 1760-1800* (New Rochelle, N.Y.: Arlington House, 1973).
           D. A. Yanchisin

19. Casper, Gerhard. AMERICAN GEHEIMNISKRÄMEREI *R. in Am. Hist. 1975 3(2): 154-158.* Raoul Berger's *Executive Privilege: A Constitutional Myth* (Cambridge: Harvard U. Pr., 1974) examines the basis in constitutional law of executive privilege and governmental *Geheimniskrämerei* (petty secretiveness) since the 18th century, particularly in light of *United States v. Nixon* (US, 1974).

20. Ceaser, James W. POLITICAL PARTIES AND PRESIDENTIAL AMBITION. *J. of Pol. 1978 40(3): 708-739.* The recent decline in the role of parties during presidential elections is a direct result of decisions by party commissions and state legislatures to open the nomination process. Both the authors of *The Federalist Papers* and the originators of permanent party competition (notably Martin Van Buren) sought electoral processes which regulated candidate behavior. On the contrary, Populist and Progressive movements (and Woodrow Wilson) sought a system which would elevate a dynamic leader above his party. A balance between these positions maintained the mixed system of candidate-oriented primaries and organization-dominated selection procedures until the post-1968 Democratic Party reforms. Primary and secondary sources; 59 notes.   A. W. Novitsky

21. Chadbourn, Erika S. DOCUMENTING THE AMERICAN LEGAL SCENE: THE MANUSCRIPT DIVISION OF THE HARVARD LAW SCHOOL LIBRARY. *Harvard Lib. Bull. 1982 30(1): 55-73.* The Harvard Law School Library Manuscript Division has some 100 collections with 1.25 million items covering 1861 to the present. Although this collection is not large, it is extremely significant. For the most part it has been processed, and inventories are available. Since the material relates to people or subjects connected with the Harvard Law School, it includes letters and papers of such familiar figures as Supreme Court justices Brandeis, Cardoza, Holmes, and Frankfurter. In addition, there are numerous groups of papers pertaining to specific episodes, such as the Sacco-Vanzetti case. Perhaps the most complete collection is that of Judge Learned Hand, who saved all of his papers concerned with his lengthy career. Largely primary documents from the library; 18 notes.   C. L. Grant

22. Chastenet, Jacques. LA PRESIDENCE DES ÉTATS-UNIS [The Presidency of the United States]. *Nouvelle Rev. des Deux Mondes [France] 1976 (12): 527-533.* Traces the evolution of the office and powers of the Presidency from the ratification of the Constitution to the term of Jimmy Carter.

23. Chaudhuri, Joyotpaul. AMERICAN INDIAN POLICY: AN OVER-VIEW OF THE LEGAL COMPLEXITIES, CONTROVERSIES, AND DILEMMAS. *Social Sci. J. 1982 19(3): 9-21.* Discusses the sources of American Indian law, including the Constitution, statutes, agreements, and court decisions; the various communities of Indians and individuals affected by Indian law; the limits of tribal authority; and the rights of Indians; and concludes that a lack of thought exists in judicial and legislative policy.

24. Chaudhuri, Joyotpaul. JEFFERSON'S UNHEAVENLY CITY: A BI-CENTENNIAL LOOK. *Am. J. of Econ. and Sociol. 1975 34(4): 397-410.* Discusses the modern concepts in Thomas Jefferson's political theory and reveals philosophical differences between Jefferson and John Locke.

25. Cohen, William. FREEDOM TO BE FOOLISH: THE DOUGLAS INQUIRY. *Center Mag. 1978 11(6): 2-6.* Discusses individual liberty as outlined in the Bill of Rights and as discussed by John Stuart Mill; on the basis of these, examines the work of the Supreme Court in upholding individual liberties, citing specific cases and issues.

26. Colbourn, H. Trevor. JOHN DICKINSON: HISTORICAL REVOLU-TIONARY. *Pennsylvania Mag. of Hist. and Biog. 1959 83(3): 271-292.* Discusses the philosophical and political background of American statesman John Dickinson, focusing on his stance toward the American Revolution, which he supported in theory, although he would not sign the Declaration of Independence in 1776, and examines how his personal library and reading could have affected his political views.

27. Commager, Henry Steele. COMMITMENT TO POSTERITY: WHERE DID IT GO? *Am. Heritage 1976 27(5): 4-7.* The United States has main-tained the institutions of the Founding Fathers while largely betraying their principles. The Founding Fathers looked to posterity for vindication, as the future belonged to America. Today Americans do not look to posterity, perhaps because with the threat of nuclear holocaust, they foresee no posterity. Illus.   J. F. Paul

28. Coontz, Stephanie. WATERGATE AND THE CONSTITUTION. *Internat. Socialist R. 1974 35(1): 12-17, 31-33.* Discussion of the Constitution, how it came into being, its interpretation by various presidents, and its relation to the Watergate Scandal.   S

29. Cover, Robert M. LEGAL TENSIONS IN THE POLITICS OF FREE-DOM. *Rev. in Am. Hist. 1974 2(4): 529-535.* Review article prompted by Thomas D. Morris' *Free Men All: The Personal Liberty Laws of the North, 1780-1861* (Baltimore: The Johns Hopkins U. Pr., 1974) which outlines the book's contents, describes its organization, discusses its shortcomings as an interpretive work, and notes its utility as an information source for antebellum political and constitutional history.

30. Cuddihy, William and Hardy, B. Carmon. A MAN'S HOUSE WAS NOT HIS CASTLE: ORIGINS OF THE FOURTH AMENDMENT TO

THE UNITED STATES CONSTITUTION. *William and Mary Q. 1980 37(3): 371-400.* Outlines developments in English statutes and common law pertaining to search, and their application. The man's-house-as-castle ideal is derived from earlier rather than later experience. The degree of discretionary intrusion varied according to one's place in the social order—the poor had little protection against search. The 18th century witnessed a vast expansion in discretionary search. Emphasizes court cases for the mid- and third quarter of the 18th century. Relates the transplanting of English methods of search and seizure to the American colonies. General search warrants were permitted; only Massachusetts had strict confinement of search. Concludes that up to the formulating of the Bill of Rights, general search was the rule. Based on legislative and court records in England and America; 128 notes.

H. M. Ward

31. Damon, Allan L. CONGRESS. *Am. Heritage 1974 25(6): 51-52, 90-93.* Congress' constitutional powers and political procedures.   S

32. Damon, Allan L. A LOOK AT THE RECORD: THE CABINET. *Am. Heritage 1976 27(3): 50-53, 90-91.* A brief history of the role of the cabinet in the executive branch of the government. Members of the cabinet are subordinate, and consequently rarely achieve great notoriety. The lack of constitutional directives has resulted in the determination of the cabinet's role largely by the will of the presidents. Includes a resumé of the types of persons (527 to date) who have served in the cabinet, and a brief history of each of the current executive departments.   J. F. Paul

33. Daniel, Josiah M., III. "CHIEF JUSTICE OF THE UNITED STATES": HISTORY AND HISTORIOGRAPHY OF THE TITLE. *Supreme Court Hist. Soc. Y. 1983: 109-112.* The title "Chief Justice of the United States" was fixed by law as early as 1787. Many are unaware of the exact title, as three variations have been used by Congress itself. In 1948, the correct title was finally recorded in the codification of the United States statutes. 36 notes, illus.   G. B. Childress

34. Daniels, O. C. Bobby. THE BICENTENNIAL: CONTRADICTIONS IN AMERICAN DEMOCRACY. *Black Scholar 1976 7(10): 2-6.* Sees contradictions inherent in the Declaration of Independence, the Constitution, and the Presidency. A passage of the initial draft of the Declaration of Independence condemning slavery was deleted from the final draft by slaveholders. This indicates that the black American was never supposed to share the unalienable rights given to white Americans. The Constitution has as its moral guardians blacks and women, although both were excluded from its writing. The blacks' constant struggle for civil rights has strengthened the nation and the Constitution. Presidents from Washington to Ford have reflected racism; even men such as Jefferson and Lincoln are frequently pictured as friends of the Negro only because of the historical myths that surround them. Based on primary and secondary sources; illus., 6 notes.   B. D. Ledbetter

35. Dauer, Manning J. THE IMPACT OF THE AMERICAN INDEPENDENCE AND THE AMERICAN CONSTITUTION: 1776-1848; WITH A

BRIEF EPILOGUE. *J. of Pol. 1976 38(3): 37-55.* Examines the political influence of the American experience with self-government from a pluralistic perspective. The American tradition can best be understood as a part of the Enlightenment. Examines several areas of change: 1) the radical advancement of Whig principles of liberty and self-government, 2) the changes in government and social structure, 3) the rejection of the state church idea, and 4) the reforms in criminal law and public education. The influence of these changes reached into Europe and may be illustrated from English, French, and Polish history and from the numerous revolutionary movements that followed the American constitutional form. 49 notes.   R. V. Ritter

36.   Dauses, Manfred A. and Wolf, Dieter O. A. DIE VERFASSUNGS-RECHTLICHE PROBLEMATIK DER "WAR POWERS" IN DEN VER-EINIGTEN STAATEN [The legal-constitutional problems of the war powers in the United States]. *Politische Vierteljahresschrift [West Germany] 1974 15(2): 213-244.* Analyzes three areas: the right to start a war, the right to carry it on, and restoring the constitutional balance through strengthened parliamentarism. Congress has the right to start a defensive war, but the President also has "sudden repulse power" and does not require the assent of Congress. As the commander-in-chief the President can carry on and end a war, but Congress controls the budget. Since Vietnam Congress has become more vocal about its right to influence foreign policy. An important recent development is the Javits Bill, 1971, which seeks to limit the presidential sudden repulse powers. This is a step toward parliamentarism as distinct from sole presidential control. Based on secondary works and newspapers; 141 notes.   A. Alcock

37.   DeWolf, L. Harold. THE DEATH PENALTY: CRUEL, UNUSUAL, UNETHICAL, AND FUTILE. *Religion in Life 1973 42(1): 37-41.*

38.   Dion, Léon. 1776-1976: LE DÉROULEMENT D'UNE RÉVOLUTION PERMANENTE [1776-1976: the unrolling of a permanent revolution]. *Tr. of the Royal Soc. of Can. [Canada] 1976 14: 71-82.* Discusses the American Revolution and its effect on the world. It has a moral essence before being either political or economic. Free speech remains a fundamental part of the revolutionary inheritance. Such rights are safeguarded by the Constitution. For Europeans the idea of natural rights remains an hypothesis, but Americans see natural rights as a fact. Also, Americans believe in the idea of Manifest Destiny, an inheritance of the covenant between God and his chosen people. In the French Revolution, the leaders recognized that there had been a preexisting government and king. Americans, when creating their country, saw themselves as in a state of nature. The American Revolution is incomplete, and as struggles continue, one wonders whether the United States or some other country will be the revolutionary influence on the world.   J. D. Neville

39.   Dippel, Horst. AMERIKANISCHE UND EUROPÄISCHE REVOLU-TIONSIDEALE BEI THOMAS PAINE [American and European revolutionary ideals in the works of Thomas Paine]. *Amerikastudien/Am. Studies [West Germany] 1976 21(2): 203-215.* Dealing with Paine's political thought, this paper not only intends to discuss his revolutionary ideas of the 1770's through the 1790's but also tries to place them within the context of contemporary

social and political realities in America as well as Europe. During this period of his life, Paine believed above all in reason and its fundamental educational value, in the dualistic structure of human life and the whole world, in the dichotomy of the "people" on one side and aristocracy on the other, in the significance of first principles, and in republicanism. An enemy of ignorance and, what seemed to him identical, of monarchy and hereditary government and a staunch defender of the ideals of the American Revolution and especially of the Pennsylvania Constitution of 1776, he advocated political egalitarianism while at the same time standing up for free enterprise, individual striving, and the idea of the self-made man. Poverty, though it existed in America, appeared to him as an individual problem only and definitely not a social one. On his return to Europe in 1787, when confronted with mass poverty in England and France, his view of poverty changed: what was an individual problem in America assumed the role of the central social problem in Europe. Enlarging his political philosophy by a social component, Paine, in his *Rights of Man,* first formulated the social obligations of property, postulating a progressive income tax as well as an inheritance tax. In no way an attack on private property, his scheme tended to improve the conditions of the lower classes and thereby to benefit society as a whole. Disappointed with the course of the French Revolution, Paine's ideas culminated—in his *Agrarian Justice*—in the demand to complete the political revolution by a social revolution in order to adjust the structure of society to the advanced political principles of a republic.
J

40. Dippel, Horst. SOURCES IN GERMANY FOR THE STUDY OF THE AMERICAN REVOLUTION. *Q. J. of the Lib. of Congress 1976 33(3): 199-217.* Only a few special collections exist in Germany which can throw light on the American Revolution. Because the *Federalist Papers* and Adams' works were never published in German editions, the constitutional aspects remained relatively unknown in Germany. Although Germany had no diplomatic representation in America, correspondence revealing the German government's attitude toward the Revolution is available, since German diplomatic representation existed in most major European centers where information on the Revolution was abundant. Many individuals were adversaries of the Revolution though the American call for independence found a ready response among the German bourgeoisie. Illus., 73 notes. E. P. Stickney

41. Dumbrell, John W. and Lees, John D. PRESIDENTIAL POCKET-VETO POWER: A CONSTITUTIONAL ANACHRONISM? *Pol. Studies [Great Britain] 1980 28(1): 109-116.* Analyzes the little-noticed but significant conflict between the US executive and Congress over President Richard M. Nixon's use of the pocket (indirect) veto, 1970-74. Intended as a modified form of the absolute veto, this provision was little used until 1929; precedents were established in 1929 and 1938. An appellate court decision of 1974 went against the executive, which finally conceded defeat in 1975. The episode illustrates the potential for anachronisms to exist in the US constitution and the increasing role played by the courts in adjudicating executive-legislative disputes. Based on congressional, presidential, Supreme Court, and appellate court papers; 27 notes. D. J. Nicholls

42. Dunne, Gerald T. PROPRIETORS—SOMETIMES PREDATORS: EARLY COURT REPORTERS. *Supreme Court Hist. Soc. Y. 1976: 61-72.* Briefly discusses the reporting of the Supreme Court's opinions from 1790 through the 19th century; discusses the law reporting of Alexander James Dallas, William Cranch, Henry Wheaton, Richard Peters, Benjamin Chew Howard, Jeremiah Black, and others.

43. Edel, Wilbur. AMENDING THE CONSTITUTION BY CONVENTION: MYTHS AND REALITIES. *State Government 1982 55(2): 51-56.* Discusses the difficulties, especially in control, in the convocation of a constitutional convention to initiate a balanced-budget amendment to the Constitution; discusses historical precedent.

44. Edelman, Martin. THE CREATIVE CONUNDRUM: LAW & SOCIAL VALUES. *Polity 1980 13(1): 113-125.* Essays in *The Moral Foundations of the American Republic,* edited by Robert H. Horwitz (Charlottesville: U. of Virginia, 1977), modify Richard Hofstadter's thesis on the framing of the Constitution by suggesting that the framers were less interested in encouraging a certain set of values than they were in establishing an enduring republic; Morton J. Horwitz, in *The Transformation of American Law, 1780-1860* (Cambridge, Mass.: Harvard U. Pr., 1977), and Grant Gilmore, in *The Ages of American Law* (New Haven, Conn.: Yale U. Pr., 1977), both view the pre-Civil War period as one of legal flexibility and innovation; Gilmore, however, sees a retreat to formalism as a result of the Civil War and a collapse of confidence in the law after World War I, while G. Edward White, in *The American Judicial Tradition* (New York: Oxford U. Pr., 1976), defines the tradition, in the 19th and 20th centuries, as one in which judges have had to justify their power and authority.

45. Eisenach, Eldon J. CULTURAL POLITICS AND POLITICAL THOUGHT: THE AMERICAN REVOLUTION MADE AND REMEMBERED. *Am. Studies 1979 20(1): 71-97.* Explores differing interpretations of the American Revolution by examining the patterns of political-cultural conflicts inherent in the sources used to write these histories. Focuses on three areas of conflict and concern: religion, the role of law in political structures, and constitutionalism. Whig interpretations seem to have been more convincing than progressive historiography. Primary and secondary sources; 60 notes.

J. A. Andrew

46. Engeman, Thomas S. PRESIDENTIAL STATESMANSHIP AND THE CONSTITUTION: THE LIMITS OF PRESIDENTIAL STUDIES. *Rev. of Pol. 1982 44(2): 266-281.* Studies such as Richard Neustadt's *Presidential Power* (1960) and Richard Pious's *The American Presidency* (1979) provide useful analyses of various elements of the presidency; however, they do not fully explain the nature of the executive. The nature of presidential government can be better understood by studying the opinions of "Publius" in the *Federalist* and the statesmanship of Lincoln as they relate to constitutional separation of powers, executive prerogative, and impeachment. While prerogative operates as the true source of executive power, providing the president with the necessary power to govern in the face of political inertia, impeach-

ment acts as the ultimate legislative power and insures democracy. The successful president combines knowledge of democratic principles with the prudent use of his prerogative powers under the Constitution. 44 notes.

G. A. Glovins

47. Ferrando Badía, Juan. EL FEDERALISMO [Federalism]. *Rev. de Estudios Pol. [Spain] 1976 (206-207): 23-76.* Discusses the rise of federalism since the American Constitution of 1787, and analyzes the differences between the federal and centralized government.

48. Foley, William E. SLAVE FREEDOM SUITS BEFORE DRED SCOTT: THE CASE OF MARIE JEAN SCYPION'S DESCENDANTS. *Missouri Hist. Rev. 1984 79(1): 1-23.* Marie Jean Scypion was the daughter of a Natchez woman and a black slave brought from what is now Illinois to St. Louis by her French master. When Spain acquired Louisiana, Governor General Alejandro O'Reilly issued a 1769 decree ending the enslavement of Indians and part Indians. Nevertheless, racism led to the assumption that all blacks and part blacks were slaves. A series of arguments and lawsuits over who, if anyone, owned her culminated in an 1838 US Supreme Court refusal to overturn the Missouri Supreme Court's decision that three of her descendants were free persons. 10 illus., 84 notes.

R. Grove

49. Funston, Richard. THE SUPREME COURT AND CRITICAL ELECTIONS. *Am. Pol. Sci. R. 1975 69(3): 795-811.* Several years ago Professor Robert Dahl argued that the traditional concern over the Supreme Court's power of judicial review was largely unfounded. Dahl demonstrated that seldom, if ever, had the Court been successful in blocking the will of a lawmaking majority. This paper argues that, had Dahl considered his data from a different perspective, he would have discovered that, by virtue of the recruitment process, the Court will rarely even attempt to thwart a law-making majority. Examining Dahl's data in the context of the Survey Research Center's election classification scheme, the paper focuses on the Court's relation to patterns of partisan change to show that the traditional philosophic concern with the counter-majoritarian nature of judicial review is largely divorced from empirical reality and has relevance only during periods of partisan realignment within the political system as a whole. The paper buttresses the argument that the Court's "yea-saying" power is more important than its "nay-saying" power, a realization which can serve as a premise from which a logically consistent justification of the Court's power of judicial review may be dialectically constructed.

J

50. Gallardo, Ricardo. THE FORGING OF A FEDERAL GOVERNMENT. *Américas (Organization of Am. States) 1976 28(11/12): 12-16.* Discusses the debates over federalism in the process of establishing a federal government in the United States and points out reasons for its relative success, while concurrently establishing a basis for its failure in Latin American countries, 1825-50.

51. García Labrado, Francisco. CONDICIONAMIENTOS DEL PROBLEMA DE LA AYUDA ECONÓMICA ESTATAL A LA PRENSA EN

ESTADOS UNIDOS [Conditions of the problem of state economic aid in the US press]. *Rev. Española de la Opinión Pública [Spain] 1974 (35): 123-152.* Discusses constitutional and historical conditions in the United States since 1791, and examines the question of state aid from the political and economic points of view, stressing the influence of economic factors and the role of the press since the 1930's.

52.   Garfinkel, Herbert. MARTIN DIAMOND: TEACHER-SCHOLAR OF THE DEMOCRATIC REPUBLIC. *Publius 1978 8(3): 123-127.* Martin Diamond, Winston M. Fisk, and Herbert Garfinkel wrote *The Democratic Republic,* an American government text, to counteract the prevailing political science orthodoxy of the 1950's and 1960's; this orthodoxy, the new formalism, portrayed the Constitution as a deliberate effort to create a nondemocratic republic and overemphasized the underlying realities and hidden motives beneath formal constitutional structures and practices.

53.   Garrett, James Leo, Jr. THE "FREE EXERCISE" CLAUSE OF THE FIRST AMENDMENT: RETROSPECT AND PROSPECT. *J. of Church and State 1975 17(3): 393-398.* Discusses legal decisions regarding the religious freedom clauses in the First Amendment of the US Constitution, 1878-1972.

54.   Gobetti, Daniela. "UNA GENEROSA COSTITUZIONE": SOCIETA E POLITICA NEGLI SCRITTI DI THOMAS PAINE ["A generous constitution": society and politics in the writings of Thomas Paine]. *Pensiero Pol. [Italy] 1983 16(1): 83-103.* Thomas Paine derived some of his themes and vocabulary from English "country Whiggism" without sharing its nostalgic conservatism. Especially as regards the social and political consequences of commercial expansion, Paine refused to share Whig pessimism and believed in the special character of American society, where circumstances had created an environment free from oppressive and unjust structures in which the common good could be achieved by the free competition of all interests. 42 notes.
                                                                        J. V. Coutinho

55.   Goetzmann, William. TIME'S AMERICAN ADVENTURES: AMERICAN HISTORIANS AND THEIR WRITING SINCE 1776. *Social Sci. Q. 1976 57(1): 3-48.* Contains a bicentennial review of the course and progress of American historical studies. Covers the rise, development, and fall of major schools of historical thought, including the early Patriotists, the Enlightenment, Romanticism, Professionalism, Progressivism, Modernism, Traditionalism, Symbolism, the Concensus School, Existentialism, and Radicalism. Increasing reports to the effect that history has served its purpose and no longer has a role to play in the modern world seem premature. History is alive and well and can face the future with confidence. Refs., 7 notes.
                                                                        V. L. Human

56.   Goldin, Claudia. AMERICAN SLAVERY: DE JURE AND DE FACTO. *J. of Interdisciplinary Hist. 1979 10(1): 129-135.* Reviews Leslie Howard Owens's *This Species of Property: Slave Life and Culture in the Old South* (New York: Oxford U. Pr., 1976) and William M. Wiecek's *The Sources of Antislavery Constitutionalism in America, 1760-1848* (Ithaca, N.Y.: Cornell U.

Pr., 1977). Wiecek's is an opus of extreme erudition which describes the changing thought of abolitionist groups with respect to slavery's constitutionalism and analyzes the events culminating in the US Constitution's 13th and 14th amendments. Owens's task is to investigate what it meant to be a slave, which goal he does not achieve. Wiecek's goal, however, is easily achieved. The strength of both works is in their narration, not analysis, thus harming somewhat their value to historians. Note.   E. R. Campbell

57.   Gollobin, Ira. THE BILL OF RIGHTS AND THE FOREIGN BORN. *Worldview 1975 18(7-8): 31-35.* Discusses provisions in the Bill of Rights and Constitutional law regarding the residency rights of foreign-born citizens, 1798-1970's, including issues in deportation during the Nixon Administration.

58.   Green, Barbara and Hurwitz, Leon. BIAS IN COLLEGE TEXTBOOKS: THE IMPACT OF CRITICAL EVENTS ON INTERPRETATIONS. *J. of Higher Educ. 1980 51(2): 184-193.* Content analysis of American government textbooks published in the post-McCarthy and post-Watergate eras demonstrates that although underlying interpretations of constitutional issues remained constant, the overall textbook presentations shifted. This highlights the danger of stressing current events to the point that they distort overall presentation of fundamental issues. Biblio.   J

59.   Guerrero, Manuel P. SUBSTANTIVE DUE PROCESS FOR RESIDENT ALIENS. *Aztlán 1979 10: 31-52.* Traces the development of congressional prerogatives in the passage of immigration laws and the Supreme Court's acceptance of Congress's plenary powers. Resident aliens lack access to due process of law because of restrictive laws that the Supreme Court approved. Court cases, statutes, and published studies; 129 notes.
                                                                A. Hoffman

60.   Harris, Robert J. JUDICIAL REVIEW: VAGARIES AND VARIETIES. *J. of Pol. 1976 38(3): 173-208.* Examines the place of judicial review in a democratic government based on "the supremacy of the people and the Constitution which was a product of their will." During the past 200 years there evolved the fiction that judicial decisions which interpret the Constitution are the authoritative Constitution. Initially, judicial review aimed at curbing prejudiced and ill-conceived legislation; now it appears to destroy that virtue the founders of the republic regarded as its basis. 67 notes.
                                                                R. V. Ritter

61.   Harvey, Gerald C. EXPATRIATION LAW IN THE UNITED STATES: THE CONFUSING LEGACY OF *AFROYIM* AND *BELLEI*. *Columbia J. of Transnational Law 1974 13(3): 406-435.* Discusses expatriation law developments during 1790-1973 with emphasis on the impact of US Supreme Court decisions in *Afroyim* v. *Rusk* (US, 1967) and *Rogers* v. *Bellei* (US, 1971).   S

62.   Hermens, Ferdinand A. THE CHOICE OF THE FRAMERS. *Presidential Studies Q. 1981 11(1): 9-27.* Instead of forming a complete constitutional republic, the Founding Fathers actually formed two different political systems.

One was a representative republic that has worked. The other is a system of divided powers that has caused many failures, including Watergate. Because of the immediate disillusionment over the British government, the Constitutional Convention (1787), largely influenced by John Adams, chose the experimental separation of powers over a cabinet government. Instead of eliminating the power of factions, this has helped factions block the democratic process. 74 notes.   D. H. Cline

63. Hogan, Harry J. THE SUPREME COURT AND NATURAL LAW. *Am. Bar Assoc. J. 1968 54(6): 570-573.* While charges that the Supreme Court has unduly arrogated to itself the role of public conscience are rampant today, Mr. Hogan commends the Court for choosing to accept this role. Our founding fathers... were influenced by John Locke's version of natural law, which assumed that there are fixed and eternal ideals and that man, who is basically good, can readily apprehend them. While science, philosophy and the disillusioning events of the 20th century have discredited the Lockean concept of man, they have not discredited the concept of natural law *per se.* Concludes that the Court is the agency best suited to assume the role, once filled by the Church, of expressing the public conscience.   J

64. Horwitz, Morton J. THE LEGACY OF 1776 IN LEGAL AND ECONOMIC THOUGHT. *J. of Law and Econ. 1976 19(3): 621-632.* By 1876, as Henry George wrote in his Centennial publication *Progress and Poverty,* the country had abandoned its original natural rights legal philosophy, and learned the political uses of law to assist economic development. Early Supreme Court decisions whittled away at the unregulated property system, in favor of a free market system. Covers 1775-1920. Primary and secondary sources; 8 notes.
                                                                          C. B. Fitzgerald

65. Hurst, William. PRACTICAL CONSTRUCTION OF THE WAR POWER. *Rev. in Am. Hist. 1978 6(1): 63-67.* Review article prompted by Abraham D. Sofaer's *War, Foreign Affairs and Constitutional Power: The Origins* (Cambridge, Mass.: Ballinger Publishing Co., 1976).

66. Hutson, James H. COUNTRY, COURT, AND CONSTITUTION: ANTIFEDERALISM AND THE HISTORIANS. *William and Mary Q. 1981 38(3): 337-368.* Surveys treatment of the antifederalists by historians. Emphasis is placed on the Progressive historians, who, following Frederick Jackson Turner's 1893 thesis, portrayed the antifederalists as democrats. Antifederalism was strongest among inland farmers and frontiersmen. The Progressive interpretation of antifederalism as a democratic movement has been challenged since the 1950's, beginning with Merrill Jensen's two works on the Confederation period, stressing radical versus conservative struggle for rule. Cecelia M. Kenyon led the way for the consensus theory. Subsequent historiography on the antifederalists, by both the new revisionists and neo-Progressives, is analyzed. With the Progressive and consensus schools now finding common ground, the best interpretation is that of "country" versus "court." Based on writings on the adoption of the Constitution; 143 notes.   H. M. Ward

67. Jacobson, Harold K. STRUCTURING THE GLOBAL SYSTEM: AMERICAN CONTRIBUTIONS TO INTERNATIONAL ORGANIZA-TION. *Ann. of the Am. Acad. of Pol. and Social Sci. 1976 428: 77-90.* There are important connections between the ideals embodied in the Declaration of Independence and the Constitution and policies that the United States pursues in the United Nations and other international institutions. The concepts inherent in the American Revolution, the doctrine that government should rest on the consent of the governed, and the doctrine of limited government, could have provided a basis for American involvement in international politics or for American isolation. During the nineteenth century, the latter was followed, except that the United States expanded its commercial relations with other countries as had been implied in the Constitution. By proposing the League of Nations, Woodrow Wilson attempted to establish an institutional framework within which American participation in international politics would be consistent with American ideals. A similar effort was made during World War II. The United States was crucial in structuring the world order that emerged. Achievement of American ideals in this world order has proved to be a complex and demanding task: early euphoria yielded to disillusionment. The U.S. now appears to have a more mature understanding of its shortcomings and the importance of other countries' ideals. It has evidenced a willingness to engage in international institutions to attain American ideals in the same way as within domestic institutions.   J

68. Jillson, Calvin C. PRESIDENTIAL POWER: THE EXECUTIVE IN REPUBLICAN GOVERNMENT: THE CASE OF THE AMERICAN FOUNDING. *Presidential Studies Q. 1979 9(4): 386-402.* The question of the proper relationship between the executive and legislative branches of a republican government dominated much of the Constitutional Convention of 1787. Factor analysis of roll-call voting during the debates over the structure of the executive branch, both before and after the compromise of 4 September, shows that political coalitions essentially and firmly determined the nature and length of the argument, as well as its ultimate resolution. The Electoral College has functioned in ways unimagined by Founding Fathers ignorant of how politics could and would change over time, but the relative success of the system accounts for its survival despite perennial criticism. 4 tables, diagram, 20 notes.   P. M. Cohen

69. Johnston, Richard E. and Thompson, John T. THE BURGER COURT AND FEDERALISM: A REVOLUTION IN 1976? *Western Pol. Q. 1980 33(2): 197-216.* In 1976, in *National League of Cities* v. *Usery* the Supreme Court of the United States, for the first time since 1936, struck down a law of Congress supported by the Commerce Clause. In so doing, the Court used (for the first time in its history) a doctrine called "intergovernmental immunities," which was a judicial construction of the late 19th century previously used to protect one level of government from the taxing power only of the other level. This paper examines the past history of the great powers of the Congress, including taxing, spending, commerce regulation, etc., and then examines the effect which *National League* might have upon the future use of taxing, spending, and commerce regulation in the United States. The conclusion is, that if the Court continues to use the rules it discusses in the case, two things

will result. 1)The Court will again (as in the 1895-1936 period) become the daily arbitrator of what is or is not permissible federal legislation, based on a belief that the Court must protect the states from a hostile federal government, and 2)the Congress will find it very difficult to effectuate national purposes through the use of delegated federal powers which it has been free to use in the past.   J

70.   Kamath, M. V. THE FUNCTIONING OF THE AMERICAN POLIT-ICAL SYSTEM. *India Q.: J. of Int. Affairs [India] 1976 32(3): 303-314.* Analyzes the structure and operations of the political system from the period of the framing of the US Constitution to the Watergate scandal. Believes that the rise of executive power has come largely due to the exigencies. The founding fathers sought to build into the Constitution a system of checks and balances which would avoid either the tyranny of the legislature or the executive.   S. H. Frank

71.   Katona, Anna. AMERICAN INFLUENCES ON HUNGARIAN PO-LITICAL THINKING FROM THE AMERICAN REVOLUTION TO THE CENTENNIAL. *Canadian-American Rev. of Hungarian Studies [Canada] 1978 5(1): 13-28.* The political developments in the United States from 1776 to 1876 influenced Hungarian efforts at achieving political democracy. The American Revolution was a model for independence movements in Hungary and early Hungarian constitutional proposals were based on the federal principle. American influence in Hungary climaxed with the dethroning of the Habsburgs and began to wane as American political corruption in the last half of the 19th century overshadowed the early democratic ideals. 71 notes.
                                                                         J. Moore

72.   Kelly, Alfred H. and Miles, Richard D. MAINTENANCE OF REVO-LUTIONARY VALUES. *Ann. of the Am. Acad. of Pol. and Social Sci. 1976 426: 25-52.* Though the values and institutional structure of the American system of constitutional liberty have to some extent exhibited extraordinary continuity, it has evolved with the growth of the American social and political order and successive political crises. The Revolutionary era saw the emergence of 2 or 3 closely related ideas about man and his relation to the state, which served as the foundations of America's constitutional democracy—the ideas of limited government, natural rights, and the concept of an open society. It is the theory of natural law, natural right, the compact theory of the state, and limited government that Jefferson incorporated in the Declaration of Independence. But it cannot be assumed that the Declaration and the Revolution completed the union between natural rights and human equality. In many respects the sociopolitical structure out of which they came was not democratic at all. For instance, it still tolerated slavery. The Bill of Rights provided a statement of natural and historical rights translated into law. Today, constitutional rights in the areas of equality, the dimensions of an open society, and nationalization of constitutional liberty have changed substantially from those of the Revolutionary era.   J

73.   Kempf, Hubert and Toinet, Marie-France. LA FIN DU FÉDÉRAL-ISME AUX ÉTATS-UNIS? [The end of federalism in the United States?].

Rev. Française de Sci. Pol. [France] 1980 30(4): 735-775. Discusses federalism in the United States, one of the "fundamental elements of the constitutional pact of 1787," attempting to determine whether, after 200 years, the theory of the original federalism has actually been realized, focusing on the criteria of federalism and the evolution of centralization (the growing and irreversible new form of federalism), from financial constraint to political control.

74. Ketcham, Ralph. PARTY AND LEADERSHIP IN MADISON'S CONCEPTION OF THE PRESIDENCY. *Q. J. of the Lib. of Congress 1980 37(2): 242-258.* James Madison (1751-1836) was concerned that faction and political parties posed the greatest threat to free republican government. In the Constitution, he strove not only to provide for an executive who would be able to recognize and possess the virtue to uphold the common good, but also to provide the means for keeping such an executive virtuous, that is, impartial, non-partisan, and able to pursue the public interest over private concerns. Madison was willing to put some restraints on direct, free government in order to provide for such leadership that he considered vital to the public good. Early (pre-1829) presidents tried to be antiparty, patriotic, with a positive conception of national leadership to provide for good republican government. Madison was guided by such a conception of the presidency as he first devised and then filled the office. 15 illus., 16 notes.   A. R. Souby

75. Klein, Milton M. NEW YORK LAWYERS AND THE COMING OF THE AMERICAN REVOLUTION. *New York Hist. 1974 55(4): 383-408.* A historiographical article surveying all writings pertaining to the role of lawyers in the American Revolution. The subject has not been treated by contemporaries nor historians. Emphasis is placed upon the transformation of constitutional monarchy into constitutional republicanism. Based on published contemporary writings and modern historical monographs; illus., 64 notes.   A. C. Aimone

76. Lea, Jimmy. THE PRESIDENCY: AUXILIARY AND PRIMARY LIMITS. *Southern Q. 1976 14(2): 133-149.* Examines the direct and indirect powers associated with the American presidency, since the writing of the Constitution. Focuses on existing judicial and legislative methods and alternatives for preventing the growth and abuse of executive power. Social, cultural, and technological factors and developments could influence public attitudes toward power and the presidency. 61 notes.   R. W. Dubay

77. LeClaire, Charles A. THE MARINES HAVE LANDED. *Marine Corps Gazette 1959 43(7): 24-30.* Describes the constitutional implications of decisions by the US government to dispatch US Marines on combat missions to foreign lands, and comments on how the matter has been viewed by US presidents since Thomas Jefferson.

78. Levitsky, Ronald and Steffen, George. SUPREME COURT SIMULATION GAME. *Social Studies 1983 74(2): 89-92.* A method utilized in teaching about the Constitution is to have students simulate proceedings of the Supreme Court, with students acting as lawyers and justices. Deviation from actual court proceedings would allow for witnesses, cross-examination, and an audience to observe. The teacher, acting as chief clerk, sets the rules for this

10-day simulation. Cases may include well-known or imaginary disputes. All participants must conduct research on their roles.   K. E. Gilmont

79. Lipson, Leslie. EUROPEAN RESPONSES TO THE AMERICAN REVOLUTION. *Ann. of the Am. Acad. of Pol. and Social Sci. 1976 428: 22-32.* The American Revolution has influenced Europe in three ways. First came the impact of the Declaration in creating a new state. This was the first occasion when a colony had rebelled and asserted its own right to self-government. In the nineteenth century, Spain and Portugal lost their colonies in Latin America, and the British began the grant of self-government to theirs. Second, the United States was imbued with the philosophy that individuals have rights which are prior to government. Equality and liberty were prized, but equality came first. The effect on those Europeans who opposed the traditional order was overwhelming, as in France in 1789. America's republicanism was a further challenge to the monarchies of Europe. So too was the movement toward democracy which gathered speed after 1830 with the transfer of political power to the masses. Thirdly, the form of government established by the Constitution offered a new model. Although the presidency was not copied, federalism was an invention which European countries could utilize. By and large, the dualism which marked the results of America's Revolution exerted contrary attractions on a divided European society. Hamilton's image of America was appealing to some Europeans, Jefferson's vision to others.   J

80. Loss, Richard. ALEXANDER HAMILTON AND THE MODERN PRESIDENCY: CONTINUITY OR DISCONTINUITY? *Presidential Studies Q. 1982 12(1): 6-25.* Tests the thesis of Edward Corwin and Clinton Rossiter that a continuity between the teachings of Alexander Hamilton and the modern theory of presidential power exists. Hamilton's thoughts cannot be seen as a primary or secondary source, however, for the theories of presidential power espoused by Theodore Roosevelt, Woodrow Wilson, and Corwin. They reduced Hamilton's complex theory to a simple quest for power, and they abandoned his belief in natural law, Christianity, moderation, and virtue. 106 notes.   D. H. Cline

81. Mason, Alpheus Thomas. EAVESDROPPING ON JUSTICE: A REVIEW ESSAY. *Pol. Sci. Q. 1980 95(2): 295-304.* Reviews the recent bestseller *The Brethren* and, citing the *Federalist,* argues that such an unauthorized and undocumented study of the inner workings of the Supreme Court impedes public understanding of the Court's constitutional role.   J

82. McWorter, Gerald. RACISM AND THE NUMBERS GAME: BLACK PEOPLE AND THE 1980 CENSUS. *Black Scholar 1980 11(4): 61-71.* From the 1787 Constitutional Convention which counted a black as three-fifths of a white man for taxation and political representation, to the 1980 Census, blacks have been undercounted, leading to underrepresentation in politics, loss of revenue sharing monies, and problems in education, specifically in mathematics, computers, and statistics; suggests solutions to the problem.

83. Meador, Daniel J. ROLE OF THE JUSTICE DEPARTMENT IN MAINTAINING AN EFFECTIVE JUDICIARY. *Ann. of the Am. Acad. of Pol. and Social Sci. 1982 (462): 136-151.* Since 1790, attorneys general have intermittently undertaken to improve the administration of justice in federal courts. Since the mid-1960's, this court reform role by the Justice Department has been relatively sustained. Focuses on the various constitutional and policy reasons that point to an active Justice Department involvement in federal judicial administration since the 1970's and describes the work of the office established for this purpose by Attorney General Bell.   J/S

84. Meyer, Howard N. *BROWN* AND "BIG FOURTEEN." *Crisis 1979 86(6): 223-225.* For more than one-half of the history of the United States, the 14th Amendment has been the focus of attention in almost as many constitutional law cases as the other 25 amendments combined. The "equal protection" clause has provided the authority for establishing democratic rights for the poor, women, blacks, aliens, the young, and accused citizens. *Brown v. Board of Education* (US, 1954) restored to the 14th Amendment the purpose and meaning for which it was intended.   A. G. Belles

85. Miller, Arthur S. THE SUPREME COURT OF THE UNITED STATES: A BIBLIOGRAPHICAL ESSAY. *Am. Studies Int. 1977 16(2): 5-14.* Discusses the most important books and articles about the Supreme Court to appear in the last 50 years. Despite the mountains of literature on the Supreme Court, no good current history of the Court exists, and biographies are available only for the Court's most famous members. Older publications view the Court as a legal rather than political body, but modern works are starting to counter that view. Contemporary studies focus on public reaction to Court decisions, the application of game theory to judicial actions, and the philosophy of law. Researchers are crippled by the secretiveness of the Court, an idealized view of justice, and the difficulty of observing the Court in action.   J. W. Leedom

86. Miller, Charles A. CONSTITUTIONAL LAW AND THE RHETORIC OF RACE. *Perspectives in Am. Hist. 1971 5: 147-200.* "Moral overstrain"— the difference between rhetoric as expressed and justified in America's major documents and a reality which contradicts that rhetoric. In a Declaration of Independence which deliberately omitted the slave trade clause America established a rhetoric of moral overstrain. And the pattern continues in the present. The Supreme Court developed its unique methods of moral overstrain in their interpretations of the Civil War amendments and in decisions such as *Plessy v. Ferguson* (1896). Constitutional semantics were used to hinder the evolution of a color-blind equality. 174 notes.   W. A. Wiegand

87. Moore, Robert B. SEXISM IN TEXTBOOKS. *Social Studies 1978 69(3): 112-116.* Discusses sexism in American textbooks and the ineffectiveness of Title IX, US Code to solve the problem, because of probable conflict with the First Amendment of the US Constitution. Outlines possible procedures to help alleviate the problem, which involve individual and group analysis of educational materials to be presented to students. Note.   L. R. Raife

88. Morgan, Edmund S. GEORGE WASHINGTON: THE ALOOF AMERICAN. *Virginia Q. Rev. 1976 52(3): 410-436.* Aloofness, self-interest, honor, and daring were characteristics of Washington. All contributed to his ability to lead effectively in the Revolution and to set domestic and foreign policies of the new constitutional government. Then and now "Americans honor the father of their country from a respectful distance."   O. H. Zabel

89. Mortensen, Mauritz Sundt. FRIHETSIDEOLOGI OG PRESSES-TRUKTUR I USA: ET HISTORISK FRAGMENT [The ideology of free-dom and the structure of the press in the USA: an historical fragment]. *Samtiden [Norway] 1976 85(3): 129-143.* Shows how the freedom of the press, guaranteed in the First Amendment to the United States Constitution, has been undermined in the United States by the growth of private commercial control over mass media. Based on American sources; biblio.   R. G. Selleck

90. Motley, Constance B. THE CONTINUING AMERICAN REVOLU-TION. *J. of Negro Hist. 1976 6(1): 7-15.* The ideological revolution begun by white colonists and Founding Fathers has been carried forward by the idealism of civil liberationists of all races throughout US history. Based on judicial opinions; 27 notes.   N. G. Sapper

91. Murphy, Walter F. CONSTITUTIONAL INTERPRETATION: TEXT, VALUES, AND PROCESSES. *Rev. in Am. Hist. 1981 9(1): 7-14.* Review essay of John Hart Ely's *Democracy and Distrust: A Theory of Judicial Review* (1980): 18th-20th centuries.

92. Nikiforov, A. S. and Savel'ev, V. A. KONSTITUTSIIA SSHA: KO-DEKS BURZHUAZNOI DEMOKRATII [The US Constitution as a code of bourgeois democracy]. *Voprosy Istorii [USSR] 1977 (9): 80-97.* The article traces the history of the creation and adoption of the Constitution of the United States, the Bill of Rights and the most important amendments to the Constitution. The author subjects to a critical examination and objective appraisal the cardinal principles and fundamental provisions of the Constitu-tion in the process of their gradual development and transformation in the practical political activity of the state.   J

93. Nikiforova, M. A. NEPRIIATNYE POPRAVKI V KONSTITUTSII S.SH.A. [Undesirable amendments to the US constitution]. *Sovetskoe Gosu-darstvo i Pravo [USSR] 1979 (4): 109-113.* Discusses the inflexibility of the US constitution as analyzed by A. A. Mishin, who mentions that only seven constitutional alterations have ever been achieved.

94. O'Brien, David M. FREEDOM OF SPEECH AND FREE GOVERN-MENT: THE FIRST AMENDMENT, THE SUPREME COURT, AND THE POLITY. *Virginia Cavalcade 1983 33(1): 30-37.* Examines the broaden-ing of 1st Amendment rights of freedom of speech and freedom of the press through decisions of the Supreme Court.

95. O'Donnell, Alice L. A LONG WAY, BABY: WOMEN AND OTHER STRANGERS BEFORE THE BAR. *Supreme Court Hist. Soc. Y. 1977:*

59-62, 114. Discusses the problems women have faced in getting admitted to the bar of the US Supreme Court and focuses on the admission of a number of women, among them Mrs. Belva Lockwood, the first in 1879, Myra Bradwell, admitted in 1892 after an 1872 decision by the court denied her right to practice before the Supreme Court of Illinois, and Katy Kane, admitted in 1890.

96. Osborne, Thomas J. 1776 AND THE NEW RADICALISM. *Thought 1973 48(188): 19-32.* The "new radicals" include Vietnam War protesters, the Weathermen, and the Black Panthers. Their intellectual spokesmen are Staughton Lynd, William O. Douglas, William M. Kunstler, C. Wright Mills, and Herbert Marcuse. The radicals, arguing that the American Revolution justifies their programs and activities, have discussed the relevance of 1776 to contemporary American society. They have not succeeded, however, in justifying the new radicalism in Revolutionary terms. The natural rights philosophy to which the men of 1776 appealed was peculiarly conservative in character, especially in its defense of property rights. The Revolution was primarily a political event, a war for national independence, not a social movement. The theory of internal colonialism, in which the government of George III *vs.* the 13 colonies is compared to the federal government *vs.* oppressed minorities within the United States, confuses the concept of imperialism with that of national sovereignty. J. C. English

97. Ostrom, Vincent. THE CONTEMPORARY DEBATE OVER CENTRALIZATION AND DECENTRALIZATION. *Publius 1976 6(4): 21-32.* Examines thought on federalism, centralization, and decentralization during the 1780's, 1880's, and 1970's to understand the apparent death of federalism and soon-to-be death of constitutional government.

98. Parrish, E. THE HUGHES COURT, THE GREAT DEPRESSION, AND THE HISTORIANS. *Historian 1978 40(2): 286-308.* Analyzes several groups of historians who have concerned themselves with the Supreme Court under Chief Justice Charles Evans Hughes in the 1930's. One group, typified by Merlo Pusey and Samuel Hendel, was inclined to be generous with the Court, especially Hughes and Owen Roberts. They blamed the New Dealers for the constitutional difficulties. Another contingent, which included Edward Corwin, Robert Stern, Thomas Reed Powell, and others, were New Dealers who defended Roosevelt at the Court's expense. A later group, the revisionist historians of the 1960's, often failed to confront judicial issues, and consequently have ignored the significant civil rights and civil liberties stands of the 1930's Court. Evaluating the quantity and quality of the works on the Hughes Court, concludes that the body of literature is small and the works are of varying significance. M. S. Legan

99. Pfeffer, Leo. THE DEITY IN AMERICAN CONSTITUTIONAL HISTORY. *J. of Church and State 1981 23(2): 215-239.* Following a history of the recognition of the deity by countries in Europe and the Near East, traces the attempts to get the United States to recognize the deity in the laws and the court's rejection of these attempts. Many cases are cited. Based mostly on court cases; 89 notes. E. E. Eminhizer

100.   Pierce, Michael D. THE INDEPENDENCE MOVEMENT IN VIR-
GINIA, 1775-1776. *Virginia Mag. of Hist. and Biog.* *1972 80(4): 442-452.*
Reviews arguments by historians accounting for Virginia's choice of revolution
in 1776. There were many contributing factors; however, the need to secure
constitutional rights and pride in the customary liberties of 18th-century
Virginia were basic motives. Based on the published letters of revolutionary
leaders; 49 notes.   C. A. Newton

101.   Pious, Richard M. THE EVOLUTION OF THE PRESIDENCY:
1789-1932. *Current Hist.* *1974 66(394): 241-245, 271-272.* One of six articles
in this issue on "The American Presidency."   S

102.   Polsby, Nelson W. IN PRAISE OF ALEXANDER M. BICKEL.
Commentary 1976 61(1): 50-54. Alexander M. Bickel (1924-74) was a lawyer
with many talents. He taught, was a legal historian, wrote political philosophy,
and entered the public arena as a political activist to educate the American
people on current political questions, which turned more and more on legal
and constitutional interpretation. Bickel believed in a government of institutions, both stable and flexible, relying on a balance between order and liberty
to preserve society. He approved of civil disobedience, which was for him a
quite different form of political behavior from revolutionary activity. He
brought his views to the public on the pages of *Commentary* and the *New
Republic,* as well as in legal journals and works such as *The Morality of
Consent.* Personal recollection.   S. R. Herstein

103.   Powell, Lewis F., Jr. OF POLITICS AND THE COURT. *Supreme
Court Hist. Soc. Y. 1982: 23-26.* Alpheus Mason wrote that the Supreme
Court has consisted mostly of politicians appointed by politicians and confirmed by politicians, which proposes a question regarding the juxtapositioning
of political success and court appointments. An analysis of the 14 chief justices
who preceded Warren Burger indicates that while men like William Howard
Taft and Earl Warren gained distinction through political office, others like
John Marshall, Roger B. Taney, and Charles Evans Hughes attained prominence initially as lawyers. The Constitution demands allegiance once an
individual is called to the court, thus preempting political ties. Address given
before the American College of Trial Lawyers, New Orleans, 8 August 1981;
11 notes, illus.   G. B. Childress

104.   Pritchett, C. Herman. WHY RISK A CONSTITUTIONAL CON-
VENTION? *Center Mag. 1980 13(2): 14-21.* Discusses the history and the
implications of efforts to convene a Constitutional convention, and emphasizes
the risks of convening a convention over such an issue as balancing the
national budget; 1787-1970's.

105.   Raphalides, Samuel J. THE PRESIDENT'S USE OF TROOPS IN
CIVIL DISORDER. *Presidential Studies Q. 1978 8(2): 180-187.* Examines the
President's constitutional and statutory authority to use federal troops during
civil disorders. Articles I and IV of the Constitution plus various statutes
passed since 1789 and surviving in sections 331-333 of Title 10 of the United
States Code provide for federal intervention with or without a state's request.

Semantical inconsistencies have given the President broad discretionary powers in determining what constitutes "domestic violence." Historic examples of federal intervention are discussed including the Whisky Rebellion, the Pullman Strike of 1894, and the civil rights disorders of the 1960's. Despite the reluctance of Presidents to exercise these extensive powers, there is concern about possible abuses. The National Emergencies Act (US, 1976) addresses this concern, but more should be done to define the circumstances where intervention may be employed. 43 notes, biblio.   S. C. Strom

106. Rogers, T. W. JUDICIAL INTERPRETATION OF INTERNAL MIGRATION AS A CONSTITUTIONAL RIGHT IN THE UNITED STATES OF AMERICA. *Int. Migration [Netherlands] 1978 16(3-4): 131-159.* Enumerates Supreme Court cases involving the right to travel; the first arose out of efforts of a state to proscribe in-movements reflecting "an interplay between welfare, poverty and travel." Justice Story admitted specifically the power of a state to repel paupers seeking entrance. Justice Field "insisted that the rights that a state extended to its own citizens must be extended to citizens of other states within its borders." The Fifth Amendment due process includes the right to travel." In *Aptheker* [the] Court interdicted a federal statute forbidding members of the Communist party to obtain passports." The discussion of the 14th Amendment includes the position of Justice Douglas "who consistently took the position that the right to travel was a privilege and immunity of national citizenship." Since 1969, welfare residency laws have been clearly judged as interfering with a constitutional right to travel. 155 notes.   E. P. Stickney

107. Romero, José Luis. LA INDEPENDENCIA DE HISPANOAMÉRICA Y EL MODELO POLÍTICO NORTEAMERICANA [Spanish-American independence and the North American political model]. *Inter-Am. Rev. of Biblio. 1976 26(4): 429-455.* Latin America had four possible political models after independence: the Spanish, the English, the French revolutionary model, or the North American. The North American model was based on a federal system and established a new equalitarian and democratic society. The 1811 Venezuelan constitution was the first to be based on the US political model, but others turned to it at times during the unrest of the 19th century. 16 notes.   B. D. Johnson

108. Roper, Donald M. SEARCHING FOR A MODEL JURISPRUDENCE: THE LIMITATIONS OF CONSTITUTIONAL THINKING. *Rev. in Am. Hist. 1978 6(3): 415-420.* Review article prompted by Gary J. Jacobsohn's *Pragmatism, Statesmanship, and the Supreme Court* (Ithaca, NY: Cornell U. Pr., 1977).

109. Rothbard, Murray N. MODERN HISTORIANS CONFRONT THE AMERICAN REVOLUTION. *Literature of Liberty 1978 1(1): 16-41.* Examines the historiography of the American Revolution in terms of interpretations (constitutional conflict, progressive, and consensus) and time periods: pre-1775 (political and economic conflicts, the frontier, the role of ideas, and local Revolutionary accounts) and post-1775 (warfare, patriotism, political history,

economic conditions, social organization, foreign policy, and results of the Revolution).

110. Rothman, Rozann. THE AMBIGUITY OF AMERICAN FEDERAL THEORY. *Publius* 1978 8(3): 103-122. To reconcile opposing factions the framers of the Constitution placed sovereignty in the people rather than in government, thus prompting dichotomous theories of federalism: dual federalism, or compact theory, held that the new government was a hybrid (partly federal and partly national) and that powers and functions should be shared by the federal government and the states; the hierarchical theory, to the contrary, held that the new government was an incomplete national government and that, as it moved toward greater centralization, functions but not powers should be shared with the states; a delicate balance has existed between these two theories, fluctuating with circumstances, during 1787-1978.

111. Runyan, C. F. OUR GOVERNMENT. *Marine Corps Gazette 1961 45(5): 20-23.* Criticism of the US government has a detrimental affect on army morale—an example of which is the indoctrination of US prisoners of war by Communists during the Korean War. Includes a discussion of the US Constitution.

112. Sandoz, Ellis. CLASSICAL AND CHRISTIAN DIMENSIONS OF AMERICAN POLITICAL THOUGHT. *Modern Age 1981 25(1): 14-25.* The thought of the founders of the United States is distinguished by a synthesis of Christian and classical theory. The American Revolution was dominated by actions intended to restore a true and just social and political order. What was to be restored was the reasonable and just ordering of human affairs to harmonize with divine governance. The rule of law rather than of men, institutionalized in the separation of powers and system of checks and balances, is an insight taken from classical theory of the just state. Taken from Christianity is the notion that divine and natural justice supplies the standard of what is lawful and within the reach of the consent of the people by their constitution. Based on writings of the founding Fathers and secondary sources; 51 notes.   R. D. Rahmes

113. Schambra, William A. THE ROOTS OF THE AMERICAN PUBLIC PHILOSOPHY. *Public Interest 1982 (67): 36-48.* Federalist and antifederalist philosophies have dominated America's political tradition in conflict over community against individual liberty. Liberalism in the 20th century was unable to reconcile devotion to a national community through big government with a commercial philosophy that would sustain economic growth. Contemporary attempts to overturn the New Deal philosophy and emphasize individual liberty are met with liberal hostility. Note.   J. M. Herrick

114. Schechter,   Stephen   L. ON   THE   COMPATIBILITY   OF FEDERALISM AND INTERGOVERNMENTAL MANAGEMENT. *Publius 1981 11(2): 127-141.* Defines and discusses the term intergovernmental management. Examines intergovernmental management as it relates to federalism, and as it developed during presidential administrations from Johnson to Carter. Primary sources; 26 notes, table.   G. Smith

115. Scheiber, Harry N. AMERICAN CONSTITUTIONAL HISTORY AND THE NEW LEGAL HISTORY: COMPLEMENTARY THEMES IN TWO MODES. *J. of Am. Hist. 1981 68(2): 337-350.* Although scholarly studies of US constitutional history lost considerable prestige during the last two decades, the field is not dead. Though many scholars view the new legal history as a threat to the narrower and more traditional constitutional history, the best of the new legal history incorporates traditional themes and concerns from constitutional history. Legal history will integrate with constitutional history in such areas as the Commerce Clause and property law. 55 notes.

T. P. Linkfield

116. Scheiber, Harry N. CENTRALIZATION OF POWER AND DEVELOPMENT OF THE AMERICAN FEDERAL SYSTEM, 1789-1979. *Czasopismo Prawno-Historyczne [Poland] 1980 32(1): 155-183.* Analyzes the development of the American federal system, focusing on the problem of centralization and diffusion of power. The original "dual federalism" while yielding some power to the states, gradually increased in concentration until 1933. The New Deal period shifted to a greater concentration in numerous policies and, since the end of World War II, the power of the federal government has increased to the point of marking a transformation of US federalism. 97 notes.

G. P. Cleyet

117. Scheiber, Harry N. FEDERALISM AND THE AMERICAN ECONOMIC ORDER, 1789-1910. *Law and Soc. Rev. 1975 10(1): 57-118.* Discusses the historiography of political and legal aspects of the relationship between federalism and the economic order in the 19th century, emphasizing the role of the Supreme Court and issues in constitutional law.

118. Scheiber, Harry N. FEDERALISM AND LEGAL PROCESS: HISTORICAL AND CONTEMPORARY ANALYSIS OF THE AMERICAN SYSTEM. *Law & Soc. Rev. 1980 14(3): 663-722.* Whether federalism is more than a legal fiction is a question that generates considerable controversy among scholars in law and the social sciences. Historians of 19th-century American federalism have differed about the workings of the federal system in the era characterized as "dual federalism." This article provides an analysis of these controversies and offers a theoretical position on the problem of real power under federalism. The historical literature, it is argued, provides legal scholars and social scientists with abundant data on the reach, diversity, and effects of governmental action in the different historical epochs of American federalism. The relationship of federalism in the United States to political freedom, governmental performance and efficiency, and the formation of public policy all receive attention.

J

119. Schlesinger, Arthur M., Jr. CONGRESS AND THE MAKING OF AMERICAN FOREIGN POLICY. *Foreign Affairs 1972 51(1): 78-113.* Traces the constitutional and historical aspects of foreign policy control by Congress and the Executive branch. The Constitution is rather ambiguous on this matter, assigning "joint possession" of war and treaty powers to the two branches of government, thereby causing a source of contention. Joint resolutions and executive agreements enhance presidential treaty powers by evading

the Senate's veto. Presidential powers increased further under Franklin D. Roosevelt, during World War II, and ultimately were carried to extreme lengths by Presidents Johnson and Nixon in Indochina. Historically neither branch has remained dominant. Congress must reassert itself, and the two branches of government must become increasingly sensitive to the joint possession of power.   J. A. Kicklighter

120. Schulte Nordholt, J. W. DE AMERIKAANSE CONSTITUTIE EN HET PRESIDENTSCHAP [The American constitution and the presidency]. *Kleio [Netherlands] 1975 16(11): 671-675.* Discusses the conflicting tendencies of "idealism" (trust) and "realism" (distrust) in American political history. The constitution, a product of distrustful politicians, provided a system of checks and balance. The executive has become increasingly independent of the legislative branch; mentions advantages and disadvantages of such a development. Cites the press and public opinion, bolstered by idealism, as a counter-weight to maintain a democratic society. Compares Wilson's idealism, with its redeeming qualities, to Nixon's extreme manifestation of distrust which led to his downfall.   R. C. Alltmont

121. Shaffer, Thomas I. FIRST AMENDMENT: HISTORY AND THE COURTS. *Rev. of Pol. 1978 40(2): 271-279.* Review article prompted by Walter Berns's *The First Amendment and the Future of American Democracy* (New York: Basic Books, 1976), argues that the Supreme Court has "drifted intolerably far away from the principles and circumstances which caused the founding generation of free Americans to amend their written Constitution by limiting the government's control of religion, assembly, and speech." He further argues that the Court "misreads law and misunderstands history." The Court can't be blamed for not following history as Berns states. Church and state problems cannot be dictated to society by Supreme Court edicts alone. 19 notes.   L. E. Ziewacz

122. Swindler, William F. JUSTICES IN ACADEME. *Supreme Court Hist. Soc. Y. 1979: 31-37.* A consideration of the educational roles, both as students and as professors, of US Supreme Court justices. The first academic chair of law was opened at William and Mary College in 1779, and Chief Justice John Marshall was one of its first students. James Wilson, an appointee of President George Washington, was the first justice to accept a professorship of law. Joseph Story was the first major academic figure in the history of the court. After the early years, scholarly contributions by justices, both before and after appointment, picked up considerably. In 1976, Justice Tom Clark was appointed to the chair at William and Mary, thus completing the circle. 5 photos, table.   V. L. Human

123. Tebbel, John. FROM RAGS TO RICHES: THE MEDIA IN AMERI-CAN SOCIETY. *Q. J. of the Lib. of Congress 1981 38(1): 42-50.* Reviews the development of the mass media in American society, from early newspapers to the development of modern newspapers, paperback books, magazines, and radio and television, and how the various media have been viewed by the public and the government. Until recently, the media have been well protected by the First Amendment. However, as indicated by the 1978 Burger Supreme

Court decisions, the media are becoming increasingly threatened by a hostile public, government, court system, and business community. Illus.

A. R. Souby

124. Tonsor, Stephen J. THE UNITED STATES AS A "REVOLUTIONARY SOCIETY." *Modern Age 1975 19(2): 136-145.* "... Two hundred years after a revolution reluctantly made and a Constitution which strengthened rather than weakened the conservative character of American political arrangements, American society and politics are still revolutionary,... Far from being a break with the past and its institutions, the new American nation sheltered, preserved and quickened political ideas, constitutional forms and polititical institutions that were temporarily in eclipse in Europe." S

125. VanDerSlik, Jack R. RESPECTING AN ESTABLISHMENT OF RELIGION IN AMERICA. *Christian Scholar's Rev. 1984 13(3): 217-235.* Argues that the intent of the 1st Amendment to the Constitution was to protect churches established by the states from interference by the federal government, not to create a wall of separation between church and state. Since *Everson v. Board of Education* (US, 1947), the Supreme Court has consistently misapplied the establishment clause.

126. Velasco, Gustavo R. ON EQUALITY AND EGALITARIANISM. *Modern Age 1974 18(1): 21-28.* Discusses the origins of the ideas and ideals of equality and egalitarianism in the United States based on the thoughts of Rousseau, Locke, Jefferson, Franklin, and Adams; provides a history of human rights protections written into constitutions, documents, and treaties since the American Revolution.

127. Vitullo-Martin, Thomas. FEDERAL POLICIES AND PRIVATE SCHOOLS. *Pro. of the Acad. of Pol. Sci. 1978 33(2): 124-135.* Federal aid to private schools has existed for almost 200 years. Initially this aid was given through direct grants. In time a type of general educational aid based on programs offering federally desired programs was substituted. More recently because of constitutional constraints aid has gone more frequently to assist the private school student rather than the private school. All federal aid to public and private schools is regulated. The Internal Revenue Code provides the most important control over federal aid to private schools. K. N. T. Crowther

128. Weber, Paul J. JAMES MADISON AND RELIGIOUS EQUALITY: THE PERFECT SEPARATION. *Rev. of Pol. 1982 44(2): 163-186.* Traces the writings of James Madison through his career, during 1780-1830, as political theorist, constitutional architect, president, and retired statesman. Madison consistently stressed the principle of equal separation in matters of public policy regarding church and state. Religious liberty did not demand structural separation; however, it was important that it remain free of government coercion and totally disestablished so that each citizen could enjoy equality. Finally, it was Madison's contention that religious liberty should enjoy equal protection and promotion, much as those other natural rights of life and property. 70 notes. G. A. Glovins

129.   Wiener, Frederick Bernays. ARE THE GENERAL MILITARY AR-
TICLES UNCONSTITUTIONALLY VAGUE? *Am. Bar Assoc. J. 1968*
54(4): 357-364. Those who would assail language in the general military
articles dealing with officers' conduct and conduct that brings discredit on the
armed forces as "void for vagueness" fail to recognize that numerous Supreme
Court decisions have upheld statutes so attacked when their meanings seemed
reasonably well-settled and understood.... The articles in question have been a
part of American military law since 1775 and that any possibilities of
vagueness are countervailed by the practical construction applied to the articles
by those who administer them.... Those who object to restriction of constitutional freedoms for members of the armed forces should give consideration to
the nature of an armed force.   J

130.   Wolfe, Christopher. JOHN MARSHALL & CONSTITUTIONAL
LAW. *Polity 1982 15(1): 5-25.* A widespread view has it that Chief Justice
John Marshall molded the Constitution so as to bring it more in accord with
his own Federalist principles. However, Marshall was faithful to the Constitution, and his carefully elaborated rules of construction worked to preserve his
fidelity. Marshall's approach to interpretation and judging, rooted in the
founders' "democratic constitutionalism," was quite different from that of
20th-century judges and commentators.   J/S

131.   Youngs, J. William T. THE FORMATIVE YEARS: A CRITICAL
REVIEW OF AUDIO-VISUAL AIDS FOR TEACHING AMERICAN
HISTORY: 1607-1789. *Hist. Teacher 1976 9(3): 379-407.* Presents an overview and evaluation of audiovisual materials covering the early period in
American history through the adoption of the Constitution. The author divides
the material into five categories: general surveys, colonization, life in early
America, the Revolution, and the Constitution. Most of the materials evaluated
are for use in high school- and introductory-level college courses. Based on
primary and secondary sources; 11 illus., 37 notes.   P. W. Kennedy

132.   Zvesper, John. THE MADISONIAN SYSTEMS. *Western Pol. Q. 1984*
37(2): 236-256. There were two "Madisonian systems": the interest-group
pluralism of the *Federalist No. 10,* and the less famous but more truly
republican system of party government that Madison advocated after 1789.
These conflicting theoretical systems corresponded to the two conflicting
tendencies of his practical politics. Studies of Madison's contradictions have
not explored the possibility that those contradictions reflected the defects of
both systems and, perhaps, Madison's own recognition of those defects.
Examination of his development and use of his basic pluralist argument shows
that he was not deeply committed to it, possibly because of its theoretical
defects. Madison displayed a similar detachment from his second system. He
was more consistently attached to the principles of liberalism and prudence
than to the devices of pluralism and party government.   J

133.   —. BOOKS BY JUSTICES: A REPRESENTATIVE LIST. *Supreme*
Court Hist. Soc. Y. 1979: 38-39. A selective bibliography of books published
by justices of the Supreme Court. The list is not comprehensive; articles are
excluded altogether. Not all listed books are concerned with law. Rather, an

effort has been made to show the wide range of subjects which have interested the justices. Fifteen authors are included; publication dates range from 1807 to 1978. 2 photos. V. L. Human

134. —. JUSTICE IN AMERICA: FACT OR FICTION? *Social Educ.* *1973 37(7): 635-643.*
O'Neil, Robert M. JUSTICE IN AMERICA: FACT OR FICTION? p. 636.
Greene, Linda. JUSTICE IN AMERICA: THE PERSISTENT MYTH, p. 637.
Banks, James A. TEACHING STRATEGIES, p. 639.
Matheson, Kenneth. SOURCES AND RESOURCES, p. 642. Discusses the nature of justice in America from the Bill of Rights to the present courts. Biblio. S

135. —. THE NUMBERS GAME. *Supreme Court Hist. Soc. Y. 1977: 86-100.* Discusses the laws that have determined the number of justices who may sit on the Supreme Court.

136. —. [POLITICAL THOUGHT OF THOMAS JEFFERSON]. *Chinese Studies in Hist. 1981 14(3): 3-37.*
Israel, John. AN INTRODUCTION TO LIU CHO-CH'ANG'S "THE DEMOCRATIC THOUGHT OF THOMAS JEFFERSON," *pp. 3-6.* A short sketch of the life and writings of Liu Zhuochang (Liu Cho-ch'ang) (1921) and his position as the foremost Jefferson scholar in China.
Liu Zhuochang. THE DEMOCRATIC THOUGHT OF THOMAS JEFFERSON, *pp. 7-37.* Explains the positive and negative aspects of such Jeffersonian ideals as the separation of powers, the right of revolution, checks and balances, an agrarian-based society, and the importance of human freedom. Based on Jefferson's writings and the analysis of his biographers; 15 notes. A. C. Migliazzo

137. —. [PREFECTORIALISM AND FEDERALISM: ARE THEY COMPATIBLE?]. *Publius 1981 11(2): 3-58.*
Elazar, Daniel J. IS FEDERALISM COMPATIBLE WITH PREFECTORIAL ADMINISTRATION?, *pp. 3-22.* Since the mid-1960's prefectorial administration, in which the federal government seeks to increase direct supervision and regulation of state and local governments has increased. Prefectorialism is not compatible with federalism. 31 notes, 3 fig.
Fried, Robert C. PREFECTORIALISM IN AMERICA?, *pp. 23-29.* Prefectorialism is not emerging, but if it did, the impact would not be negative. 6 notes, table.
Sundquist, James L. IN DEFENSE OF PRAGMATISM: A RESPONSE TO "IS FEDERALISM COMPATIBLE WITH PREFECTORIAL ADMINISTRATION?," *pp. 31-37.*
Goldwin, Robert A. THAT MAY BE ALL RIGHT IN PRACTICE, BUT IT DOESN'T WORK IN THEORY: COMMENTS ON "IS FEDERALISM COMPATIBLE WITH PREFECTORIAL ADMINISTRATION?," *pp. 39-45.* Agrees with Elazar in terms of practical aspects, but disagrees with Elazar's theory.

Oakerson, Ronald J. RECIPROCITY, CONSUMERISM, AND COLLEC-
TIVE ACTION: A RESPONSE TO "IS FEDERALISM COMPATIBLE
WITH PREFECTORIAL ADMINISTRATION?," *pp. 47-53.* Basically
agrees with Elazar's central contention on the increasing coordinating
capabilities of the federal government over the provision of public services
to local clientele leading to greater federal domination of state and local
governments, but questions other portions of the work. 14 notes.

Elazar, Daniel J. PREFECTS, PRAGMATISM AND PRACTICE: A RE-
SPONSE TO THE RESPONDENTS, *pp. 55-58.*   G. Smith

138.   —. [THEORIES OF US CONSTITUTIONAL HISTORY]. *J. of Pol.
1981 43(2): 292-325.*

Wolfe, Christopher. A THEORY OF U.S. CONSTITUTIONAL HISTORY,
pp. 292-316. Two fundamentally different kinds of judicial review, rather
than a series of eras under dominant Supreme Court chief justices, have
characterized the constitutional history of the United States. Through the
Civil War period, a traditional view required fidelity to an intelligible,
broad and substantive Constitution and was characterized by rules of
interpretation, the search for intelligible standards and infrequent judicial
review. After the Civil War, a modern view adapted the Constitution to
new and changing circumstances. Modern interpretation has given a
legislative character to judicial review, deemphasized rules of interpretation, raised questions of degree and the balancing of interests, and
expanded the frequency of such review. The modern perspective is
especially evident in cases concerning due process and the 14th Amendment. 46 notes.

Carter, Lief H. THINK THINGS, NOT WORDS, *pp. 317-321.* Despite
Christopher Wolfe's construction of a traditional view of constitutional
history, pre-Civil War Supreme Court decisions such as *Swift* v. *Tyson,
Marbury* v. *Madison, Fletcher* v. *Peck, Dartmouth College* v. *Woodward,*
and *Dred Scott* v. *Sandford* indicate that the court's rhetoric of strict
interpretation was overshadowed by its expansive actions. 10 notes.

Wolfe, Christopher. A REJOINDER TO CARTER, *pp. 322-325.* Asserts
that those cases cited by Carter were decided in accord with a strict
interpretation of the Constitution. Modern judicial review is characterized
by greater frequency, expansion of judicial power, and judicial involvement in an increasingly broad range of public policy issues. 3 notes.

A. W. Novitsky

Books

139.   Abraham, Henry J. *Freedom and the Court: Civil Rights and Liberties
in the United States.* 2nd ed., New York: Oxford U. Pr., 1972. 397 pp.

140.   Adler, Mortimer J. and Gorman, William. *The American Testament.*
(Institute for Philosophical Research.) New York: Praeger, 1975. 160 pp.

141. Anastaplo, George. *The Constitutionalist: Notes on the First Amendment.* Dallas: Southern Methodist U. Pr., 1971. 826 pp.

142. Anderson, Terry L. and Hill, Peter J. *The Birth of a Transfer Society.* Stanford: Hoover Inst. Pr., 1980. 114 pp.

143. Antieau, Chester James. *States' Rights under Federal Constitutions.* Dobbs Ferry, N.Y.: Oceana, 1984. 169 pp.

144. Baldwin, Leland D. *Reframing the Constitution: An Imperative for Modern America.* Santa Barbara, Calif.: ABC-Clio, 1972. 145 pp.

145. Barber, Sotirios A. *On What the Constitution Means.* Baltimore: Johns Hopkins U. Pr., 1984. 245 pp.

146. Berger, Raoul. *Executive Privilege: A Constitutional Myth.* Cambridge, Mass.: Harvard U. Pr., 1974. 430 pp.

147. Berkson, Larry Charles. *The Concept of Cruel and Unusual Punishment.* Lexington, Mass.: Lexington, 1975. 252 pp.

148. Berns, Walter. *The First Amendment and the Future of American Democracy.* New York: Basic, 1976. 266 pp.

149. Berry, Mary Frances. *Black Resistance/White Law: A History of Constitutional Racism in America.* New York: Appleton-Century-Crofts, 1971. 268 pp.

150. Bessette, Joseph M. and Tulis, Jeffrey, ed. *The Presidency in the Constitutional Order.* Baton Rouge: Louisiana State U. Pr., 1981. 349 pp.

151. Bickel, Alexander M. *The Morality of Consent.* New Haven, Conn.: Yale U. Pr., 1975. 156 pp.

152. Bobbitt, Philip. *Constitutional Fate: Theory of the Constitution.* New York: Oxford U. Pr., 1982. 285 pp.

153. Breckenridge, Adam Carlyle. *The Executive Privilege: Presidential Control Over Information.* Lincoln: U. of Nebraska Pr., 1974. 188 pp.

154. Coleman, Frank M. *Hobbes and America: Exploring the Constitutional Foundations.* Toronto: U. of Toronto Pr., 1977. 159 pp.

155. Collins, Ronald K. L., ed. *Constitutional Government in America.* Durham, N.C.: Carolina Acad., 1980. 504 pp.

156. Cord, Robert L. *Separation of Church and State: Historical Fact and Current Fiction.* New York: Lambeth, 1982. 307 pp.

157.   Duker, William F. A Constitutional History of Habeas Corpus. (Contributions in Legal Studies, no. 13). Westport, Conn.: Greenwood, 1980. 349 pp.

158.   Eastland, Terry and Bennett, William J., ed. Counting by Race: Equality from the Founding Fathers to Bakke and Weber. New York: Basic, 1979.

159.   Eckhardt, Bob and Black, Charles L., Jr. The Tides of Power: Conversations on the American Constitution. New Haven: Yale U. Pr., 1976. 225 pp.

160.   Ehrlich, Walter, ed. Presidential Impeachment: An American Dilemma. St. Charles, Mo.: Forum Pr., 1974. 136 pp.

161.   Ely, John Hart. Democracy and Distrust: A Theory of Judicial Review. Cambridge, Mass.: Harvard U. Pr., 1980. 268 pp.

162.   Fehrenbacher, Don E. The Dred Scott Case: Its Significance in American Law and Politics. New York: Oxford U. Pr., 1978. 741 pp.

163.   Fisher, Louis. A Constitution Between Friends: Congress, the President, and the Law. New York: St. Martin's, 1978. 274 pp.

164.   Flower, Milton E. John Dickinson: Conservative Revolutionary. Charlottesville: U. Pr. of Virginia for Friends of the John Dickinson Mansion, 1983. 338 pp.

165.   Fowler, Dorothy Ganfield. Unmailable: Congress and the Post Office. Athens: U. of Georgia Pr., 1977. 266 pp.

166.   Friedrich, Carl J. Limited Government: A Comparison. Englewood Cliffs, N.J.: Prentice-Hall, 1974. 139 pp.

167.   Goebel, Julius, Jr. History of the Supreme Court of the United States. Vol. 1: Antecedents and Beginnings to 1801. New York: Macmillan, 1971. 864 pp.

168.   Goldwin, Robert A. and Schambra, William A., ed. How Democratic Is the Constitution? (A Decade of Study of the Constitution.) Washington: Am. Enterprise Inst. for Public Policy Res., 1981. 150 pp.

169.   Graham, George J., Jr. and Graham, Scarlett G., ed. Founding Principles of American Government: Two Hundred Years of Democracy on Trial. Bloomington: Indiana U. Pr., 1976. 395 pp.

170.   Grimes, Alan P. Democracy and the Amendments to the Constitution. Lexington, Mass.: Lexington, 1978. 190 pp.

171.   Grundfest, Jerry. George Clymer: Philadelphia Revolutionary, 1739-1813. (Dissertations in American Biography.) New York: Arno, 1983. 554 pp.

172.   Haller, Walter. *Supreme Court und Politik in den USA: Fragen der Justiziabilität in der Höchstrichterlichen Rechtsprechung* [Supreme Court and politics in the USA: Questions on justiciability in the reviewing of the administration of justice]. Bern, Switzerland: Stämpfli, 1972. 384 pp.

173.   Harmon, M. Judd, ed. *Essays on the Constitution of the United States.* (National University Publications Multi-Disciplinary Studies in the Law.) Port Washington, N.Y.: Kennikat, 1978. 202 pp.

174.   Hentoff, Nat. *The First Freedom: The Tumultuous History of Free Speech in America.* New York: Delacorte, 1980. 323 pp.

175.   Kristol, Irving et al. *America's Continuing Revolution: An Act of Conservation.* (Distinguished Lecture Series on the Bicentennial.) Washington: American Enterprise Inst. for Public Policy Res., 1975. 398 pp.

176.   Lees, J. D.; Maidment, R. A.; and Tappin, M. *American Politics Today.* Manchester, England: Manchester U. Pr., 1982. 189 pp.

177.   Lieberman, Jethro K. *Milestones! 200 Years of American Law: Milestones in Our Legal History.* New York: Oxford U. Pr., 1976. 422 pp.

178.   Lofton, John. *The Press as Guardian of the First Amendment.* Columbia: U. of South Carolina Pr., 1980. 358 pp.

179.   Marke, Julius J. *Vignettes of Legal History, Second Series.* South Hackensack, N.J.: Rothman, 1977. 274 pp.

180.   Miller, Robert T. and Flowers, Ronald B., ed. *Toward Benevolent Neutrality: Church, State, and the Supreme Court.* Waco, Tex.: Baylor U. Pr., Markham Pr. Fund, 1977. 601 pp.

181.   Pritchett, C. Herman. *Constitutional Law of the Federal System.* Englewood Cliffs, N.J.: Prentice-Hall, 1984. 382 pp.

182.   Radcliffe, James E. *The Case-or-Controversy Provision.* University Park: Pennsylvania State U. Pr., 1978. 285 pp.

183.   Regan, Richard J. *Private Conscience and Public Law: The American Experience.* New York: Fordham U. Pr., 1972. 245 pp.

184.   Rossum, Ralph A. and McDowell, Gary L., ed. *The American Founding: Politics, Statesmanship, and the Constitution.* Port Washington, N.Y.: Kennikat, 1981. 190 pp.

185.   Simpson, William. *Vision and Reality: The Evolution of American Government.* London: Murray, 1978. 243 pp.

186.   Smith, Page. *The Constitution: A Documentary and Narrative History.* New York: Morrow, 1978. 564 pp.

187. Stephens, Otis H., Jr. *The Supreme Court and Confessions of Guilt.* Knoxville: U. of Tennessee Pr., 1973. 236pp.

188. Stevens, John D. *Shaping the First Amendment: The Development of Free Expression.* Beverly Hills, Calif.: Sage, 1982. 157pp.

189. Thomas, Ann Van Wynen and Thomas, A. J. *The War-Making Powers of the President: Constitutional and International Law Aspects.* Dallas: Southern Methodist U. Pr., 1982. 177pp.

190. Wiecek, William M. *The Guarantee Clause of the U.S. Constitution.* (Cornell Studies in Civil Liberty.) Ithaca, N.Y.: Cornell U. Pr., 1972. 324 pp.

191. Wiecek, William M. *The Sources of Antislavery Constitutionalism in America, 1760-1848.* Ithaca, N.Y.: Cornell U. Pr., 1977. 306pp.

192. Worton, Stanley. *Freedom of Religion.* Rochelle Park, N.J.: Hayden, 1975. 160pp.

Dissertations

193. Asbury, Charles Joseph. "The Right to Keep and Bear Arms in America: The Origins and Application of the Second Amendment of the Constitution." U. of Michigan 1974. 198 pp. *DAI 1974 35(7): 4346-A.*

194. Auer, A. "Les Noirs, les écoles publiques et le système constitutionnel aux Etats-Unis" [Blacks, public schools and the constitutional system in the United States]. U. de Neuchâtel [Switzerland] 1975. *DAI-C 1980 41(2): 251; 5/ 1701c.*

195. Conner, Jett Burnett. "Thomas Paine and the First Principles of Democratic Republics." U. of Colorado, Boulder 1980. 245 pp. *DAI 1981 41(8): 3704-A.* DA8103082

196. Curry, Thomas John. "The First Freedoms: The Development of the Concepts of Freedom of Religion and Establishment of Religion in America from the Early Settlements to the Passage of the First Amendment to the Constitution." Claremont Grad. School 1983. 898 pp. *DAI 1983 44(5): 1547-1548-A.* DA8321047

197. DiSarro, Joseph. "The Ninth Amendment and the Expansion of Natural Rights and Liberties in American Constitutional Law: A Case Study." West Virginia U. 1979. 228 pp. *DAI 1980 41(1): 382-383-A.* DA8012915

198. Dynia, Philip A. "Senate Rejection of Supreme Court Nominees: Factors Affecting Rejection, 1795-1972." Georgetown U. 1973. 914 pp. *DAI 1974 35(4): 2351-A.*

199. Elm, Lloyd Martin. "American Indian Education: A Constitutional Right." Pennsylvania State U. 1983. 140 pp. *DAI 1984 44(10): 2938-A.* DA8327484

200. Farmer, Richard Franklin. "The Operational Relationship of the First Amendment Establishment and Free Exercise Clause to Public Education: An Analysis of Judicial Criteria Employed by Federal Courts." Southern Illinois U. 1973. 218 pp. *DAI 1974 34(9): 5523-A.*

201. Feigel, Richard Eugene. "Liberalism and Ideology." Pennsylvania State U. 1984. 258 pp. *DAI 1985 45(8): 2548-A.* DA8419591

202. Granato, Leonard Alan. "Prior Restraint: Resurgent Enemy of Freedom of Expression." Southern Illinois U. 1973. 538 pp. *DAI 1974 34(9): 5895-5896-A.*

203. Greenfield, Steven L. "The Application of the First and Fourteenth Amendments to the United States Constitution to the Legal Rights of Students." Northwestern U. 1973. 149 pp. *DAI 1974 34(9): 5527-A.*

204. Heafer, Dianne Lewis. "A Historiographical Study of the Taney Court and the Dred Scott Decision." U. of Houston 1983. 253 pp. *DAI 1984 44(12): 3781-A.* DA8403909

205. Johannesen, Stanley Karl. "Constitution and Empire in the Life and Thought of John Dickinson." U. of Missouri, Columbia 1973. 222 pp. *DAI 1974 34(11): 7154-A.*

206. Keating, Pamela Jane. "An Investigation of a Constitutionally Protected Right of Education." U. of Washington 1981. 228 pp. *DAI 1981 42(1): 111-A.* DA8113451

207. Kiley, Michael Mills. "The Republic of Reason: The Political Ideas of Thomas Paine." U. of California, Santa Barbara 1979. 262 pp. *DAI 1980 40(11): 5989-5990-A.* DA8010916

208. Latzer, Barry. "The Constitutional Authority of the President to Commence Hostilities without a Congressional Declaration of War." U. of Massachusetts 1977. 530 pp. *DAI 1978 38(8): 5023-5024-A.*

209. Lienesch, Michael Frederick. "The Concept of Time in American Political Thought: 1783-1800." U. of California, Berkeley 1977. 613 pp. *DAI 1978 38(8): 5024-A.*

210. Lowry, Stephen Michael. "A Small Group Study of the Supreme Courts of the United States, 1803-1971." U. of Pennsylvania 1974. 385 pp. *DAI 1975 36(1): 513-514-A.*

211. McCaughey, Elizabeth Peterken. "William Samuel Johnson, Loyalist and Founding Father." Columbia U. 1976. 824 pp. *DAI 1978 39(4): 2487-A.*

212. Mell, Wayne Allan. "James Wilson, Alexander Hamilton, William Blackstone: Organic Principles of Constitutional Liberty." U. of Oregon 1976. 150 pp. *DAI 1977 37(9): 6013-6014-A.*

213. Murphy, Brian Michael. "The American Ideology and the Supreme Court: The Quality of Equality." Miami U. 1980. 166 pp. *DAI 1981 41(7): 3245-A.* DA8100399

214. Pullen, Ricky D. "A Comparison and Contrast of the Libertarian and Social Responsibility Theories of the Press Based on United States Supreme Court Decisions." Southern Illinois U. 1973. 352 pp. *DAI 1974 34(9): 5897-A.*

215. Samson, Steven Alan. "Crossed Swords: Entanglements between Church and State in America." U. of Oregon 1984. 667 pp. *DAI 1985 45(7): 2247-A.* DA8422869

216. Slabbert, Christian. "Non-Obviousness as a Requirement for Patentability in South Africa and in the United States of America: A Comparative Study." U. of the Witwatersrand [South Africa] 1980. *DAI 1981 41(8): 3699-A.*

217. Smith, Dale Patrick. "Interstate Extradition: A Case Study in Constitutional Interpretation." U. of Georgia 1984. 162 pp. *DAI 1984 45(2): 630-A.* DA8411980

218. Sullivan, Francis Leo. "The News Media and Crime Reporting: The Issue of Free Press vs. Fair Trial." U. of Massachusetts 1982. 488 pp. *DAI 1983 43(8): 2769-A.* DA8229614

219. Wilson, Bradford Pentony. "Judicial Enforcement of the Fourth Amendment: A Constitutional History." Catholic U. of Am. 1981. 167 pp. *DAI 1982 42(8): 3727-A.* DA8202574

2

EARLY EXPERIENCES WITH CONSTITUTIONALISM, 1777-1787

Article Abstracts

220. Agresto, John T. LIBERTY, VIRTUE AND REPUBLICANISM, 1776-1787. *Rev. of Pol. 1977 39(4): 473-504.* Recent academic studies have demonstrated renewed interest in the relation of virtue to republicanism in the decade following the Revolutionary War. The founding fathers sought to avoid the two dilemmas of republicanism—anarchy or tyranny—by emphasizing civic virtue which meant frugality and restraint. Americans, however, loved liberty and profit more than sacrifice and duty. The Constitutional Convention provided a "way of achieving a viable self-government that did not require virtue as its base." 108 notes.   L. E. Ziewacz

221. Bailyn, Bernard. 1776: A YEAR OF CHALLENGE: A WORLD TRANSFORMED. *J. of Law and Econ. 1976 19(3): 437-466.* Surveys significant publications in 1776, including works by Edward Gibbon, Thomas Paine, Jeremy Bentham, John Adams, and most important, Adam Smith's *Wealth of Nations.* Describes these books within the context of the flood of peasant emigration that alarmed Great Britain, and of worsened Anglo-American relations which made the American Revolution inevitable. 47 notes.
C. B. Fitzgerald

222. Banning, Lance. THE HAMILTONIAN MADISON: A RECONSIDERATION. *Virginia Mag. of Hist. and Biog. 1984 92(1): 2-28.* A revisionist discussion of James Madison's nationalist ideals. Alexander Hamilton felt that his ally made a complete policy reversal when, in 1790, Madison opposed the creation of a national bank. Hamilton's analysis has colored historians' interpretations of Madison's behavior, and Irving Brant's biography of the Virginia statesman added to the confusion. Closer examination of Madison's writings reveal, however, that he was never the nationalist others have portrayed him to be. Instead, he sought a balance between democracy and centralized government. Based on the *Papers of Alexander Hamilton,* pub-

lished federal and Constitutional Convention records, and the *Letters of Members of the Continental Congress;* 50 notes, illus.   D. J. Cimbala

223. Banning, Lance. JAMES MADISON AND THE NATIONALISTS, 1780-1783. *William and Mary Q. 1983 40(2): 227-255.* Questions the traditional appraisal of Madison during these years as a total nationalist. At the time he favored keeping the government of the Articles of Confederation. Madison's positions on the proposal for a national bank, the impost amendment, and various issues relating to the west followed Virginia special interests rather than a nationalist stance. Only in 1783 did Madison emerge as a nationalist, chiefly because of the financial crises. Experience in Congress led Madison to conclude that the union was threatened by congressional reliance on the states for revenue. Madison's aversion to British commercial policy injurious to American interests also helped shape Madison's nationalist principles. Based on congressional records and Madison's correspondence; 98 notes.   H. M. Ward

224. Beitzinger, A. J. REVOLUTIONARY THOUGHT REVISITED AND REVISED. *Rev. of Pol. 1979 41(3): 428-436.* Review article prompted by Garry Wills's *Inventing America: Jefferson's Declaration of Independence* (Garden City, N. Y.: Doubleday, 1978), Morton White's *The Philosophy of the American Revolution* (New York: Oxford U. Pr., 1978), and Ronald M. Peters's Jr. *The Massachusetts Constitution of 1780: A Social Compact* (Amherst, Mass.: U. of Massachusetts Pr., 1978). Wills's theory is that Jefferson was basically anti-Lockean, White perceives Jefferson as a "rational intuitionist," while Peters finds that in Massachusetts, "the primacy of individual autonomy [is] in American Revolutionary Thought." Wills's book is flawed by lack of documentation and proper evaluation of existing facts. White's work is the most thorough and able philosophical analysis yet made of the philosophy of the American Revolution. Peters's book is the type of analysis "needed in the quest for further understanding of the American revolutionary generation's intent."   L. Ziewacz

225. Bender, Paul and Field, Martha A. REPORT ON COMMITTEE I. *Ann. of the Am. Acad. of Pol. and Social Sci. 1976 426: 70-80.* [Reports the conclusions of the "Maintenance of Revolutionary Values"committee at the April 1976 Bicentennial Constitutional Conference of the AAPSS.] It was suggested that a way of clarifying constitutional values might be to look closer at the framers of the Constitution—what were their views and background. They were elitists, from diverse backgrounds, representing a relatively broad spectrum for the time. Particular revolutionary values were discussed, beginning with equality. Discussion particularly centered on whether equality referred to "equality of opportunity" or "equality of result." It was expressed that equality of result was not in conflict with equality of opportunity but a necessary tool to achieve it. Generally, equality of opportunity was preferred to equality of result, except that there should be a certain amount of result equality in order to ensure real equality of opportunity, and it was agreed that quotas were sometimes necessary to correct past discrimination. Other values were discussed briefly, including domestic tranquility, exporting democracy, free speech, constitutional respect for individual autonomy and privacy, and

fairness of treatment by government. Revolutionary values were summarized as falling into 3 categories: freedom of expression, equality, and protection from government arbitrariness.   J

226. Berkeley, Edmund, Jr. THE NAVAL OFFICE IN VIRGINIA, 1776-1789. *Am. Neptune 1973 33(1): 20-33.* A review of the post-independence customs rules and procedures in Virginia. As the individual states were virtually autonomous, Virginia created regulations designed primarily to accumulate revenue. The ease of smuggling caused regular revisions of the law in the hope of forcing compliance, although such measures served only to exacerbate and complicate the situation. Nothing worthwhile was accomplished until the federal government established a uniform customs law under provisions granting it such authority in the new Constitution. 35 notes.
                                                                V. L. Human

227. Bloom, John Porter. THE CONTINENTAL NATION—OUR TRINITY OF REVOLUTIONARY TESTAMENTS. *Western Hist. Q. 1975 6(1): 4-15.* Discusses the Declaration of Independence, a brief cry of defiance and inspiration; the Constitution and its first 10 amendments, a masterpiece of "celebrated compromises" that harnessed the Declaration to "grubby reality"; and the Ordinance of 1787 (the Northwest Ordinance), the "most creative" of the three. Reviews the historiography of the Ordinance of 1787 and calls for "its proper celebration" as a part of the observance of the bicentennial. Illus.
                                                                D. L. Smith

228. Borden, Morton. FEDERALISTS, ANTIFEDERALISTS, AND RELIGIOUS FREEDOM. *J. of Church and State 1979 21(3): 469-482.* Discusses why no statement on religious liberty appeared in the first-proposed Constitution; Federalists and Antifederalists differed less on philosophy than on implementation. Based on the Federalists' papers, Antifederalists' writings, and printed studies of the people involved, and of the period; 49 notes.
                                                                E. E. Eminhizer

229. Brown, Jonathan. THE ARTICLES OF CONFEDERATION: TOWARDS A FIRST CONSTITUTION. *A. N. U. Hist. J. [Australia] 1976 12: 24-31.* Discusses the significance of the Articles of Confederation which led to the drafting of the Constitution of the United States.

230. Brown, Richard D. THE FOUNDING FATHERS OF 1776 AND 1787: A COLLECTIVE VIEW. *William and Mary Q. 1976 33(3): 465-473.* Discusses the status and other factors related to the 99 men who either signed the Declaration of Independence or the Constitution. Various quantitative data are given as to a profile of collective identity. Similarities noted: for example, concerning birth, region, ethnic background, family, occupation, climatic conditions, and longevity. Includes a list of personnel examined, background information, occupations, cohort groups, family size, and factors relating to deaths. Based on secondary sources, including population studies; 9 tables, 33 notes.   H. M. Ward

231. Brown, Wallace. AN ENGLISHMAN VIEWS THE AMERICAN REVOLUTION: THE LETTERS OF HENRY HULTON, 1769-1776. *Huntington Lib. Q. 1972 36(1): 1-26, (2): 139-151.* Part I. An introduction to and a series of letters written by Henry Hulton, an English customs commissioner in Boston, to his friend Robert Nicholson in Liverpool during April 1769-November 1771. The letters include descriptions of some of the main revolutionary events in Boston and his analysis of those events and of British policy. Hulton was proud of Britain's constitution and way of life, both of which he feared were being destroyed by the "demogogues" of Boston. The letters are located in Manchester College, Oxford, and Unitarian College, Manchester; 80 notes. Part II includes 10 letters dated from 21 November 1772, when Hulton was customs commissioner in Boston, to 22 August 1776, when he had returned to England. 21 notes.   S. R. Smith

232. Campbell, William F. THE SPIRIT OF THE FOUNDING FATHERS. *Modern Age 1979 23(3): 246-250.* Textually analyzes the *Federalist* in terms of its intellectual underpinnings and references to classical political theory and in terms of the philosophers contemporary to their authors. The Founding Fathers are seen by many as arguing for a constitution to serve as a vehicle for the positive channeling of man's innate pride and vanity. The author agrees with those who offer a more positive interpretation and contends that this view of human nature will not lead to mild federal government. A view of man as a possessor of divine grace must be substituted. 5 notes.
C. A. D'Aniello

233. Chaffin, Robert J. THE DECLARATORY ACT OF 1766: A REAPPRAISAL. *Historian 1974 37(1): 5-25.* To view the Declaratory Act of March 1766 primarily as a means of introducing repeal of the Stamp Act (1765) is to ignore both the motives leading to its passage, and its immediate effect upon the British government. A primary purpose was to settle a constitutional question: the supreme authority of parliament over the colonies. The consequences of the act were that the principle it embodied was rendered sacrosanct, compromise became difficult, and enforcement intensified antagonism. Indeed, the Declaratory Act became a barrier to reconciliation between mother country and American colony. 50 notes.   N. W. Moen

234. Chouillet, Jacques. DIDEROT AND AMERICA. *Studies in Eighteenth-Century Culture 1983 12: 223-230.* The great American interest in Denis Diderot is attributable to the work of American scholars such as Otis Fellows and Arthur Wilson and to Diderot's own interest in American affairs. Numerous passages in Raynal's *Histoire des Deux Indes* can be attributed to him. The American Revolution confirmed Diderot's preexisting theory of the relation between the individual and the state. He followed American events closely. With the Declaration of Independence, he called the revolt "the legitimate use of an unalienable and natural right of oppressed men." A comparison of Diderot's political texts and those which inspired the American revolt reveals similarities, though one did not inspire the other. A community of thought existed that enables us to understand the enthusiasm of a French *philosophe* for 4 July 1776. Based on Diderot material in the Bibliotheque

Nationale, published primary sources, and secondary sources; 27 notes.

T. F. Moriarty

235. Conniff, James. THE ENLIGHTENMENT AND AMERICAN PO-
LITICAL THOUGHT: A STUDY OF THE ORIGINS OF MADISON'S
FEDERALIST NUMBER 10. Pol. Theory 1980 8(3): 381-402. James Madison's innovations in political theory have not been recognized, as scholars have
attempted to tie him to Enlightenment ideology; responding to the needs
particular to the American experience, he determined that effective authority
rather than virtue was central to republicanism, as recorded in *Federalist No.
10.*

236. Dangerfield, George. FOR GOD AND/OR REASON. *Rev. in Am.
Hist. 1981 9(3): 330-335.* Review essay of Pauline Maier's *The Old Revolutionaries: Political Lives in the Age of Samuel Adams* (1980), which examines
the roles of Samuel Adams (b. 1722), Isaac Sears (b. 1730), D. Thomas Young
(b. 1731), Richard Henry Lee (b. 1732), and Charles Carroll (b. 1737) during
1763-76.

237. Dennison, George M. HISTORICAL HIDE AND SEEK: OR, THE
SEARCH FOR THE HISTORICAL AMERICA. *R. in Am. Hist. 1975 3(2):
159-163.* Paul K. Conkin's *Self-Evident Truths: Being a Discourse on the
Origins & Development of the First Principles of American Government—
Popular Sovereignty, Natural Rights, and Balance & Separation of Powers*
(Bloomington: Indiana U. Press, 1974) discusses the origins and American
adaptations of popular sovereignty, natural rights, and separation of powers in
the constitutional history of the 1760's-80's.

238. Dennison, George M. THE "REVOLUTIONARY PRINCIPLE":
IDEOLOGY AND THE CONSTITUTION IN THE THOUGHT OF
JAMES WILSON. *Rev. of Pol. 1977 39(2): 157-191.* American Revolutionary
theorist James Wilson assumed that "the social order in the United States
would persist despite experimentation with political arrangements. Government, in other words, was separate and distinct from state and society."
However, Wilson altered his view and by the 1790's abandoned order and
security for an ideology that envisioned society "as a community of individuals
who assured decency and viability by pursuing their own interests in an active
and enlightened way." Wilson's theory of peaceful revolution was perceived by
the American people as more of a "threat than a promise." 103 notes.

L. E. Ziewacz

239. Deren, Štefica. PODRIJETLO AMERIČKOG STRANAČKOG SUS-
TAVA (S POSEBNIM OSVRTOM NA RAZVOJ FEDERALISTA) [The
origins of the American party system (with special regard to the development
of the federalists)]. *Politička Misao [Yugoslavia] 1972 9(2-3): 216-228.*
Examines the antagonisms between George Washington and Alexander Hamilton on one side, and Thomas Jefferson on the other, which split the nation
between federalists and antifederalists (later republicans), and argues that the
major reason for the short existence of federalists was the conflict between
Hamilton and John Adams, and not any external factors.

240. Dickson, Charles Ellis. JAMES MONROE'S DEFENSE OF KEN-
TUCKY'S INTERESTS IN THE CONFEDERATION CONGRESS: AN
EXAMPLE OF EARLY NORTH/SOUTH PARTY ALIGNMENT. *Regis-
ter of the Kentucky Hist. Soc. 1976 74(4): 261-280.* Political party divisions
may have begun earlier than generally believed. James Monroe defended the
interests of the West, particularly Kentuckians, in Congress under the Articles
of Confederation. In the debates over negotiations under way with Spain in
regard to the use of the Mississippi River, as early as 1785 Monroe and others
fought diligently to protect the future economic development of the region.
Primary and secondary sources; 60 notes.   J. F. Paul

241. Drakeman, Donald L. RELIGION AND THE REPUBLIC: JAMES
MADISON AND THE FIRST AMENDMENT. *J. of Church and State 1983
25(3): 427-445.* James Madison was not responsible for the written form
adopted for the First Amendment. His interest centered on concern over
infringement of freedom of conscience, and his willingness to be involved in
what is now called "civil religion" was rooted in his intense patriotism. 74
notes.   E. E. Eminhizer

242. Edwards, George. THE PRESIDENT, THE MEDIA AND THE
FIRST AMENDMENT. *Presidential Studies Q. 1982 12(1): 42-47.* To understand the formation of the American Constitution, it is necessary to understand
the tyranny experienced by the colonists. This led to the adoption of the Bill of
Rights, particularly the 1st Amendment. Based on the author's experience as
chief judge of the US Court of Appeals.   D. H. Cline

243. Elazar, Daniel J. CONFEDERATION AND FEDERAL LIBERTY.
Publius 1982 12(4): 1-14. American federalism as expressed in the Constitution
had roots in the Whig-inspired Articles of Confederation, but represented a
different approach to central authority. The Articles of Confederation was a
pact to insure operating freedom for its constituent polities, whereas the
federation also sought to insure the individual liberties of the entire population.
This expansion of central power engendered a need for restraint of central
authority. These new needs were met by the Bill of Rights and by the
mechanism of separation of powers.   D. Powell

244. Ferguson, Robert A. THE EMULATION OF SIR WILLIAM JONES
IN THE EARLY REPUBLIC. *New England Q. 1979 52(1): 3-26.* Sketches
William Jones's (1746-94) career as a linguist, jurist, orientalist, and poet.
During the 1780's, his writings were filled with warnings of civic corruption,
increased central authority and executive prerogative, and the danger of
factions in Great Britain. Such language would form the basis of Republican
rhetoric for 40 years thereafter. Literary lawyers dominated American journals
and criticism during the era, and a second cause for his influence in America
was his life as an attorney and jurist. In this field he was important in gaining
acceptance of Blackstone's *Commentaries on the Laws of England.* Based on
Jones's writings and secondary sources; 56 notes.   J. C. Bradford

245. Ferguson, Robert A. "MYSTERIOUS OBLIGATIONS": JEFFER-
SON'S *NOTES ON THE STATE OF VIRGINIA. Am. Literature 1980*

52(3): 381-406. Notes on the State of Virginia (London, 1787) represents Thomas Jefferson's attempt to define America as a republic, utilizing themes and techniques common to Enlightenment thinkers of the 18th century. Jefferson demonstrates how the compilation of factual knowledge would lead to a larger coherence. The legal philosophy of the Enlightenment and English common law provided Jefferson with a structure with which he could connect the natural world (America) and the political order (the new Republic). *Notes* deserves critical attention because it possesses both theme and structure that reflect Jefferson's mastery of Enlightenment thought. Table, 58 notes.

T. P. Linkfield

246.   Ferling, John. THE SENATE AND FEDERAL JUDGES: THE IN-TENT OF THE FOUNDING FATHERS. *Capitol Studies 1974 2(2): 57-70.*

247.   Fifer, J. Valerie. UNITY BY INCLUSION: CORE AREA AND FEDERAL STATE AT AMERICAN INDEPENDENCE. *Geographical J. [Great Britain] 1976 142(3): 462-470.* The United States provides a valuable case study in political process-area interaction, and the bicentennial year is an appropriate point at which to retrace the state's initial approaches to the integration of people, land and power by political means. The internal structure of the country's core area at independence is examined as the product of an extraordinarily varied colonial, revolutionary and post-revolutionary political experience; as a result, the successful innovative model of federalism was to provide the means of projecting, connecting and controlling new social and political networks extending beyond the core area into new land.   J

248.   Franklin, John Hope. THE NORTH, THE SOUTH, AND THE AMERICAN REVOLUTION. *J. of Am. Hist. 1975 62(1): 5-23.* In the 1840's and 1850's northern and southern politicians, writers, and public speakers were engaged in vituperative debates on the relative merits of the northern and southern contributions to the war of independence and the principles of the constitution. The tenor of the debates was more reflective of contemporary sectional biases and interests, particularly on the issue of slavery, than of interest in historical accuracy. Two major combatants were William Gilmore Simms, a South Carolina novelist, and Lorenzo Sabine, a Massachusetts historian. Based on contemporary memoirs, letters, newspapers, and secondary works; 61 notes.

J. B. Street

249.   Fulcher, J. Rodney. COMMON SENSE VS. *PLAIN TRUTH:* POLITICAL PROPAGANDA AND CIVIL SOCIETY. *Southern Q. 1976 15(1): 57-74.* Explains the reasons behind the selection of the name for Thomas Paine's pamphlet *Common Sense.* The primary issue was the role of a constitution in civil society and the concept of political revolution as a vehicle for social change. 41 notes.

R. W. Dubay

250.   Funston, Janet and Funston, Richard. CESARE BECCARIA AND THE FOUNDING FATHERS. *Italian Americana 1976 3(1): 73-92.* Italian penological reformer Cesare Bonesana, Marchese di Beccaria, had an impact on the political thought of the American Founding Fathers, 1764-83.

251. Goldman, Eric F. THE PRESIDENT, THE PEOPLE, AND THE POWER TO MAKE WAR. *Am. Heritage 1970 21(3): 28-35.* The Constitution states that the power to make war is a congressional prerogative, but the Korean War and the Vietnam War were conducted without congressional sanction.   S

252. Greene, Jack P. VALUES AND SOCIETY IN REVOLUTIONARY AMERICA. *Ann. of the Am. Acad. of Pol. and Social Sci. 1976 426: 53-69.* The original principles and values of the American Republic and how they were rooted in and were reflections of the particular social conditions in early America are the subjects of this paper. The foundation of the "American science of politics" was a hardheaded and realistic view of human nature. The founding fathers saw America as having in its power the ability to begin the world over by discovering the "constant and universal principles" of government. What emerged from America's adaptation of the body of theory and tradition available was a system that was distinctively American. The American system incorporated the concept of the natural rights of man, existing independently of government. The government was limited by constitutions and by its representative nature; it was to be responsive and responsible to the people. The sovereignty resided within the people themselves. America would be safe from the tyranny of a majority faction by its multiplicity of interests. The primary purpose of government, according to the Declaration, was to secure man's inalienable rights—life, liberty, and the pursuit of happiness—and other values sought were unity and public virtue. These values expressed and reflected the social conditions of early America.   J

253. Greene, Jack P. WILLIAM KNOX'S EXPLANATION FOR THE AMERICAN REVOLUTION. *William and Mary Q. 1973 30(2): 293-306.* In 1778 William Knox, an undersecretary of state for the colonies, began to reflect on the results of British policy since the Stamp Act crisis. He believed that a new colonial constitution would quiet the colonists. His ideas were embodied in a paper which he submitted to various British dignitaries. Reproduces Part One of the document, "Considerations on the great Question, what is to be done with America?" written 1778-79. This modern-sounding document ascribes the deterioration of relations between the colonies and the mother country to social circumstances and a deficient political arrangement. Knox believed that the colonists resented what they saw as the ultimate intentions of British policy. 23 notes.   H. M. Ward

254. Guggisberg, Hans R. THE MEANING OF THE AMERICAN BICENTENNIAL. *Swiss Am. Hist. Soc. Newsletter 1976 12(2): 7-13.* The true meaning of the American Bicentennial is that it recalls the success of the American Revolution and the durability of the constitutional institutions created by the Founding Fathers.

255. Hamowy, Ronald. JEFFERSON AND THE SCOTTISH ENLIGHTENMENT: A CRITIQUE OF GARRY WILLS'S *INVENTING AMERICA: JEFFERSON'S DECLARATION OF INDEPENDENCE. William and Mary Q. 1979 36(4): 503-523.* Takes issue with Garry Wills's thesis (New York: 1978) that Thomas Jefferson's philosophical views in the Declaration of

Independence are derived from the Scots Enlightenment—the works of Thomas Reid, David Hume, Adam Smith, Lord Kames, Adam Ferguson, and Francis Hutcheson—rather than from the influence of John Locke. Sees similarities in language of the Declaration with the Scots philosophers, but says that they reflect statements in Locke's writings. The author criticizes Wills's use of booklists. There is no evidence that Jefferson was even remotely familiar with the Scots philosophers at the time of writing the Declaration. The author clarifies the meaning of certain phrases in the Declaration, such as the "pursuit of happiness." Collates the Declaration of Independence and Jefferson's writings with the works of Locke and the Scots philosophers. 69 notes.

H. M. Ward

256. Hancock, Harold B., ed. LETTERS TO AND FROM CAESAR RODNEY. *Delaware Hist. 1966 12(2): 147-168.* Letters to and from Caesar Rodney, 1777-81. Important items include a letter from Thomas Rodney describing the Battle of Germantown; requests for supplies, especially horses and flour; a letter from Henry Laurens urging Delaware to ratify the Articles of Confederation; a request from the Council of Maryland that Delaware cooperate with that state, Virginia, and Pennsylvania in enacting legislation forbidding the distilling of grain into spirits, and requests by George Washington and Nicholas Van Dyke for flour, cattle, and militia. Rodney reported that obstructions in Delaware Bay prevented shipment of the small amount of provisions to be sent to Washington for the projected southern campaign of 1781. 40 notes.

R. M. Miller

257. Heffer, Jean and Kaspi, André. AUTOUR DE LA RÉVOLUTION AMÉRICAINE [About the American Revolution]. *Annales: Écon., Sociétés, Civilisations 1975 30(1): 219-225.* A review article prompted by recent works on the American Revolution. These include works on the origins of the movement for Independence, the Loyalists, the Confederation and the Constitution, and the ideology of the Revolution. There seems to be widespread agreement that class conflict played a weak role in the movement toward Independence. 6 notes.

J. C. Billigmeier

258. Heinrichs, Terry. HOBBES & THE COLEMAN THESIS. *Polity 1984 16(4): 647-666.* In his well-known book, *Hobbes and America: Exploring the Constitutional Foundations* (1977), Frank Coleman characterized Hobbes's political theory as liberal democratic and, therefore, as an appropriate model for understanding American liberalism. Hobbes's theory is neither liberal nor democratic, and is actually in opposition to, not in harmony with, liberal thought and practice in America.

J/S

259. Hoxie, R. Gordon. THE PRESIDENCY IN THE CONSTITUTIONAL CONVENTION. *Presidential Studies Q. 1985 15(1): 25-32.* The most remarkable and a unique creation of the framers of the Constitution was the presidency. Principally pushed by six crucial members of the convention (George Washington, Alexander Hamilton, James Madison, Rufus King, James Wilson, and Gouverneur Morris), the convention created the presidency with four basic characteristics that have survived to this day: a single executive,

no constitutional cabinet or council, popular election, and broad presidential powers. 19 notes. D. H. Cline-Burnett

260. Hutson, James H. INTELLECTUAL FOUNDATIONS OF EARLY AMERICAN DIPLOMACY. *Diplomatic Hist. 1977 1(1): 1-19.* In 1776 a consensus about foreign policy existed among American Revolutionary leaders. It endured through the adoption of the Federal Constitution. "American leaders operated in foreign politics according to the assumptions of power politics that dominated contemporary European statecraft. They believed that the balance of power was 'natural'... and that it was their duty to manipulate it for their country's advantage." Historian Felix Gilbert's contention, therefore, that at its inception American foreign policy was motivated by a crusading internationalistic idealism is inadmissible. Nor is it correct to interpret early American foreign policy as an incipient liberalism which was devoured by a conservative reaction in 1787, only to resurrect itself in 1801. Primary and secondary sources; 104 notes. G. H. Curtis

261. Igarashi, T. PENNSYLVANIA KYOWAHA NO SEIJISHIDO (1)— AMERICA GASHUKOKU RENPOTAISEI KEISEIKATEI NOIKOUK— [The political leadership of the Pennsylvania Republicans: a study of the evolution of federalism in the United States]. *Kokkagakkai Zasshi [Japan] 1976 89(3-4): 34-92, (5-6): 45-120, (7-8): 39-120.* Part 1. Investigates the factors that contributed to the operation of the federal system after the Constitution was promulgated. Part 2. Pennsylvania Republicans aimed at preventing the formation of despotism by a check and balance system, and attempted to facilitate the operation of the state government by training competent personnel. Part 3. The Constitution was firmly established by the time the change of regime was accomplished in 1800 when Jefferson became president.

262. Kashatus, William C., III. THOMAS PAINE: A QUAKER REVOLUTIONARY. *Quaker Hist. 1984 73(2): 38-61.* Thomas Paine's writings, 1776-77, reflect William Penn's and other Quakers' influence with respect to loyalty to legitimate government, greater avoidance of violence than Lockean "commonwealth" political theory or Enlightenment rationalism proposed, a millennial spirit, and plain language. Paine was raised a Quaker in Thetford, England, and was caught up in Whig republican agitation as a customs officer in Lewes, 1768-74. In Philadelphia, 1774-77, he sympathized with Quakers supporting violent revolution, who were eventually disowned by orthodox Quakers. As editor of the *Pennsylvania Magazine,* 1774-76, and as aide-de-camp to General Nathaniel Greene (also of Quaker background), Paine's Quaker heritage appeared, too, in his antislavery, antidueling, and feminist sentiments. Secondary sources; 108 notes. T. D. S. Bassett

263. Katz, Stanley N. THOMAS JEFFERSON AND THE RIGHT TO PROPERTY IN REVOLUTIONARY AMERICA. *J. of Law and Econ. 1976 19(3): 467-488.* Jefferson believed widespread landowning and a farming economy essential to a republic. His Virginia legislation (prohibiting entail, primogeniture, etc.) exemplified his brief-lived dream of pure republicanism in government. His vision, enacted as the Articles of Confederation, survived only

during 1776-87. Based on primary and secondary sources; 52 notes.

C. B. Fitzgerald

264. Kirkpatrick, Jeane J. MARTIN DIAMOND AND THE AMERICAN IDEA OF DEMOCRACY. *Publius 1978 8(3): 7-31.* The late Martin Diamond attempted to disprove the notion that the majoritarian-democratic principle established by the American Revolution and reflected in the Declaration of Independence conflicted with the libertarian, republican, conservative emphasis of the Constitution; according to Diamond, charges brought against the Electoral College are precisely those leveled at the Constitution by utopian socialists whose unrealistic expectations led to pessimism, whereas the more moderate expectations of the Founders of the Constitution led to optimism.

265. Knight, Carol Lynn H. A CERTAIN GREAT COMMONER: THE POLITICAL IMAGE OF WILLIAM PITT, FIRST EARL OF CHATHAM, IN THE COLONIAL PRESS. *Pro. of the Am. Phil. Soc. 1979 123(2): 131-142.* Examines articles published in 54 colonial newspapers during 1756-78 which related to three periods of William Pitt's work: as war minister (1756-61), an opponent of the Stamp Act in the 1760's, and defender of American liberties in the 1760's and 1770's. Most of the articles were copied from British publications, thus giving a rather similar appraisal of Pitt across the colonies and in both Whig and Tory papers. Thirteen categories of characteristics attributed to Pitt are described: political independence, opposition to patronage, support of the British Constitution, support of the "American Constitution," accepting office only when consistent with principle, entering the opposition only to defend principle, tolerating religious nonconformity, representing imperial interests, possessing private virtues, possessing public virtues, deference to public opinion, winning public esteem, demonstrating patriotism, and unselfishly serving his country when called. These virtues formed a set of political ideals widely found in 18th-century Britain and America. Based on colonial newspapers; 68 notes, 2 appendixes.

H. M. Parker, Jr.

266. Koch, Adrienne. JAMES MADISON AND THE LIBRARY OF CONGRESS. *Q. J. of the Lib. of Congress 1980 37(2): 159-161.* James Madison (1751-1836), regarded as the "father of the Constitution," was also the first to propose a Library of Congress. He drew up the first book list of the legislators' library, worked to get Thomas Jefferson's private library for the nation, and worked closely with the Librarian of Congress. A philosopher-statesman, Madison advocated the American experiment and combined theory and practice into a new political institution based on his knowledge of human nature and the normal course of social change. His native intelligence, reasoning power, command of learning, and devotion to liberty combined to allow him to make his unique contributions.

A. R. Souby

267. Lambert, Paul F. FROM FEDERALISM TO JEFFERSONIANISM, THE CONSISTENCY OF BENJAMIN RUSH. *New Scholar 1974 4(2): 191-203.* Rush's link to the Federalists was their mutual support of the federal Constitution. His personal and political differences with Alexander Hamilton and John Adams strengthened his ideal of a republican utopia with the

exportability and perfectibility of American institutions, held since the early days of the Revolution.   D. K. Pickens

268. Lawson, Philip. BRITISH TRADITIONS AND REVOLUTIONARY AMERICA. *Can. Rev. of Am. Studies [Canada] 1983 14(2): 165-173.* Reviews *In Defiance of the Law: The Standing-Army Controversy, Two Constitutions, and the Coming of the American Revolution* (1981), by John Philip Reid; *American Patriots and the Rituals of Revolution* (1981), by Peter Shaw; and *Shay's Rebellion: The Making of an Agrarian Insurrection* (1980), by David P. Szatmary. Conceptually and methodologically disparate, the books reach similar conclusions: American revolutionary ideology in the 1760's and 70's suffered from discord and hesistancy to rebel. 8 notes.   H. T. Lovin

269. Lechtreck, Roy. WHO CREATED WHOM? THE MYTH OF STATE SOVEREIGNTY. *Midwest Q. 1983 24(2): 182-187.* Contrary to the accepted myth that the states created the federal government, the states never existed prior to the central government, nor were they ever sovereign. Delegates to the Constitutional Convention never considered themselves as members of individual states during the Revolution; instead, they acted as citizens of one sovereign nation after the break with England. Throughout American history, those who have been loudest to proclaim state sovereignty and states' rights have been those who have opposed certain economic policies of the federal government. The myth of state sovereignty has been used as a propaganda weapon by these people in their struggle for supremacy.   D. H. Cline

270. Lienesch, Michael. HISTORICAL THEORY AND POLITICAL REFORM: TWO PERSPECTIVES ON CONFEDERATION POLITICS. *Rev. of Pol. 1983 45(1): 94-115.* From their understanding of both classical and British history, republicans, both revolutionaries and constitutionalists, acknowledged a cyclical theory of history in which governments from their founding went through periods of corruption and renewal. Seen from a revolutionary perspective, government under the Articles of Confederation confirmed fears that standing armies, unwarranted taxation, and the rise of aristocracy could jeopardize honest government. From the constitutionalist perspective, the problems of debt, factional squabbles, and popular protests were seen as disruptive to constitutional balance. Conservative constitutionalists called for a new and stronger central government. In 1787, republicans found themselves lodged precariously between the forces of revolution and counterrevolution. The Constitution became a triumph for balance and the conservative cause; both sides, viewing events from their historical perspectives, realized that something dramatic needed to be done. 78 notes.
G. A. Glovins

271. Lofgren, Charles A. COMPULSORY MILITARY SERVICE UNDER THE CONSTITUTION: THE ORIGINAL UNDERSTANDING. *William and Mary Q. 1976 33(1): 61-88.* Looks into the legal permissibility of military conscription in the late 18th century. Notes the acceptance of a form of compulsory military service in the colonial and Revolutionary periods. Analyzes the intent of members of the Constitutional Convention. Discusses various issues regarding the use of militia and armies. The Federalists and

Antifederalists accepted compulsory military service, although they differed on limitations of federal power. Comments on the extent to which the militia could be federalized. 87 notes.   H. M. Ward

272. Lutz, Donald S. FROM COVENANT TO CONSTITUTION IN AMERICAN POLITICAL THOUGHT. *Publius 1980 10(4): 101-134.* In a study of American constitutional history, the state constitutions in force before 1789 are examined. Terminology is dealt with in some detail. The earliest founding documents in America are discussed in relation to "covenants" or "compacts." The shift to the use of "constitution" is examined. 29 notes, appendix.   A. C. Drysdale

273. MacMaster, Richard K. OF MODERN DUST-JACKETS AND FOUNDING MYTHS: THE MEN OF THE CONSTITUTIONAL CON-VENTION OF 1787. *Fides et Hist. 1984 16(1): 83-86.* Reviews M. E. Bradford's *A Worthy Company: Brief Lives of the Framers of the United States Constitution* (1982). Based primarily on the reviewed work and secondary sources; 16 notes.   D. B. Raymond

274. Małajny, Ryszard M. DOKTRYNA WOLNOŚCI RELIGIJNEJ "OJCÓW KONSTYTUCJI" USA [The doctrine of the freedom of religion of the "Fathers of the Constitution" of the United States]. *Czasopismo Prawno-Historyczne [Poland] 1982 34(2): 111-138.* Largely restricting the article to John Adams, Thomas Jefferson, James Madison, and Thomas Paine, deals with the intellectual background leading to the affirmation of the freedom of religion in the Bill of Rights. Basing their assertions in philosophy, law, and even theology, the "fathers" outdistanced such European thinkers as John Locke and Montesquieu when, for example, Jefferson's calling for independence of political laws from religious opinions, or Madison's holding that religious uniformity is undesirable even when achievable. 69 notes. French summary.   L. A. Krzyzak

275. Malsberger, John W. THE POLITICAL THOUGHT OF FISHER AMES. *J. of the Early Republic 1982 2(1): 1-20.* Massachusetts Federalist Fisher Ames adhered to the classical, 17th-century strain of republicanism, which stressed mixed and balanced government and virtue. His critique of postrevolutionary Jeffersonian ideology was not the hysterical raving of a paranoid conservative. Although Ames accepted the notion of popular sovereignty, he hoped for a government based on a natural aristocracy, believing that the common man was depraved and incapable of self-rule and in need of a codified law to protect government conduct. Through most of his political career, Ames remained cautiously optimistic that public virtue would survive the tumultuous events of the time. Political pessimism clouded Ames's perception in his final years. Persistent factionalism, the rise of Napoleon, and Jeffersonian political maneuvers combined to raise fear in Ames that true republicanism would perish. Primary and secondary sources; 46 notes.
                                                        G. A. Glovins

276. Marks, Frederick W., III. AMERICAN PRIDE, EUROPEAN PREJ-UDICE AND THE CONSTITUTION. *Historian 1972 34(4): 579-595.* Such

scholars as J. Allen Smith, Merrill Jensen, and Charles A. Beard tend to emphasize socioeconomic aspects of the American Confederation period, seeing class conflict, civil disorder, vested interests, and Shays' Rebellion as paramount influences deeply affecting the motives and objectives of the founding fathers. An additional and positive influence was national pride. Although socioeconomics are important, the framers of the Constitution were convinced that they had a significant and historic opportunity to correct the shortcomings of the Articles of Confederation and to create a system more likely to help young America succeed. 50 notes.   N. W. Moen

277. Marty, Martin E. FREEDOM OF RELIGION AND THE FIRST AMENDMENT. *Virginia Cavalcade 1983 32(4): 158-171.* Details the history of the 1st Amendment, 1776-91, and reviews the ways in which it is still being questioned and tested in modern court decisions.

278. Mathur, Mary E. Fleming. TIYANOGA OF THE MOHAWKS: FATHER OF THE UNITED STATES. *Indian Historian 1970 3(2): 59-62, 66.* Tiyanoga (Hendrick), Mohawk chief in New York, fought for the English in the French and Indian War and was to influence the writing of the Articles of Confederation.   S

279. McColley, Robert. RADICAL POLITICAL THOUGHT IN THE AMERICAN REVOLUTION. *J. of the Illinois State Hist. Soc. 1976 69(2): 91-99.* A survey of origins and development of the political ideas of the Founding Fathers. Whereas the progressive historians emphasized economic factors, historians since the 1950's have elaborated the intellectual maturity of Revolutionary America, and especially the masterful adaptation of the English Whig or libertarian tradition. Especially discussed are books by Caroline Robbins, H. Trevor Colbourn, Robert R. Palmer, and Bernard Bailyn. 3 illus., 12 notes.   J

280. McDowell, Gary L. THE LOSERS' LEGACY. *Virginia Q. Rev. 1984 60(3): 550-561.* Reviews *What the Anti-Federalists Were for: The Political Thought of the Opponents of the Constitution. Volume 1 of the Complete Anti-Federalist* (1981) by Herbert J. Storing, and also reviews *The Complete Anti-Federalist* (1982), a seven-volume compilation of the writings of the Antifederalists edited by Storing. The Federalist papers contain only "half the story" of the Constitution's adoption. The "other half lies in the reservations and doubts about the Constitution voiced by the losers." The legacy of these losers is "still very much to be reckoned with in American political thinking."
                                                                    O. H. Zabel

281. McGuire, Robert A. and Ohsfeldt, Robert L. ECONOMIC INTERESTS AND THE AMERICAN CONSTITUTION: A QUANTITATIVE REHABILITATION OF CHARLES A. BEARD. *J. of Econ. Hist. 1984 44(2): 509-519.* An important change in the structure of US institutions occurred when the government under the Articles of Confederation was replaced by a new government under the Constitution. In 1913, Charles A. Beard proposed an economic interpretation of the formation of the Constitution that remains a much discussed yet unresolved explanation of the behavior

and motives of the men who wrote the document. Summarizes the relationship between the voting behavior of individual delegates involved in the making of the Constitution and their economic and personal characteristics. Significant patterns related to economic interests are found in the voting, with the division of interests generally consistent with that outlined by Charles A. Beard 70 years ago.   J

282. Middlekauf, Robert. ATTEMPTS TO PUT THE AMERICAN REVO-
LUTION BACK TOGETHER AGAIN. *Early Am. Lit. 1983 18(1): 102-109.*
Reviews Edward Countryman's *A People in Revolution: The American Revolution and Political Society in New York, 1760-1790* (1981); Roger Ekirch's *"Poor Carolina": Politics and Society in Colonial North Carolina, 1729-1776* (1981); John Philip Reid's *In Defiance of the Law: The Standing Army Controversy, the Two Constitutions, and the Coming of the American Revolution* (1981); and *The Briefs of the American Revolution* (1981), edited by John Philip Reid. All four histories are too confining and fragmented in their approach to the broad sweep of the American Revolution. 4 notes.
T. P. Linkfield

284. Morgan, Robert J. MADISON'S ANALYSIS OF THE SOURCES OF POLITICAL AUTHORITY. *Am. Pol. Sci. Rev. 1981 75(3): 613-625.* James Madison believed that political institutions are not the effects of conflicts among private groups in society. He traced political authority to human nature. It is the ultimate source of both public opinion and the motives which impel some individuals to hold government offices. Prudently contrived governmental institutions can moderate the countervailing tendencies arising from these two sources of authority, although they are necessarily in a state of continuing tension. Strict accountability of representatives to the whole range of diverse opinion in society is in conflict with the tendency of government to become autonomous.   J/S

285. Morgan, Robert J. MADISON'S THEORY OF REPRESENTATION IN THE TENTH FEDERALIST. *J. of Pol. 1974 36(4): 852-885.* Madison's tenth *Federalist* has been interpreted by the progressives and their heirs as proof that the Constitution is a barrier to majority rule, especially by political parties responsive to a landless urban electorate. Pluralists have construed it so as to demonstrate that majority rule is rendered benign when an increase in the size of a democratic system spontaneously multiplies and diversifies political groups. In [this essay the author] argues that the essay contains a probabilistic causal theory of representation intended to prove that some fundamental cleavages can be stabilized in a federal republic by electing legislators in large, heterogeneous districts. Madison revised republican theory to prove that constitutional government is just and stable because it incorporates all interests into the legislative process on a continuing basis, contrary to the theories of Harrington, Hume, and Montesquieu.   J

286. Morris, Richard Brandon. "WE THE PEOPLE OF THE UNITED STATES": THE BICENTENNIAL OF A PEOPLE'S REVOLUTION. *Am. Hist. Rev. 1977 82(1): 1-19.* Most muted during the bicentennial year of the American Revolution were the words "people" and "revolution." Argues that

to explain so complex and multidimensional an epoch as the American Revolution and how a durable constitutional order derived, one must recognize the movement's many popular aspects. Focuses on the ordinary person, without slighting the patriot elite, whose contributions are widely accepted. "People" means those who contributed to the decisionmaking process of revolution, change, and reform. While finding a good deal of inequality in America, shows how the lower ranks of society targeted different grievances in different areas. Town meetings and county conventions transformed into mass meetings of the "Body of the People" supplanted royal governments by a popular movement. This is central to understanding 1) the formation of the Union, in which the Congress preceded the States and called them into being; and 2) the crucial role of the people in transforming the American Revolution from a war for independence to a broad-based movement of change and reform.   A

287. Nelson, Jeffrey M. IDEOLOGY IN SEARCH OF A CONTEXT: EIGHTEENTH-CENTURY BRITISH POLITICAL THOUGHT AND THE LOYALISTS OF THE AMERICAN REVOLUTION. *Hist. J. [Great Britain] 1977 20(3): 741-749.* A review article based on Robert McCluer Calhoon, *The Loyalists in Revolutionary America, 1760-1781* (New York: Harcourt, Brace & Jovanovich, 1973); Carol Berkin, *Jonathan Sewall. Odyssey of an American Loyalist* (New York: Columbia U. Pr., 1974); and Bernard Bailyn, *The Ordeal of Thomas Hutchinson* (Cambridge: Belknap Press of Harvard U. Pr., 1974). Calhoon's book is severely criticized; Berkin's is commended; Bailyn's is highly praised. 7 notes.   L. A. McGeoch

288. Noyes, Richard. A NOTE ON A FOUNDING FATHER'S LIBRARY: THE BOOKS OF BENJAMIN GILES. *Hist. New Hampshire 1979 34(3-4): 244-252.* Benjamin Giles (1717-87), as a central figure in the development of New Hampshire's constitution, can further the understanding of New Hampshire's unique role in this field. Few of Giles's papers have survived, but an inventory of his library, included in his probate records, is revealing. It includes works by Jonathan Edwards and George Whitefield not commonly read by the founding fathers. His library had a strongly Calvinistic bias, which, with Giles's known persistence, suggests that the founding fathers may have been driven, at least in part, by Puritan energy. 15 notes.   D. F. Chard

289. Onuf, Peter. TOWARDS FEDERALISM: VIRGINIA, CONGRESS, AND THE WESTERN LANDS. *William and Mary Q. 1977 34(3): 353-374.* Virginia's surrender of claims to lands north of the Ohio River strengthened the federal system. Congress' acceptance of Virginia's dictation of terms provided a means to defend states' rights and claims against other states. Thus Virginia and Congress were not competitors. Treats the background of the territorial question and the development of ideas of state sovereignty. Comments on the various land companies. Relates cessions policy and politics to constitutional issues. Primary and secondary sources; 63 notes.
                                                                          H. M. Ward

290. Onuf, Peter S. FROM COLONY TO TERRITORY: CHANGING CONCEPTS OF STATEHOOD IN REVOLUTIONARY AMERICA. *Pol.*

Sci. Q. 1982 97(3): 447-459. Early American concepts of statehood were molded by three main factors: colonialism and the concept of states as territorial entitities; revolution and the concept of states as independent, self-governing, autonomous communities; and constitutionalism and the concept of states as entities within a community of states and subservient to federal authority. The transition from the first concept to the last was difficult because many revolutionaries did not welcome the idea of subservience to a central authority. Secondary sources; 45 notes.   J. Powell

291. Peltier, Michel. 1775: NAISSANCE D'UNE NATION [1775: birth of a nation]. *Écrits de Paris [France] 1975 (348): 40-46.* Discusses the emergence of the United States as a sovereign nation, focusing on the American Revolution, France's contribution to the war, and the pragmatic spirit of the federal Constitution.

292. Pfisterer, K. Dieterich. RELIGION ALS EIN FERMENT DER FRE-IHEIT IN DER AMERIKANISCHEN REVOLUTION [Religion as a ferment of liberty in the American Revolution]. *Amerikastudien/Am. Studies [West Germany] 1976 21(2): 217-238.* The controversy over religious liberty was comprised of two movements of independence, one of political liberation from the threat of an English state church, the other of social emancipation from the European state church system. The unconditional and resourceful support of the majority of the clergy throughout the colonies was devoted to this movement and provided an indispensable second line of leadership in staving off Imperial interference with the rule of the clergy and magistrates as the natural aristocracy of the parishes. By the time of the Revolution, heirs of the 'Great Awakening' in New England and Virginia had, on the other hand, launched drives for the abolition of the traditional mainstay of social order in Western Christendom by demanding the very separation of religious and civil authority in the parishes. From the perspective of religious liberty, the American Revolution embraced intellectual, political, and social movements which appealed to different publics. The Baptists provide the clearest illustration of religious liberty as a social movement. They rejected deference in favor of conversion, the parish aristocracy and its coercion for congregational democracy and persuasion. In their drawn-out fight against New England ecclesiastical establishments they insisted on the church as a voluntary association and projected the communicative evangelist rather than the condescending cleric as the successful new leader thus stemming the tide of secularization. They quickly grew into a mass movement during the Revolution and did much to promote the voluntary association approach as a major institution in American civilization. In Virginia they provided much of the pressure that made it possible for Thomas Jefferson's *Bill for Establishing Religious Freedom* (1786) to pass the legislature and they urged James Madison to work for a clearly-worded constitutional guarantee of religious liberty in the First Amendment (1791). On the basis of their voluntary associations they built a culture which included the poor whites and the negroes, and they added conversion to honor and virtue as central values in Southern civilization. Finally Baptist history serves as a reminder that New England and Virginia are not identical with the American experience. The early radical anti-authoritarianism of the Baptists was modified by the example

of Pennsylvania which taught them that voluntary association was an adequate institutional expression both locally and regionally for a religious experience that had been an integral part of the settlement process in America and which had not been distorted by the interference of the state.   J

293.   Rainbolt, John C. AMERICANS' INITIAL VIEW OF THEIR REVO-LUTION'S SIGNIFICANCE FOR OTHER PEOPLES, 1776-1788. *Historian* *1973 35(3): 418-433.* A study of sermon and tract literature during and immediately following the American Revolution. During the first decade of independence, separatist views, belief in the westward movement of culture and power, and the theory that nations pass through fixed cycles of growth and decline all combined to prevent most Americans from expecting that their revolution would provoke violent political change in other countries. 30 notes.
                                                                                      N. W. Moen

294.   Rakove, Jack N. FRENCH DIPLOMACY AND AMERICAN POLI-TICS: THE FIRST CRISIS, 1779. *Mid-America 1978 60: 27-35.* Foreign policy dominated the Continental Congress during 1779. Events during this year were felt in the 1780's when the Constitution was written, giving the executives foreign policy initiative. The Arthur Lee-Silas Deane quarrel precipitated controversies in Congress over foreign policy. French minister Conrad Gérard's activities with the Silas Deane faction led to Congressional stalemate. The Constitution defused the divisiveness in foreign policy by giving prerogatives to the president rather than Congress. Primary and secondary sources; 13 notes.   J. M. Lee

295.   Rashid, Salim. "HE STARTLED AS IF HE SAW A SPECTRE": TUCKER'S PROPOSAL FOR AMERICAN INDEPENDENCE. *J. of the Hist. of Ideas 1982 43(3): 439-462.* Examines the ideas concerning American independence of the Reverend Josiah Tucker, a neglected British political and economic essayist with strong Christian commitments. Most scholars have had a hard time placing Tucker's opinions because of the diversity of his targets; Pitt the Elder, Benjamin Franklin, and Edmund Burke. He was an opponent of colonial wars partially because he believed even successful ones did more harm than good to the economy. His free-trade notions may have influenced Turgot and Adam Smith. While realizing that the Americans' protests against the Navigation and Stamp acts did not actually stem from a Whig desire for full representation in Parliament, he urged his countrymen to agree to the colonists' separation on the grounds that it was inevitable, that it would not harm trade, and that all colonial peoples would and should eventually strive for autonomy. 61 notes.   W. J. Reedy

296.   Reardon, Paul C. THE MASSACHUSETTS CONSTITUTION MARKS A MILESTONE. *Publius 1982 12(1): 45-55.* The constitution of the state of Massachusetts, ratified in 1780, is an important historical document, as it had a profound effect on the ratification of the Federal Constitution. John Adams was the draftsman of the Massachusetts constitution after becoming an expert by studying constitutions, both ancient and modern. In drafting the Massachusetts constitution, he borrowed from the Pennsylvania Declaration and the 1776 Virginia Bill of Rights. Primary sources; 27 notes.   J. Powell

297.   Reichley, John A. YORKTOWN: THE BRIDGE. *Military Rev. 1981 61(10): 15-22.* The Battle of Yorktown during the American Revolution served as a bridge between the Declaration of Independence and the US Constitution. It was the crowning battle of the revolution and was a major stepping-stone toward the formation of the new republic. 9 pictures, 2 maps, 4 notes.
                                                                          D. H. Cline

298.   Richardson, Elliot. THE REVOLUTION THAT BEGAN IN 1215: FORCES BEHIND THE WAR OF INDEPENDENCE. *Round Table [Great Britain] 1976 (263): 225-231.* Examines the influence of English political and constitutional theory on the American Revolution, focusing on the influence of the Magna Carta and John Locke's *Second Treatise on Government* (1690). The revolution was inspired by 561 years of English political theory and institutional development.   C. Anstey

299.   Riley, Patrick. MARTIN DIAMOND'S VIEW OF *THE FEDERAL- IST. Publius 1978 8(3): 71-101.* In *"The Federalist's* View of Federalism" (1961) the late Martin Diamond argued that *The Federalist Papers* were not defending federal government as conceived by Montesquieu and others, 1748-87, but were attacking the idea of a *foedus* of small republics on the ground that such an arrangement led to factious turbulence; in order to gain support for their own combination of nationalism and federalism, however, Hamilton and Madison had to distort earlier ideas about federalism, which actually supported their opponents to make it appear they had tradition on their side.

300.   Rougé, Robert. LE DROIT DE RÉSISTANCE PENDANT LA RÉV- OLUTION AMÉRICAINE: THÉORIE ET PRATIQUE [The right of resis- tance during the American Revolution: theory and practice]. *Rev. Française d'Etudes Américaines [France] 1976 (2): 109-118.* Examines the origins of the theory of the "right of resistance" in the British North American colonies during 1763-76, reviewing its more practical rather than theoretical implica- tions.

301.   Royster, Charles; Palmer, R. R. (commentary). MILITARY DISCI- PLINE AND THE WINNING OF THE REVOLUTIONARY WAR. *Consortium on Revolutionary Europe 1750-1850: Pro. 1981: 202-208.* Discuss- es the necessity during the American Revolution to create a well-disciplined standing army. Such a force was created in defiance of revolutionary dogma that inspired, informal citizen-soldiers were the only proper defenders of freedom. In practice, however, revolutionary zeal, which tended to erode quickly, did not provide the margin of victory. Commentary, pp. 209-215. 18 notes.   D. Powell

302.   Rutland, Robert A. FREEDOM OF THE PRESS AND THE FIRST AMENDMENT. *Virginia Cavalcade 1983 32(3): 134-143.* Focuses on 18th- century arguments for freedom of the press, especially during the 1770's and 80's, and the legal protection gained with the ratification of the Bill of Rights.

303.   Ryerson, Richard Alan; Palmer, R. R. (commentary). FROM SOCIAL ACCIDENT TO POLITICAL DESIGN: THE TRANSFORMATION OF PUBLIC OFFICEHOLDING DURING THE AMERICAN REVOLU-TION. *Consortium on Revolutionary Europe 1750-1810: Pro. 1981: 193-201.* Describes changes in American leadership criteria during the 1770's. Prior to the American Revolution, European-style elites held positions of authority to such an extent that, in some colonies, most legislators were related. Since these leaders mostly favored the status quo, including British rule, they were largely displaced in the new order. The new US Constitution did not discriminate against the elite, but it canceled their birthright of leadership. Comments, pp. 209-215. 26 notes.   D. Powell

304.   Saage, Richard. PROBLEME DER SOZIALGESCHICHTE DER AMERIKANISCHEN REVOLUTION [Problems of the social history of the American Revolution]. *Neue Politische Literatur [West Germany] 1974 19(3): 310-339.* Review article of 24 books. Examines in the light of recent research the constitutional ideas and social reality of the American Revolution and demonstrates the erosion of these ideas by class interests in the course of the Revolution. As the distinction between workers and owners of the means of production was not yet clearly marked, a petty-bourgeois mentality could prevail even in the "mob." 88 notes.   G. Hollenberg

305.   Schambra, William A. MARTIN DIAMOND'S DOCTRINE OF THE AMERICAN REGIME. *Publius 1978 8(3): 218.* The late Martin Diamond taught that the American regime, though founded on self-interest as academic orthodoxy maintains, permits an ascent to the philosophic virtues its critics would say it sacrificed; according to Diamond, the acquisitiveness of *The Federalist* (1787-88) led to the adoption of bourgeois virtues, the federal-national compound of the Constitution led to the adoption of republican virtues, and the Declaration of Independence, by not suggesting men were equal in every respect, encouraged a natural aristocracy to create "enclaves of excellence."

306.   Schilfert, Gerhard. ZEITGENÖSSISCHE DEUTSCHE HISTORIKER ÜBER DIE AMERIKANISCHE BÜRGERLICHE REVOLUTION [Contemporary German historians on the American bourgeois revolution]. *Zeitschrift für Geschichtswissenschaft [East Germany] 1979 27(8): 736-750.* During the 18th century, professional historians in Germany based their positive or negative evaluations of the American Revolution on Enlightenment philosophy. Matthias Christian Sprengel (1746-1803) recognized the world historical importance of the Revolution. Daniel Ebeling (1741-1817) lectured and published on constitutional and economic developments in North America. Julius August Remer (1738-1803) and Johann Christian Schmohl (b. 1736) were also pro-American. In contrast, the prominent historian August Ludwig von Schlözer was critical of the rebellious Americans. 73 notes.
                                                              J. T. Walker

307.   Schulte Nordholt, J. W. THE EXAMPLE OF THE DUTCH REPUB-LIC FOR AMERICAN FEDERALISM. *Bijdragen en Mededelingen Betreffende de Geschiedenis der Nederlanden [Netherlands] 1979 94(3): 437-449.*

The Founding Fathers admired the Dutch Republic and its heroic struggle for independence against Spain. Yet, they were rather critical of its political structure. James Madison and others felt that the Dutch Republic was an example of a tragic failure of a Republic which allowed for too much individualism, placed the local and provincial interest above national concerns, and did not recognize the quality of the provinces. Primary sources; 28 notes.

G. D. Homan

308. Schwartz, Barry. GEORGE WASHINGTON AND THE WHIG CONCEPTION OF HEROIC LEADERSHIP. *Am. Sociol. Rev. 1983 48(1): 18-33.* Before George Washington had a chance to display his skill in pitched battle, he became a focal point for the *rage militaire* that swept through America in 1775. By the end of the American Revolution, however, Washington had been transformed from a military hero into the new republic's great moral symbol. This transformation is studied by looking at Washington's wartime conduct in light of a political culture that fostered intense suspicion of all forms of power and belief in "virtue" as an antidote for man's innate corruptibility. Refusing time and again to convert his military prestige into political power, Washington personified the heroic archetype of the Anglo-American Whig tradition. J

309. Shalhope, Robert E. THE IDEOLOGICAL ORIGINS OF THE SECOND AMENDMENT. *J. of Am. Hist. 1982 69(3): 599-614.* Analyzes the origins of the 2d Amendment to the Constitution in the context of libertarian thought and the American revolutionary tradition. Libertarian writers in the 17th and 18th centuries, motivated by fear of monarchical authority, linked standing, professional armies and a disarmed citizenry with loss of liberty. Dedication in the 18th century to republicanism assumed a strong relationship between agrarianism and the possession of arms. James Madison blended two distinct but related rights, the individual's right to possess arms and the need for state militias of ordinary citizens, into the same amendment. Based on 17th- and 18th-century libertarian writings and American Revolutionary Era essays and pamphlets; 47 notes. T. P. Linkfield

310. Slaughter, Thomas P. THE TAX MAN COMETH: IDEOLOGICAL OPPOSITION TO INTERNAL TAXES, 1760-1790. *William and Mary Q. 1984 41(4): 566-591.* Antifederalists opposed the Constitution's granting to the federal government the power to regulate external and internal commerce, including the levying of imposts and taxes. Their opposition stemmed from the distinction the colonists made between internal and external taxes during the Stamp Act crisis of 1765 and from broader antifederalist views on questions of representation and sovereignty. Reviews localist positions during the Confederation period and in relation to the Constitutional Convention and the ratification of the Constitution. To antifederalist localists, the issues were little different from those of the 1760's. The developing "court" and "country" factions of the 1790's differed chiefly as to their stands on the distinction between external and internal taxation. Based on the political literature and pamphlets; 75 notes. H. M. Ward

311. Stourzh, Gerald. VOM ARISTOTELISCHEN ZUM LIBERALEN VERFASSUNGSBEGRIFF: ZUR ENTWICKLUNG IN ENGLAND UND NORDAMERIKA IM 17. UND 18. JAHRHUNDERT [From an Aristotelian to a liberal concept of constitutions: its evolution in England and North America in the 17th and 18th centuries]. *Wiener Beiträge zur Geschichte der Neuzeit [Austria] 1975 2: 97-122.* Examines the influence of Aristotelian teachings about forms of government on 17th- and 18th-century political terminology, considers the origins and spread of the term "constitution," and describes fundamental rights in Great Britain, and individual rights in North America.

312. Swindler, William F. OF REVOLUTION, LAW AND ORDER. *Supreme Court Hist. Soc. Y. 1976: 16-24.* Describes the debate between 1775 and 1789 in the Continental Congress over the formation of some type of independent agency to handle disputes between states or disputes between citizens of different states, which resulted in the establishment of the Federal courts under the Judiciary Act of 1789.

313. Swindler, William F. TOWARD 1787: BETWEEN WAR AND PEACE IN 1782. *Supreme Court Hist. Soc. Y. 1982: 101-103.* The surrender of the British army under Cornwallis at Yorktown in 1781 did not end the American Revolution. A formal peace was not signed for another 16 months. Diplomatic relations only compounded the problems of a new government operating under the Articles of Confederation. The Continental Army continued to exist, and the lack of money hampered the new nation. The nation's lack of direction during 1782 led to a struggle for economic and political survival for the next five years. Illus.   G. B. Childress

314. Swindler, William F. TOWARD 1987: A "PRE-CONSTITUTIONAL" LAW CASE. *Supreme Court Hist. Soc. Y. 1983: 113-116.* The 1783 case involving the Wyoming Valley border dispute between Connecticut and Pennsylvania was the only complete "constitutional" case under the Articles of Confederation. It was settled by an ad hoc legislative court set up to settle land disputes between states. 5 illus.   G. B. Childress

315. Swindler, William F. TOWARD 1987—TWO MILESTONES IN 1781. *Supreme Court Hist. Soc. Y. 1981: 117-120.* Discusses the impact of the ratification of the Articles of Confederation and the victory at Yorktown in 1781 on the political process that led to the Constitutional Convention of 1787 in Philadelphia. The government created by the articles was severely limited and clumsy; but their ratification helped create a climate of unity that made possible the drafting of the Constitution in 1787. Includes excerpts from the Articles of Confederation and a list of signers; 4 photos.   G. V. Wasson

316. Tarter, Brent. VIRGINIANS AND THE BILL OF RIGHTS. *Virginia Cavalcade 1982 32(2): 62-75.* George Mason authored the Declaration of Rights at the Virginia Convention in 1776, which later formed one of the bases for the Bill of Rights in 1791.

317. Van Atta, John R. CAUTION, CRISIS, AND EXILE: THE UP-ROOTING OF THE AMERICAN LOYALISTS. *Indiana Social Studies Q. 1974/75 27(3): 44-56.* Examines the political theory of the loyalists during the American Revolution. S

318. Wendel, Jacques M. TURGOT AND THE AMERICAN REVOLU-TION. *Modern Age 1979 23(3): 282-289.* Anne Robert Turgot (1727-81) was minister of finance to Louis XVI from 1774 to 1776, the early years of the American Revolution. He believed in the virtue and inevitable success of the revolution but warned that France could neither financially nor socially afford to overtly aid it. French intellectuals saw America as the hope of mankind and magnified American virtues to demonstrate the validity of their ideals. Turgot, however, was not blinded to what he believed were American inadequacies. He complained that state constitutions failed to adopt the physiocratic principle of distinguishing for purposes of taxation between those who owned land and those who did not, the principle of direct taxation of property holders had not been followed, and a complicated legal and administrative structure had been created to regulate commerce. On the social level Turgot and the philosophes suffered further disappointment: a religious oath was required of elected officials and slavery was not abolished. Turgot died in 1781 before the conclusion of the war. Although disappointed, Turgot never doubted positive evolution. Based on Turgot's letters and published works; 57 notes.

C. A. D'Aniello

319. Wendel, Thomas. AMERICA'S RISING SUN: THE HUMANITIES AND ARTS IN THE FRAMING OF CONSTITUTIONAL LIBERTY. *San José Studies 1984 10(2): 4-13.* Reviews the role of the arts and humanities in American culture at the time of the Constitutional Convention, highlighting the humanist studies of the signers of the Constitution.

320. Wilson, Gary E. THE FIRST AMERICAN HOSTAGES IN MOS-LEM NATIONS, 1784-1789. *Am. Neptune 1981 41(3): 208-224.* Surveys American foreign relations with Morocco and Algiers. In October 1784 Morocco captured the *Betsey* and held its crew for almost 10 months before releasing them unharmed at the urging of Spain. In 1787 a treaty was signed with Morocco, whose forces seized only one more US vessel, the *Polly,* which was returned immediately, during the next decade. Algiers captured two American ships in 1785, treated the crews badly, and rejected all attempts to gain their release until the new government under the Constitution took office. Describes negotiations and debates over policy. 46 notes. J. C. Bradford

321. Wood, Gordon S. EIGHTEENTH-CENTURY AMERICAN CON-STITUTIONALISM. *This Constitution 1983 (1): 9-13.* From the beginning of colonial protest in the 1760's, American colonists diverged from English thinking which regarded constitutional law as equal to other legislative acts, to regard it as law that precedes and is of a higher authority than legislative actions.

322. Wright, Esmond. THE REVOLUTION AND THE CONSTITUTION: MODELS OF WHAT AND FOR WHOM? *Ann. of the Am. Acad. of Pol.*

and Social Sci. 1976 428: 1-21. The United States won its independence by war, but without the social upheaval that today usually is associated with "revolution." If the documents of 1776 and 1787 are examined objectively, their value for revolutionary "models" is limited. The units of self-government in 1787 were ready-made, thanks to 150 years of loose and liberal imperial control. The struggle was defended in terms of a parallel: seventeenth-century "Commonwealth Men" against the Stuarts, using familiar English concepts. The emphasis on the separation of powers and the primacy of the legislature had little to commend itself to the post-1945 republics, where power has been concentrated at the top—personal and charismatic. If "1787" was democracy at all, it was for men only, and then only if they were white and propertied. Nothing was planned either for imitation or for export. But images count in politics and history. Ideas are believed to be transferable and phrases quotable. Throughout the nineteenth century, the United States was seen as a model, however erroneously. Now there are other, cruder models for imitation. It is unlikely that any of these will produce the remarkable—because unique— liberal society that emerged in the United States in and after 1787.   J

323. Yarbrough, Jean. REPRESENTATION AND REPUBLICANISM: TWO VIEWS. *Publius 1979 9(2): 77-98.* Examines the political theories of Antifederalists Melancton Smith and Richard Henry Lee, and Federalists James Madison and Alexander Hamilton during the 1780's, focusing on the latter pair. The Antifederalists believed that the public good was served when representatives reflected and had to reconcile private interests, while the Federalists believed that representatives could rise to serve the public good regardless of their private interests. Hamilton and Madison adopted the British interest in virtual representation to meet the requirements of republicanism. The British conceived that an official was representative if he shared the interests of his constituents and that consequently the disfranchisement of large sections of the population did not matter, while the Federalists refined representation by extending the electoral districts: by increasing the ratio of constituents to representatives they insured that the best men would be elected and still allowed widespread suffrage. Unlike the British they contended that representation was based on election and not on mutuality of interest. 46 notes.
                                                                                          S

Books

324. Conkin, Paul K. *Self-Evident Truths: Being a Discourse on the Origins and Development of the First Principles of American Government—Popular Sovereignty, Natural Rights, and Balance and Separation of Powers.* Bloomington: Indiana U. Pr., 1974. 211 pp.

325. Corner, George W., ed. *Aspects of American Liberty: Philosophical, Historical, and Political.* Philadelphia, Pa.: Am. Phil. Soc., 1977. 233 pp.

326. Crosskey, William Winslow and Jeffrey, William, Jr. *Politics and the Constitution in the History of the United States. Vol. 3: The Political*

Background of the Federal Convention. Chicago: U. of Chicago Pr., 1981. 592 pp.

327. Davis, Joseph L. *Sectionalism in American Politics, 1774-1787.* Madison: U. of Wisconsin Pr., 1977. 239 pp.

328. Derry, John. *English Politics and the American Revolution.* New York: St. Martin's, 1976. 215 pp.

329. Ferris, Robert G., ed. *Signers of the Constitution: Historic Places Commemorating the Signing of the Constitution.* (National Survey of Historic Sites and Buildings, vol. 19.) Washington: Natl. Park Service, 1976. 355 pp.

330. Gephart, Ronald M., comp. *Revolutionary America, 1763-1789: A Bibliography.* 2 vol. Washington: Lib. of Congress, 1984. 1672 pp.

331. Griffin, Edward M. *Old Brick: Charles Chauncy of Boston, 1705-1787.* (Minnesota Monographs in the Humanities, vol. 11.) Minneapolis: U. of Minnesota Pr., 1980. 248 pp.

332. Jensen, Merrill, ed. *The Documentary History of the Ratification of the Constitution. Vol. 1: Constitutional Documents and Records, 1776-1787.* (National Historical Publications Commission and University of Wisconsin.) Madison: State Hist. Soc. of Wisconsin, 1976. 391 pp.

333. Madison, James. *The Papers of James Madison. Vol. 9: 9 April 1786-24 May 1787 with Supplement, 1781-1784.* Robert A. Rutland and William M. E. Rachal, ed. Chicago: U. of Chicago Pr., 1975. 446 pp.

334. Main, Jackson Turner. *Political Parties before the Constitution.* Chapel Hill: U. of North Carolina Pr. for the Inst. of Early Am. Hist. and Culture, 1973. 481 pp.

335. Marks, Frederick W., III. *Independence on Trial: Foreign Affairs and the Making of the Constitution.* Baton Rouge: Louisiana State U. Pr., 1973. 256 pp.

336. Onuf, Peter S. *The Origins of the Federal Republic: Jurisdictional Controversies in the United States, 1775-1787.* Philadelphia: U. of Pennsylvania Pr., 1983. 284 pp.

337. Rakove, Jack N. *The Beginnings of National Politics: An Interpretive History of the Continental Congress.* New York: Knopf, 1979. 484 pp.

338. Storing, Herbert J. and Dry, Murray, ed. *The Complete Anti-Federalist. Vol. 2: Objections of Non-Signers of the Constitution and Major Series of Essays at the Outset.* Chicago: U. of Chicago Pr., 1981. 452 pp.

339. Storing, Herbert J. *What the Anti-Federalists Were For: The Political Thought of the Opponents of the Constitution. Vol. 1 of the Complete Anti-Federalist.* Chicago: U. of Chicago Pr., 1981. 111 pp.

340. Wood, Gordon S. *The Confederation and the Constitution: The Critical Issues.* 1973. Reprint ed., Washington: U. Pr. of Am., 1979. 205 pp.

Dissertations

341. Bell, Barry Ray. "The Ideology and Rhetoric of the American Revolution." U. of Virginia 1977. 237 pp. *DAI 1978 39(2): 879-880-A.*

342. Bogin, Ruth. "Abraham Clark and the Idea of Equality in Revolutionary New Jersey." Union Grad. School 1978. 349 pp. *DAI 1978 39(3): 1781-A.*

343. Bordelon, Joseph Michael. "The Antifederalists and the Agrarian Republic: Securing the Blessings of Liberty through a Less Perfect Union." U. of Dallas 1974. 252 pp. *DAI 1976 36(8): 5506-A.*

344. diZerega, Augustus, VI. "Citizenship and Participation: A Reformulation of Democratic Theory." U. of California, Berkeley 1984. 448 pp. *DAI 1985 45(9): 2979-2980-A.* DA8426938

345. Jacobs, Roberta Tansman. "The Treaty and the Tories: The Ideological Reaction to the Return of the Loyalists, 1783-1787." Cornell U. 1974. 252 pp. *DAI 1975 35(7): 4384-4385-A.*

346. Kessler, Sanford Harvey. "John Locke and the Founding of American Civil Religion." Boston Coll. 1979. 283 pp. *DAI 1979 40(3): 1666-1667-A.*

347. Landi, Alexander R. "The Politics of James Madison." U. of Dallas 1973. 327 pp. *DAI 1974 35(2): 1182-A.*

348. Lence, Ross Marlo. "The American Declaration of Independence: A Study of Its Polemical and Philosophical Antecedents." Indiana U. 1973. 278 pp. *DAI 1974 34(9): 6071-A.*

349. Lynch, Edward John. "The Character and Conduct of Representative Government: The Political Thought of *The Federalist.*" Duke U. 1977. 234 pp. *DAI 1977 38(4): 2326-2327-A.*

350. Miller, Joshua I. "Local Autonomy in Early American Politics: Decentralist Ideas and Practices, 1630-1789." Princeton U. 1984. 155 pp. *DAI 1984 44(11): 3483-A.* DA8405122

351. O'Brien, William Arthur. "Challenge to Consensus: Social, Political and Economic Implications of Maryland Sectionalism, 1776-1789." U. of Wisconsin, Madison 1979. 523 pp. *DAI 1979 40(6): 3492-3493-A.*

352. Rowland, John Kenneth. "Origins of the Second Amendment: The Creation of the Constitutional Rights of Militia and of Keeping and Bearing Arms." Ohio State U. 1978. 463 pp. *DAI 1979 39(8): 5106-5107-A.*

353. Saar, Doreen. "Crèvecoeur's Lucubration on the Meaning of America: A Study of *Letters from an American Farmer.*" State U. of New York, Buffalo 1983. 255 pp. *DAI 1983 44(1): 170-A.* DA8312442

354. Shumer, Sara Mayhew. "The Political Republic and America: Essays in Retrieval." U. of California, Berkeley 1978. 447 pp. *DAI 1979 40(1): 440-A.*

3

THE CONVENTION AND RATIFICATION OF THE CONSTITUTION, 1787-1790

Article Abstracts

355. Adler, Mortimer J. and Gorman, William. A COMMENTARY ON THE PREAMBLE TO THE CONSTITUTION OF THE UNITED STATES. *Center Mag. 1976 9(1): 38-65.* Analyzes key political, governmental, and legal points in the Preamble to the US Constitution, and outlines the historical background of its formulation, 1775-91.

356. Agresto, John. "A SYSTEM WITHOUT PRECEDENT"—JAMES MADISON AND THE REVOLUTION IN REPUBLICAN LIBERTY. *South Atlantic Q. 1983 82(2): 129-144.* The challenge confronting the new nation after winning its independence from Great Britain was to effect a system that had no political precedent. In the *Federalist No. 10* James Madison urged the exploitation of factionalism since it had a great deal to do with personal freedom. The new republic would allow for growth and expansion of individual rights as the popular version of itself grew. Americans could indulge themselves with the notion that democracy and liberty were complementary and progressive forces—the true radicalism that Madison proposed as the solution to the new nation's political exigencies. Based on published letters of some of the founding fathers; 54 notes.   H. M. Parker, Jr.

357. Alberts, Robert C. BUSINESS OF THE HIGHEST MAGNITUDE OR DON'T PUT OFF UNTIL TOMORROW WHAT YOU CAN RAM THROUGH TODAY. *Am. Heritage 1971 22(2): 48-53, 101-103.* Describes the struggle between the Democrats and Federalists in Pennsylvania over ratification of the US Constitution in 1787.   S

358. Alberts, Robert C. THE CANTANKEROUS MR. MACLAY. *Am. Heritage 1974 25(6): 48-50, 84-89.* Excerpts from William Maclay's diary written during the First Congress.   S

359. Anderson, James L. THE QUEST FOR ORDER IN FEDERALIST AMERICA. *Consortium on Revolutionary Europe 1750-1850: Pro. 1976 29-41.* The quest for order in Federalist America created symbols of control. Concomitant public support for actual institutions did not, however, materialize. The result was a continuing suspicion of the army, militia, law enforcement agencies, and judicial systems. Based on Congressional records, printed sources, and secondary sources; 60 notes.   R. Howell, Jr.

360. Archer, John B. THE FIRST NEW HAMPSHIRE CONVENTION TO RATIFY THE CONSTITUTION, FEBRUARY, 1788, AND THE TOSCAN REPORT. *Hist. New Hampshire 1981 36(1): 38-57.* The first New Hampshire convention called to debate the proposed Constitution in 1788 adjourned after nine days of discussion when it became apparent that the majority opposed ratification. Jean Toscan, French vice-consul at Portsmouth, drafted a report, printed here, on the proceedings. Toscan's account drew on New Hampshire newspapers, which published parts of the debates. The most striking thing about Toscan's account is that it demonstrates how similar the New Hampshire debates were to the Massachusetts debates on the Constitution. 26 notes.   D. F. Chard

361. Babu, B. Ramesh. THE EPHEMERAL AND THE ETERNAL IN THE FEDERALIST. *Indian J. of Am. Studies [India] 1979 9(1): 3-14.* Explores the enduring political themes found in the 85 essays of Alexander Hamilton, James Madison, and John Jay published as *The Federalist.* Such themes include: union and liberty, the federal system of government, the separation of powers, the system of checks and balances, and elections. In all this, the single overriding concern was the freedom of the individual. The complex system of government was proposed to secure the blessings of liberty. In the mixture of the ephemeral and the eternal found in *The Federalist,* the latter outweighs the former. 17 notes.   L. V. Eid

362. Baldasty, Gerald J. FLIRTING WITH SOCIAL SCIENCE: METHODOLOGY AND VIRGINIA NEWSPAPERS, 1785-86. *Journalism Hist. 1974 1(3): 86-89.* Uses press articles to examine the later First Amendment's provision for freedom of the press, as a means of verifying historiographical questions.

363. Baldasty, Gerald J. TOWARD AN UNDERSTANDING OF THE FIRST AMENDMENT: BOSTON NEWSPAPERS, 1782-1791. *Journalism Hist. 1976 3(1): 25-30, 32.* Examines the meaning of the First Amendment regarding freedom of the press by reference to the views expressed in Boston newspapers at the time and the legal constraints against the press as shown by court cases relating to defamation.

364. Banning, Lance. JEFFERSONIAN IDEOLOGY AND THE FRENCH REVOLUTION: A QUESTION OF LIBERTICIDE AT HOME. *Studies in Burke and His Time 1976 17(1): 5-26.* Events of the French Revolution were interpreted in America in terms of the domestic struggle between Federalists and Republicans. Republicans viewed the Revolution as a fight against executive tyranny and the destruction of liberty and believed

themselves to be engaged in the same struggle against the Federalists. Primary sources; 61 notes.   H. T. Blethen

365.   Banning, Lance. REPUBLICAN IDEOLOGY AND THE TRIUMPH OF THE CONSTITUTION, 1789 TO 1793. *William and Mary Q. 1974 31(2): 167-188.* Antifederalists thought the Constitution would endanger Republican government, yet they acceded to the Constitution. The Republican party of the 1790's Americanized English opposition thought, and with the Federalists found a meeting ground in classical constitutionalism. Analyzes historiography on the ratification of the Constitution and Republican ideology. Comments on the origin of political parties in America. Based on correspondence of period and secondary sources; 45 notes.   H. M. Ward

366.   Barrett, C. Waller. THE MIRACLE OF THE CONSTITUTION. *Supreme Court Hist. Soc. Y. 1978: 97-102.* Discusses the brilliance of the Founding Fathers in writing the Constitution in 1787.

367.   Best, Judith A. THE ITEM VETO: WOULD THE FOUNDERS APPROVE? *Presidential Studies Q. 1984 14(2): 183-188.* In the *Federalist*, both Alexander Hamilton and James Madison expressed concern for executive defense against legislative tyranny; both saw the veto as the means to prevent the enactment of improper laws. The veto has become a crucial check in the system of separation of powers. Based on the *Federalist;* 27 notes.
                                                        D. H. Cline-Burnett

368.   Birkby, Robert H. POLITICS OF ACCOMMODATION: THE ORIGIN OF THE SUPREMACY CLAUSE. *Western Pol. Q. 1966 19(1): 123-135.* Views the emergence of the Supremacy Clause in the 1787 Constitutional Convention as a compromise between nationalists and states' righters.
                                                                          S

369.   Black, Frederick R. THE AMERICAN REVOLUTION AS "YARDSTICK" IN THE DEBATES ON THE CONSTITUTION, 1787-1788. *Pro. of the Am. Phil. Soc. 1973 117(3): 162-185.* The Federalists and Antifederalists used the American Revolution "as a rhetorical strategy with the aim of influencing public opinion in their favor. Attention has been focused on explicit references to the Revolution in public speeches and writings. Direct allusions to the Revolution appear much more frequently in public statements than in private correspondence, suggesting calculated use of the Revolution to mobilize support." 85 notes.   C. W. Olson

370.   Boston, Ray. THE IMPACT OF "FOREIGN LIARS" ON THE AMERICAN PRESS (1790-1800). *Journalism Q. 1973 50(4): 722-730.* Examines the influence of British exile journalists, who vilified John Adams and the Federalists, on the Democratic-Republican press, run by William Duane (1790-1800).   S

371.   Bourke, Paul F. THE PLURALIST READING OF JAMES MADISON'S TENTH FEDERALIST. *Perspectives in Am. Hist. 1975 9: 271-295.* In his 10th *Federalist*, James Madison exhibited a modern understanding of the

character of political groupings and their inherent machinations. Many modern pluralists have cited the 10th *Federalist* as evidence of Madison's early perception of political expression, but the author believes this lifts Madison out of historical perspective. Calls for a reexamination of the accuracy of pluralists' views. 28 notes.   W. A. Wiegand

372. Bowling, Kenneth R. THE BIDDLE SALE OF RUSH PAPERS AND OTHER LETTERS FROM PENNSYLVANIA MEMBERS OF THE FIRST FEDERAL CONGRESS TO THEIR CONSTITUENTS. *Manuscripts 1972 24(3): 172-181.* Reviews the manuscript papers of the members of the First Congress, particularly those of the Pennsylvania delegates. "Evidence in the Benjamin Rush Papers (the political portion of which was sold by Parke-Bernet in the three-part Alexander Biddle Sale in 1943 and 1944) and the restricted Tench Coxe Papers at the Historical Society of Pennsylvania" indicates that the Philadelphia Federalists: 1) "served as a national clearing house for news about ratification of the proposed United States Constitution in 1788"; 2) considered the First Congress to be "a second session of the Constitutional Convention of 1787"; and 3) were vitally concerned with the location of the national capital. 3 notes.   D. A. Yanchisin

373. Boyd, Steven R. ANTIFEDERALISTS AND THE ACCEPTANCE OF THE CONSTITUTION: PENNSYLVANIA, 1787-1792. *Publius 1979 9(2): 123-137.* Pennsylvanian Antifederalists prepared the way for their own defeat by participating in the ratification process according to the rules established by the Federalists. They participated in the ratification convention and ran for offices in the federal election. Rather than reject outright the concept of the Constitution, they proposed revisions and a second constitutional convention; consequently, they legitimized the concept of the federal government to the voters. 42 notes.   S

374. Boyett, Gene W. DEVELOPING THE CONCEPT OF THE REPUBLICAN PRESIDENCY, 1787-1788. *Presidential Studies Q. 1977 7(4): 199-208.* Concerns the conflicting views of the presidency during 1787-88. Antifederalists, particularly, feared the office as potentially monarchical, while Federalists pointed out obvious differences between their concept of a president and the British crown. Other fears concerned the mingling of branches of government, as in treaty making, and the presidential power of veto. Providing for presidential impeachment undercut proponents of a multiple rather than a unitary executive branch. There was, however, almost unanimous agreement on the president's indirect election. The result was a strong, though limited, executive, independent of Congress, but not controlled by the people. 85 notes.   J. Tull

375. Buel, Richard, Jr. THE DEMISE OF ANTIFEDERALISM. *Rev. in Am. Hist. 1980 8(3): 334-338.* Review essay of Steven R. Boyd's *The Politics of Opposition: Antifederalists and the Acceptance of the Constitution* (Millwood, N.Y.: KTO Pr., 1979) and John E. O'Connor's *William Paterson: Lawyer and Statesman, 1745-1806* (New Brunswick, N.J.: Rutgers U. Pr., 1979).

376. Campbell, Leon G. THE POLITICS OF PREPARATION: A COMPARISON OF THE POLITICAL THOUGHT OF ALEXANDER HAMILTON AND JUAN BAUTISTA ALBERDI. *R. Interamericana R. [Puerto Rico] 1974 4(1): 85-95.* The careers of Hamilton (1755-1804) in the United States and Alberdi (1814-86) in Argentina are very much alike. Both men laid the philosophical groundwork for the constitutions of their countries. Secondary sources; 4 notes, biblio.   J. Lewis

377. Carey, George W. ON INVENTING AND EXPLAINING AMERICA. *Modern Age 1982 26(2): 122-135.* Critiques Garry Wills's *Explaining America: The Federalist* (1981), particularly with respect to the significance of the Scottish Enlightenment upon the thought of James Madison and Alexander Hamilton. Although there was a consensus on the need for a strong national government, it is difficult to show a singular or unified impact of the Scottish Enlightenment upon both Madison and Hamilton. There are also difficulties in resolving the problem of explaining how the extended republic proposed in the *Federalist* will check factious majorities while allowing virtuous majorities to rule. Wills's interpretation is that the *Federalist* believes that the republican genius of the people will result in selecting representatives who will promote national rather than local interests. A more adequate interpretation is that the *Federalist* envisions the goal to be achieved through the character of the representational institution itself. 41 notes.   R. D. Rahmes

378. Carey, George W. PUBLIUS—A SPLIT PERSONALITY? *Rev. of Pol. 1984 46(1): 5-22.* Debunks the theory that two writers known to have used the pseudonym Publius in the *Federalist*, Alexander Hamilton and James Madison, differed in political theory sufficiently to describe Publius as a split personality. Tensions in a consensual work such as the *Federalist* arise from inherent contradictions in republicanism, rather than theoretical differences among its authors. 20 notes.   R. Grove

379. Carey, George W. SEPARATION OF POWERS AND THE MADISONIAN MODEL: A REPLY TO THE CRITICS. *Am. Pol. Sci. Rev. 1978 72(1): 151-164.* This article critically examines the commonly held proposition that Madison advocated separation of powers as a means of thwarting majority rule, or, conversely, of protecting identifiable minority interests. Rather, Madison's chief purpose in advancing the doctrine of separation of powers— one which was shared by the majority of his contemporaries—was to prevent governmental tyranny whose characteristic feature was seen as arbitrary and capricious rule resulting in government of men, not of laws. Many modern critics' analyses of the Madisonian model (most notably, Burns, Dahl, and advocates of a responsible party system) are seriously deficient because they fail to take into account this dimension of the model. Madison's writings, principally in *The Federalist*, as well as his remarks at the Philadelphia convention, clearly indicate that one of his central concerns was simultaneously to provide for protection against governmental tyranny and to guarantee popular control of government. This article examines in some detail certain critical aspects of this endeavor.   J

380.   Carey, George W. THE SUPREME COURT, JUDICIAL REVIEW AND FEDERALIST SEVENTY-EIGHT. *Modern Age 1974 18(4): 356-369.* Hamiltonian theory, apparently quaint and outdated, possesses virtue and dignity of a sound philosophic and moral basis, notably lacking in the fatuous, fashionable theories which justify judicial usurpation of power in the name of democracy. Based on secondary documents and *Federalist* No. 78 (1788); 27 notes.   M. L. Lifka

381.   Clark, Jonathan. THE MYTH OF CONSOLIDATING FEDERAL-ISTS. *Hist. Reflections [Canada] 1977 4(1): 111-135.* Illuminates the original tendencies and aims of the Federalists who formed the US Constitution, in relation to the attitudes toward states' sovereignty.

382.   Conniff, James. ON THE OBSOLESCENCE OF THE GENERAL WILL: ROUSSEAU, MADISON, AND THE EVOLUTION OF REPUBLI-CAN POLITICAL THOUGHT. *Western Pol. Q. 1975 28(1): 32-58.* James Madison revolutionized the political theory of the Republican form of government in *Federalist* No. 10. Republican theory before Madison's formulation was based on classical examples and on the idea that society could achieve an objective good. In addition it was thought that a Republic must have a homogeneous population and possess a small land area. The author shows how Jean Jacques Rousseau fitted into this pattern. The varied population and great expanse of the United States made it difficult for the Federalists to defend the new Constitution. Madison's solution was to reject the idea of the government enacting the general will and to maintain that its job was to balance competing interests. In that case the stronger the central government was and the greater was the size of the country, the smaller the chance that any social group could gain unacceptable levels of power. Based on published works including the *Federalist Papers*; 116 notes.   G. B. McKinney

383.   Cress, Lawrence Delbert. A WELL-REGULATED MILITIA: THE ORIGINS AND MEANING OF THE SECOND AMENDMENT. *Virginia Cavalcade 1983 33(2): 64-71.* Traces the 2d Amendment from its roots in Anglo-American political and constitutional theory through American political events, such as the Boston Massacre, which led to the condemnation of standing armies and to the desire for a well-regulated militia as expressed in Virginia's 1776 Declaration of Rights; to the generation that ratified it, the amendment was at once a declaration of a fundamental principle of good government and a means to protect the stability of republican institutions.

384.   Crosby, Richard W. THE NEW YORK STATE RATIFYING CON-VENTION: ON FEDERALISM. *Polity 1976 9(1): 97-116.* Discusses issues in forms of government in debates between Federalists and anti-Federalists over ratification of the proposed Constitution at the New York State Ratifying Convention in 1788.

385.   Cuddihy, William. A MAN'S HOUSE IS HIS CASTLE: UNDUE SEARCH AND SEIZURE AND THE FOURTH AMENDMENT. *Virginia Cavalcade 1984 33(4): 174-183.* Traces the English and American colonial

traditions and cases on illegal search and seizure that were embodied in the 4th Amendment to the Constitution.

386.   Denenberg, Dennis. THE MISSING LINK: NEW ENGLAND'S IN-FLUENCE ON EARLY NATIONAL EDUCATIONAL POLICIES. *New England Q. 1979 52(2): 219-233.* The educational provisions in the Ordinance of 1785 and the Northwest Ordinance (1787) reflect New England ideas. They were included at the urgings of New Englanders, and in the case of the Northwest Ordinance, at the insistence of the Ohio Company (organized in Massachusetts) which was negotiating a large land purchase at the time. The absence of this New England "education lobby" is the missing link which explains the lack of any specific education clauses in the Constitution. Primary and secondary sources; 45 notes.   J. C. Bradford

387.   De Pauw, Linda Grant. THE ANTICLIMAX OF ANTIFEDERAL-ISM: THE ABORTIVE SECOND CONVENTION MOVEMENT, 1788-89. *Prologue 1970 2(2): 98-114.* Traces the attempted actions of a segment of antifederalists to convene a second Constitutional Convention to correct oversights in the first, primarily in the realm of state and individual rights. Although men like Randolph of Virginia and Pinckney of South Carolina desired conditional ratification by states with proposed amendments included, the evolution of Madison's Bill of Rights, adopted by the First Congress, gradually silenced the demands of those desiring a second convention. Documents the various political postures and maneuverings of the years studied. Based on primary sources; 70 notes.   D. G. Davis, Jr.

388.   Diamond, Ann Stuart. A CONVENTION FOR PROPOSING AMENDMENTS: THE CONSTITUTION'S OTHER METHOD. *Publius 1981 11(3-4): 113-146.* Examines Senator Orrin Hatch's state-oriented propos-al, the Constitutional Convention Implementation Act of 1981, the history of Article 5 of the Constitution, the convention method, and the legislative procedures for calling an Article 5 convention. Based on a paper prepared for a conference on The Constitution and the Budget at the American Enterprise Institute, May 1979. Primary sources; 90 notes.   G. Smith

389.   Diamond, Ann Stuart. THE ZENITH OF SEPARATION OF POW-ERS THEORY: THE FEDERAL CONVENTION OF 1787. *Publius 1978 8(3): 45-70.* Critics of the Constitution fall prey to the Adams fallacy—the belief that separation of powers is a form of balanced government dividing the powers of government according to class rather than function—or to the deadlock syndrome—the notion that out of excessive fear of tyranny and a concern for liberty the framers of the Constitution devised a system of checks and balances which prevented government from governing effectively; a study of debate at the Federal Convention of 1787, however, reveals that the purpose of checks and balances was to prevent deadlocks and to entrust vast powers to popular government without threatening liberty.

390.   Diamond, Martin. THE SEPARATION OF POWERS AND THE MIXED REGIME. *Publius 1978 8(3): 33-43.* Contrary to popular belief, the separation of powers is a modern conception: to insure justice, the mixed

regime of ancient Greece combined undivided power with a people divided into the few and the many; to insure individual liberty, the separation of powers, as conceived by John Locke, Montesquieu, and the framers of the US Constitution, combined divided governmental power with an undivided people.

391. Donahoe, Bernard and Smelser, Marshall. THE CONGRESSIONAL POWER TO RAISE ARMIES: THE CONSTITUTIONAL AND RATIFYING CONVENTIONS, 1787-1788. *R. of Pol. 1971 33(2): 202-211.* Raising and administering an army was an important question in 1787, given the traditional opposition to a standing army. Proponents of the Constitution argued that an army administered by Congress was necessary for defense. Opponents offered accusations rather than arguments in rebuttal. Both sides agreed on the principle of civilian control over the military. Based on primary and secondary sources; 49 notes.   N. A. Kuntz

392. Draper, Theodore. HUME & MADISON: THE SECRETS OF FEDERALIST PAPER NO. 10. *Encounter [Great Britain] 1982 58(2): 34-47.* Examines James Madison's debt to David Hume for the concept of the "extended republic" which Madison used as a guiding principle and check against factionalism in Federalist No. 10; and comments on 20th-century studies of this connection by Douglass Adair (in 1957) and Garry Wills in his *Expanding America: The Federalist* (1981).

393. Dumbauld, Edward. OLMSTEAD'S CLAIM: THE CASE OF THE MUTINOUS MARINER. *Supreme Court Hist. Soc. Y. 1977: 52-58, 69.* Background of the Supreme Court decision in the case of Connecticut seaman Gideon Olmsted, imprisoned by the British in 1778, who mutinied along with three other prisoners and took the 14 British on board the sloop *Active* captive, and then claimed the *Active* and its cargo as theirs; the court found in 1809 that Olmsted was legally able to collect the money from the sale of the sloop and its cargo as a reward for his brave actions against his British captors.

394. Einhorn, Lois J. BASIC ASSUMPTIONS IN THE VIRGINIA RATIFICATION DEBATES: PATRICK HENRY VS. JAMES MADISON ON THE NATURE OF MAN AND REASON. *Southern Speech Communication J. 1981 46(4): 327-340.* Discusses Antifederalist Henry Clay's assumptions that man and government were inherently evil, and that to an absolutist, reasoning was unnecessary, and James Madison's assumptions that man was a combination of good and bad, and a balanced government could control people, based on his support of the power of reason and logical thinking; focuses on their speeches at the Virginia Ratification Convention on the Federal Constitution in 1788.

395. Erler, Edward J. THE PROBLEM OF THE PUBLIC GOOD IN *THE FEDERALIST. Polity 1981 13(4): 649-667.* James Madison insisted in *The Federalist* (1787-88) that the public good derives not from virtue but from the diversity and rivalry of private interests. Yet by 1792 Madison had argued the necessity of a political party as the permanent representative of republican virtue. The author traces these changes and argues that it is doubtful if American political practices ever conformed to *The Federalist* position.   J/S

396. Eulau, Heinz. POLARITY IN REPRESENTATIONAL FEDERAL-
ISM: A NEGLECTED THEME OF POLITICAL THEORY. *Publius 1973
3(2): 153-171.* Discusses the principle of administrative polarity in representational governmental bodies from 1787 to the 20th century, emphasizing the
political theory of the *Federalist Papers.*

397. Ferguson, E. James. POLITICAL ECONOMY, PUBLIC LIBERTY,
AND THE FORMATION OF THE CONSTITUTION. *William and Mary
Q. 1983 40(3): 389-412.* America and Great Britain faced similar problems at
the end of the 18th century, including payment of the public debt and the
regulation of taxes, banking, and currency. British solutions to these problems
were emulated by American financial experts, such as Alexander Hamilton and
Robert Morris, who believed that Britain's nationalist system suited American
needs. The system embodied strong government, general and uniform laws,
elite guidance, and promotion of commercial and financial development. Based
on contemporary periodicals, political documents, and correspondence; 67
notes.   H. M. Ward

398. Furtwangler, Albert. STRATEGIES OF CANDOR IN *THE FEDER-
ALIST. Early Am. Literature 1979 14(1): 91-109.* When Alexander Hamilton,
James Madison, and John Jay wrote the *Federalist* papers, they deliberately
created a mood based on an appeal to *candor,* defined as "polite deference,
freedom from malice, kindliness." Wishing to rise above the level of petty,
factional, and intemperate squabbling, the *Federalist*'s authors went out of
their way to defer to any conceivable opposition argument against the new
constitution. Their objective was to dispel doubt and promote confidence in the
new governmental framework, and to accomplish this, they adopted the tactic
of deference toward any likely opposition. 18 notes.   T. P. Linkfield

399. Gaugush, Bill. PRINCIPLES GOVERNING THE INTERPRETA-
TION AND EXERCISE OF ARTICLE 5 POWERS. *Western Pol. Q. 1982
35(2): 212-221.* Looks closely at the 1787 Constitutional Convention debates as
well as at the various United States Supreme Court decisions dealing with the
interpretation of Article 5 provisions. The records of the 1787 Convention
debates lend credence to the proposition that Congress's role in the convention
process was intended to be minimal, its power to call a convention being
merely perfunctory. In interpreting various Article 5 provisions the high court
has enunciated two major principles which, if applied to the convention
provision, would recognize the states' ascendancy vis-à-vis the Congress in the
convention process.   J/S

400. Gazell, James A. ONE MAN, ONE VOTE: ITS LONG GERMINA-
TION. *Western Pol. Q. 1970 23(3): 445-462.* Discusses the origin of the
American "one man, one vote" voting tradition, including English law and
arguments put forth in the *Federalist Papers,* 1787-92.

401. Graymont, Barbara. NEW YORK STATE INDIAN POLICY AFTER
THE REVOLUTION. *New York Hist. 1976 57(4): 438-474.* Tells how New
York State induced the Iroquois to give up almost all of their lands in the
central and western parts of the state, thereby destroying the Iroquois

Confederacy as a sovereign power. Reveals the conflicting jurisdiction over Indian affairs in New York between the state government and the United States Congress under both the Articles of Confederation and the US Constitution. 4 illus., 75 notes. R. N. Lokken

402. Hardy, B. Carmon. A FREE PEOPLE'S INTOLERABLE GRIEV-ANCE: THE QUARTERING OF TROOPS AND THE THIRD AMEND-MENT. *Virginia Cavalcade 1984 33(3): 126-135.* Troop billeting, a point of contention in English law since the Middle Ages, was among the major grievances that precipitated the American Revolution; protection against the billeting of troops was subsequently incorporated into the Bill of Rights.

403. Haw, James A. SAMUEL CHASE'S "OBJECTIONS TO THE FED-ERAL GOVERNMENT." *Maryland Hist. Mag. 1981 76(3): 272-285.* Many contemporaries and most historians have ascribed Samuel Chase's Antifederalism primarily to motives of self-interest, based on his unsuccessful movement for paper money and debt relief in the Maryland legislature between 1785 and 1787. It is not true, however, that Chase never made any thorough critique of the Constitution, as this reprinting of his series of rough notes entitled "Objections to the Federal Government" and intended for delivery at the state ratifying convention on 24 April 1788, shows. "It deserves to be ranked with the more impressive pieces of Antifederalist analysis," in its strong warnings against the "aristocratic danger" of the new system. From a copy made by George Bancroft; 35 notes. G. J. Bobango

404. Hobson, Charles F. THE NEGATIVE ON STATE LAWS: JAMES MADISON, THE CONSTITUTION, AND THE CRISIS OF REPUBLI-CAN GOVERNMENT. *William and Mary Q. 1979 36(2): 215-235.* James Madison, "Father of the Constitution," persistently sought a power to be given to the national legislature to veto state laws—a view of Madison that has been neglected by historians. Madison thought that the negative would be beneficial to controlling the internal affairs of the state. Such a negative would prevent recklessness and despotism on the part of the state legislatures and would promote stablity necessary for maintaining republican government. Discusses Madison's arguments. He was a stronger nationalist before 1790 than he has been credited with. Based on Madison's writings, records of the Constitutional Convention, and *The Federalist;* 46 notes. H. M. Ward

405. Hobson, Charles F. THE VIRGINIA PLAN OF 1787: A NOTE ON THE ORIGINAL TEXT. *Q. J. of the Lib. of Congress 1980 37(2): 210-214.* The original version of the Virginia Plan, introduced to the Federal Convention on 29 May 1787, and eventually transformed into the Constitution in September, has never been found. Scholars have tried to reconstruct it from existing copies made by delegates during the course of the convention, but have not yet agreed upon a completely accurate text. J. Franklin Jameson (1903) and Homer C. Hockett (1955) both concluded that none of the variant texts then known could be viewed as an accurate copy of the original text. However, after examining eight extant manuscript copies of the Virginia Plan and the changes made in the ninth resolution, amended on 4 June and 12 June, the author agrees with Max Farrand (1911) that James Madison's (1751-1836)

copy of the Virginia Plan contains the original text. The author argues that if Jameson had used the manuscript version instead of the two printed versions of David Brearley's copy of the resolutions, Jameson would have reached this same conclusion. Based on various papers in the Manuscript Division of the Library of Congress; 8 illus., 28 notes.   A. R. Souby

406.   Huston, James H. ROBERT YATES' NOTES ON THE CONSTITU-TIONAL CONVENTION OF 1787: *CITIZEN GENET'S EDITION. Q. J. of the Lib. of Congress 1978 35(3): 173-182.* Two pages of the notes taken during the Constitutional Convention of 1787 by Robert Yates and copied by John Lansing, Jr., were found in the papers of Edmond C. Genet in the Manuscript Division of the Library of Congress. Comparison with the 1821 publication edited by Genet, *Secret Proceedings and Debates of the Convention Assembled at Philadelphia in the Year 1787,... from Notes taken by the late Robert Yates,.. . and copied by John Lansing,... ,* reveals that Genet took many liberties with the original Yates-Lansing notes, rendering the published version inaccurate, incomplete, and polemical, portraying James Madison in an unfavorable light. Madison recognized some of the inaccuracies, but changed his own notes to agree with the published version in many places. Madison's notes published in 1840 and the Yates-Lansing published notes are the primary sources of information about the Constitutional Convention of 1787; both must now be examined more carefully, as parts may be unreliable. Based on documents in the Rare Book and Special Collections Division of the Library of Congress and secondary sources; 7 illus., 16 notes.   A. R. Souby

407.   Hutson, James H. THE INCOMPLETE ANTIFEDERALIST. *Rev. in Am. Hist. 1983 11(2): 204-207.* Reviews *The Complete Anti-Federalist* (1981), edited by Herbert J. Storing, which reprints antifederalist writings of 1787-88.

408.   Hutson, James H. JOHN DICKINSON AT THE FEDERAL CON-STITUTIONAL CONVENTION. *William and Mary Q. 1983 40(2): 256-282.* The convention documents of John Dickinson indicate Dickinson's positions on the issues at the convention. His own plan shows that Dickinson offered a compromise between the Virginia and New Jersey plans. Principally, he argued for a bicameral legislature, with one house popularly based and the other having state representation. Dickinson favored a sectional, tripartite executive. The 16 documents represented here reveal the major contributions of Dickinson to the convention's debates. The document is at the Historical Society of Pennsylvania; 53 notes.   H. M. Ward

409.   Hutson, James H. PIERCE BUTLER'S RECORDS OF THE FEDER-AL CONSTITUTIONAL CONVENTION. *Q. J. of the Lib. of Congress 1980 37(1): 64-73.* Pierce Butler (1744-1822), an Anglo-Irish aristocratic South Carolina planter, attended the Federal Constitutional Convention in Philadelphia in 1787. His notes on the debates are not very valuable to scholars; they are sketchy, very cryptic, inaccurate in dates, and are covered with doodling and sketched profiles of the speakers. However, Butler's records also contain plans, committee reports, motions, resolutions, and incidental papers that will supplement other records of the 1787 Federal Convention. Reprints Butler's notes on the debates, Mason's suggested revisions of the

Constitution, and an unknown author's objections to the Constitution. Based on photostatic copies of the 1787 Federal Convention papers of Pierce Butler in the Library of Congress Manuscript Division; illus., 29 notes.

A. R. Souby

410. Ireland, Owen. PARTISANSHIP AND THE CONSTITUTION: PENNSYLVANIA, 1787. *Pennsylvania Hist. 1978 45(4): 315-332.* During the debate over ratifying the US Constitution in Pennsylvania, Antifederalists were members of the state's Constitutional Party, but other Constitutionalists cooperated with Republicans and formerly nonaligned individuals in supporting the Federalist cause. A high degree of Republican versus Constitutionalist partisanship briefly characterized the discussion of the Federal Constitution as a result of methods employed by its legislative supporters on 28-29 September 1787 to call a ratifying convention. Based on newspapers, *Minutes of the Pennsylvania General Assembly,* and other materials; 3 tables, fig., 33 notes.

D. C. Swift

411. Jacobsohn, Gary J. HAMILTON, POSITIVISM, & THE CONSTITU-TION: JUDICIAL DISCRETION RECONSIDERED. *Polity 1981 14(1): 70-88.* There is no incompatibility between what Raoul Berger rightly perceives as a principal concern of the founders, that discretionary judicial power be carefully circumvented, and the intent of these men to establish a Constitution embodying certain principles of natural right and justice. Alexander Hamilton's jurisprudential reflections suggest that the commitment to a written constitution did not rule out natural law as an appropriate source for constitutional adjudication. Hamilton's writings are infused with this understanding; thus they help us avoid confusing a commitment to positive law with a commitment to positivistic jurisprudence.

J/S

412. Jayne, Edward. OLIVER ELLSWORTH. *Daughters of the Am. Revolution Mag. 1977 111(7): 702-705.* Oliver Ellsworth, a delegate to the Constitutional Convention from Connecticut, helped frame the Constitution, 1787.

413. Jillson, Calvin and Anderson, Thornton. REALIGNMENTS IN THE CONVENTION OF 1787: THE SLAVE TRADE COMPROMISE. *J. of Pol. 1977 39(3): 712-729.* The Commerce and Slave Trade Compromise was a turning point in the Constitutional Convention, and inaugurated a major realignment of voting blocs among the participating states. Factor analysis indicates five blocs before the compromise 1) New Hampshire, Massachusetts, North and South Carolina, and Georgia; 2) Massachusetts, Pennsylvania, Delaware, and Virginia; 3) New York, New Jersey, and Delaware; 4) Connecticut; and 5) New Hampshire and Maryland. (Some states are classified in multiple blocs.) After the compromise, power shifted toward the northern states. Use of statistical techniques may indicate further refinements of this study, which supports a theory of state voting behavior first proposed by George Mason to Thomas Jefferson in 1792. Based on Max Farrand, ed., *Records of the Federal Convention of 1787* (New Haven: Yale U. Pr., 1911) and secondary sources; 5 tables, 20 notes.

A. W. Novitsky

414. Jillson, Calvin. THE REPRESENTATION QUESTION IN THE FEDERAL CONVENTION OF 1787: MADISON'S VIRGINIA PLAN AND ITS OPPONENTS. *Congressional Studies 1981 8(1): 21-41.* Discusses the elements of James Madison's Virginia Plan, which would strengthen nation authority over states' rights, presented at the Constitutional Convention of 1787, focusing on the controversy over the issue of representation in Congress.

415. Jillson, Calvin C. CONSTITUTION-MAKING: ALIGNMENT AND REALIGNMENT IN THE FEDERAL CONVENTION OF 1787. *Am. Pol. Sci. Rev. 1981 75(3): 598-612.* Offers an empirical description of the voting alignments that dominated the American Constitutional Convention. Processes analogous to V. O. Key's conception of "critical elections" at the macrolevel of national politics can also be identified and analyzed at the microlevel of the constituent assembly. Therefore, the critical election phenomenon permeates all levels of the American political system and not simply the national level of electoral mass politics. More specifically, this clear description of coalition alignment, operation, and realignment in the Constitutional Convention, when informed and enlightened by the "critical realignment" model, greatly facilitates the more traditional discussion of debate, conflict, and ultimate decision on the central issues before that body: representation, federalism, senatorial authority, and the nature of the executive in a republican government.   J/S

416. Jillson, Calvin C. and Eubanks, Cecil L. THE POLITICAL STRUCTURE OF CONSTITUTION MAKING: THE FEDERAL CONVENTION OF 1787. *Am. J. of Pol. Sci. 1984 28(3): 435-458.* A "rationalist" line of interpretation has consistently argued for the centrality of ideas and political principles to the outcome of the Constitutional Convention's debates, while a "materialist" tradition has consistently stressed the importance of practical politics and economic interests. Integrates these alternative traditions of analysis and explanation by demonstrating that a dynamic relationship of mutual interdependence existed between philosophical and material influences in the convention.   J/S

417. Jillson, Calvin and Anderson, Thornton. VOTING BLOC ANALYSIS IN THE CONSTITUTIONAL CONVENTION: IMPLICATIONS FOR AN INTERPRETATION OF THE CONNECTICUT COMPROMISE. *Western Pol. Q. 1978 31(4): 535-547.* This paper attempts to test empirically several contradictory hypotheses that have traditionally been offered to explain the occurrence of the Connecticut Compromise in the American Constitutional Convention of 1787: large vs. small states, northern vs. southern, holders of western lands vs. those who held little or none, carrying vs. non-carrying states, etc. Quantitative techniques are used to array the data (roll-call votes) in as parsimonious a form as possible. It is found that none of these hypotheses is satisfactory since the nationalists had enough votes to base representation on population in both houses, yet failed to do so. It is argued that a dominant coalition made up of the three largest states and the three southernmost states broke down early in July, when a few delegates from Massachusetts and North Carolina estimated the determination of the small landless states to maintain equality of states in at least one house of Congress to be such that refusal would break the union. It is also argued that the knowledge of some in the

Convention of the simultaneous work of Congress on the Northwest Ordinance facilitated the Connecticut Compromise.   J

418. Jones, Robert F. GEORGE WASHINGTON AND THE POLITICS OF THE PRESIDENCY. *Presidential Studies Q. 1980 10(1): 28-35.* One of the oldest extra-official roles of the president is that of leader of his political party. The only president who could not be labeled a party leader was the first: George Washington. Nevertheless, he did not remain entirely above politics; in 1794 he joined the Federalists. At the end of his administration he embraced politics propagated by extreme, or Hamiltonian, Federalists. His acceptance of their politics started the politicizing of the presidency. 29 notes.

G. E. Pergl

419. Kaminski, John P. ANTIFEDERALISM AND THE PERILS OF HOMOGENIZED HISTORY: A REVIEW ESSAY. *Rhode Island Hist. 1983 42(1): 30-37.* The *Complete Anti-Federalist,* 7 vols. (1981), edited by Herbert J. Storing, with the assistance of Murray Day is a seriously flawed work. Among other defects, it is far from complete, it lumps Antifederalists together as if they formed a monolith, and it pays scant attention to the plurality, state-by-state, of the opposition to the ratification of the Constitution. Based on unpublished manuscripts and archival records; 7 notes.   P. J. Coleman

420. Kaminski, John P. CONTROVERSY AMID CONSENSUS: THE ADOPTION OF THE FEDERAL CONSTITUTION IN GEORGIA. *Georgia Hist. Q. 1974 58(2): 244-261.* Georgia's ratification of the Constitution was not without some controversy. There were both federalist and antifederalist forces in the state which attempted to sway public opinion through newspaper articles under such names as "A Georgian," "Demosthenes Minor," "A Citizen," "A Farmer," and "A Briton." The arguments related to the Indian menace and to the question of state sovereignty. The delegates to the ratification convention accepted the Constitution in short order and completed their work in approximately 10 days. Based on primary sources; 43 notes.

M. R. Gillam

421. Kaminski, John P. POLITICAL SACRIFICE AND DEMISE: JOHN COLLINS AND JONATHAN J. HAZARD, 1786-1790. *Rhode Island Hist. 1976 35(3): 91-98.* Analyzes the Rhode Island struggle to ratify the Constitution of the United States. The Antifederalists devised a strategy to secure ratification at little political cost to their party's popularity. John Collins and Jonathan J. Hazard were made scapegoats. Based on manuscripts, newspapers, and secondary sources.   P. J. Coleman

422. Kaplan, Lawrence S. THE FOUNDING FATHERS AND THE TWO CONFEDERATIONS. THE UNITED STATES OF AMERICA AND THE UNITED PROVINCES OF THE NETHERLANDS, 1783-1789. *Bijdragen en Mededelingen betreffende de Geschiedenis der Nederlanden [Netherlands] 1982 97(3): 423-438.* Most American statesmen disliked the Dutch political and constitutional system. They considered it a "species of failed confederacies" which resembled the American Confederation too closely. Holland, in its

suffering, provided a "crowd of lessons," according to Jefferson. Published primary materials; illus., 56 notes.

G. D. Homan

423.   Lettieri, Ronald J. CONNECTICUT'S "PUBLIUS": OLIVER ELLS-WORTH, *THE LANDHOLDER SERIES*, AND THE FABRIC OF CONNECTICUT REPUBLICANISM. *Connecticut Hist. 1982 (23): 24-45.* Describes 13 anonymous essays published in the *Connecticut Courant* beginning in 1787 by "A Landholder," who was really Oliver Ellsworth, that provided the vehicle for Ellsworth "to emerge as the leader of the Federalist forces to ratify the Constitution in Connecticut."

424.   Lieberman, Carl. GEORGE WASHINGTON AND THE DEVELOPMENT OF AMERICAN FEDERALISM. *Social Sci. 1976 51(1): 3-10.* The origins and development of American federalism can be explained by reference to such factors as the existence of a common culture, favorable geographical conditions, and the shared experience of a war for independence. However, the actions of national leaders, including the president of the United States, have also affected the development of the federal system. This article describes some of the ways in which George Washington influenced the federal order while serving as the country's first chief executive.   J

425.   Lienesch, Michael. IN DEFENCE OF THE ANTIFEDERALISTS. *Hist. of Pol. Thought [Great Britain] 1983 4(1): 65-87.* Historians have portrayed the Antifederalists as provincial paranoids of second-rate intelligence and ability, obstructionist demagogs who lacked vision and courage, and men of little faith. The Antifederalists have been misunderstood. Their reform notions were rational responses that reverenced republican ideology. Accepting the Articles of Confederation government as legitimate, they were convinced that the Articles could be amended. As classical republicans, the Antifederalists accepted the cyclical theory that a corrupt government would fall to revolutionary designs. In their eyes, Federalist initiatives were anarchical propositions that breached the confederation compact. The Antifederalists were not progressives, and, though they feared for the future of the republic, they did not oppose democracy, rather they disdained degeneracy. 112 notes.

G. A. Glovins

426.   Lienesch, Michael. INTERPRETING EXPERIENCE: HISTORY, PHILOSOPHY, AND SCIENCE IN THE AMERICAN CONSTITUTIONAL DEBATES. *Am. Pol. Q. 1983 11(4): 379-401.* Relying primarily on debates in federal and state ratifying conventions, reviews the intellectual conflicts that took place between Federalists and Antifederalists concerning the roles of historical, philosophical, and scientific theories in the creation of the constitution.   J/S

427.   Loss, Richard. PRESIDENTIAL POWER: THE FOUNDERS' INTENTION AS A PROBLEM OF KNOWLEDGE. *Presidential Studies Q. 1979 9(4): 379-386.* Scholarly efforts to decipher the Founding Fathers' intended meaning in the Constitution are misguided when they oversimplify the theoretical and practical differences between 1787 and the 20th century. Nonetheless, an openly objective attempt to recover the insights of the

Founders should clarify the principles involved in debating the superiority of the original versus the organic understanding of the Constitution, with subsequent implications regarding presidential power. 40 notes.

P. M. Cohen

428. Lutz, Donald S. THE COMPLETE ANTI-FEDERALIST, REVIEWED. *Publius 1982 12(3): 127-129.* Reviews *The Complete Anti-Federalist* (1981), edited, with commentary and notes, by Herbert J. Storing and Murray Dry, which assembles all the major writing surrounding the ratification of the US Constitution. J. Powell

429. Marks, Frederick W., III. FOREIGN AFFAIRS: A WINNING ISSUE IN THE CAMPAIGN FOR RATIFICATION OF THE UNITED STATES CONSTITUTION. *Pol. Sci. Q. 1971 86(3): 444-469.* Analyzes the methods and issues used to promote acceptance of a completely new frame of government. The proponents demonstrated that the exigencies of foreign affairs were sufficient to justify the significant and risky increase in federal power represented by the Constitution. Thomas Jefferson expressed well the purpose of the central power as being "to make us one nation as to foreign concerns, and keep us distinct in domestic ones." 97 notes. R. V. Ritter

430. Marsella, Paul D. PROPAGANDA TRENDS IN THE *ESSEX JOURNAL AND NEW HAMPSHIRE PACKET,* 1787-1788. *Essex Inst. Hist. Collections 1978 114(3): 161-178.* Historians agree that prerevolutionary American newspapers were a medium for propaganda, but none have analyzed the role of newspapers during the Ratification controversy. Here a system of content analysis was devised to study the *Essex Journal and New Hampshire Packet* of Newburyport, Massachusetts. News items were grouped under the general symbolic categories of identification (referring to persons or groups), demand (expressions of preference and volition), and expectation (assumptions of fact). Every fourth issue of the *Journal* printed from May 1787 to September 1788 was examined in detail. Anxiety evoked by negative reports of Shays' Rebellion, tender laws, and Indian raids provided the emotional backdrop for favorable reports on the Constitution. The use of positive and negative symbols by the newspaper inevitably influenced the reader's conception and reception of the Constitution. Concludes that the *Journal* was a propaganda medium and a reflection of the political and economic divisions in the society. Based on the *Essex Journal* and on secondary sources; 7 tables, 36 notes. R. S. Sliwoski

431. Marshall, Jonathan. EMPIRE OR LIBERTY: THE ANTIFEDERALISTS AND FOREIGN POLICY, 1787-1788. *J. of Libertarian Studies 1980 4(3): 233-254.* Discusses the role which the Antifederalists had in early foreign policy debates and their impact on the ratification of the Constitution.

432. Martin, Philip L. THE APPLICATION CLAUSE OF ARTICLE FIVE. *Pol. Sci. Q. 1970 85(4): 616-628.* A chronological study of the convention mode for amending the Constitution determines why it has not been successfully initiated. "For reasons of political suspicion, public disinterest, and theoretical uncertainty, the application clause will probably remain an unused part of the Constitution." 42 notes. R. V. Ritter

433. McGraw, Joseph. TO SECURE THESE RIGHTS: VIRGINIA RE-PUBLICANS ON THE STRATEGIES OF POLITICAL OPPOSITION, 1788-1800. *Virginia Mag. of Hist. and Biog. 1983 91(1): 54-72.* Describes the conception of the Democratic Republican Party and its development as an opposing political force. The Virginia Republicans, who included Thomas Jefferson, John Taylor, James Madison, and James Monroe sought to defeat Federalist policies using three methods: increased electoral power through better Republican representation in the Legislative and Executive branches, strong state response to federal legislation via nullification or interposition, and voter education through published pamphlets, the use of a partisan press, and open lines of communication between voters and legislators. Based on pub-lished papers and writings of Jefferson, Taylor, Madison, and Monroe, congressional proceedings, contemporary newspapers, and manuscripts at the University of Virginia; 48 notes.   D. J. Cimbala

434. Meyers, Marvin. REVOLUTION AND FOUNDING: ON PUBLIUS-MADISON AND THE AMERICAN GENESIS. *Q. J. of the Lib. of Congress 1980 37(2): 192-200.* James Madison (1751-1836), writing as "Publi-us" in *The Federalist*, defended the work of the Philadelphia convention of 1787 against charges of a counterrevolutionary coup by saying that they were working under the supreme authority of the people and their rights to point out a system capable of securing the country's happiness, a system which the people would approve or disapprove. His view of history as a graveyard of lost republican hopes led him to understand that "a measure of popular and local liberty... must be reconciled with that full measure of authority necessary to secure the rights, the safety, and the happiness of society." The problem of the republic was that the right of the people to institute new government was accompanied by their right to alter and abolish old government. Madison warned that the instability of government must be protected against or the republic could not last. 3 illus., 19 notes.   A. R. Souby

435. Morgan, Edmund S. THE WITCH AND WE, THE PEOPLE. *Am. Heritage 1983 34(5): 6-11.* An incident in Philadelphia during the Constitu-tional Convention, in which a woman was killed by a mob for supposed witchcraft, helps to illustrate the difficult task faced by the fathers of the Constitution. American culture in 1787 was still beset by old superstitions and a penchant for mob violence; these problems provided the rationale for the antidemocratic fears and biases of some of the participants in the convention. 3 illus.   J. F. Paul

436. Morris, Richard B. JOHN JAY AND THE ADOPTION OF THE FEDERAL CONSTITUTION IN NEW YORK: A NEW READING OF PERSONS AND EVENTS. *New York Hist. 1982 63(2): 133-164.* Traditional accounts have exaggerated Alexander Hamilton's role in winning New York's ratification of the Constitution at the Poughkeepsie Convention. John Jay, a man who expressed his strong opinions in temperate language and whose moderation and willingness to compromise disarmed the anti-Federalist opposi-tion, was most effective in securing ratification from a convention which had a large majority of anti-Federalist delegates. The Jay strategy of having the convention consider the Constitution clause by clause prolonged deliberation

and prevented rejection. Most delegates were willing to compromise. Jay opposed conditional ratification, but accepted the anti-Federalist proposal for a second convention to amend the Constitution. Based on Jay Papers, Columbia University, and other primary sources; 2 illus., 75 notes.   R. N. Lokken

437.   Nall, Charles T., ed. A LETTER FROM PETERSBURG, VIRGINIA, JANUARY 10, 1789. *Virginia Mag. of Hist. and Biog. 1974 82(2): 144-149.* Letter from François Xavier Dupont (1762-93) to Etienne Clavière, Genevan financier, describing business conditions, climate, the new constitution, geography, and politics in the young republic. From the Etienne Clavière Papers, Archives Nationales, Paris; 10 notes.   R. F. Oaks

438.   Nicgorski, Walter. THE ANTI-FEDERALISTS: COLLECTED AND INTERPRETED. *Rev. of Pol. 1984 46(1): 113-125.* Reviews the edition in seven volumes of *The Complete Anti-Federalist* (1981), by Herbert J. Storing with the assistance of Murray Dry. The edition rescues the writings of the anti-federalists from the obscurity to which US history consigned them and which neither their historical role nor their political theory deserves. Note.

R. Grove

439.   Papenfuse, Edward C. AN UNDELIVERED DEFENSE OF A WIN-NING CAUSE: CHARLES CARROLL OF CARROLLTON'S "REMARKS ON THE PROPOSED FEDERAL CONSTITUTION." *Maryland Hist. Mag. 1976 71(2): 220-251.* Analyzes and reprints a full transcription of a recently acquired manuscript of a proposed speech by Charles Carroll to the Maryland ratifying convention in the spring of 1788. Carroll stressed most of all the need for a strong central government to oversee and ensure the revival of public credit, and for years had fought the Maryland group led by Samuel Chase which urged easy credit and inflated paper money. Surprisingly Carroll was not elected to the convention. but his arguments prevailed in the end, for Chase's ambiguous stands during the elections finished his political career. The manuscript itself is a detailed defense of each portion of the new constitution, with emphasis as to how the state legislatures will act as a check on the Senate and House and keep the people informed of any wrong-doing. Lengthy examination of the judicial power follows, concluded by a long digression on Greek history, and the general wisdom of the new plan. Several lengthy footnotes comment on the text. Primary sources; illus., 40 notes.

G. J. Bobango

440.   Pate, Zeph Eugenia. MEN WHO FRAMED THE CONSTITUTION. *Daughters of the Am. Revolution Mag. 1983 117(7): 718-720.* Briefly examines the backgrounds of the delegates to the Constitutional Convention.

441.   Patrick, John J. and Remy, Richard. FOR THE CLASSROOM: WASHINGTON'S DECISION TO ATTEND THE CONSTITUTIONAL CONVENTION. *This Constitution 1983 (1): 19-22.* Presents materials and a lesson plan on George Washington's decision in March 1787 to attend the Constitutional Convention in Philadelphia.

442. Patterson, Kirby W. THE MAKING OF A PRESIDENT: THE THINKING IN 1787. *Am. Bar Assoc. J. 1974 60: 1357-1362.* "The nation is now in the unique position of having a president chosen with the approval of Congress and will soon have a vice president who must receive similar approval. But this situation is not an aberration. Many members of the Constitutional Convention of 1787 favored just such a plan, and its advantages are worth considering today."   J

443. Peterson, Paul. THE MEANING OF REPUBLICANISM IN *THE FEDERALIST. Publius 1979 9(2): 43-75.* Republicanism was defined in various ways in *The Federalist* (1787). In common usage, the term meant that all power was derived from the people, that offices were held for short duration, and that there should be a multiplicity of officeholders. The Federalists' definition of republicanism eliminated the concept of political offices of short duration and numerous officeholders. 72 notes.   S

444. Rapport, Leonard. PRINTING THE CONSTITUTION: THE CONVENTION AND NEWSPAPER IMPRINTS, AUGUST-NOVEMBER 1787. *Prologue 1970 2(2): 69-89.* Details the bibliographical and publishing history of the US Constitution from the first printed draft (probably 6 August), to the first public printings of 18-19 September, and to mid-October 1787 when three-quarters of the nation's newspapers had published the new document. Virtually every newspaper, most of which were weeklies, had published the Constitution by the time the first state, Delaware, held its ratification convention on 3 December. Based on primary sources; illus., 33 notes.   D. G. Davis, Jr.

445. Renner, Richard Wilson. CONSCIENTIOUS OBJECTION AND THE FEDERAL GOVERNMENT, 1787-1792. *Military Affairs 1974 38(4): 142-145.* James Madison recognized conscientious objection to military service in his initial draft of the Second Amendment, but it was removed by the Senate. A similar proposal by him for inclusion in the Federal militia laws lost in the House after extensive debate. While some of the opposition reflected animosity toward the Quakers for their passivity in the patriot cause during the Revolution, most reflected the desire of the states to retain full powers over their militia. Based upon the Congressional debates and contemporary comment; 33 notes.   K. J. Bauer

446. Rexine, John E. CLASSICAL POLITICAL THEORY AND THE UNITED STATES CONSTITUTION. *Greek Orthodox Theological Rev. 1976 21(4): 321-340.* Investigates the influence of classical political theory on the Founding Fathers during the framing of the Constitution, 1787.

447. Riccards, Michael P. THE PRESIDENCY AND THE RATIFICATION CONTROVERSY. *Presidential Studies Q. 1977 7(1): 37-46.* During the debate over ratifying the Constitution of 1787, Federalists and Antifederalists argued over the role of the Presidency, discussing the President's relationship with the Senate, term of office, and treaty, pardoning, veto, and military powers. Federalists and Antifederalists chose George Washington for President and drafted the Bill of Rights to protect against abuses of executive power.

Based on Federalist and Antifederalist pamphlets, letters, addresses, and legislative debates; 39 notes. R. D. Hurt

448. Riker, William H. THE HERESTHETICS OF CONSTITUTION-MAKING: THE PRESIDENCY IN 1787, WITH COMMENTS ON DETERMINISM AND RATIONAL CHOICE. *Am. Pol. Sci. Rev. 1984 78(1): 1-16.* One method of reconciling the conflict in methodology between determinism and indeterminism is the notion of rational choice, which allows for both regularities in behavior and artistic creation. Artistry within the rational choice context is explained in terms of the notion of heresthetics or the dynamic manipulation of the conditions of choice, using as an example the decision of the Constitutional Convention of 1787 on the method of selecting the president. J

449. Risjord, Norman K. and DenBoer, Gordon. THE EVOLUTION OF POLITICAL PARTIES IN VIRGINIA, 1782-1800. *J. of Am. Hist. 1974 60(4): 961-984.* Analysis of roll call votes in the Virginia House of Delegates reveals that by the time of the Constitutional Convention a political group had emerged which could be designated "creditor/nationalist" in its orientation toward payment of prewar debts, a lenient attitude toward returned Loyalists, tax powers to the national government, and judicial reforms to assist debt collection. Another group oriented around Patrick Henry could be considered "debtor/anti-nationalists." The Henry faction tended to become Antifederalists in the debate over the constitution, while Madison and the "creditor/nationalist" faction became Federalists. In later debates over Hamilton's fiscal policies some Federalists became Republicans, but within the state a clearly large majority of 1788's Federalists remained Federalists by 1791. A similar continuity is to be noted when issues of neutrality and Jay's Treaty were raised. By 1800 more cohesive and disciplined political parties had emerged, making conscious appeals to the electorate. 9 tables, 76 notes. K. B. West

450. Risjord, Norman K. VIRGINIANS AND THE CONSTITUTION: A MULTIVARIANT ANALYSIS. *William and Mary Q. 1974 31(4): 613-632.* Uses the technique of multiple classification to determine reasons for supporting the Constitution in Virginia. Profile of Assembly members from 1788 to 1791 adds further evidence. Attributes investigated are wealth, mercantile interests, family background, age, military service, and personal viewpoints (whether cosmopolitan or provincial). Party affiliation after the adoption of the Constitution is related to personal attributes and environmental factors. Based on tax lists and secondary sources; 34 notes. H. M. Ward

451. Robinson, Donald Allen. JENSEN'S MONUMENT: DOCUMENTS ON CONSTITUTIONAL RATIFICATION. *Rev. in Am. Hist. 1977 5(3): 326-334.* Review article prompted by Merrill Jensen, ed., *The Documentary History of the Ratification of the Constitution,* Vol. 1, *Constitutional Documents and Records, 1776-1787.* and Vol. 2, *Ratification of the Constitution by the States: Pennsylvania* (Madison: State Historical Society of Wisconsin, 1976).

452. Robinson, Donald L. THE INVENTORS OF THE PRESIDENCY. *Presidential Studies Q. 1983 13(1): 8-25.* The 55 delegates to the 1787 constitutional convention fell into three ideological groups. The radicals wanted a separate, solitary executive who would be popularly elected and have broad powers. The old republicans, espousing the spirit of the revolution, pushed for a plural executive, chosen by the legislature and having mainly administrative powers. The men in the middle held no specific viewpoint, but did hold the balance of votes. The radicals, with their starkly new image of the executive, prevailed in the convention because, although in the minority, they had clearly formulated recommendations and the circumstances of the times created an opportunity for a new, fresh approach. Chart, 45 notes.

D. H. Cline

453. Rodrigues, Leda Boechat. JOSE JOAQUIM DA MAIA E THOMAS JEFFERSON [Jose Joaquim da Maia and Thomas Jefferson]. *Rev. Hist. e Geog. Brasileira [Brazil] 1981 (333): 53-70.* Describes the meetings and correspondence between Thomas Jefferson, then American ambassador to France, and Brazilian medical student in the University of Montpelier, Jose Joaquim da Maia, in 1786. Da Maia used the pseudonym "Vendek" in his writings, and he and Jefferson exchanged information and opinion on both political matters and on questions of natural history. Jefferson was especially interested in the social and natural-history information about Brazil provided by da Maia, information that Jefferson shared with John Jay. The life, career, and writings of Jefferson are also reviewed, and he is eulogized as one of the greatest American thinkers and doers. 19 notes.   R. Garfield

454. Rogers, George C., Jr., ed. THE LETTERS OF WILLIAM LOUGH-TON SMITH TO EDWARD RUTLEDGE, JUNE 8, 1789 TO APRIL 28, 1794. *South Carolina Hist. Mag. 1968 69(1): 1-25, (2): 101-138, (4): 225-242, 1969 70(1): 38-58.* Part I. Reprints five letters from William Loughton Smith to Edward Rutledge, written while he was working in Congress on the passage of the 10th amendment. Part II. Reprints 14 more letters of William Loughton Smith to Edward Rutledge, dealing with the assumption of state debts by the new US Congress, and his own efforts to get the assumption of South Carolina's debts. Part III. Nine further letters from William Loughton Smith to Edward Rutledge, primarily concerned with his efforts to take advantage of Alexander Hamilton's economic program for the advantage of South Carolina. Part IV. Nine letters from William Loughton Smith to Edward Rutledge, dealing with Smith's activities in getting reelected for Congress.   S

455. Rogers, George C., Jr. SOUTH CAROLINA FEDERALISTS AND THE ORIGINS OF THE NULLIFICATION MOVEMENT. *South Carolina Hist. Mag. 1970 71(1): 17-32.* Discusses how the Federalists, the elites of South Carolina, changed their political attitudes from pro-Union to pro-Secession as slavery and an agricultural economy became more entrenched.   S

456. Schultz, Harold S. JAMES MADISON: FATHER OF THE CONSTITUTION? *Q. J. of the Lib. of Congress 1980 37(2): 215-222.* Praises James Madison (1751-1836) for his character and mind, his influences at the

Constitutional Convention of 1787, and his concern for nationalism, republicanism, stability, and the protection of the private property rights of individuals, but feels that he cannot truly be considered the Father of the Constitution because he was not able to achieve what he thought was most important in the new plan of government and did not contribute either to the "Great Compromise" or to the provision for the judicial veto of state and federal laws. Madison's major influence was in his insistence on a strong national government elected by popular vote. 2 illus.   A. R. Souby

457. Shiriaev, B. A. TOMAS DZHEFFERSON I AMERIKANSKAIA KONSTITUTSIIA [Thomas Jefferson and the American constitution]. *Vestnik Leningradskogo U.: Seriia Istorii, Iazyka i Literatury [USSR] 1977 (8): 49-55.* The atmosphere and the style of work of the constitutional convention strongly emphasized its antidemocratic tendencies. Thomas Jefferson understood some of the reasons for this, while admitting that the constitution had its good and its bad articles. The absence of a bill of rights, however, troubled him. He was compelled to compromise and accept many of the articles that he disagreed with, but on the condition that a bill of rights be added to the document. 21 notes.   G. F. Jewsbury

458. Shriver, Phillip R. AMERICA'S OTHER BICENTENNIAL. *Old Northwest 1983 9(3): 219-235.* The Northwest Ordinance of 1787, like the Declaration of Independence and the Constitution, deserves to be honored in a bicentennial celebration. The general public has tended to ignore the Northwest Ordinance because of its complex and legalistic language, the obscurity of its authors, its passage by the Confederation Congress, and its association with land speculation. As one of the three most fundamental documents in American history, however, the Northwest Ordinance was instrumental in determining how the nation was to grow. Based on a presidential address presented to the 51st annual conference of the Ohio Academy of History, Columbus, Ohio, 23 April 1983. Primary sources; 46 notes.   P. L. McLaughlin

459. Shulhafer, Lucia. JAMES IREDELL, PATRIOT. *Daughters of the Am. Revolution Mag. 1979 113(9): 994-999.* English-born James Iredell (1751-99) arrived in North Carolina as a youth, became an American patriot, constitutional lawyer, and US Supreme Court justice.

460. Smith, Dennis C. THE APPEAL OF A VIRTUOUS GOVERNMENT, A CONTENT ANALYSIS OF SOME CONNECTICUT NEWSPAPERS DURING THE RATIFICATION CONTROVERSY, 1787. *New Scholar 1974 4(2): 135-151.* Argues that ideology was of greater public concern during the ratification controversy than economic interests as reflected in the newspapers examined. Within this ideological framework, morality and religion were referred to most often with civil unrest a distant third. Eight tables; note.   D. K. Pickens

461. Spencer, Martin E. RULE OF LAW IN AMERICA. *Southern Q. 1976 14(4): 333-349.* Traces the concept of law in America from 1787 to the present. Emphasizes such principles as democracy, authoritarianism, and

constitutionalism. American views of law are examined in terms of individuals and groups. 6 notes.   R. W. Dubay

462.   Sprague, Stuart Seely. KENTUCKY POLITICS AND THE HERI-TAGE OF THE AMERICAN REVOLUTION: THE EARLY YEARS, 1783-1788. *Register of the Kentucky Hist. Soc. 1980 78(2): 98-114.* The statehood movement in Kentucky was a three-cornered affair (United States, Virginia, and Kentucky) in the 1780's, and each participant had its own problems and priorities. The struggle for statehood was not resolved successfully by 1788, at least in part due to internal uncertainties, national ratification of the Constitution, and the machinations of General James Wilkinson. Primary sources; 2 illus., 30 notes.   J. F. Paul

463.   Stampp, Kenneth M. THE CONCEPT OF A PERPETUAL UNION. *J. of Am. Hist. 1978 65(1): 5-33.* The Constitutional Convention of 1787 invalidated the historical argument for a perpetual union by destroying the existing one. When the present Union was created in 1789, the question whether a state could secede from that Union remained unresolved. The Constitution was ambiguous on the subject, and the Founding Fathers left the dilemma of perpetuity to posterity. An organized body of thought supporting the concept of perpetuity took decades to develop, partly because many Americans viewed the Union as an experiment, as a means to an end, and not an end in itself. The nullification controversy in South Carolina (1830-33), however, initiated an explosion of unionist rhetoric affirming perpetual union. Daniel Webster, James Madison, Edward Livingston, and Andrew Jackson, among others, argued vigorously for perpetuity. By 1833 the Union had become, for nationalists, an end in itself. 107 notes.   T. P. Linkfield

464.   Stuart, Reginald C. WAR POWERS OF THE CONSTITUTION IN HISTORICAL PERSPECTIVE. *Parameters 1980 10(4): 65-71.* The war clauses of the American Constitution, which divide the powers to declare and wage war between Congress and the president, were an outgrowth of the idealism and pragmatism of the 18th century. The separation of powers was based on perception that most wars occurred due to disputes between monarchs rather than because of national interests. Yet, the framers and ratifiers of the Constitution also recognized that an armed defense was a necessity. "There was a rough consensus that the country was weak and vulnerable, that republicanism was worth defending, that specific interests should be pursued, and that future wars were likely." Based on letters and other writings of the framers and ratifiers of the Constitution, and on secondary sources; 27 notes.   L. R. Maxted

465.   Swindler, William F. THE SELLING OF THE CONSTITUTION. *Supreme Court Hist. Soc. Y. 1980: 49-54.* The struggle for ratification of the Constitution during 1787-88 was fought in the press by influential essayists. The most enduring work was the *Federalist,* a series of 85 essays favoring ratification written by Alexander Hamilton, James Madison, and John Jay. It cannot be conclusively demonstrated that the *Federalist* affected decisively the outcome of the ratification debate, but it has since become a fundamental

document of government often cited as precedent by state and national courts on constitutional matters. Illus.   S

466. Thomson, Harry C. THE FIRST PRESIDENTIAL VETOES. *Presidential Studies Q. 1978 8(1): 27-32.* Discusses the early history of the veto during the presidency of George Washington. After considering action against several bills including the establishment of the national bank, Washington invoked the first presidential veto on 5 April 1792 against a bill reapportioning the House of Representatives. The grounds were constitutional and compromise legislation was quickly adopted. In February 1797, a second veto was applied to a bill for the reduction of the Army. Washington based his action on military considerations and again his veto was upheld proving the viability of the constitutional division of authority. 5 notes.   S. C. Strom

467. Turner, John J., Jr. THE REVOLUTION, THE FOUNDING FATHERS, AND THE ELECTORAL COLLEGE. *West Georgia Coll. Studies in the Social Sci. 1976 15: 31-42.* Discusses the Constitutional Convention in 1787, particularly the Founding Fathers' decision to choose a president through the electoral college.

468. VanBurkelo, Sandra Frances. "HONOUR, JUSTICE, AND INTEREST": JOHN JAY'S REPUBLICAN POLITICS AND STATESMANSHIP OF THE FEDERAL BENCH. *J. of the Early Republic 1984 4(3): 239-274.* Portrayed as an intellectual lightweight—an incompetent and unimaginative jurist on a weak court—John Jay has suffered in the hands of constitutional historians. Equipped with a pessimistic pietism and a Federalist disdain for the common elements and self-interested politicians, Jay was an 18th-century conservative who distrusted republicanism, yet found it plausible. Cognizant of the incomplete nature of the American Revolution, Jay argued for a comprehensive political economy that combined ultraconservative domestic politics with economic liberalism. A seasoned diplomat, Jay understood that domestic unification was a crucial prerequisite to prosperity. Public morality and harmony were preferable to self-centered obstructionism and immobilization. Advocating reciprocal connections among nations which fostered healthy dependency rather than protectionism and indebtedness, Jay argued for a national vision. Illus., 84 notes.   G. A. Glovins

469. Vance, Roger P. THE FIRST FEDERAL CUSTOMS. *US Naval Inst. Pro. 1976 102(3): 46-53.* The new Constitution of the United States authorized Congress to collect taxes on imports, but did not spell out how Congress was to implement its authority. Still, revenue was badly needed by the new government, and one of its first acts of business in the first Congress was the import problem. Eventually, in July and August 1789, Congress began the revenue collection under four separate acts, each embracing a part of the subject. But in carrying out the acts, the Treasury Department ran into the problem of physically collecting and securing the revenue. A new collection law was passed on 4 August 1790, an improved version of the old, and it also provided for 10 "swift-cruising cutters empowered to board and examine merchantmen... and small enough to appear suddenly at any secluded anchorage." The cutters more than paid for themselves and the cumulative

total of receipts from the federal customs increased tremendously. And it was those cutters "to which today's Coast Guard can trace its lineage." 6 photos.

A. N. Garland

470. Warren, Earl. ADDRESS BY THE HONORABLE EARL WARREN, CHIEF JUSTICE OF THE UNITED STATES, DELIVERED AT THE NATIONAL ARCHIVES ON SEPTEMBER 22, 1964. *Natl. Arch. Accessions 1965 59: 1-4.* Address at the opening of the Archives' Supreme Court Exhibit in Washington, D.C., paid tribute to Dr. Wayne C. Grover, Archivist of the United States, and his staff. Concludes by saying: "it is appropriate... to honor the Judiciary Act of September 24, 1789, as well as the Supreme Court, which it established, and the Bill of Rights, which the same Congress that passed the Judiciary Act submitted to the States for ratification. Each of these by itself has had immense meaning to us as a nation."   D. D. Cameron

471. Wilhelm, Stephen J. THE ORIGINS OF THE OFFICE OF THE VICE PRESIDENCY. *Presidential Studies Q. 1977 7(4): 208-214.* Discusses origins of the Vice Presidency concept in colonial America. A deputy executive was an optional feature, but did exist in many colonies. Its appearance as a feature of the Constitution is a mystery in terms of existing documents, suggesting that it was put in as a minor detail. The Vice President's powers are meager, but he assumes the Presidency in the event of the President's death. 17 notes, biblio.   J. Tull

472. Williams, James B. and Carey, George W. THE FOUNDING FATHERS AND "THE FEDERALIST." *Modern Age 1982 26(3-4): 315-317.* Modern liberals have focused on *The Federalist* in their criticism of American government, claiming that Madison, Hamilton, and Jay did not believe in popular rule because they feared mob tyranny. Actually, they only feared the popular control of "pure" or direct democracy, particularly in small republics in which a small majority could oppress a large minority. In the extended republic of the United States, however, with its plurality of interests and parties, majority decisions are invariably for the common good. Therefore, the authors of *The Federalist* were not antirepublican. The United States now has the technological capability to institute direct popular rule through national referenda and initiatives. The potential consequences of deploying this capability should be carefully considered.   J. Powell

473. Wills, Garry. GEORGE WASHINGTON AND "THE GUILTY, DANGEROUS AND VULGAR HONOR." *Am. Heritage 1980 31(2): 4-11.* After the American Revolution, Henry Knox formed an influential society of retired military officers called the Society of the Cincinnati which so closely allied itself to George Washington that he almost failed to attend the 1787 Constitutional Convention simply because the society would also be present in Philadelphia.

474. Winkle, John W., III. DIMENSIONS OF JUDICIAL FEDERALISM. *Ann. of the Am. Acad. of Pol. and Social Sci. 1974 416: 67-76.* "Distribution of power between national and subnational judiciaries is a significant yet often overlooked dimension of American federalism. Jurisdictional overlap between

state and federal courts has long generated administrative and political tensions that strike at the heart of intergovernmental viability. Acute questions of intersystem equilibrium arise in the consideration of judicial federalism. The dual court configuration materially affects litigant behavior, judicial policy making, and court administration. Intersystem reconciliation assumes greater importance in light of modern demands of spiraling litigation. This article seeks to raise some of the myriad issues of judicial federalism."   J

475. Wolfe, Christopher. ON UNDERSTANDING THE CONSTITU- TIONAL CONVENTION OF 1787. *J. of Pol.* 1977 39(1): 97-118. In "What the Framers Meant by Federalism" in Robert A. Goldwin, ed., *A Nation of States* (Chicago: Rand McNally & Co., 1963) and Martin Diamond, Winston Fisk, and Herbert Garfinkel, *The Democratic Republic* (Second ed., Chicago: Rand McNally & Co., 1970) Martin Diamond argues that the crucial issue in the first part of the Constitutional Convention was not a division between large and small state interests, but a deeper theoretical cleavage between advocates of a small and an extended republic. Although the small-republic argument was raised during the various state ratification debates, analysis of the proceedings of the convention indicates that the traditional interpretation is more accurate. Based on primary and secondary sources; 6 notes.   A. W. Novitsky

476. Wood, Gordon S. THE AUTHORSHIP OF THE *LETTERS FROM THE FEDERAL FARMER. William and Mary Q.* 1974 31(2): 299-308. Denies that Richard Henry Lee was the author of the *Letters.* Compares Lee's other writings with reference to style, syntax, punctuation, and revelation of his personality. Asserts Lee first received copies of the *Letters* from John Lamb. Concludes that the real author will probably never be known. Traces the reasons why Lee became regarded as the author. Based on the original documents, essays, and correspondence; 27 notes.   H. M. Ward

477. Worcester, Donald E. THE SIGNIFICANCE OF THE REGENCY PERIOD. *Rev. do Inst. Hist. e Geográfico Brasileiro [Brazil]* 1975 (307): 196-205. Compares and contrasts Brazil in the Regency period, 1831-40, with the United States under the Confederation government, 1781-89. Both were periods when federalism and republicanism were introduced, although later abandoned, and represented important stages in the evolution of government. Both governments went too far in establishing provincial autonomy, were hampered by restrictions, were ended by unconstitutional means, and included several remarkable statesmen who helped establish political stability. Biblio.   P. J. Taylorson

478. Wozniak, Chad J. THE NEW WESTERN COLONY SCHEMES: A PREVIEW OF THE UNITED STATES TERRITORIAL SYSTEM. *Indiana Mag. of Hist.* 1972 68(4): 283-306. Deals with the numerous territorial schemes during the decades preceding the American Revolutionary War that were unsuccessful, but whose major ideas were eventually incorporated in the Northwest Ordinance of 1787. These early plans presaged the territorial system guaranteeing equality for the new colonies by insuring that their inhabitants would preserve the political rights enjoyed by the old colonies, becoming integral parts of a single, unified national community. Concludes that the

schemes for new western colonies were an important phase in the development of American constitutionalism. Primary and secondary sources; 92 notes.

N. E. Tutorow

479.   Wunder, John R. CONSTITUTIONAL OVERSIGHT: CLARKE V. BAZADONE AND THE TERRITORIAL SUPREME COURT AS COURT OF LAST RESORT. *Old Northwest* 1978 4(3): 259-284. George Rogers Clark (1752-1818) had "appropriated" supplies from trader Laurent Bazadone at Vincennes in the 1786 Shawnee war. In 1801 the Northwest Territory General Court (supreme court) awarded Bazadone $12,000 from Clark's land holdings, after which Clark appealed to the Supreme Court. In a landmark decision, *Clarke v. Bazadone* (US, 1802), only slightly modified by Congress in 1805, Chief Justice John Marshall (1755-1835) held that the Supreme Court lacked appellate jurisdiction over territorial courts. However, Congress created a new state, Ohio, where Bazadone had won judgment and a new territory, Indiana, where Clark's holdings were. Bazadone got nothing. Based on national and Virginia archives and secondary works; 57 notes.

J. N. Dickinson

480.   Yarbrough, Jean. THOUGHTS ON THE *FEDERALIST'S* VIEW OF REPRESENTATION. *Polity* 1979 12(1): 65-82. Frequent criticism of our political institutions as unrepresentative leads the author of this article to examine the Founding Fathers' understanding of representation as expressed in the *Federalist.* By analyzing Nos. 35, 36 and 57 in addition to the often discussed No. 10 she makes an important contribution to the clarification of this controversial issue. Her position is that the *Federalist* was more concerned with the "refinement" of the people's views than with their reflection. Since the interest of society is served best by the most qualified persons, the authors of the *Federalist* have a preference for representation by the more enlightened and educated classes, particularly lawyers who—unaffected by any particular economic interest—are most likely to transcend interest group politics.   J

481.   —. [THE CONSTITUTIONAL TRADITION]. *J. of Pol.* 1980 42(1): 2-48.
Lienesch, Michael. THE CONSTITUTIONAL TRADITION: HISTORY, POLITICAL ACTION, AND PROGRESS IN AMERICAN POLITICAL THOUGHT 1787-1793, *pp. 2-30.* Before 1787, Revolution and Constitution had been discontinuous; later they were inseparable. Leaders distorted history to support the new federal institutions. The Constitution, having ended tyranny and corruption and limited governmental power, eliminated the need for republican activism. There were ramifications in education, psychology, and even the idea of progress. A Constitutional tradition was created, but the campaign to erase Revolutionary ambition failed. 38 notes.
McDonald, Forrest. A COMMENT, *pp.31-35.* The above article, while of value, ignores the 18th century theory of passions. Constitutional theory was premised on the passions of ambition and avarice. Lienesch also oversimplifies the historical idea of fame. Note.
Carey, George W. COMMENT: CONSTITUTIONALISTS AND THE CONSTITUTIONAL TRADITION SO WHAT?, *pp. 36-46.* Disputes

Lienesch's claim that, until 1787, most Americans saw the proposed Constitution as a rejection of the Revolution and that constitutionalists denied the value of classical education. The repeated and cumulative failures of the Articles of Confederation, due to basic structural defects, required a Constitution. 15 notes.

Lienesch, Michael. RESPONSE TO COMMENTS ON "THE CONSTITU-TIONAL TRADITION.. . ," *pp. 47-48.* Disputes Carey's characterization of Benjamin Rush as a crackpot, and his claim that the Constitution was "a logical outgrowth of the Revolution and the problems arising from independence."

Books

482. Aptheker, Herbert. *Early Years of the Republic from the End of the Revolution to the First Administration of Washington (1783-1793).* (A History of the American People.) New York: International, 1976. 167 pp.

483. Bennett, Walter Hartwell, ed. *Letters from the Federal Farmer to the Republican.* University: U. of Alabama Pr., 1978. 145 pp.

484. Boyd, Steven R. *The Politics of Opposition: Antifederalists and the Acceptance of the Constitution.* Millwood, N.Y.: KTO, 1979. 178 pp.

485. Epstein, David F. *The Political Theory of* The Federalist. Chicago: U. of Chicago Pr., 1984. 234 pp.

486. Furtwangler, Albert. *The Authority of Publius: A Reading of the Federalist Papers.* Ithaca, N.Y.: Cornell U. Pr., 1984. 151 pp.

487. Jensen, Merrill, ed. *The Documentary History of the Ratification of the Constitution. Vol. 2: Ratification of the Constitution by the States: Pennsylvania.* Madison: State Hist. Soc. of Wisconsin, 1976. 779 pp.

488. Jensen, Merrill, ed. *The Documentary History of the Ratification of the Constitution. Vol. 3: Ratification of the Constitution by the States: Delaware, New Jersey, Georgia, Connecticut.* Madison: State Hist. Soc. of Wisconsin, 1978. 669 pp.

489. Kaminski, John P. and Saladino, Gaspare J., ed. *The Documentary History of the Ratification of the Constitution. Vol. 13: Commentaries on the Constitution: Public and Private. Vol. 1: 21 February to 7 November 1787.* Madison: State Hist. Soc. of Wisconsin, 1981. 632 pp.

490. Kaminski, John P. and Saladino, Gaspare J., ed. *The Documentary History of the Ratification of the Constitution. Vol. 14: Commentaries on the Constitution: Public and Private. Vol. 2: 8 November to 17 December 1787.* Madison: State Hist. Soc. of Wisconsin, 1983. 565 pp.

491. Lomask, Milton. *The Spirit of 1787: The Making of Our Constitution.* New York: Farrar, Straus and Giroux, 1980. 213 pp.

492. Seed, Geoffrey. *James Wilson: Scottish Intellectual and American Statesman.* Millwood, N.Y.: KTO, 1978. 229 pp.

493. Wills, Garry. *Explaining America:* The Federalist. (America's Political Enlightenment Series, vol. 2.) Garden City, N.Y.: Doubleday, 1981. 286 pp.

Dissertations

494. Boyd, Steven Ray. "The Constitution in State Politics: From the Calling of the Constitutional Convention to the Calling of the First Federal Elections." U. of Wisconsin 1974. 305 pp. *DAI 1974 35(3): 1588-1589-A.*

495. Goldstone, Lawrence S. "The Slavery Effect at the Philadelphia Convention of 1787." New School for Social Res. 1973. 161 pp. *DAI 1974 34(8): 5265-A.*

496. Jillson, Calvin Clarence. "Compromise and Critical Realignment in the American Constitutional Convention of 1787." U. of Maryland 1979. 339 pp. *DAI 1980 41(2): 786-A.* DA8016722

497. Marmon, Sharon Marie. "Sword of Damocles: The Federalists, the Antifederalists and the American Experiment with the Good Republic." U. of Texas, Austin 1983. 309 pp. *DAI 1983 44(4): 1195-A.* DA8319641

498. Naroll, Raoul Soskin. "Clio and the Constitution: The Influence of the Study of History on the Federal Convention of 1787." U. of California, Los Angeles 1953. 277 pp. *DAI 1976 37(6): 3857-A.*

499. Parsons, Theophilus, Jr. "The Old Conviction Versus the New Realities: New York Antifederalist Leaders and the Radical Whig Tradition." Columbia U. 1974. 527 pp. *DAI 1975 35(7): 4398-A.*

500. Patterson, David L. "The Constitution: An Exslave Interpretation." U. of California, Berkeley 1978. 370 pp. *DAI 1979 40(1): 437-A.*

501. Peterson, Paul Carson. "The Political Science of *The Federalist.*" Claremont Grad. School 1980. 174 pp. *DAI 1980 41(1): 386-387-A.* DA8015615

502. Smyth, Linda Q. *"The Federalist:* The Authorship of the Disputed Papers." U. of Virginia 1978. *Doctoral Dissertations in Hist. 1978 3(1): 20.*

503. Wagner, Donald Rolland. "'The Extended Republic' of *The Federalist;* An Examination of Publius' Rhetoric." U. of Georgia 1979. 151 pp. *DAI 1979 40(4): 2246-A.*

504. Zagorski, Paul Walter. "The Separation of Powers and the U.S. Constitution: Original Intention and Present-Day Significance." Claremont Grad. School 1975. 306 pp. *DAI 1975 36(2): 1074-A.*

4

THE DEVELOPMENT OF THE CONSTITUTION, 1790-1900

Article Abstracts

505. Alberts, Robert C. THE NOTORIOUS AFFAIR OF MRS. REYN-OLDS. *Am. Heritage 1973 24(2): 8-11, 89-93.* Alexander Hamilton's alleged adultery in 1791 with Maria Lewis Reynolds led to blackmail, which in turn led to a quarrel, a near duel, an incident in Federalist and Anti-Federalist politics, and charges of dishonesty against Hamilton, the secretary of the treasury. In 1971 Julian Boyd reexamined the Hamilton-Reynolds incident and called for a reassessment of Hamilton's character and of his services to the early republic. Illus.   D. L. Smith

506. Antell, Joan B. THE SUFFRAGE MOVEMENT. *Current Hist. 1976 70(416): 203-205, 231-232.* Outlines the history of the woman suffrage movement nationally and on a state-by-state basis 1848-1920, including the role of Congress and the Supreme Court.

507. Barney, William L. JOHNSON AND RECONSTRUCTION: SWING-ING AROUND THE CIRCLE AGAIN. *Rev. in Am. Hist. 1980 8(3): 366-371.* Review essay of Albert Castel's *The Presidency of Andrew Johnson* (Lawrence: Regents Pr. of Kansas, 1979), Patrick W. Riddleberger's *1866: The Critical Year Revisited* (Carbondale: Southern Illinois U. Pr., 1979) and James E. Sefton's *Andrew Johnson and the Uses of Constitutional Power,* edited by Oscar Handlin (Boston: Little, Brown, 1980).

508. Baumann, Roland M. JOHN SWANWICK: SPOKESMAN FOR "MERCHANT-REPUBLICANISM" IN PHILADELPHIA, 1790-1798. *Pennsylvania Mag. of Hist. and Biog. 1973 97(2): 131-182.* Detailed biographical sketch of Democratic-Republican John Swanwick (1759-98) reveals that Philadelphia Republicans were supported by new entrepreneurial groups ("merchant-Republicans") as well as by persons with little or no property. These "merchant-Republicans" clashed with their Federalist counterparts over policy issues, "demanding greater protection of trade from foreign shippers, freer banking facilities, cheaper marine insurance, and a foreign policy that was

immune from foreign domination." As spokesman at the national level for these "merchant-Republicans," Swanwick often was at odds with Jefferson on foreign and domestic issues. Swanwick's disagreements with Jefferson's policies sometimes reshaped Jefferson's thinking and are significant for revealing the strands of Democratic-Republicanism in the early National Period. Based on primary and secondary sources; 238 notes.   E. W. Carp

509. Benedict, Michael Les. PRESERVING THE CONSTITUTION: THE CONSERVATIVE BASIS OF RADICAL CONSTRUCTION. *J. of Am. Hist. 1974 61(1): 65-90.* In formulating means to protect the rights of ex-slaves, Republicans were conservative in their desire not to develop a permanent expansion of national power at the expense of states' rights. The 14th Amendment and the Civil Rights Act rested upon the assumption of state legislative supremacy and gave Congress no permanent power where laws were equal. More radical insistence on black suffrage was an attempt to give blacks the power to protect themselves once states were left to their own government again. The 15th Amendment limited powers of the states but did not confer powers on the national government. After 1868, though Reconstruction reeled toward disaster, Republicans would not shake off their conservative state-centeredness. 60 notes.   K. B. West

510. Bergesen, Albert. NATION-BUILDING AND CONSTITUTIONAL AMENDMENTS: THE ROLE OF THE THIRTEENTH, FOURTEENTH, AND FIFTEENTH AMENDMENTS IN THE LEGAL RECONSTITUTION OF THE AMERICAN POLITY FOLLOWING THE CIVIL WAR. *Pacific Sociol. Rev. 1981 24(1): 3-15.* The amendments (1865, 1866, 1870) solved two problems in social reconstruction: 1) establishing the ultimate political authority of the federal government over state governments and 2) legally transforming slaves into citizens.

511. Berindei, Dan. CONSTITUŢIA AMERICANĂ ŞI ECOURILE EI IN TĂRILE ROMÂNE [The US Constitution and its echoes in the Romanian Principalities]. *Magazin Istoric [Romania] 1976 10(7): 50-51.* Finds echoes of the Constitution in the Romanian Principalities in the view of 19th-century Romanian intellectuals.

512. Bloomfield, Maxwell. TWO CHEERS FOR 1787. *Rev. in Am. Hist. 1983 11(2): 208-213.* Reviews Harold M. Hyman and William M. Wiecek's *Equal Justice under Law: Constitutional Development, 1835-1875* (1982), which synthesizes recent scholarship on the development of federal power with respect to civil rights and the regulation of business.

513. Borden, Morton. THE CHRISTIAN AMENDMENT. *Civil War Hist. 1979 25(2): 156-167.* Heeding Protestants' criticism since 1787 of the US Constitution's failure to acknowledge national dependence on God, and specifically on Christ, and accepting the common opinion that the Civil War was a punishment not only for slavery but also for that omission, Protestant fundamentalists in 1863 founded the National Reform Association to support a Christian constitutional amendment. President Abraham Lincoln proclaimed National Fast Day (30 April 1863), acknowledged the truth of the Scriptures,

and urged repentance for sin, but he never supported the National Reform Association; nor did Congress. As their goal became less attainable, their supporters fell away and those who remained became fanatical. The National Reform Association persisted until 1945; its members believed that the proclamation and observance of National Fast Day had turned the tide in the Civil War and that a similar constitutional proclamation of dependence on Christ would save the nation. The public never concurred. 37 notes.   S

514. Bridges, Roger D. EQUALITY DEFERRED: CIVIL RIGHTS FOR ILLINOIS BLACKS, 1865-1885. *J. of the Illinois State Hist. Soc. 1981 74(2): 82-108.* Slavery predated statehood in Illinois by nearly a century, and discriminatory "Black Laws" were continuously passed between 1819 and 1853. In 1861, Illinois was the first state to ratify a proposed constitutional amendment prohibiting abolition. Post-Civil War politics centered on the repeal of the Black Laws and recognition of black civil rights in judicial, electoral, political, and educational spheres. While the Illinois Republican Party supported the national policy toward the South, it was reluctant to pursue the same policy at home. Black suffrage in Illinois came only with the ratification of the 15th Amendment. In 1876, John W. E. Thomas became the first black Illinois state representative. Only in the 1880's, when blacks appeared ready to bolt the Republican Party, did Republicans and Democrats begin to support civil rights and equality. 17 illus., 104 notes.

A. W. Novitsky

515. Burke, Joseph C. WHAT DID THE PRIGG DECISION REALLY DECIDE? *Pennsylvania Mag. of Hist. and Biog. 1969 93(1): 73-85.* A fresh analysis of the Supreme Court's decision in the *Edward Prigg v. Pennsylvania* case, a test of the constitutionality of an 1826 Pennsylvania law which placed limitations on a slave owner in his attempts to recover a runaway slave from within the borders of the state. Challenges the traditional interpretation of the case that "states lacked the power to pass any laws on fugitive slaves, including laws to aid their recovery, and that the Constitution did not obligate state officials to assist owners in regaining their runaway slaves." Shows that this view "ignores the differences between the judges on these two issues," and also "disregards the subtleties of Justice Joseph Story's opinion, turning insinuations into legal doctrines." 44 notes.   R. V. Ritter

516. Campbell, Bruce A. JOHN MARSHALL, THE VIRGINIA POLITICAL ECONOMY AND THE *DARTMOUTH COLLEGE* DECISION. *Am J. of Legal Hist. 1975 19(1): 40-65.* Chief Justice John Marshall wrote the majority opinion of the Supreme Court in the *Trustees of Dartmouth College v. Woodward* (US, 1819), ruling "that the charter of a private corporation was a contract protected by the federal constitution from arbitrary legislative amendment or repeal." Explores Marshall's experiences with Virginia corporations, 1801-18, to provide an understanding of why he assumed "that the contracts clause of the federal constitution extended to business corporations." Includes a critical assessment of previous literature on the subject. 43 notes.

L. A. Knafla

517.   Clayton, James L. THE SUPREME COURT, POLYGAMY AND THE ENFORCEMENT OF MORALS IN NINETEENTH CENTURY AMERICA: AN ANALYSIS OF *REYNOLDS V. UNITED STATES.* *Dialogue 1979 12(4): 46-61.* The 1879 Supreme Court decision on the case of Mormon George Reynolds upheld the constitutionality of the antipolygamy act passed by Congress in 1862. The Mormons held that polygamy was protected under the First Amendment guarantee of the free exercise of religion. The Court held that religious belief could not be used to justify an overt act made criminal by the law of the land. The significant basis for the Court's decision, however, was that deviant sexual behavior which offended majority sentiment could not be tolerated. In light of changed public attitudes, the Court's decision could soon be modified. Based on Utah District Court and US Supreme Court records and on secondary sources; 66 notes.   R. D. Rahmes

518.   Cobb, W. Montague. FROM THE CRADLE OF LIBERTY TO THE CRADLE OF MANKIND. *Crisis 1977 84(7): 359-365.* The formation of statements on human rights in the United States Constitution was an innovation above the concept of democracy. But these statements did not include blacks, Indians, or Orientals. Blacks continued to live under slavery or unofficial apartheid until the 1960's. But if America is the cradle of liberty, then Africa is the cradle of mankind and the roots of us all go back to an African heritage.   A. G. Belles

519.   Cohen, Naomi W. ANTISEMITISM IN THE GILDED AGE: THE JEWISH VIEW. *Jewish Social Studies 1979 41(3-4): 187-210.* Testimonies by Jews who reported on or experienced anti-Semitism offer important new insights into the causes of the phenomenon. As reflected in the writings of American Jews, anti-Semitism began earlier than generally assumed and was caused by more than social competition and agrarian radicalism. Instead, they lay major blame on Christian religious teachings and actions, the proposed Christian amendment to the Constitution, and ministerial sermons. They also blamed economic stereotypes, envy, ignorance, and bigotry. Based largely on Jewish newspapers; 100 notes.   J. D. Sarna

520.   Contee, Clarence G. TEACHER, HEALER, LAWYER: THE SU-PREME COURT BAR'S FIRST BLACK MEMBER. *Supreme Court Hist. Soc. Y. 1976: 82-85.* Biography of the first black lawyer to be admitted to the Supreme Court bar, Dr. John S. Rock (1825-66), a freeman from birth, who was admitted in 1865.

521.   Coray, Michael S. "DEMOCRACY" ON THE FRONTIER: A CASE STUDY OF NEVADA EDITORIAL ATTITUDES ON THE ISSUE OF NONWHITE EQUALITY. *Nevada Hist. Soc. Q. 1978 21(3): 189-204.* The State Constitution and subsequent legislation established political and cultural supremacy for whites in Nevada by 1865. However, Congress passed the Civil Rights Act of 1866, and that law, alongside other federal legislation passed in 1867 and 1868, threatened the preferential sociopolitical position of whites in Nevada. As spokesmen for white supremacy, the *Daily Territorial Enterprise* (Virginia City) and the *Humboldt Register* saw little danger from the Indians. The journals rated Chinese intrusions in Nevada a more serious threat, but

believed that it was readily surmountable. On the other hand, the newspapers considered Black intrusions calamitous to Nevada whites, for Congress had enfranchised Blacks, and Nevadans could not resist the federal will. Based on Nevada state documents and newspapers; 59 notes.   H. T. Lovin

522. Cresswell, Stephen. THE ATTORNEY GENERALSHIP OF CHARLES DEVENS. *Hayes Hist. J. 1982 3(6): 32-45.* Charles Devens, the Massachusetts jurist who served as attorney general during the presidency of Rutherford B. Hayes, is a relatively obscure historical figure owing to a paucity of surviving personal information. As attorney general, he argued cases before the Supreme Court concerning state versus federal court jurisdiction, including two important arguments for upholding black civil rights in jury trials. He was also instrumental in defending black voting rights. Despite his obscurity, Devens was a competent official in upholding federal laws during the Hayes administration. Based on records of the Department of Justice, the Charles Devens and Rutherford B. Hayes manuscript collections in the Hayes Presidential Center, and contemporary newspapers; 38 notes.   R. G. Frederick

523. Cresswell, Stephen. THE CASE OF TAYLOR STRAUDER. *West Virginia Hist. 1983 44(3): 193-211.* Discusses the case *Strauder* v. *West Virginia* in which the United States Supreme Court decided that it was unconstitutional to exclude blacks from juries, and also portrays the lives of Taylor Strauder, accused of murdering his wife, and George O. Davenport and Blackburn B. Dovener, his white lawyers. Only white males were allowed to serve on juries in West Virginia and, after nine years of incarceration during appeals, Strauder, who had been sentenced to death, was freed by the decision because blacks were excluded from juries. Newspapers, correspondence, court records.   J. D. Neville

524. Cullen, Charles T. TOWARD A HISTORY OF AMERICAN LAW: A REVIEW ESSAY. *New York Hist. 1973 54(2): 191-199.* Reviews *History of the Supreme Court of the United States,* volume 1, *Antecedents and Beginnings to 1800* by Julius Goebel, Jr. (New York: Macmillan, 1972), ed. Ray Roberts. This series should put American legal history, long in its infancy, into adolescence. Warns against the pitfalls that mar Goebel's book, particularly his highly technical writing style. The use of jargon in legal history will widen, not narrow, the gulf between historians and lawyers. Based on secondary sources; 8 notes.   G. Kurland

525. Davis, Julia. A FEISTY SCHOOLMARM MADE THE LAWYERS SIT UP AND TAKE NOTICE. *Smithsonian 1981 11(12): 133-150.* Outlines the career of Belva Ann Lockwood (1830-1917), a headstrong woman who overcame seemingly insurmountable barriers in order to practice before the Supreme Court; she also ran for president in 1884.

526. Dearmont, Nelson S. FEDERALIST ATTITUDES TOWARD GOVERNMENTAL SECRECY IN THE AGE OF JEFFERSON. *Historian 1975 37(2): 222-240.* Shows that the issue of secrecy in government is a bedrock question dating not merely from the Nixon and other recent administrations, but back to the early years of the Constitution when controversies over foreign

policy (Jefferson's embargo, acquisition of West Florida, war with Britain in 1812), parliamentary practice (voting the previous question), and the increasing use of closed congressional sessions led to popular suspicion of governmental power, and debate of the doctrine that publicity is essential to republicanism. Although traditionally associated with advocacy of aristocratic principles, the Federalists took the affirmative in this debate in part, perhaps, because they learned the importance of publicity to an out-of-office party during Jefferson's administration. Annals of Congress, 1789-1824; 57 notes.   N. W. Moen

527. Decker, Raymond G. THE SECULARIZATION OF ANGLO-AMERICAN LAW, 1800-1970. *Thought 1974 49(194): 280-298.* Anglo-American constitutional, family, and criminal law have absorbed from the Christian tradition, especially in its Protestant form, metaphysical constructs, moral standards, and linguistic forms. In a pluralistic society a value consensus is lacking. In order to protect individual freedom under these circumstances, the religious elements in the law are being removed.   J. C. English

528. Dennison, George M. THE DORR WAR AND POLITICAL QUES-TIONS. *Supreme Court Hist. Soc. Y. 1979: 45-62.* Reviews *Luther* v. *Borden* (1849), a Supreme Court decision affecting the Dorr Rebellion, the effort of Rhode Islanders in 1842 to establish a shadow government because of restrictive voting regulations which they perceived as making legal change impossible. An influx of immigrants and an exodus of natives had changed the demographic face of the state, but the old agricultural laws remained in force. A league formed to go directly to the people voted into office its own state government, which resulted in the charter government calling out the national guard. The Suffragists, failing politically, turned to the courts. But the Supreme Court ruled against them, arguing that the constitutional right to change governments was unquestioned, but that the US Supreme Court did not have the authority to interfere in state matters. 5 illus., 77 notes.
V. L. Human

529. Dennison, George M. THE DORR WAR AND THE TRIUMPH OF INSTITUTIONALISM. *Social Sci. J. 1978 15(2): 39-58.* Examines the Dorr Rebellion, 1842, in Rhode Island and assesses its implications for American constitutional development.

530. Dougan, Michael B. THE DOCTRINE OF CREATIVE DESTRUC-TION: FERRY AND BRIDGE LAW IN ARKANSAS. *Arkansas Hist. Q. 1980 39(2): 136-158.* Discusses ferry and bridge law cases in Arkansas ca. 1837-1940 as they related to the landmark Supreme Court decision in the Massachusetts case, *Charles River Bridge* v. *Warren Bridge* (US, 1837). The last Arkansas toll bridge was discontinued in 1940. Mainly primary sources; 106 notes.   G. R. Schroeder

531. Dunleavy, Janet E. and Dunleavy, Gareth W. RECONSTRUCTION, REFORM, AND ROMANISM, 1865-85: AMERICA AS SEEN BY CHARLES O'CONOR AND CHARLES OWEN O'CONOR DON, M.P. *Éire-Ireland 1980 15(3): 15-35.* Compares the views of the US political system held by Charles O'Conor (1804-84), distinguished Irish American attorney,

and Charles Owen O'Conor Don (1838-1906), his prominent Irish kinsman and correspondent. A lawyer's lawyer, Charles O'Conor rose to prominence in the New York Bar and in national affairs. He saw reconstruction as an opportunity for political reform against the special interest groups of political parties and office-holders who had been able to 1) gain undemocratic power by taking advantage of English-modeled aspects of the US Constitution, and 2) discriminate against Irish American Catholics. The Irish Charles Owen O'Conor (whose title "Don" designated him head of the O'Conors of Connacht), a member of parliament and familiar with the role of parties in the English system, favored not reform of the US political system but solutions worked out by realignment of political factions. Based on the writings of both O'Conors; 50 notes.   D. J. Engler

532.   Ebright, Malcolm. THE SAN JOAQUÍN GRANT: WHO OWNED THE COMMON LANDS? A HISTORICAL-LEGAL PUZZLE. *New Mexico Hist. Rev. 1982 57(1): 5-26.* Traces litigation leading to *Rio Arriba Land and Cattle Company* v. *United States,* a landmark case decided in 1897 by the US Supreme Court, to show how the question of ownership under Spanish law of the common lands of a community land grant was handled. The Supreme Court made its decision lacking all the facts and previous legal authority. Based on US Bureau of Land Management records, Surveyor General's Reports, and other primary sources; illus., map, 74 notes.   A. C. Dempsey

533.   Finkelman, Paul. *PRIGG V. PENNSYLVANIA* AND NORTHERN STATE COURTS: ANTI-SLAVERY USE OF A PRO-SLAVERY DECISION. *Civil War Hist. 1979 25(1): 5-35.* This 1842 US Supreme Court decision, written by Justice Joseph Story himself, first upheld the 1793 Fugitive Slave Law and the masters' power over runaways. It struck down personal liberty laws, but the decision's *dicta* allowed state noncompliance. The slave power seemed victorious; it turned out, though, to be an antislavery tool. Chief Justice Roger Taney feared this from the start. Story's decision accelerated a legal and legislative movement against the prospect of kidnapped free blacks. It was interpreted to mean that property rights and due process could not coexist. It forced Northerners to choose free men rather than Union harmony. Based on national and state statute books and secondary sources; 100 notes.
                                                                                R. E. Stack

534.   Finkleman, Paul. WHAT DID THE DRED SCOTT CASE REALLY DECIDE? *Rev. in Am. Hist. 1979 7(3): 369-374.* Review article prompted by Don E. Fehrenbacher's *The Dred Scott Case: Its Significance in American Law and Politics* (New York: Oxford U. Pr., 1978) discusses the impact of the 1857 Supreme Court decision on the Democratic Party, legal decisions involving the question of black citizenship, and the Missouri Compromise.

535.   Finley, S. W. DANIEL WEBSTER PACKED 'EM IN. *Supreme Court Hist. Soc. Y. 1979: 70-78, 83.* Reviews the character of Daniel Webster, and of his cases which appeared before the US Supreme Court. Notes that he ranks as high in the making of constitutional law as Justices Marshall and Storey; it is remarkable how often his arguments were much the same as the judicial opinions of the court's majority. Covers the cases of *Darthmouth*

College v. *Woodward* (US, 1819), *M'Culloch* v. *Maryland* (US, 1819), and *Gibbons* v. *Ogden* (US, 1824), complete with Webster's argument and the court's majority opinion. Perhaps Webster was even more important in the making and clarification of constitutional law when on the floor of the Senate, where some of his greatest orations were made. Covers ca. 1819-40's. 3 photos.

V. L. Human

536. Forman, William H., Jr. CHIEF JUSTICE EDWARD DOUGLASS WHITE. *Am. Bar Assoc. J. 1970 56(3): 260-262.* Louisiana's "most illustrious legal son" [1845-1921] served his country as a lawyer, in government and as both an Associate Justice and Chief Justice of the United States.   J

537. Fraga, Alberto. ALGUNAS CONSIDERACIONES SOBRE EL MOV-IMIENTO NEGRO EN LOS ESTADOS UNIDOS DURANTE EL PERIO-DO DE RECONSTRUCION (1865-1877) [Some remarks on the Negro movement in the United States during Reconstruction, 1865-77]. *Santiago [Cuba] 1982 (45): 83-98.* The end of the Civil War and the defeat of the slave-owning Southern oligarchy seemed to create conditions favorable to the integration of four million freedmen as full citizens according to the 13th, 14th and 15th amendments to the Constitution. In fact, Reconstruction was only a period of adaptation of the Southern landed aristocracy to the new conditions imposed by capitalism on agricultural production. The Compromise of 1877 liquidated the few gains the poor whites and the blacks had obtained during Reconstruction. 14 notes.

J. V. Coutinho

538. Franklin, John Hope. THE ENFORCEMENT OF THE CIVIL RIGHTS ACT OF 1875. *Prologue 1974 6(4): 225-235.* Surveys evidence of negligence in the enforcement of the act from its inception in 1875 until the Supreme Court declared it unconstitutional in 1883. Paramount was the "lukewarm-to-indifferent attitude of the federal officials toward the Civil Rights Act." Respect for it was largely destroyed by adverse decisions by lower courts and the six-year delay by the Supreme Court in rendering a final decision. It had already "become a casualty in the war waged by white supremacists." 63 notes.

R. V. Ritter

539. Freyer, Tony. THE SOCIAL MATRIX OF LEGAL CHANGE. *Rev. in Am. Hist. 1979 7(3): 319-324.* Review article prompted by Randall Bridwell and Ralph U. Whitten's *The Constitution and the Common Law: The Decline of Doctrines of Separation of Powers and Federalism* (Lexington: U. of Kentucky Pr., 1977); analyzes the legal theory behind *Swift* v. *Tyson* (US, 1842) and its implications for the doctrines of federalism and separation of powers, 1840's-1930's.

540. Frizzell, George E. REMARKS OF MR. THOMAS, OF JACKSON. *J. of Cherokee Studies 1982 7(2): 64-68.* William Holland Thomas, a leading influence in the eastern band of Qualla Town Oconaluftee River Cherokee Indians, appealed in a speech to the North Carolina senate for the safeguarding of Cherokee rights won by allegiance to General Andrew Jackson at the Battle of the Horse Shoe, by a US Supreme Court decision, *Euchella* vs. *Welch,* and by the treaties of 1817, 1819, and 1835. By using the example of the heroism

and patriotic gallantry under fire of Cherokee leader Janulska in the War of 1812, Thomas emphasized the Cherokee desire to live within the laws established in North Carolina. 13 notes.   K. E. Gilmont

541. Furlong, Patrick J. THE INVESTIGATION OF GENERAL AR-THUR ST. CLAIR, 1792-1793. *Capitol Studies 1977 5(2): 65-86.* The Congressional investigation of General Arthur St. Clair's 1791 defeat in the Old Northwest by the confederated Indian tribes established a constitutional precedent for the House of Representatives to examine executive conduct, 1792-93.

542. Gammon, Tim. BLACK FREEDMEN AND THE CHEROKEE NATION. *J. of Am. Studies [Great Britain] 1977 11(3): 357-364.* From the inception of the Cherokee Nation in 1839, the Cherokees and other Indians practiced racism against blacks. Blacks were enslaved and, after 1866, discriminations against the black freedmen were practiced despite constitutional and treaty provisions to the contrary. James Milton Turner (1840-1915), a black lawyer from Missouri and sometime American Consul General in Liberia, challenged the restrictions successfully. In 1888, the US Congress indemnified the victims of racism. Government documents and secondary sources; 28 notes.
H. T. Lovin

543. Gelpi Barrios, Juan. PERSONALIDAD JURÍDICA DE LA IGLESIA EN PUERTO RICO [Juridical personality of the Catholic Church in Puerto Rico]. *Rev. Española de Derecho Canónico [Spain] 1977 33(95-96): 395-415.* Until 1863, when the "congregational corporation" was defined in the United States, the difference in Church and State relations between the United States and Europe consisted in the American notion of trusteeship. Under trusteeship the Catholic Church had opposed denial of its legal status and the undermining of its religious mission, gratefully confirming the new status in the Third Plenary Council in Baltimore, 1884. In Puerto Rico, the 1898 Treaty of Paris concluding the Spanish-American War assured the continued application of the 1851 concordat between Spain and the Holy See to the Church in Puerto Rico. This juridical status of the Church in Puerto Rico was approved by the US Supreme Court in 1908.   R. D. Rodríguez

544. Gold, David M. REDFIELD, RAILROADS, AND THE ROOTS OF "LAISSEZ-FAIRE" CONSTITUTIONALISM. *Am. J. of Legal Hist. 1983 27(3): 254-268.* The career of Isaac F. Redfield of Vermont contradicts the orthodox view that railroads and big business effected a revolution in constitutional thought in the last quarter of the 19th century by securing the support of state legislatures, judiciaries, and the Supreme Court to protect their economic interests and attain unabashed capitalist power. Redfield was chief justice of Vermont during 1852-60, and editor of the *American Law Register* during 1860-76. Redfield strove to preserve the powers of the state, encouraged the work of the courts in protecting private rights, and supported Thomas A. Cooley's commitment to Jacksonian equality. While Redfield never solved the problem of defining the limits of legislative authority, he became one of the most insistent jurists of the era on the regulation of railroads. Recognizing the inability of legislatures to perform this function, he called for a greater role for

the courts. Based on Redfield's writings, contemporary treatises, and case reports; 70 notes.   L. A. Knafla

545. Grant, C. L. SENATOR BENJAMIN HAWKINS: FEDERALIST OR REPUBLICAN? *J. of the Early Republic 1981 1(3): 233-247.* Benjamin Hawkins, first senator from North Carolina during 1790-95, usually has been classified as a Federalist because of his friendship with George Washington, his opposition to radical economic demands, his support of excise taxes, and his identification with the Federalist faction in North Carolina. A nationalist and a diligent senator who was at his best in committee assignments, Hawkins is more correctly viewed as an independent whose friendship with Thomas Jefferson, James Madison, and James Monroe increasingly led him to vote with the Jeffersonian faction for a permanent capital on the Potomac and against a national bank and the appointment of John Jay to England in 1794. Hawkins admired France and hated Great Britain, positions consistent with the views of his North Carolina constituents. Based on contemporary correspondence and *Annals of Congress;* 42 notes.   C. B. Schulz

546. Gressman, Eugene; Douglas, William O.; and Thompson, William S. THE WORLD OF EARL WARREN. *Am. Bar Assoc. J. 1974 60(10): 1228-1236.* "Earl Warren, the fourteenth chief justice of the United States, died on July 9. Thus ended a unique public career—the 'epitome of the American dream,' to use Chief Justice Burger's words—that took Earl Warren from lawyer, to prosecuting attorney, to state attorney general, to governor, to chief justice of the United States. On these pages three phases of that career are touched—his legal and judicial achievements, his role as chief justice, and his contribution to the world peace through law movement."   J

547. Hancock, Harold B. THE STATUS OF THE NEGRO IN DELA-WARE AFTER THE CIVIL WAR, 1865-1875. *Delaware Hist. 1968 13(1): 57-66.* Because slavery in Delaware was not economically profitable, there were numerous manumissions prior to the Civil War; indeed, the free black population outnumbered the slave population over eight to one. However, Delaware was reluctant to abolish slavery. During the Civil War slavery became a symbol of defiance against the northern government, and so the state clung to the institution. Reconstruction race relations were strained. Responsible Democrats' unwilling to give blacks no more than limited rights, rejected the 13th, 14th, and 15th Amendments. An 1873 law, establishing complicated tax procedures necessary for individuals to be placed on the voting rolls, effectively disfranchised blacks and served as the base of Democratic Party power for the next 25 years. In education blacks made modest gains, largely due to the support of Quakers and philanthropic individuals who underwrote black education. Little progress was made in advancing social status; the 1873 legislature took a Jim Crow stand in refusing blacks admittance to white juries, public conveyances, public parks, and hotels. Not surprisingly, blacks continued in a subservient economic status. 23 notes.   R. M. Miller

548. Hardaway, Roger D. HOWELL EDMUNDS JACKSON: TENNES-SEE LEGISLATOR AND JURIST. *West Tennessee Hist. Soc. Papers 1976 (30): 104-119.* Tennessee has had six jurists serve on the bench of the US

Supreme Court. One of these was Howell Edmunds Jackson (1832-95), who served a short time (4 March 1893-8 August 1895) before his death. Prior to his appointment to the Supreme Court bench Jackson had served as representative to the state legislature, US Senator, and US Circuit Court Judge, where he gained a reputation as a rigid constructionist and an expert in patent law. While he was not one of the great associate justices, no charge has ever been laid against his integrity. While tending to be biased toward corporations, at the same time he felt that railroads should pay their fair share of taxes. Because of the brevity of his term, plus his low seniority on the Court, he was not assigned important cases. His opinions reveal, however, that he thought the judicial branch of government should leave lawmaking to the legislative branch. He attained several positions of power on the state and federal levels, serving with distinction in each capacity. Thus he stands as an important figure in Tennessee political history. Based largely on US Supreme Court decisions and secondary sources; illus., 118 notes.   H. M Parker, Jr.

549. Higginbotham, A. Leon, Jr. RACISM AND THE EARLY AMERI-
CAN LEGAL PROCESS, 1619-1896. *Ann. of the Am. Acad. of Pol. and
Social Sci. 1973 (407): 1-17.* "An understanding of the early American legal process is central to dealing with the racial disparities of today. From 1619 to 1860 the American legal process was one which expanded and protected the liberties of white Americans—while at the same time the legal process became increasingly more harsh as to the *masses* of blacks, with a steady contraction of their liberties. The United States Constitution sanctioned slavery, so that under federal law the slave 'had no rights which the white man was bound to respect.' Though the Emancipation Proclamation and the Thirteenth, Fourteenth, and Fifteenth Amendments significantly expanded the actual rights and options of blacks, nevertheless from 1865 to 1896 the legal process failed to effectuate the full potential of the rights intended and assured under the constitutional amendments."   J

550. Hoadley, John F. THE EMERGENCE OF POLITICAL PARTIES IN
CONGRESS, 1789-1803. *Am. Pol. Sci. Rev. 1980 74(3): 757-779.* Although the political leaders who wrote the Constitution did not hold the idea of party in high regard, these same individuals (according to many historians) became the founders of a new party system within the first decade of the new government. This article considers the question (on which no consensus exists) of whether parties did develop. The analysis focuses upon one aspect of party development, namely, the agreement among members of Congress in their roll-call voting records. Spatial analysis (multidimensional scaling) permits a visual picture of the increased clustering of congressmen into two party blocs from 1789 to 1803, especially after the Jay Treaty debate in 1796. This very clear trend supports the idea that politics was moving away from a sectional basis to one founded more clearly on partisan grounds.   J

551. Hochman, Steven H. ON THE LIBERTY OF THE PRESS IN VIR-
GINIA: FROM ESSAY TO BLUDGEON, 1798-1803. *Virginia Mag. of Hist.
and Biog. 1976 84(4): 431-445.* Although Virginia Republicans opposed the Sedition Act and denied the authority of the Federal government to restrict the press, their attitudes toward state restriction of the press were less clear. The

attempts of George Hay to prevent James Thomson Callender from publishing derogatory material on the Republican Party brought about a milestone decision and a victory for freedom of the press when First Amendment restrictions were applied to the state of Virginia. Based largely on contemporary newspapers; 41 notes.   R. F. Oaks

552. Hoffer, Peter C. IS PSYCHOHISTORY REALLY HISTORY? *Psychohistory Rev. 1979 7(3): 6-12.* Responds to critics of psychohistory by suggesting that psychohistorians could become more rigorous in their analyses of the past by borrowing from several academic psychological fields in addition to psychoanalysis. Both cognitive psychology and trait psychology offer psychohistorians theoretical frameworks which may be utilized to explain causality. Trait psychology creativity utilized by political scientists has led to innovative studies of voting behavior and the functioning of the US Supreme Court. The author's studies of psychological determinants of political affiliation in revolutionary New York are examples of the creative application of academic psychological theories and measurements to study of the past. The author describes how social psychological measurements may be applied to historical data. 36 notes.   J. M. Herrick

553. Hoffman, Daniel. CONTEMPT OF THE UNITED STATES: THE POLITICAL CRIME THAT WASN'T. *Am. J. of Legal Hist. 1981 25(4): 343-360.* An analysis of how the founders of the United States understood the First Amendment ramifications of government secrecy. The author assesses the early criminal prosecutions during 1794-98, focusing on events involving freedom of the press and political libel: the Cobbett Case (1797), Bache's Case (1798), Duane's Case (1800), and the Sedition Act of 1798. The founders believed fervently that the First Amendment protected the people in their right to know what the government did, and that the disclosure of government secrets was not a criminal offense as long as the facts were true. Based on court records, government documents, and newspapers; 50 notes.
L. A. Knafla

554. Hoffman, Richard J. CLASSICS IN THE COURTS OF THE UNITED STATES. *Am. J. of Legal Hist. 1978 22(1): 55-84.* Analyzes the classical allusions and citations in the arguments and opinions of the US Supreme Court and the Virginia High Court of Chancery in the first decade of the federal court system, 1790-1800. The sources, techniques, and significance of these allusions and citations are listed and discussed at great length, particularly those of Chancellor George Wythe of the Virginia Court. Allusions and quotes were drawn frequently from Greek and Roman literature, history, and mythology. The chief purpose in most instances was to buttress the role of national institutions and of a judicial system that was rational and humane. The classics provided an alternative to English sources and a new model for action in a new nation. Collectively, they "played a critical part in the struggle at the beginning of the Republic over the form and function of law and the judiciary." There are three appendixes: classical allusions drawn from memory, from literary sources, and allusions of the Supreme Court. Based on court cases and biographical studies; 93 notes.   L. A. Knafla

555. Holt, Michael F. ANTISLAVERY AND THE LAW: THE STORY OF A RECIPROCAL RELATIONSHIP. *Rev. in Am. Hist. 1978 6(4): 512-517.* Review article prompted by William M. Wiecek's *The Sources of Antislavery Constitutionalism in America, 1760-1848* (Ithaca, N.Y.: Cornell U. Pr., 1977).

556. Hulse, James W. THE CALIFORNIA-NEVADA BOUNDARY: THE HISTORY OF A CONFLICT. *Nevada Hist. Soc. Q. 1980 23(2): 87-109, (3): 157-178.* Part I. Congress passed laws in 1850 and 1861 that located the portion of the California-Nevada boundary north of Lake Tahoe at different points; thus it initiated boundary controversies between the two states that persist today. Legislation passed by the California and Nevada legislatures in the 1860's complicated the dispute. Greater ambiguity developed as a result of surveys commissioned by the US General Land Office in 1871 and 1872. Based on archival materials, federal publications, and California and Nevada state documents; 66 notes. Part II. After 1872, Congress authorized new surveys. Although one by Alexey von Schmidt raised questions, the controversy seemed to end when the two state legislatures accepted lines drawn by the US Coast and Geodetic Survey, 1893-1900. In 1977, California revived the boundary dispute, which was decided in its favor by the US Supreme Court on 10 June 1980. Photo, 125 notes.   H. T. Lovin

557. Huntley, Horace. A REVIEW ESSAY OF DANIEL A NOVAK, *THE WHEEL OF SERVITUDE. UMOJA: A Scholarly J. of Black Studies 1978 2(3): 183-187.* Review essay of *The Wheel of Servitude* (Lexington: U. of Kentucky Pr., 1978) discusses attitudes and institutions affecting the status of black workers, government agencies, and a Supreme Court decision which has attempted to equalize employment opportunities, 1865-1960's.

558. Hyman, Harold M. MARS AND THE CONSTITUTION. *Civil War Times Illus. 1973 12(3): 36-42.* The debate over Lincoln's constitutional power to wage the Civil War.   S

559. Jackson, W. Sherman. THE COLLAPSE OF THE PECULIAR IN-STITUTION THROUGH MILITARY AND LEGAL ACTION. *Ohio Hist. 1974 83(3): 183-191.* Reviews the emancipation controversy from 1857 to the ratification of the 13th Amendment in 1865. Early in the Civil War partial emancipation was accomplished by military commanders in certain regions, and by congressional action in certain cases. Democrats in Ohio opposed these wartime emancipation measures. The 13th Amendment was the first amend-ment to deal directly with nationwide social reform, and it provided the constitutional basis for the first Civil Rights Act (1866) and the 14th Amendment. Based on congressional records, and on secondary works; 27 notes.   J. B. Street

560. Jackson, W. Sherman. REPRESENTATIVE JAMES M. ASHLEY AND THE MIDWESTERN ORIGINS OF AMENDMENT THIRTEEN. *Lincoln Herald 1978 80(2): 83-95.* Although the 13th Amendment helped revolutionize the federal Constitution concerning human rights and equality, its adoption did not signify a departure from the traditional growth of

American constitutionalism. Instead it marked "a resumption of the nationalizing constitutional views of Hamilton, Marshall and the early Supreme Court." In the struggle to secure the amendment's passage in Congress in 1865, Representative James M. Ashley of Ohio played a key role. An ardent Free Soiler before turning Republican, Ashley served as House floor manager of the 13th Amendment and persuaded a number of Democrats to support it. 3 photos, 71 notes.   T. P. Linkfield

561.   Jacobsohn, Gary J. ABRAHAM LINCOLN "ON THIS QUESTION OF JUDICIAL AUTHORITY": THE THEORY OF CONSTITUTIONAL ASPIRATION. *Western Pol. Q. 1983 36(1): 52-70.* Examines the constitutional theory of Abraham Lincoln by contrasting it with the recent work of John Hart Ely. This contrast illustrates changes in constitutional jurisprudence and clarifies Lincoln's controversial and frequently misunderstood reaction to the *Dred Scott* opinion. Lincoln's position on the nature and limits of judicial authority is predicated upon a commitment to natural rights principles that manifests itself in an insistence upon the importance of the Declaration of Independence for constitutional interpretation. The relationship between these two documents in Lincoln's thought is the basis for characterizing his public law philosophy the theory of constitutional aspiration.   J/S

562.   James, Joseph B. IS THE FOURTEENTH AMENDMENT CONSTITUTIONAL? *Social Sci. 1975 50(1): 3-9.* Traces the questionable procedures in 1866-68 which led to the ratification of the 14th Amendment during Reconstruction.   S

563.   Johnston, Richard E. SOME COMPARATIVE STATISTICS ON U.S. CHIEF JUSTICE COURTS. *Rocky Mountain Social Sci. J. 1972 9(1): 89-100.* A statistical analysis of the decisions of the US Supreme Court justices. Examines Court action concerning the invalidation of national law; the invalidation of state constitutional provisions, state laws and city ordinances; and the reversal of previous Court positions. After analyzing 1,021 cases, devises a series of tables which reflect the behavior of the 11 US Chief Justice Courts, through Earl Warren, concerning the above actions. Reveals that the Warren Court has struck down 50% more national laws than any other Court, and that the Warren Court led in number of non-unanimous decisions. 6 tables, note.   N. E. Ramirez

564.   Jordan, Christine. LAST OF THE JACKSONIANS. *Supreme Court Hist. Soc. Y. 1980: 78-88.* John Archibald Campbell, a native of Georgia, was educated at the University of Georgia and at West Point before being admitted to the Georgia bar in 1829. He developed a very successful private law practice in Alabama and was appointed to the Supreme Court in 1853. He resigned his seat in 1861 and the following year became Assistant Secretary of War for the Confederacy. After the war Campbell returned to private practice with great success and at the time of his death was considered one of the nation's leading lawyers. Campbell was a Jacksonian Democrat whose juridical career on both sides of the bench was marked by strong adherence to state sovereignty, strict construction of federal power, opposition to the power of corporations, and

judicial guardianship of individual rights. Based on court records and other
primary and secondary sources; illus., 53 notes.   S

565. Kaushik, R. P. THE ISSUE OF POLITICAL RIGHTS OF THE
BLACKS: THE FORMATIVE PERIOD, 1865-1877. *Indian J. of Am. Studies [India]* 1980 10(1): 58-64. Examines some historiographical aspects of the
political rights that the 13th, 14th, and 15th Constitutional Amendments
conferred on newly freed black slaves. The historian cannot reach an absolute
conclusion in assessing the motives of the politicians who passed these
amendments, yet the provisions of the 14th and 15th Amendments remained
practically in abeyance after they had been passed. Secondary sources; 20
notes.   L. V. Eid

566. Kerp, Thomas Bland. WERE THE LINCOLN CONSPIRATORS
DEALT JUSTICE? *Lincoln Herald* 1978 80(1): 38-46. The eight Abraham
Lincoln assassination alleged conspirators, especially Edwin Spangler, Dr.
Samuel Mudd, and Samuel Arnold, were deprived of due process of law. In
1866 Federal judge Willard Hull decided in *United States* v. *Commandant of
Fort Delaware* that because the Civil War had ended, civilians could not be
tried before a military commission, and he ordered the civilians in question
released. This established a precedent that should have applied in the cases of
Arnold, Mudd, and Spangler, who were imprisoned on the Dry Tortugas,
Florida. Instead, another judicial decision, *Ex parte Mudd et al.* (1868),
deprived the three civilians of their constitutional right of due process. 9
photos, 35 notes.   T. P. Linkfield

567. Lee, R. Alton. INDIAN CITIZENSHIP AND THE FOURTEENTH
AMENDMENT. *South Dakota Hist.* 1974 4(2): 198-221. Traces the American Indian's status with regard to citizenship rights. Often considered "aliens
in their own land," the 14th Constitutional Amendment (1866) and the debate
which preceded its passage displayed the wide range of feelings that white
Americans held toward Indians. Despite the fact that the amendment defined
citizenship for all, further legal confrontations were necessary to make clear
the US position in regard to earlier Indian treaties, criminal jurisdiction on
reservations, authority to homestead, voting rights, and the citizenship status
of reservation versus non-reservation Indians. In 1924, all Indians were granted
citizenship, but Indians still do not hold first-class citizenship rights. Based on
secondary sources; photo, 49 notes.   A. J. Larson

568. Lizanich, Christine M. "THE MARCH OF THIS GOVERNMENT":
JOEL BARLOW'S UNWRITTEN HISTORY OF THE UNITED STATES.
William and Mary Q. 1976 33(2): 315-330. At the suggestion of Thomas
Jefferson, Joel Barlow began to write a history of the American Republic.
Discusses Barlow's views on politics and government, and his efforts at the
organization and writing of the project. Reprints four essays intended as part
of the history. They cover 1) differences between Federalists and Republicans,
2) political science in America, 3) the novelty of the American system, and 4)
faith in the American government. Barlow considered the work a successor to
The Federalist. Based on primary sources. 27 notes.   H. M. Ward

569.   Lucie, Patricia. ON BEING A FREE PERSON AND A CITIZEN BY CONSTITUTIONAL AMENDMENT. *J. of Am. Studies [Great Britain] 1978 12(3): 343-358.* During the American Civil War, feminist reformers attempted, to no avail, to fuse the issues of citizenship rights for former slaves and women's demands for political and social equality. Then the postwar constitutional amendments dealing with citizenship matters simply lifted the slaves from their earlier bondage and formally accorded them citizen privileges and immunities. In the 1870's, the US Supreme Court ruled in several cases such as *Minor* v. *Happersett* (1874) against contentions by women reformers that the new constitutional guarantees in the 14th and 15th Amendments buttressed their claims to political and civil equality with males. Based on judicial writings and secondary sources; 48 notes.   H. T. Lovin

570.   Lucie, Patricia M. L. CONFISCATION: CONSTITUTIONAL CROSSROADS. *Civil War Hist. 1977 23(4): 307-321.* Congressional debates on confiscation were more useful than the 1861-62 Acts they produced. Little property was confiscated, and the emancipation clauses were made redundant by Proclamation and Amendment. However, the debates were a seminar in Reconstruction problems. Congress developed much expertise in matching rights with remedies. The federal courts were utilized to enforce new-found constitutional rights. The courts became the "nuts and bolts" of Reconstruction legislation. Secondary sources; 35 notes.   R. E. Stack

571.   Lunardini, Christine A. and Knock, Thomas J. WOODROW WILSON AND WOMAN SUFFRAGE: A NEW LOOK. *Pol. Sci. Q. 1980-81 95(4): 655-671.* Reinterprets the role of Woodrow Wilson in the passage of the 19th Amendment guaranteeing women the right to vote. Wilson, originally opposed to the amendment, was converted through the efforts of women suffragists and became an advocate of critical importance.   J

572.   Lurie, Jonathan. THE "NEW" LEGAL HISTORY. *Pennsylvania Mag. of Hist. and Biog. 1983 107(2): 293-298.* Reviews Harold M. Hyman and William M. Wiecek's *Equal Justice under Law: Constitutional Development 1835-1875,* which analyzes the dominant constitutional values of the mid-19th century and examines the emergence of a strong state police power and a body of law favorable to industry and railroads. Secondary sources; 5 notes.   T. H. Wendel

573.   Maccraken, Brooks W. ALTHEA AND THE JUDGES. *Am. Heritage 1967 18(4): 60-63, 75-79.* Divorce trial of Sarah Althea Hill and Senator William Sharon preceded the ambush of Supreme Court Justice Stephen J. Field and killing of lawyer David S. Terry in 1889.   S

574.   Maidment, Richard A. *PLESSY V. FERGUSON* RE-EXAMINED. *J. of Am. Studies [Great Britain] 1973 7(2): 125-132.* Assesses the controversy over the Supreme Court's ruling on racial segregation in the case of *Plessy vs. Ferguson* (1896). The court approved segregation by race as a matter of "judicial restraint and respect for precedent" when it ruled that a Louisiana law was not in violation of the 14th Amendment. Critics contend that the

court's judgment was "mere camouflage" of the judges' segregation "policy predilections." 24 notes.   H. T. Lovin

575. Maness, Lonnie E. and Chesteen, Richard D. THE FIRST ATTEMPT AT PRESIDENTIAL IMPEACHMENT: PARTISAN POLITICS AND INTRA-PARTY CONFLICT AT LOOSE. *Presidential Studies Q. 1980 10(1): 51-62.* Studies the role of impeachment in the American constitutional system. Sixty-six impeachment attempts reached the investigative stage; many others never advanced beyond their introduction. Some involved presidents; the first (1843) was against President John Tyler, the second and third were against President Herbert C. Hoover in 1932 and 1933. Already in 1787, voices were warning that impeachment power could be abused for partisan reason. 65 notes.   G. E. Pergl

576. McCoy, Drew R. AMERICAN POLITICAL IDEOLOGY IN THE 1790S: TWO APPROACHES. *Rev. in Am. Hist. 1978 6(4): 496-502.* Review article prompted by Lance Banning's *The Jeffersonian Persuasion: Evolution of a Party Ideology* (Ithaca, N.Y.: Cornell U. Pr., 1978) and John Zvesper's *Political Philosophy and Rhetoric: A Study of the Origins of American Party Politics* (Cambridge, Eng.: Cambridge U. Pr., 1977) which discuss American political ideology in the 1790's.

577. McCurdy, Charles W. AMERICAN LAW AND THE MARKETING STRUCTURE OF THE LARGE CORPORATION, 1875-1890. *J. of Econ. Hist. 1978 38(3): 631-649.* This paper employs the techniques of legal history to explore the relationship between the rise of big business and the size of the American market. It emphasizes law as a determinant of market size, and it analyzes judicial construction of the Constitution's commerce clause over time to delineate the role of integrated corporations in generating legal change. Specifically, the paper suggests that if the American market is defined as a free-trade unit, enlargement of the market was a result of, rather than a prerequisite for, the post-Civil War revolution in business organization.   J

578. McCurdy, Charles W. JUSTICE FIELD AND THE JURISPRU-DENCE OF GOVERNMENT-BUSINESS RELATIONS: SOME PARAME-TERS OF LAISSEZ-FAIRE CONSTITUTIONALISM, 1863-1897. *J. of Am. Hist. 1975 61(4): 970-1005.* Analyzes the role of Supreme Court Justice Stephen J. Field in influencing the Court's attitude toward government-business relations in the 30 years after the Civil War. Field's interpretation of the 14th Amendment and his contribution to the "public trust" doctrine embodied a new constitutional view which was designed to separate the public and private sectors and to limit government involvement in both subsidizing and regulating private business. Field's government-business jurisprudence provided solutions for policy issues of the 1870's, but in the next generation his doctrines proved incompatible with a changing capitalist society. Based on court cases and secondary works; 180 notes.   J. B. Street

579. McCurdy, Charles W. THE KNIGHT SUGAR DECISION OF 1895 AND THE MODERNIZATION OF AMERICAN CORPORATION LAW, 1869-1903. *Business Hist. Rev. 1979 53(3): 304-343.* The conventional histori-

cal wisdom that the 1896 Knight Sugar Trust decision of the Supreme Court was a manifestation of a judicial commitment to laissez faire is in error. The Fuller court believed state governments were competent to proceed against business combinations through *quo warranto* prosecutions, and it believed Pennsylvania would do so in this instance. To decide the case in favor of the Justice Department would have, in the court's view, interfered with state control of foreign corporations. In state after state, however, authorities declined to use those powers for fear of local economic consequences. Based on judicial decisions and other public documents; 122 notes.   C. J. Pusateri

580. Mccurdy, Charles W. LEGAL INSTITUTIONS, CONSTITUTION-AL THEORY, AND THE TRAGEDY OF RECONSTRUCTION. *Rev. in Am. Hist. 1976 4(2): 203-211.* Review article prompted by Phillip S. Paludan's *A Covenant With Death: The Constitution, Law, and Equality in the Civil War Era* (Urbana: U. of Illinois Pr., 1975); discusses the careers of five constitutional law theorists and their influence on psychological and legal concepts of Reconstruction, 1868-80's.

581. McCurdy, Charles W. STEPHEN J. FIELD AND PUBLIC LAND LAW DEVELOPMENT IN CALIFORNIA, 1850-1866: A CASE STUDY OF JUDICIAL RESOURCE ALLOCATION IN NINETEENTH-CENTU-RY AMERICA. *Law and Soc. Rev. 1976 10(2): 235-266.* A case study of California courts engaged in regulating competing economic interests that were exploiting the resources of public lands. Especially involved and influential in establishing policies with respect to these competing interests was the California Supreme Court. As that Court's Chief Justice, Stephen J. Field established the successful doctrinal balance among the competing interests.
                                                                      H. R. Mahood

582. Mcginty, Brian. WAR IN THE COURT. *Civil War Times Illus. 1980 19(5): 22-25, 39-41.* From the *Dred Scott* decision of 1857 through the *Legal Tender Cases* of 1870-71, the US Supreme Court dealt with many controversial constitutional law questions under the leadership of Chief Justices Roger Brooke Taney (1777-1864) and Salmon Portland Chase (1808-73).
                                                                      D. P. Jordan

583. McKay, E. Douglas. PENNSYLVANIA VS. WHEELING AND BEL-MONT BRIDGE COMPANY. *Upper Ohio Valley Hist. Rev. 1980 9(2): 2-8.* The suspension bridge built on the Ohio River at Wheeling, [West] Virginia, 1847-49, by the Wheeling and Belmont Bridge Company, obstructed navigation along the Ohio River; this culminated in a lawsuit by Pennsylvania decided against the Company by the US Supreme Court in 1852, although in 1856 it was decided that the bridge should remain standing.

584. Mendelson, Wallace. A NOTE ON THE CAUSE AND CURE OF THE FOURTEENTH AMENDMENT. *J. of Pol. 1981 43(1): 152-158.* While the three chief congressional sponsors of the 14th Amendment agreed that they were not merely constitutionalizing the provisions of the Civil Rights Act, they disagreed on the exact meaning of the amendment. Representative John Bingham saw the amendment as protecting the privileges and immunities of all

citizens and the inborn rights of all persons. Congressman Thaddeus Stevens argued that it permitted Congress to correct unjust state legislation, applying all laws equally to all persons. Senator Jacob Howard believed that it would cover all the personal rights secured by the first eight amendments. The amendment may be understood only in the context of the antiracist measures, which include all the Civil War amendments, the Civil Rights Acts of 1866, 1870, 1871, and 1875, as well as the five Reconstruction acts and Freedmen's Bureau provisions. 35 notes.   A. W. Novitsky

585. Middleton, Kent R. THE PARTISAN PRESS AND THE REJEC-TION OF A CHIEF JUSTICE. *Journalism Q. 1976 53(1): 106-110.* John Rutledge, a South Carolina Federalist, was nominated and rejected for Chief Justice of the Supreme Court. Before notice of the nomination reached him, he attacked the Jay Treaty (1794) with England in a speech. The *Columbian Centinel*, a Federalist newspaper, printed a long response to the speech. The Philadelphia *Aurora*, a Republican newspaper, supported him. In the Senate the vote on his nomination followed the lines of the vote on the treaty. Based on primary and secondary sources; 49 notes.   K. J. Puffer

586. Miles, Edwin A. AFTER JOHN MARSHALL'S DECISION: *WORCESTER V. GEORGIA* AND THE NULLIFICATION CRISIS. *J. of Southern Hist. 1973 39(4): 519-544.* Gives the history of the *Worcester* v. *Georgia* case in which the Supreme Court ruled that missionaries Samuel A. Worcester and Dr. Elizur Butler had the right to reside in Cherokee lands, and that Georgia had no right to extend her laws over these lands within her borders. Georgia disregarded the decision and did not release the missionaries, but Worcester and Butler refused to abandon efforts to have the decision enforced. The situation was aggravated in 1833 during the nullification crisis with South Carolina, and associates of Vice President Martin Van Buren acted to solve the dispute. The federal government was thus enabled to use force to put down nullification in South Carolina without added controversy in Georgia, and aided in the preservation of the Union in 1833. Based on contemporary newspaper reports, Georgia and US government documents, and primary and secondary sources; 56 notes.   N. J. Street

587. Morris, Jeffrey B. MORRISON WAITE'S COURT. *Supreme Court Hist. Soc. Y. 1980: 36-48.* The 1870's-80's were turbulent years of economic uncertainty, expansion of big business, labor unrest, the failure of the post-Civil War commitment to black civil rights, and government corruption. The Supreme Court during these difficult times was hard-working and dominated by impressive jurists, including Chief Justice Morrison R. Waite, John Marshall Harlan, Samuel F. Miller, and Stephen J. Field. The high court's jurisprudence was marked by the overturning of much Reconstruction legisla-tion, the determination that the 14th Amendment provided protection for corporations, and the decision that states had some power to regulate businesses affected by the public interest. Waite, the chief justice during 1874-88, was an energetic jurist and an effective leader and manager. Mainly secondary sources; 7 illus., 40 notes.   S

588. Nikiforova, M. A. ROL' PRETSEDENTA V KONSTITUTSION-
NOM PRAVE SSHA [The role of precedent in US constitutional law].
Sovetskoe Gosudarstvo i Pravo [USSR] 1980 (9): 130-134. In addition to the
Constitution itself, precedents found in the so-called common law are the basis
for the administration of justice and for the decisions of the Supreme Court in
the United States. Analysis of the court's activities shows that the rule of
precedent is often applied to disguise political decisions by referring to little-
known and poorly understood precedents. 20 notes.   S

589. Oates, Stephen B. THE SLAVES FREED. *Am. Heritage 1980 32(1):
74-83.* A step-by-step account of President Abraham Lincoln's move toward
emancipation. Responding to pressures from radical Republicans, Lincoln
agreed to demands that the Civil War result in the eradication of the South's
peculiar institution. His role in that effort, from the war's beginning to the
passage of the 13th Amendment by Congress in 1865, is covered. 11 illus.
J. F. Paul

590. Owens, Mackubin T., Jr. A FURTHER NOTE ON CERTAIN OF
HAMILTON'S PSEUDONYMS: THE "LOVE OF FAME" AND THE
USES OF PLUTARCH. *J. of the Early Republic 1984 4(3): 275-286.*
Alexander Hamilton's use of "Catullus" and "Metallus" as signatures to essays
written in 1792 intimated a true patriotic defense of the republic and
Constitution against Jeffersonian partisanship. In Plutarch's life of Caius
Marius, Catullus and Metallus stand as principled pillars of republican virtue
against the factious designs of Marius. Douglass Adair and other historians
have questioned Hamilton's ulterior motives and desire for power and have
attempted to link him to Caesarism. Hamilton, however, did not admire Caesar
and he feared tyranny, not from Jefferson, but from Aaron Burr. Hamilton
understood that real fame accrued to the individual who would sacrifice his
reputation for the sake of principle, knowing that history would ultimately
vindicate the principled man. In Hamilton's estimation, Burr lacked an
appreciation for fame, was devoid of principle, and was motivated strictly by
short-term self-interest. Illus., 27 notes.   G. A. Glovins

591. Paludan, Phillip S. LINCOLN, THE RULE OF LAW, AND THE
AMERICAN REVOLUTION. *J. of the Illinois State Hist. Soc. 1977 70(1):
10-17.* Analyzes Abraham Lincoln's "political religion" as revealed through
his *Collected Works.* That religion was based on his self-proclaimed reverence
for law and the constitutional system. He saw the crucial test of democracy as
a balance between liberty and order. 2 illus., 18 notes.   J

592. Paul, Ellen. TAKING LIBERTY. *Reason 1984 15(11): 45-49.* Despite
constitutional guarantees to the contrary, governments take property without
just compensation; the courts remain the only viable institution to protect
endangered property rights.

593. Perry, James R. and Buchanan, James M. ADMISSION TO THE
SUPREME COURT BAR, 1790-1800: A CASE STUDY OF INSTITUTION-
AL CHANGE. *Supreme Court Hist. Soc. Y. 1983: 11-16.* Admission to
practice of law before the Supreme Court in the last decade of the 18th century

was decided by the chief justice and the US attorney general, as well as other members of the court. John Jay as chief justice was especially influential in the admission of new lawyers to practice before the Supreme Court. 22 notes; 5 illus.   G. B. Childress

594.   Phillips, Harry. TENNESSEE AND THE U.S. COURT OF AP-PEALS: THE SIXTH CIRCUIT. *Tennessee Hist. Q. 1954 33(1): 22-33.* Tennessee has been well represented on the US Court of Appeals for the Sixth Circuit. One of the most famous meetings of the court was the unusual one-week session of the court held in Nashville in 1897. The judges were three of the court's most famous: John Marshall Harlan, known for his support of civil rights in the post-Civil War period; William Howard Taft, the only man to be both Chief Justice of the Supreme Court and President; and Horace H. Lurton, Tennessean and formerly a distinguished law professor at Vanderbilt University. 30 notes.   M. B. Lucas

595.   Poland, Charles P., Jr. ABRAHAM LINCOLN AND CIVIL LIBER-TIES: A REAPPRAISAL. *Lincoln Herald 1974 76(3): 119-132.* Explores President Abraham Lincoln's attitude on the Constitution and his attempt to square unconstitutional acts with the Constitution. Lincoln contended that the application of the Constitution was not the same in times of "rebellion or invasion" as in peacetime. Civil liberty policies during the administration were left for his cabinet secretaries and the military to handle. Lincoln violated the Constitution in order to preserve the Union. Based on Lincoln's collective works and J. G. Randall's works; illus., 93 notes.   A. C. Aimone

596.   Poulson, Barry W. SUBSTANTIVE DUE PROCESS AND LABOR LAW. *J. of Libertarian Studies 1982 6(3-4): 267-277.* Describes the extension to economic subjects of judicial examination of 5th and 14th Amendment rights to equal protection under the law.

597.   Pratt, Walter F. RHETORICAL STYLES ON THE FULLER COURT. *Am. J. of Legal Hist. 1980 24(3): 189-220.* A study of the variety, and richness of styles, among the justices of the Supreme Court under the tenure of Chief Justice Melville Fuller, 1895-1905. The database consists of the 286 cases involving a challenge to the constitutionality of state, territorial, and federal statutes. The information quantified includes voting patterns, length of opinion, and the average number of cases cited per page of opinion. The results reveal differences in the justices' style of argument and reasoning. Three groups are described, with justices Holmes and Peckham at each end. Holmes wrote epigrammatical opinions that relied on the frequent citation of opinions to demonstrate the extent to which governments should be given great latitude in making law, while Peckham used a principal-essay style to protect individual and corporate liberties from the unreasonable, unnecessary, and arbitrary acts of legislatures. Based on the Supreme Court Reports; 159 notes.

                                                                    L. A. Knafla

598.   Preston, L. E. SPEAKERS FOR WOMEN'S RIGHTS IN PENNSYL-VANIA. *Western Pennsylvania Hist. Mag. 1971 54(3): 245-263.* Profiles the

careers and achievements (1837-1920) of pro-feminists in Pennsylvania, culminating in the ratification of the 19th Amendment.   S

599.   Price, Edward. THE BLACK VOTING RIGHTS ISSUE IN PENN-SYLVANIA, 1780-1900. *Pennsylvania Mag. of Hist. and Biog. 1976 100(3): 356-373.* Constitutionally disenfranchised in 1838, black Pennsylvanians did not regain the right to vote until ratification of the 15th Amendment in 1870. Although at first meeting with hostility from whites, by 1900 blacks could vote without hindrance and were exercising a small degree of political power. The franchise was useful to blacks to improve their condition but was not a panacea. Primary and secondary sources; 67 notes.   E. W. Carp

600.   Rau, Donald. *CUMMINGS V. MISSOURI:* THREE CHEERS FOR FATHER CUMMINGS. *Supreme Court Hist. Soc. Y. 1977: 20-28.* Discusses the Supreme Court decision in *Cummings* v. *Missouri* (US, 1867) that found unconstitutional the test oath and registry act required of priests and ministers in the state of Missouri prior to conducting services or ceremonies, and which also found Father John Cummings of St. Joseph's Catholic Church in Louisiana, Missouri, not guilty for refusing to take the oath.

601.   Relyea, Harold C. NATIONAL EMERGENCY POWERS: A BRIEF OVERVIEW OF PRESIDENTIAL SUSPENSIONS OF THE HABEAS CORPUS PRIVILEGE AND INVOCATION OF MARTIAL LAW. *Presidential Studies Q. 1977 7(4): 238-243.* Chronicles outstanding examples of executive power to suspend habeas corpus and invoke martial law. The issue of his right to suspend habeas corpus is based on precedent, not being clearly outlined in the Constitution. Martial law has often merely meant placing soldiers at the disposal of civil authorities. Hawaii was placed under both martial law and suspension of habeas corpus by its governor at the outbreak of hostilities with Japan, a condition lasting until late 1944. An open question is whether a congressional declaration or presidential proclamation would be mandatory for suspension or martial law in case of wars or national emergencies. 19 notes.   J. Tull

602.   Richard, K. Keith. UNWELCOME SETTLERS: BLACK AND MU-LATTO OREGON PIONEERS. *Oregon Hist. Q. 1983 84(1): 29-55, (2): 172-205.* Part 1. Examines white attitudes and legislation that were adverse toward blacks and mulattoes in Oregon. When Oregon was admitted as a state in February 1859, its constitution was antislavery but reflected an antiblack and mulatto bias. Passage of the 13th and 14th Amendments to the US Constitution occurred at a time when many blacks and mulattoes were settling in the Portland area. Interracial marriages plus the attitudes of whites toward these people resulted in several discriminatory laws. Although the 15th Amendment guaranteed many freedoms to blacks and mulattoes, the private opinions of many whites were not favorable toward them. Based primarily on 1850, 1860, and 1870 US census data; 2 photos, table, 2 fig., 62 notes. Part 2. Discusses fluctuating economic conditions for blacks and mulattoes in Oregon and the attitudes of white Oregonians toward them. Most Oregon blacks and mulattoes lived in Multnomah County and the city of Portland. Ratification of the 15th Amendment brought enfranchisement, but failed to change racial

attitudes and practices entirely. Religion and education were the major vehicles used to bring about cooperative efforts. Based on 1850, 1860, and 1870 US census data and Oregon newspapers; 3 photos, plate, 10 tables, 40 notes.

C. R. Gunter, Jr./S

603. Riegel, Stephen J. THE PERSISTENT CAREER OF JIM CROW: LOWER FEDERAL COURTS AND THE "SEPARATE BUT EQUAL" DOCTRINE, 1865-1896. *Am. J. of Legal Hist. 1984 28(1): 17-40.* The "separate but equal" doctrine of race relations, which was enshrined by the 1896 Supreme Court decision in *Plessy* v. *Ferguson,* has long been regarded by legal historians as a turn-of-the-century development whose genesis in the South was due to legislative action. However, many lower federal court judgments on Reconstruction civil-rights amendments and laws legitimatized segregation. The cases involved public accommodations, transportation, and education. In a society opposed to social equality, the operative judicial phrase became: equal accommodations do not mean identical accommodations. Nonetheless, judges often provided relief to black plaintiffs who were excluded altogether from accommodations. In this perspective, the *Plessy* decision did not represent a change from *de facto* to *de jure* segregation, but only the persistence of Jim Crow in the 2d Reconstruction. Based on judicial and legislative records; 94 notes.   L. A. Knafla

604. Robbins, Peggy. SUSAN B. ANTHONY. *Am. Hist. Illus. 1971 6(5): 36-43.* Susan Brownell Anthony (1820-1906) was born in Adams, Massachusetts, of Quaker parents. In the late 1840's, she became active in temperance, antislavery movements, and women's rights, devoting her full time after 1849 to "social action." Although the years 1855-65 were devoted to the American Antislavery Society in New York, Susan also led the fight which resulted in an 1860 New York law granting property rights to married women. After the Civil War, she concentrated on winning woman suffrage, and 14 years after she died the 19th Amendment was ratified, 26 August 1920, often called the "Susan Anthony Amendment." Secondary sources; 5 illus.   D. Dodd

605. Rosenberg, Norman L. ALEXANDER ADDISON AND THE PENN-SYLVANIA ORIGINS OF FEDERALIST FIRST-AMENDMENT THOUGHT. *Pennsylvania Mag. of Hist. and Biog. 1984 108(4): 399-419.* The statements of Alexander Addison, a Pennsylvania Federalist judge, on freedom of expression are a good indication of the course of Federalist thought on the matter. Addison accepted free speech, but in a responsible manner and condemned irresponsible journalism and outright libel. His ideas express the philosophical basis behind the Federalists' Sedition Act of 1798.   S

606. Rosenberg, Norman L. THE LAW OF POLITICAL LIBEL AND FREEDOM OF PRESS IN THE NINETEENTH CENTURY AMERICA: AN INTERPRETATION. *Am. J. of Legal Hist. 1973 17(4): 336-352.* During 1824-70 political libel ceased to be a main issue in constitutional law.

607. Russell, Kay. THE FALLBROOK IRRIGATION DISTRICT CASE. *J. of San Diego Hist. 1975 21(2): 23-40.* Describes the historical background to the Fallbrook Irrigation District Case (US, 1896), concerning the constitution-

ality of the California Irrigation District Law and the use of the Santa Margarita River by citizens of Fallbrook for their avocado orchards.   S

608. Scheiber, Harry N. THE ROAD TO *MUNN:* EMINENT DOMAIN AND THE CONCEPT OF PUBLIC PURPOSE IN THE STATE COURTS. *Perspectives in Am. Hist. 1971 5: 329-402.* When the Supreme Court decided in *Munn v. Illinois* (US, 1877) that business could affect the public interest, it was not offering a novel interpretation of the law. Rather, members of the court logically extended interpretations rendered in earlier decisions of lower courts. State courts had exercised eminent domain law extensively prior to the Civil War, and *Munn v. Illinois* merely validated state court dictates. 242 notes.   W. A. Wiegand

609. Schultz, L. Peter. WILLIAM HOWARD TAFT: A CONSTITUTIONALIST'S VIEW OF THE PRESIDENCY. *Presidential Studies Q. 1979 9(4): 402-414.* An examination of the theory of presidential power advanced by William Howard Taft casts doubt on the prevalent assumption that strict adherence to the Constitution implies severely limited presidential authority. Citing John Marshall, Taft argued that political law substantively differed from law properly treated in the courts. Execution of treaties, for example, as well as decisions required of the commander in chief, involved the political discretion of the president, whose quasi-legislative and quasi-judicial responsibilities were in such cases beyond dispute. Theodore Roosevelt's stewardship theory is perhaps unduly broad; Taft's arguments suggest that the constitutionalist's view is not so narrow as presumed. 102 notes.   S

610. Schweninger, Loren. BLACK CITIZENSHIP AND THE REPUBLICAN PARTY IN RECONSTRUCTION ALABAMA. *Alabama R. 1976 29(2): 83-103.* Throughout the Reconstruction era the Republican Party in Alabama was badly divided on the question of enfranchising the freedmen. A moderate wing defended the federal government and the 14th and 15th Amendments, while a conservative wing, led in part by Judge J. Haralson, an ex-slave, opposed the Constitution, the Grant Administration, and several federal patronage appointees. Tension and conflict plagued the party, and "doomed Alabama Reconstruction to failure from the outset." Based on primary and secondary sources; 88 notes.   J. F. Vivian

611. Sernett, Milton C. THE RIGHTS OF PERSONHOOD: THE DRED SCOTT CASE AND THE QUESTION OF ABORTION. *Religion in Life 1980 49(4): 461-476.* Discusses two Supreme Court decisions: *Roe v. Wade* (US, 1973), which legalized abortion, and *Dred Scott v. Sandford* (US, 1857), which certified that blacks were not US citizens—in other words that they were nonpersons without legal recourse.

612. Smith, Dean. 300 POUNDS OF SOLID CHARITY: WILLIAM HOWARD TAFT. *Am. Hist. Illus. 1976 11(1): 10-17.* "300 Pounds of Solid Charity" was Will Rogers' tribute to William Howard Taft as he was leaving the Presidency in 1913. At the end of the 1912 campaign, Taft reached his highest weight, 335 pounds. When he graduated from Yale Law School in 1878, he weighed 243 pounds. As a circuit judge in the 1890's, he bulged to the

290's and on returning to the United States in 1904, after four years in the Philippines, he weighed 326. Taft had a passion for food and ate more when faced with difficulties. Once he was out of politics and became a professor of Law at Yale, he lost weight; and, after eight years on the Supreme Court, he was down to 244. 7 illus.   D. Dodd

613. Smith, George P. REPUBLICAN RECONSTRUCTION AND SEC-TION TWO OF THE FOURTEENTH AMENDMENT. *Western Pol. Q. 1970 23(4): 829-853.* Discusses Reconstruction and the Republican Party's attempt to maintain its ascendency through passage of black suffrage, entailed in section two of the Fourteenth Amendment.

614. Snyder, K. Alan. FOUNDATIONS OF LIBERTY: THE CHRISTIAN REPUBLICANISM OF TIMOTHY DWIGHT AND JEDIDIAH MORSE. *New England Q. 1983 56(3): 382-397.* Within the Federalist-Republican battles of the 1790's, historians have commonly viewed Jedidiah Morse and Timothy Dwight as aristocrats. Modern scholarship suggests that Federalists used a different concept of republicanism, one that might be termed "republican ideologue." Examined against this new concept, the thought of Morse and Dwight on Christian republicanism, while grounded in liberty, was alert to the possible abuses of it. Although virtue and absolute truth were the foundations of liberty, a Christian sense of morality was essential to its vitality. Morse and Dwight both reacted against the French Revolution and America of the 1790's when they saw Christian values disregarded. They were not manipulators for political advantage, but rather champions within the dominant Congregational-ist-Federalist framework of liberty. 38 notes.   R. S. Sliwoski

615. Sogrin, V. V. IDEOLOGIIA FEDERALISTSKOI PARTII S.SH.A. (KONETS XVIII-NACHALO XIX V.) [Ideology of the Federalist Party in the late 18th and early 19th centuries]. *Amerikanskii Ezhegodnik [USSR] 1981: 65-92.* The Federalist Party was the party of government during 1789-1801, and played a key role in opposing the Republicans until 1815. The federalists were the descendants of the moderate conservative wing of the American Revolution. They represented the interests of financial, trade, and manufacturing circles of the Northeast, as well as Southern planters. The Federalists stood for the conservation of recent bourgeois transformations and the maintenance of the supremacy of the capitalist upper classes. Based on congressional records, the papers of Alexander Hamilton, and on secondary sources; 76 notes.   J. Bamber

616. Spackman, S. G. F. AMERICAN FEDERALISM AND THE CIVIL RIGHTS ACT OF 1875. *J. of Am. Studies [Great Britain] 1976 10(3): 313-328.* Describes racial considerations and social and political pressures that influenced the Civil Rights Act of 1875 when Congress considered and passed it and the courts reviewed it. Authored by Charles Sumner (1811-1874) and designed to prevent discrimination against blacks, the legislation caused major constitutional disputes about the nature and extent of federal powers to enforce the 13th and 14th Amendments. In 1883 the US Supreme Court struck down the Civil Rights Act, thus setting back the achievement of racial equality by

substantially expanding federal powers to punish individuals. Based on government documents and secondary sources; 49 notes.   H. T. Lovin

617. Spector, Robert M. WOMAN AGAINST THE LAW: MYRA BRAD-WELL'S STRUGGLE FOR ADMISSION TO THE ILLINOIS BAR. *J. of the Illinois State Hist. Soc. 1975 68(3): 228-242.* The unsuccessful effort of Myra Bradwell to gain admission to the Illinois bar led to her appeal to the US Supreme Court in 1873. The Court ruled that her case was not justified under the Fourteenth Amendment or the privileges and immunities clause of Section IV of the United States Constitution. Bradwell's case, however, did prepare the way for other women to be admitted to law practice in Illinois and in other states. She successfully edited the *Chicago Legal News* until her death in 1894, making this legal publication one of the most respected in the country.
                                                                          N. Lederer

618. Staley, Laura. SUFFRAGE MOVEMENT IN ST. LOUIS DURING THE 1870S. *Gateway Heritage 1983 3(4): 34-41.* An organized movement to secure feminine suffrage in Missouri began when reformers, led by Virginia Minor, formed an association on 8 May 1867 to gain the ballot for women. The group claimed that the 14th Amendment had already enfranchised women, and, citing such legal theories, the suffrage association initiated litigation to compel Missouri civil authorities to honor these asserted voting rights of women. Finally, in *Minor* v. *Happersett* (29 March 1875), the US Supreme Court denied the suffrage movement's theories, holding that 14th Amendment provisos never superseded state constitutions, which all restricted suffrage rights to some degree. Based on legal documents, government publications, and secondary sources; 17 photos, 36 notes.   H. T. Lovin

619. Stange, Douglas C. ABOLITION AS TREASON: THE UNITARIAN ELITE DEFENDS LAW, ORDER, AND THE UNION. *Harvard Lib. Bull. 1980 28(2): 152-170.* Describes pre-Civil War opposition of Unitarian conservative clergymen in Boston and St. Louis to the abolitionist movement. By championing law and order, respect for the US Constitution and state law, and separation of politics from moral influence, the ministers upheld the view of businessmen, who were mainly responsible for the fiscal well-being of the churches. The clergy, however, did accept in principle proposals to colonize slaves in foreign lands, realizing the impracticality of the idea because slaveholders would lose too much to agree. Any strong attempt at colonization would generate national disunion, a much worse evil, in the clergy's view, than slavery. Based on the James Freeman Clarke Papers, Houghton Library, Harvard University; William G. Elliot Collection, University Archives, Olin Library, Washington University, St. Louis; and files of the Missouri Historical Society, St. Louis; 81 notes.   D. J. Mycue

620. Stern, Madeleine B., ed. TWO UNPUBLISHED LETTERS FROM BELVA LOCKWOOD. *Signs: J. of Women in Culture and Soc. 1975 1(1): 269-272.* These letters present a biography and the political philosophy of Belva Bennett Lockwood (1830-1917), the first woman attorney to practice law in the federal courts and before the US Supreme Court and the first woman campaigner for the presidency. Reprints her 1884 letter to the National Equal

Rights Party in which she accepted the presidential nomination. In her strongly feminist and humanist platform she advocated equal political and civil rights regardless of sex or race, equitable distribution of money and power, uniform marriage and divorce laws upholding equality of the sexes, temperance, universal peace through a court of arbitration, and citizenship for American Indians. Her vigorous campaign garnered more than 4,000 votes and helped establish the place of women in the political arena. Based on primary and secondary sources; note.   T. Simmerman

621. Swindler, William. HIGH COURT OF CONGRESS: IMPEACH-MENT TRIALS, 1797-1936. *Am. Bar Assoc. J. 1974 60(4): 420-428.* History shows that impeachment trials have moved from barely disguised political vendettas to quasi-judicial proceedings.   J

622. Swindler, William F. MR. CHISHOLM AND THE ELEVENTH AMENDMENT. *Supreme Court Hist. Soc. Y. 1981: 14-18.* Discusses the impact of the case of *Chisholm* v. *Georgia* (US, 1792) on the question of states' rights and the power of the federal government. The issues raised by the case resulted in the ratification of the 11th Amendment, which freed states from the sort of litigation that Alexander Chisholm had brought against Georgia and acted as a buffer for states' rights against encroachments by the federal government, after it had been ratified in 1795 and put into effect in 1798. Relies on the records of several court cases; photo.   G. V. Wasson

623. Swindler, William F. ROSCOE CONKLING AND THE FOUR-TEENTH AMENDMENT. *Supreme Court Hist. Soc. Y. 1983: 46-52.* Roscoe Conkling argued two cases before the Supreme Court in 1882. Conkling's interpretation of the word "person" in the 14th Amendment to include corporations is significant in the later history of the court. 7 illus.
G. B. Childress

624. Szasz, Ferenc M. ANTEBELLUM APPEALS TO THE "HIGHER LAW," 1830-1860. *Essex Inst. Hist. Collections 1974 110(1): 33-48.* Because slavery was written into the Constitution, Northerners and Southerners debated the nature of a "higher law" on which all law was based.   S

625. Taylor, John M. JUSTICE STEPHEN J. FIELD. *Am. Hist. Illus. 1974 9(6): 35-38.* An account of the life and career of Stephen Johnson Field (1816-99). When gold was discovered in California, Field left his New York law practice and arrived in San Francisco at the end of 1849, settling in Marysville. In 1863 President Lincoln named him to the Supreme Court where he served until 1887. "Among his colleagues Stephen J. Field was a picture of judicial dignity. ... In his judicial opinions, Field was often spokesman for a conservative minority which later became a majority on the Court.... Field was one of the most influential justices of his generation, and saw many of his early dissents become the law of the land. His judicial philosophy was not without inconsistencies, and his decisions concerning the Federal regulatory power would be reversed in later Court decisions." Illus., 3 photos.
D. D. Cameron

626. Teaford, Jon C. TOWARD A CHRISTIAN NATION: RELIGION, LAW AND JUSTICE STRONG. *J. of Presbyterian Hist. 1976 54(4): 422-437.* William Strong (1808-95) was an Associate Justice of the US Supreme Court from 1870 until his resignation in 1880. A prosperous entrepreneur and expert in business law, he was also a Presbyterian Elder and loyal layman in a country which was beginning to deviate from traditional Christian values and the Christian way of life. He was a member of the National Reform Association which in 1864 unsuccessfully proposed an amendment to the preamble of the US Constitution which would give formal recognition to God and Jesus Christ so that there would be no doubt that the US was a Christian nation ruled by a Christian government. His efforts to promote personal piety in the midst of great social change characterized his own zeal for the moral and spiritual welfare of his country. At the same time he was woefully aware of the shortcomings of the Christian cause in the US in failing to provide religious and social provisions for the masses. He served on the boards of numerous interdenominational agencies in addition to his Presbyterian responsibilities. Based largely on Strong's writings; illus., 40 notes.   H. M. Parker, Jr.

627. Tollett, Kenneth S.; Leonard, Jeanette J.; and James, Portia P. A COLOR-CONSCIOUS CONSTITUTION: THE ONE PERVADING PURPOSE *REDUX. J. of Negro Educ. 1983 52(3): 189-212.* The "one pervading purpose" of constitutional amendments and civil rights legislation passed during Reconstruction was to protect blacks' rights. Supreme Court decisions of 1871-99 established the precedent of a "color-blind Constitution," denying the primacy of blacks by extending protection to other minorities and even to corporations. A return by federal courts to the original aim of these amendments and laws, especially in desegregation and affirmative action suits, would insure justice and equality for blacks. Based on court decisions and federal law; 68 notes.   R. G. Sherer

628. Turner, John J., Jr. THE TWELFTH AMENDMENT AND THE FIRST AMERICAN PARTY SYSTEM. *Historian 1973 35 (2): 221-237.* The 12th Amendment partly was intended to extend and strengthen the safeguards against factionalism which were institutionalized in the Electoral College. In fact, the amendment facilitated the emergence of the modern party system by legalizing party control of both officers in the executive branch. Shows the state of opinion about political parties at this stage in American history. Based on records of the Constitutional Convention, the Federalist papers, and secondary sources; 61 notes.   N. W. Moen

629. Turner, Justin G. THE STROHM LETTERS AND LINCOLN'S THIRTEENTH AMENDMENT. *Lincoln Herald 1976 78(1): 24-26.* Presents copies of four letters written by the daughters of Isaac Strohm, Chief Engrossing Clerk, authenticating the manuscript copy of the Thirteenth Amendment owned by the Henry E. Huntington Library.   B. J. LaBue

630. VanDeburg, William L. FREDERICK DOUGLASS: MARYLAND SLAVE TO RELIGIOUS LIBERAL. *Maryland Hist. Mag. 1974 69(1): 27-43.* Young Frederick Douglass was convinced of the omnipotence of God and His role as "Supreme Judge of the Universe." By the 1840's, however, the influence

of Reason, Transcendentalism, and Unitarianism convinced him that the abolition movement must be primarily a human enterprise. Despising the passive attitude displayed by many black ministers, Douglass even criticized Henry Ward Beecher's reliance on God to end slavery. Increasingly enlightenment terminology crept into Douglass' writings and speeches, and his move to a humanistic theology climaxed with his address in Philadelphia's Horticultural Hall on 26 April 1870 when he lauded Wendell Phillips, Elijah Lovejoy, John Brown, and Abraham Lincoln in celebrating the recently ratified 15th Amendment. Primary and secondary sources; 8 illus., 59 notes.

G. J. Bobango

631.   Weeks, Louis and Hickey, James C. "IMPLIED TRUST" FOR CONNECTIONAL CHURCHES: *WATSON V. JONES* REVISITED. *J. of Presbyterian Hist. 1976 54(4): 459-470.* Unravels and recounts the complicated history of the famous case of *Watson* v. *Jones*, which dealt with the control and ownership of the property of the Walnut Street Presbyterian Church, Louisville, Kentucky, in the post-Civil War period. The thrust of the case for ecclesiastical as well as civil law is that the governing body of a local church (in this case the session) holds the property and the rights to decision-making in behalf of the highest judicatory of the denomination among those churches that are connectional in their polity. In the more recent *Presbyterian Church in the US* v. *Mary Elizabeth Blue Hull Memorial Presbyterian Church* (1969) the Supreme Court ruled that the First Amendment prohibits civil courts from awarding church property on the basis of the court's interpretation of church doctrine. Thus the basic legal doctrines spawned by *Watson* v. *Jones* over a century ago will probably continue to help determine the role of civil courts in church disputes. Based on the minutes of the Walnut Street Presbyterian Church and secondary materials; 34 notes.   H. M. Parker, Jr.

632.   Westin, Alan F. POPULISM AND THE SUPREME COURT. *Supreme Court Hist. Soc. Y. 1980: 62-77.* The conflict between late 19th-century Populism and large capitalist interests was clearly drawn in legal and political battles that pitted farmers and the states against the railroads. These battles were waged over states' attempts to regulate railroad bond subscriptions, to recover public lands made available to promoters of internal improvements who defaulted on projects, to exercise control over railroad rates, and other issues. The Supreme Court of this period generally favored corporate interests, and in so doing often broke with its long-established policy of accepting state court constructions of state constitutions and laws. The attitude of the Supreme Court was a major campaign issue in the election of 1896, when the Democratic Party platform condemned "government by judges." The Supreme Court's consistent support of the corporations turned the focus of progressive forces from local to national issues, sheltered corporate development during its years of expansion and consolidation, and revived the antilegal farmer-debtor tradition. Abridged reprint of an article published in the *Journal of Politics* (1953). Based on court records and other primary sources; 2 illus., 87 notes.

S

633.   White, G. Edward. JOHN MARSHALL HARLAN I: THE PRECURSOR. *Am. J. of Legal Hist. 1975 19(1): 1-21.* Examines Harlan's Supreme

Court career, 1877-1911, focusing on his responses to the Reconstruction amendments and to the growth of large-scale industrial enterprise. Harlan evolved from an orthodox Whig to a paternalist, gradually accepting government regulation of the economy, civil rights, and liberal interpretations of the 13th, 14th, and 15th amendments. Includes a brief account of his earlier political career from the late 1850's to the mid-1870's. 104 notes.

L. A. Knafla

634. White, Jean Bickmore. WOMAN'S PLACE IS IN THE CONSTITUTION: THE STRUGGLE FOR EQUAL RIGHTS IN UTAH IN 1895. *Utah Hist. Q. 1974 42(4): 344-369.* Reviews Utah women's struggle to acquire voting rights when the territory became a state in 1895. Initially, both political parties supported universal suffrage, but opposition soon developed. Militancy was wholly absent, and the women won because their leaders were respected members of the Mormon Church. 5 photos, 58 notes.   V. L. Human

635. Wiecek, William M. A PECULIAR CONSERVATISM AND THE DORR REBELLION: CONSTITUTIONAL CLASH IN JACKSONIAN AMERICA. *Am. J. of Legal Hist. 1978 22(3): 237-253.* The Rhode Island conservatives in the Dorr Rebellion of 1842 were significantly different than the "consensus interpretation" of Whig conservatism during 1835-55. Using court records, grand jury charges, house reports and addresses, and local newspapers, concludes that this peculiar conservatism extolled the law, compact theory, and social hierarchy. The key issue was expanding the suffrage, which the conservatives opposed as a threat to the social order. 57 notes.

L. A. Knafla

636. Wiecek, William M. SLAVERY AND ABOLITION BEFORE THE UNITED STATES SUPREME COURT, 1820-1860. *J. of Am. Hist. 1978 65(1): 34-59.* The notoriety surrounding *Dred Scott* v. *Sandford* (US, 1857) has frequently hindered historians' efforts to understand the policy-making role of the antebellum Supreme Court. The *Dred Scott* case was neither exceptional nor anomalous. It was, however, the natural result of judicial doctrines and tendencies that had been developing for several years. John Marshall, though opposed to slavery in the abstract, believed that a judge's moral instincts should not influence his rulings in light of the law. Roger Taney, as Chief Justice, was determined to destroy antislavery constitutional ideas argued in cases before him. Even before the famous *Dred Scott* case, Supreme Court decisions involving *Groves* (1841), *Prigg* (1842), and *Van Zandt* (1847) consistently undermined antislavery constitutional ideas argued before the Court. The *Dred Scott* decision was no aberration. 89 notes.

T. P. Linkfield

637. Wright, Almon R. THE DAY THE INCOME TAX WAS DECLARED UNCONSTITUTIONAL. *Mankind 1976 5(6): 36-39.* The Populist thrust to punish the rich and tap their resources through the imposition of an income tax was thwarted by the decision of the Supreme Court in the case of *Pollock* v. *Farmer's Loan and Trust Company* (US, 1895). The five-member majority of the Court ruling against the tax reasoned that it represented a

direct tax and was unconstitutional owing to the fact that it was not apportioned on the basis of the population of each state.   N. Lederer

638.   Young, James Harvey. THIS GREASY COUNTERFEIT: BUTTER VERSUS OLEOMARGARINE IN THE U.S. CONGRESS, 1886. *Bull. of the Hist. of Medicine 1979 53(3): 392-414.* In 1886, Congress enacted a law taxing oleomargarine. The debates leading to the final vote constituted the first prolonged discussion in Congress involving a pure food issue. The major themes of the debate were the farmer's and the consumer's welfare, fraud, the role of big business in American society, and constitutionality. The next year, Dr. Harvey Wiley published the first part of the Bureau of Chemistry's Bulletin 13 on *Food and Food Adulterants,* and this began the campaign which culminated in the passage of the Pure Food and Drug Act (US, 1906). 139 notes.   M. Kaufman

639.   —. EQUAL JUSTICE UNDER LAW: DOCUMENTARY FILMS ON THE SUPREME COURT. *Supreme Court Hist. Soc. Y. 1978: 25-30.* Discusses the series of five films about our "constitutional heritage" based on four cases heard under Chief Justice John Marshall: *Marbury* v. *Madison* (1803), the Burr treason trial (1807), *McCulloch* v. *Maryland* (1819), and *Gibbons* v. *Ogden* (1824), which were released in 1977 by the Bicentennial Committee of the Judicial Conference of the United States.

640.   —. A GENTILE REPROVES AN ANTI-SEMITE: FRESNO—1893. *Western States Jewish Hist. Q. 1977 9(4): 299-300.* During a murder trial in Fresno, California, defense lawyer William D. Foote attempted to undermine the testimony of a Jewish prosecution witness by abusing Jews generally. Grove L. Johnson, prosecuting attorney, in offering a rejoinder to Foote's anti-Semitic views, emphasized traditional American religious tolerance and Constitutional rights and privileges. Johnson's speech is quoted at length. 9 notes.
    B. S. Porter

Books

641.   Baxter, Maurice G. *The Steamboat Monopoly: Gibbons v. Ogden, 1824.* (Borzoi Series in United States Constitutional History.) New York: Knopf, 1972. 146 pp.

642.   Belz, Herman. *Emancipation and Equal Rights: Politics and Constitutionalism in the Civil War Era.* New York: Norton, 1978. 171 pp.

643.   Berger, Raoul. *Government by Judiciary: The Transformation of the Fourteenth Amendment.* Cambridge, Mass.: Harvard U. Pr., 1977. 483 pp.

644.   Berry, Mary Frances. *Military Necessity and Civil Rights Policy: Black Citizenship and the Constitution, 1861-1868.* (Series in American Studies.) Port Washington, N.Y.: Kennikat, 1977. 132 pp.

645. Bridwell, Randall and Whitten, Ralph U. *The Constitution and the Common Law: The Decline of the Doctrines of Separation of Powers and Federalism.* Lexington, Mass.: Heath, 1977. 206 pp.

646. Bringhurst, Bruce. *Antitrust and the Oil Monopoly: The Standard Oil Cases, 1890-1911.* (Contributions in Legal Studies, no. 8.) Westport, Conn.: Greenwood, 1979. 296 pp.

647. Burch, Philip H., Jr. *Elites in American History. Vol. 2: The Civil War to the New Deal.* New York: Holmes & Meier, 1981. 496 pp.

648. Chase, James S. *Emergence of the Presidential Nominating Convention, 1789-1832.* Urbana: U. of Illinois Pr., 1973. 332 pp.

649. Cortner, Richard C. *The Jones and Laughlin Case.* (Borzoi Series in United States Constitutional History.) New York: Knopf, 1970. 191 pp.

650. deAlvarez, Leo Paul S., ed. *Abraham Lincoln, The Gettysburg Address, and American Constitutionalism.* Irving, Tex.: U. of Dallas Pr., 1976. 203 pp.

651. Dewey, Donald O. *Marshall versus Jefferson: The Political Background of Marbury v. Madison.* (Borzoi Series in United States Constitutional History.) New York: Knopf, 1970. 195 pp.

652. Ehrlich, Walter. *They Have No Rights: Dred Scott's Struggle for Freedom.* (Contributions in Legal Studies, no. 9.) Westport, Conn.: Greenwood, 1979. 266 pp.

653. Eidelberg, Paul. *A Discourse on Statesmanship: The Design and Transformation of the American Polity.* Urbana: U. of Illinois Pr., 1974. 472 pp.

654. Elsmere, Jane Shaffer. *Justice Samuel Chase.* Muncie, Ind.: Janeva, 1981. 370 pp.

655. Goff, John S. *The Supreme Court Justices, 1863-1912: Arizona Territorial Officials, Vol. 1.* Cave Creek, Ariz.: Black Mountain, 1975. 200 pp.

656. Haskins, George Lee and Johnson, Herbert A. *Foundations of Power: John Marshall, 1801-1815.* (History of the Supreme Court of the United States Series, vol. 2.) New York: Macmillan, 1981. 687 pp.

657. Hoffman, Daniel N. *Governmental Secrecy and the Founding Fathers: A Study in Constitutional Controls.* Westport, Conn.: Greenwood, 1981. 339 pp.

658. Horowitz, Robert F. *The Great Impeacher: A Political Biography of James M. Ashley.* New York: Brooklyn Coll. Pr., 1979. 227 pp.

659.   Hyman, Harold M. and Wiecek, William M. *Equal Justice under Law: Constitutional Development, 1835-1875.* (New American Nation series.) New York: Harper & Row, 1982. 571 pp.

660.   Hyman, Harold M. *A More Perfect Union: The Impact of the Civil War and Reconstruction on the Constitution.* (Impact of the Civil War: The Civil War Centennial Commission Series.) New York: Alfred A. Knopf, 1973. 562 pp.

661.   James, Joseph B. *The Ratification of the Fourteenth Amendment.* Macon, Ga.: Mercer U. Pr., 1984. 331 pp.

662.   Kutler, Stanley I. *Privilege and Creative Destruction: The Charles River Bridge Case.* Philadelphia: Lippincott, 1971. 191 pp.

663.   Lawhorne, Clifton O. *The Supreme Court and Libel.* Carbondale: Southern Illinois U. Pr., 1981. 140 pp.

664.   Linden, Glenn M. *Politics or Principle: Congressional Voting on the Civil War Amendments and Pro-Negro Measures, 1838-69.* Seattle: U. of Washington Pr., 1976. 88 pp.

665.   Marshall, John. *The Papers of John Marshall. Vol. 4: Correspondence and Papers, January, 1799-October, 1800.* Charles T. Cullen, ed. Chapel Hill: U. of North Carolina Pr.; Williamsburg, N.C.: Inst. of Early Am. Hist. and Culture, 1984. 365 pp.

666.   O'Connor, John E. *William Paterson: Lawyer and Statesman, 1745-1806.* New Brunswick, N.J.: Rutgers U. Pr., 1979. 351 pp.

667.   Paludan, Phillip S. *A Covenant with Death: The Constitution, Law, and Equality in the Civil War Era.* Urbana: U. of Illinois Pr., 1975. 309 pp.

668.   Schwartz, Bernard. *From Confederation to Nation: The American Constitution, 1835-1877.* Baltimore: Johns Hopkins U. Pr., 1973. 243 pp.

669.   Sefton, James E. *Andrew Johnson and the Uses of Constitutional Power.* Oscar Handlin, ed. Boston: Little, Brown, 1980. 212 pp.

670.   Semonche, John E. *Charting the Future: The Supreme Court Responds to a Changing Society, 1890-1920.* (Contributions in Legal Studies, no. 5.) Westport, Conn.: Greenwood, 1978. 470 pp.

671.   Sisson, Daniel. *The American Revolution of 1800.* New York: Knopf, 1974. 468 pp.

672.   Sofaer, Abraham D. *War, Foreign Affairs and Constitutional Power: The Origins.* Cambridge, Mass.: Ballinger, 1976. 533 pp.

673. Stites, Francis N. *John Marshall: Defender of the Constitution.* Boston: Little, Brown, 1981. 181 pp.

674. Stites, Francis N. *Private Interest and Public Gain: The Dartmouth College Case, 1819.* Amherst: U. of Massachusetts Pr., 1972. 176 pp.

675. Swindler, William F. *The Constitution and Chief Justice Marshall.* New York: Dodd, Mead, 1979. 414 pp.

676. Swisher, Carl B. *History of the Supreme Court of the United States. Vol. 5: The Taney Period, 1835-1864.* New York: Macmillan, 1974. 1041 pp.

677. Tugwell, Rexford G. *The Compromising of the Constitution.* Notre Dame, Ind.: U. of Notre Dame Pr., 1976. 188 pp.

678. Zvesper, John. *Political Philosophy and Rhetoric: A Study of the Origins of American Party Politics.* Cambridge, England: Cambridge U. Pr., 1977. 237 pp.

Dissertations

679. Annis, David Leslie. "Mr. Bushrod Washington, Supreme Court Justice on the Marshall Court." U. of Notre Dame 1974. 302 pp. *DAI 1974 35(5): 3021-A.*

680. Finkelman, Paul. "A More Perfect Union? Slavery, Comity, and Federalism, 1787-1861." U. of Chicago 1976. *DAI 1976 37(6): 3850-3851-A.*

681. Gordon, Benjamin Laurence. "The Federalists: Principle and the Political Marketplace." New York U. 1979. 381 pp. *DAI 1979 40(5): 2837-A.*

682. Hart, Mary Johnson. "Privacy and Media Encroachment." U. of Denver 1980. 321 pp. *DAI 1981 41(8): 3309-3310-A.* DA8101699

683. Hawkins, Seth Clayton. "Garfield at the Bar: An Architectonic Rhetorical Criticism of Selected Speeches by James A. Garfield before the U.S. Supreme Court." Bowling Green State U. 1975. 162 pp. *DAI 1975 36(2): 597-A.*

684. Hoemann, George Henry. "What God Hath Wrought: The Embodiment of Freedom in the Thirteenth Amendment." Rice U. 1982. 350 pp. *DAI 1982 43(2): 525-A.* DA8216322

685. Jessup, Dwight Wiley. "Reaction and Accommodation: The United States Supreme Court and Political Conflict, 1809-1835." U. of Minnesota 1978. 491 pp. *DAI 1978 39(6): 3776-3777-A.*

686.   Lasser, William. "Crisis and the Supreme Court: Judicial Politics in Periods of Critical Realignment." Harvard U. 1983. 309 pp. *DAI 1983 44(6): 1911-A.* DA8322395

687.   Luce, Willard Ray. "*Cohens v. Virginia* (1821) The Supreme Court and State Rights: A Reevaluation of Influences and Impacts." U. of Virginia 1978. 254 pp. *DAI 1979 40(2): 1031-A.*

688.   Martin, Bert Edmon. "Freedom and the Puritan Conscience: American Destiny and the Defenders of the *Amistad* Africans." Baylor U. 1979. 149 pp. *DAI 1980 40(8): 4636-A.*

689.   McDonough, Judith Rene. "William Henry Moody." Auburn U. 1983. 236 pp. *DAI 1984 44(11): 3468-A.* DA8404477

690.   Moffit, Robert Emmet. "Metaphysics and Constitutionalism: The Political Philosophy of Orestes Brownson." (Volumes I and II) U. of Arizona 1975. 934 pp. *DAI 1975 36(3): 1776-1777-A.*

691.   Sawrey, Robert Dixon. "Ohio and Reconstruction: The Search For Future Security, 1865-1868." U. of Cincinnati 1979. 271 pp. *DAI 1979 40(4): 2230-A.*

692.   Schimmel, Barbara Barlin. "The Judicial Policy of Mr. Justice McReynolds." Yale U. 1964. 252 pp. *DAI 1983 44(2): 557-A.* DA8313252

693.   Schotten, Peter Max. "A Government of Laws: The Constitutional Understanding of Mr. Justice Story." Claremont Grad. School 1974. 352 pp. *DAI 1974 35(1): 542-543-A.*

694.   Suits, David Bowden. "The Political Theory of Lysander Spooner." U. of Waterloo 1977. *DAI 1978 38(10): 6174-6175-A.*

695.   Tagg, James Douglas. "Benjamin Franklin Bache and the Philadelphia *Aurora.*" Wayne State U. 1973. 749 pp. *DAI 1974 34(11): 7171-A.*

696.   Tarpley, James Douglas. "Fair Use as Copyright Doctrine: Judicial and Statutory Interpretation." Southern Illinois U., Carbondale 1983. 199 pp. *DAI 1984 44(7): 1960-A.* DA8326571

697.   Tenney, Craig Davidson. "Major General A. E. Burnside and the First Amendment: A Case Study of Civil War Freedom of Expression." Indiana U. 1977. 288 pp. *DAI 1977 38(4): 2311-2312-A.*

698.   Trimpe, Dale Wilbur. "The History of Illinois Equalization Aid." U. of Illinois, Urbana-Champaign 1973. 141 pp. *DAI 1974 34(12): 7503-7504-A.*

699.   Whiteside, Ruth Ann. "Justice Joseph Bradley and the Reconstruction Amendments." Rice U. 1981. 355 pp. *DAI 1981 42(2): 826-A.* DA8117006

700.   Winitsky, Marvin Laurence. "The Jurisprudence of Roger B. Taney."
U. of California, Los Angeles 1973. 358 pp. *DAI 1974 34(11): 7175-7176-A.*

701.   Wolfe, Nancy Travis. "The Fuller Court and Employer's Liability." U.
of Delaware 1974. 261 pp. *DAI 1974 35(5): 2924-A.*

702.   Yow, Thomas Sidney, III. "'State Action' and Private Higher Education: An Analysis of Judicial Application of the Fourteenth Amendment."
Duke U. 1982. 210 pp. *DAI 1983 44(1): 88-A.* DA8313275

5

THE DEVELOPMENT OF THE CONSTITUTION, 1900-1985

Article Abstracts

703. Abraham, Henry J. EFFECTIVENESS OF GOVERNMENTAL OPERATIONS. *Ann. of the Am. Acad. of Pol. and Social Sci. 1976 426: 81-97.* The Judiciary has always received a higher rating of esteem and regard than the other two branches of government. However, it is not free from pragmatic or philosophical operational problems. Two of these are finding a line between judging and legislating and court reform. Suggestions for reform fall into three categories: (1) those dealing with the institution and modus operandus of the courts, (2) those concerned with court staff, and (3) those dealing with the legal framework mandated by lawmakers and the Constitution. A matter of infinitely more pressing concern is how to confine judges to judging rather than legislating. The Supreme Court must possess the power to interpret legislation, but a line must be drawn between the imposition of judicial judgment and the exercise of judicial will. Our federal system underlies both the disappointments and the accomplishments of the American government. The apparent trend toward centralization of federal power is both an axiom of modern American federalism and irreversible. However, since excessive rigidity of centralization is a weakness, regional, state, and local governments should retain a substantial sphere of independence. [Report of Committee II of AAPSS Bicentennial Conference]. J

704. Abrams, Norman. LIBERTY AT BAY: THE SUPREME COURT AND SEARCH AND SEIZURE. *Center Mag. 1977 10(1): 16-20.* Discusses the legal and constitutional implications of the Supreme Court's recent interpretations of the Fourth Amendment in favor of the prosecution and against the accused; analyzes search and seizure issues.

705. Adams, Bruce. THE UNFINISHED REVOLUTION: BEYOND ONE PERSON, ONE VOTE. *Natl. Civic Rev. 1978 67(1): 19-25.* Political and racial gerrymandering have reduced electoral competition, diluted the value of political participation, weakened parties and denied representation to minority groups. Common Cause has proposed a model reapportionment process

designed to achieve the Supreme Court's goal of "fair and effective representation" by eliminating gerrymandering and having lines drawn by a nonpartisan, independent commission.   J

706. Adamson, Agar. THE FULTON-FAVREAU FORMULA: A STUDY OF ITS DEVELOPMENT 1960 TO 1966. *J. of Can. Studies 1971 6(1): 45-55.* Discusses the development of the movement to construct a system for amendment of the British North America Act (1867), known as the Fulton-Favreau Formula, concentrating primarily on the development of this formula 1960-66.

707. Adkison, Danny. PRESIDENTIAL VACANCIES AND SECTION TWO OF THE TWENTY-FIFTH AMENDMENT. *Social Sci. J. 1979 16(3): 41-57.* Describes presidential succession and evaluates the effectiveness of Section Two of the 25th Amendment, adopted 1967, which provides for presidential nomination and congressional confirmation of vice-presidents; covers 1789-1970's.

708. Alciatore, Robert T. FEDERAL AID TO CHURCH-RELATED SCHOOLS AND THE CONSTITUTION. *Catholic Educ. R. 1967 65(6): 383-395.* Argues that the only way to interpret the First Amendment without encountering contradiction is to allow federal aid to church-related schools. 26 notes.   J. M. McCarthy

709. Alexander, Herbert E. RETHINKING ELECTION REFORM. *Ann. of the Am. Acad. of Pol. and Social Sci. 1976 425: 1-16.* Occasionally, a public issue surfaces which relates to the basic fibers of our democratic system, an issue whose resolution further translates the democratic theory of 1776 into actual practice. Such is the issue of election reform. The problem is how to apply democratic principles to elections in an age of media politics seemingly dominated by dollar politics. The electoral process presents perhaps a classic conflict between the democratic theory of full public dialogue in free elections and the conditions of an economic marketplace. Election law reform has become a high priority issue; within the last five years, federal laws regulating election campaigns have been changed twice, and 44 states have revised theirs. More revisions are occurring in the wake of the landmark Supreme Court decision in *Buckley* v. *Valeo.* Reform is not neutral but works to change institutions and processes, sometimes in unforeseen ways. Laws regulating relationships between candidates and political parties, and citizens and politicians, and affecting the relative power of interest groups, are bound to influence the entire political process and change the participation of citizens, candidates, parties, and other groups in elections. Recent changes are certain to have direct consequences for the two-party system, constitutional protections, and levels of participation and confidence in the electoral system.   J

710. Anawalt, Howard C. IS THE MACBRIDE COMMISSION'S APPROACH COMPATIBLE WITH THE US CONSTITUTION? *J. of Communication 1981 31(4): 122-128.* The MacBride Commission Report on a New World Communication Order (1980), submitted to UNESCO by the Interna-

tional Commission for the Study of Communication Problems (the MacBride Commission), in general is compatible with the US Constitution and US laws.

711.   Anderson, Douglas A. DREW PEARSON: A NAME SYNONY-MOUS WITH LIBEL ACTIONS. *Journalism Q. 1979 56(2): 235-242.* During 1932-69, when he wrote his syndicated newspaper column, "Washington Merry-Go-Round," Drew Pearson defended himself against at least 108 libel suits brought against him or newspapers publishing his column. The US Supreme Court decision in *New York Times* v. *Sullivan* (US, 1964) overrode the state-to-state variations in libel law that had encouraged scattered court actions against Pearson, and it provided a more substantial defense against libel charges than had been available previously. Judging from his success in the courts, Pearson was able to play his investigative role within the constraints of perpetually developing libel law. Based on federal and state court rulings, and on interviews; 88 notes.   R. P. Sindermann, Jr.

712.   Arendale, Marirose. TENNESSEE AND WOMEN'S RIGHTS. *Tennessee Hist. Q. 1980 39(1): 62-78.* While the Tennessee legislature dragged its feet in adopting the proposed 19th Amendment to the Constitution, it was the 10th legislature to pass on the Equal Rights Amendment. But reaction set in, and two years later, in 1974, the legislature rescinded its action. The arguments in both campaigns suggest that Tennessee, a border state with ties to the deep South, retains the regional conviction that a woman is the fulcrum around which family life revolves. Buttressed by Biblical references, this concept has stubbornly resisted contemporary pressures for change. Based largely on contemporary newspaper accounts; 2 illus., 44 notes.   H. M. Parker, Jr.

713.   Armstrong, Virginia and Johnson, Charles A. CERTIORARI DECISIONS BY THE WARREN & BURGER COURTS: IS CUE THEORY TIME BOUND? *Polity 1982 15(1): 141-150.* In 1963, Joseph Tanenhaus and associates presented a "cue theory" explaining how the US Supreme Court decides whether or not to grant certiorari, the calling up of records from a lower court. Tanenhaus's research, however, analyzed certiorari decisionmaking in the 1940's and 1950's. Tests the applicability of cue theory in light of the changes in the ideological makeup of the Supreme Court. The relationships proposed by Tanenhaus prevail in the later terms of the court. Furthermore, other factors interact to influence decisions, especially the ideological drift of lower court decisions. Secondary sources; 5 tables, 20 notes.   J. Powell

714.   Arons, Stephen and Katsch, Ethan. RECLAIMING THE FOURTH AMENDMENT IN MASSACHUSETTS. *Civil Liberties Rev. 1975 2(1): 82-89.* Legislative action in Massachusetts countermanded a US Supreme Court decision to allow police searches without warrants, opting instead in favor of the individual's right to privacy, 1974.

715.   Arons, Stephen. THE SEPARATION OF SCHOOL AND STATE: *PIERCE* RECONSIDERED. *Harvard Educ. R. 1976 46(1): 76-104.* Notes that in *Pierce* v. *Society of Sisters* (US, 1925) the Supreme Court affirmed that the Constitution "protect(s) parents' rights to pass along their values to their

children," and argues that a First Amendment reading of that decision may prove present forms of compulsory education to be unconstitutional.

716. Ashbrook, John M. AGAINST COMPREHENSIVE GUN CON-TROL. *Current Hist.* *1976 71(418): 23-25, 31.* Cites the 2nd Amendment right of the people to keep and bear arms and argues that gun control has no relation to crime control, 1975.

717. Atkins, Burton M. and Zavoina, William. JUDICIAL LEADERSHIP ON THE COURT OF APPEALS: A PROBABILITY ANALYSIS OF PANEL ASSIGNMENT IN RACE RELATIONS CASES ON THE FIFTH CIRCUIT. *Am. J. of Pol. Sci.* *1974 18(4): 701-711.* "Since courts of appeals use a three-member panel system for deciding cases, it is entirely possible for a decision of the court to represent a minority preference of the sitting active judges. This fact is crucial in understanding the role played by the intermediate appellate courts in the implementation of the Supreme Court's desegregation decisions. It has been widely accepted, for example, that the fifth circuit was vital in achieving a national goal of integration in reversing decisions of locally oriented district courts. But in explaining the role played by the fifth circuit it is necessary to determine whether or not the policy of the fifth circuit was engineered by a majority, in which case it would be legitimate to assume that it held a perspective more in tune with a national orientation than the local positions taken by the district courts, or if the policy was the outgrowth of a minority of the court made possible by the panel system. Indeed the specific charge had been levied against that court that Chief Justice Tuttle had purposefully gerrymandered the panel assignments in order to assure pro-civil rights decisions. With the aid of probability analysis we assessed the validity of the charge. Our data show that from 1961 to 1963 a *minority* of the active judges decided a disproportionate number of race relations cases and that these decisions were usually in support of the black plaintiffs. Moreover, the relationships were statistically significant; indeed, such a distribution would occur by chance one time in ten thousand! By contrast, our data show that such a skewed distribution did not occur when a sample of cases under a previous chief judge was analyzed."   J

718. Atwater, Tony. NEWSROOM SEARCHES: IS "PROBABLE CAUSE" STILL IN EFFECT DESPITE NEW LAW? *Journalism Q. 1983 60(1): 4-9.* On 31 May 1978, the US Supreme Court ruled in *Zurcher* v. *Stanford Daily* that constitutional rights did not render newspapers immune to search warrants. The Privacy Protection Act of 1980 reversed some aspects of that decision, although loopholes remained. Analyzes the probable cause concept in the Fourth Amendment in relation to searches of press property and confidentiality of journalists' sources. 34 notes.   R. Grove

719. Baer, Judith A. THE BURGER COURT AND THE RIGHTS OF THE HANDICAPPED: THE CASE FOR STARTING ALL OVER AGAIN. *Western Pol. Q. 1982 35(3): 339-358.* Addresses the emerging issue of disability rights. The few cases that the Supreme Court has decided so far have either been sent back to lower courts or decided against the disabled

claimants on the merits. These rulings are due to the judges' failure to think creatively about the issues.   J/S

720. Ball, Howard. CARELESS JUSTICE: THE UNITED STATES SU-PREME COURT'S SHOPPING CENTER OPINIONS, 1946-1976. *Polity 1978 11(2): 200-228.* Although an indispensable means of correcting error and adapting the law to changing conditions, judicial reversals of precedents harbor the danger of legal instability. For this reason direct overturns of past opinions by a later court occur rather infrequently. Instead, courts prefer to release themselves from the straitjacket of *stare decisis* by distinguishing a case at hand from its precedent altogether. In examining a series of cases involving the right of free expression on private property from 1946 to 1976, the author finds that in addition to impersonal forces and correction of prior error, majority consensus of the bench plays a vital part in reducing the sense of instability that is easily aroused by the direct overturn of precedents.   J

721. Barnett, Stephen R. NEWSPAPER MONOPOLY AND THE LAW. *J. of Communication 1980 30(2): 72-80.* Examines the effects of "anticompeti-tive economic practices" and "government intervention in the media market-place through the Newspaper Preservation Act" passed in 1970, on monopoly in the newspaper industry in the United States since the Supreme Court decision, *Times-Picayune Publishing Co.* v. *United States* (US, 1953), which upheld the legality of combination rates for advertisers in newspapers.

722. Bartholomew, Paul C. THE SUPREME COURT OF THE UNITED STATES 1970-1971. *Western Pol. Q. 1971 24(4): 687-701.* Reviews the issues that faced the court this term.   S

723. Bellow, Gary. THE TROUBLE WITH THE BURGER COURT. *Working Papers for a New Soc. 1978 6(5): 16, 18-21.* The ideology of the Supreme Court, 1968-78, under Chief Justice Warren Burger, subscribes to the legal theory that a just constitutional system depends on a clear distinction among "public," "personal," and "private."

724. Belz, Herman. CHANGING CONCEPTIONS OF CONSTITUTION-ALISM IN THE ERA OF WORLD WAR II AND THE COLD WAR. *J. of Am. Hist. 1972 59(3): 640-669.* A broad analysis of political theory and ideas concerning constitutionalism reveals a reaction against the "realist" concept of the Constitution as a "parchment barrier against social reform and a defense of the laissez-faire status quo," and of law as a static justification of economic self-interest. The rise of Nazi and Communist totalitarian movements led many earlier realists such as Charles Beard and Carl Becker to reassess the constitution more positively as a valuable restraint on the power of govern-ment. Even radical movements of the 1960's, while proclaiming the need for more opportunities for political action on the part of citizens, worked within the structure of constitutionalism as a normative mode of conducting public affairs. 117 notes.   K. B. West

725. Belz, Herman. THE REALIST CRITIQUE OF CONSTITUTIONAL-ISM IN THE ERA OF REFORM. *Am. J. of Legal Hist. 1971 15(4): 288-306.*

"Constitutional realism in the latter years of the 19th century formed the basis for and was continuous with a more far-reaching critical attack on constitutional law and institutions in the Era of Reform." Provides a critique of positive and negative traditions formulated by the works of constitutional writers in the first third of the 20th century. 53 notes.   L. A. Knafla

726. Bender, Paul. THE RELUCTANT COURT. *Civil Liberties R. 1975 2(4): 86-103.* The present Court's creative energies are going to be concentrated on middle-class rights: rights of privacy, speech, procedural due process. These are the rights with which the justices feel most comfortable; they are also rights which do not seem dangerous in the hands of the wrong people.
J

727. Bendiner, Robert. THE LAW AND POTTER STEWART: AN INTERVIEW WITH JUSTICE POTTER STEWART. *Am. Heritage 1983 35(1): 98-104.* An interview with retired Supreme Court justice Potter Stewart, in which Stewart tells of his views on numerous legal issues. Included are his opinions on desegregation, affirmative action, criminal procedures, censorship, school prayer, and capital punishment. 2 photos.   J. F. Paul

728. Berkson, Larry C. CRUEL AND UNUSUAL PUNISHMENT: THE PARAMETERS OF THE EIGHTH AMENDMENT. *Policy Studies J. 1975 4(2): 131-136.* Distinguishes between corporeal and incorporeal punishment and shows how the Eighth Amendment has been interpreted in the courts to limit the use of either.

729. Berry, Mary F. BOOK REVIEW ESSAY. *Afro-Americans in New York Life and Hist. 1982 6(1): 55-59.* Reviews J. Harvie Wilkinson III's *From Brown to Bakke: The Supreme Court and School Integration, 1954-1978* (1979), and Harvard Sitkoff's *A New Deal for Blacks: The Emergence of Civil Rights as a National Issue. Vol. I: The Depression Decade* (1978).

730. Beth, Loren P. MR. JUSTICE BLACK AND THE FIRST AMENDMENT: COMMENTS ON THE DILEMMA OF CONSTITUTIONAL INTERPRETATION. *J. of Pol. 1979 41(4): 1105-1124.* Justice Hugo Black attempted to confine substantive due process within the limits set by the first eight amendments, to prevent judges from substituting their policy preferences for those of the legislature or executive. His theory of the first amendment implied a place-oriented exemption covering the performance of legitimate governmental functions. While his attempts at defining the limits of the first amendment were not successful, of all recent justices, Black came closest to balancing the rule of law and the imprecise limitation it imposes on constitutional interpretation. 61 notes.   A. W. Novitsky

731. Bickel, Alexander M. THE CONSTITUTION AND THE WAR. *Commentary 1972 54(1): 49-55.* Examines the constitutionality of the Tonkin Gulf Resolution and US involvement in the Vietnam War.   S

732. Binion, Gayle. AN ASSESSMENT OF POTTER STEWART. *Center Mag. 1981 14(5): 2-5.* A commitment to states' rights and to narrow,

nonanticipatory judicial opinions were the hallmarks of Potter Stewart's Supreme Court work, 1958-81; Stewart's justice-as-lawyer role was unrealistic because it "suggests that the Constitution is simply a legal code requiring no theoretical exegesis and/or that the development of constitutional theory is to be avoided whenever possible."

733. Binion, Gayle. THE BURGER COURT AND THE RIGHTS OF THE POOR. *Center Mag. 1982 15(2): 2-7.* Decisions of the Burger court in poverty cases have been closely related to the "constitutionally protected rights of indigent criminal defendants" and voting rights; the court has failed to "apply equal-protection scrutiny consistently."

734. Binion, Gayle. THE IMPLEMENTATION OF SECTION 5 OF THE 1965 VOTING RIGHTS ACT: A RETROSPECTIVE ON THE ROLE OF COURTS. *Western Pol. Q. 1979 32(2): 154-173.* The 1965 Voting Rights Act (amended 1970, 1975) has proven to be the most important federal legislation protecting the right to vote. The specific focus here is on the roles played by the courts in the implementation of Section 5 of the Act, which was virtually ignored during the first five years after its passage. It was not until the U.S. Supreme Court rendered decisions interpreting broadly the reach of Section 5 that compliance began. Three specific functions of the courts are analyzed: first, they were crucial actors in securing compliance when covered jurisdictions refused to submit their electoral changes for preclearance. Second, they have been important in immunizing court-ordered electoral changes (i.e., reapportionment) from the preclearance requirements of Section 5. Third, the decisions of the U.S. Supreme Court in 1975 and 1976 have placed limitations on the power of the Attorney General to object to electoral changes which he has reviewed. The paper involves both an analysis of all of the reported decisions of courts on Section 5 and a critique of their strengths and weaknesses.   J

735. Birkby, Robert H. TEACHING CONGRESS HOW TO DO ITS WORK: MR. JUSTICE MCREYNOLDS AND MARITIME TORTS. *Congressional Studies 1981 8(1): 11-20.* Traces the 10-year-long effort beginning in 1917 by Supreme Court Justice James Clark McReynolds to convince Congress through legal decisions that a more comprehensive maritime benefits law was necessary to provide for compensation to seamen and their heirs for accidental injury or death, which resulted in the Longshoremen's and Harbor Worker's Compensation Act (US, 1927).

736. Bishop, David W. THE AFFIRMATIVE ACTION CASES: *BAKKE, WEBER,* AND *FULLILOVE. J. of Negro Hist. 1982 67(3): 229-244.* After 1937, the Supreme Court moved from protection of property rights to concern about civil and political rights. Some decisions attacked racial discrimination by striking down laws and rules that mandated segregation. Other decisions applied a "rational basis" test to determine whether a situation was related to legitimate state goals. Three recent court cases—*Regents of the University of California* v. *Bakke* (US, 1978), *Kaiser Aluminum and Chemical Company* v. *Weber* (US, 1979), and *Fullilove et al.* v. *Klutznick, Secretary of Commerce, et*

al. (US, 1980)—illustrate a new, changing mood in support of racial equality.
69 notes.   A. G. Belles

737. Bishop, Joseph W., Jr. POLITICS & ACLU. *Commentary 1971 52(6): 50-58.*

738. Bittner, John R. POLITICS AND INFORMATION FLOW: THE OREGON SHIELD LAW. *Western Speech 1975 39(1): 51-59.* Concern for First Amendment rights and for the protection of confidential news sources was a major reason for the passage of a shield law in 1974.   S

739. Black, Elizabeth S. HUGO BLACK: A MEMORIAL PORTRAIT. *Supreme Court Hist. Soc. Y. 1982: 72-94.* Hugo Black was a justice on the Supreme Court during 1937-71. An Alabamian who had at one time been a member of the Ku Klux Klan, Black was one of the most respected justices in the long history of the Supreme Court. In September of 1968, Black agreed to a CBS taped television interview to discuss his personal and legal philosophy. Black, then aged 82, was skeptical about the session but its impact was phenomenal. Aired in December, 1968, the interview brought a massive response from other jurists, Black's law clerks, and hundreds of private citizens. The media also responded favorably, and the broadcast has since been used as a teaching device. Based on the transcriptions of the television interview; 118 notes, 5 illus.   G. B. Childress

740. Blackman, Paul H. PRESIDENTIAL DISABILITY AND THE BAYH AMENDMENT. *Western Pol. Q. 1967 20(2, part 1): 440-455.* Examines the instances of presidential disability in US history in light of the recent constitutional amendment which provides for the vesting of executive power.   S

741. Blanchard, Margaret A. THE FIFTH-AMENDMENT PRIVILEGE OF NEWSMAN GEORGE BURDICK. *Journalism Q. 1978 55(1): 39-46, 67.* Invoking the Fifth, rather than the First, Amendment, George Burdick of the New York *Tribune* refused in 1914 to answer a federal grand jury's questions about the sources of his paper's stories on the dealings of a customs appointee of President Woodrow Wilson. Burdick refused the presidential pardon issued to encourage him to cooperate with Assistant US Attorney Frank Carstarphen. Federal district judge Learned Hand held that the pardon could not be refused. The Supreme Court in *Burdick* v. *United States* (US, 1915) ruled, however, that because a pardon imputes guilt, no one can be forced to accept one. Primary and secondary sources; 41 notes.   R. P. Sindermann, Jr.

742. Blumrosen, Alfred W. LABOR ARBITRATION AND DISCRIMI-NATION: THE SITUATION AFTER GRIGGS AND RIOS. *Arbitration J. 1973 28(3): 145-158.* "To the proverbial man on the street, race discrimination is a matter of evil intent. But the Supreme Court has made it clear in the Griggs case that the target of the Civil Rights Act of 1964 is not the deliberate wrongdoer or racist alone, but the whole body of attitudes and practices that even well-intentioned individuals may exhibit. Thus, 'the law has focused over the years on reforming systems which discriminate,' the author points out. On

the basis of his study of published awards three years ago, he concluded that arbitrators have dealt effectively with discriminatory practices which also constituted contractual violations. But where the contract was inherently discriminatory, arbitrators had felt obliged to uphold the agreement, at whatever cost to the statutory rights of employees. Now, three years later, he finds some improvement, based upon 'consciousness raising experience,' particularly in cases involving discrimination against women. But if arbitration awards are to be deferred to, in the manner anticipated by the Fifth Circuit decision in the Rios case, it might become advisable for parties to broaden the scope of arbitral authority so as to permit them to strike down provisions that are clearly repugnant to the purpose of the Civil Rights Act."   J

743.   Boles, Donald E. CHURCH AND STATE AND THE BURGER COURT: RECENT DEVELOPMENTS AFFECTING PAROCHIAL SCHOOLS. *J. of Church and State 1976 18(1): 21-38.* The Burger Court has been more strict in its interpretations of the first amendment than the Warren Court. Discusses the voting record of the justices on church-state relations and the reasons for their stands on various cases. Points out that the Burger Court has practically ended legislative subterfuge to get around the constitution. Also discusses the fact that higher education cases are approached from a different philosophy. 85 notes.   E. E. Eminhizer

744.   Boodhoo, Ken I. and Harnanan, Ivan C. THE U.S.-BAHAMIAN LOBSTER DISPUTE: INTERNATIONAL LEGAL PERSPECTIVES. *Caribbean Studies [Puerto Rico] 1980 20(1): 57-67.* Discusses the legal implications of the dispute concerning the harvesting of the spine lobster that lives on the Bahama Banks and which led to a confrontation between the Bahamas Marine Patrol and Cuban-American lobstermen in 1978. Examines the significance of the lobster in the international law of the sea, the basis of the Bahamian government claims and the claims of Cuban Americans and their US constitutional rights. Concludes by suggesting possible solutions in the light of past experiences and treaties. 32 notes.   J. V. Coutinho

745.   Borosage, Robert. SECRECY VS. THE CONSTITUTION. *Society 1975 12(3): 71-75.* By constitutional law the executive protects the secrets of intelligence services, like the Central Intelligence Agency.   S

746.   Brady, David W. Schmidhauser, John Berg, Larry L. HOUSE LAWYERS AND SUPPORT FOR THE SUPREME COURT. *J. of Pol. 1973 35(3): 724-729.* Voting records for 1937-60 do not substantiate the assumption that lawyers in the House are protective of the Supreme Court. The "legal-professionalization" hypothesis should be reformulated. Fig., 4 tables, 6 notes.   A. R. Stoesen

747.   Brauer, Carl M. ORDER AND STRUGGLE IN RECENT RACE RELATIONS. *Rev. in Am. Hist. 1980 8(4): 553-560.* Review essay of William H. Chafe's *Civilities and Civil Rights: Greensboro, North Carolina, and the Black Struggle for Freedom* (New York: Oxford U. Pr., 1980) and J. Harvie Wilkinson III's *From Brown to Bakke: The Supreme Court and School Integration: 1954-1978* (New York: Oxford U. Pr., 1979).

748. Brenner, Saul. FLUIDITY ON THE UNITED STATES SUPREME COURT: A REEXAMINATION. *Am. J. of Pol. Sci. 1980 24(3): 526-535.* What is the extent and impact of fluidity on the Supreme Court? To answer this question partially the court's original vote on the merits is compared with its final vote during the period Harold Burton served as a justice (1945-1958). It is found that in 88% of the situations the justices voted the same way at both stages. There are no significant differences between the number of vote changes in major cases and in nonmajor ones. The fluidity that occurred was more likely to affect the size of a majority that was already winning at the original vote than to transform a minority at the original vote into a majority at the final vote. The vote changes also created a more attitudinally grounded vote, for the final vote scales generate better scale correlations than the original vote scales. These differences, however, disappear when the consensus cases are omitted.   J

749. Brenner, Saul. FLUIDITY ON THE SUPREME COURT: 1956-1967. *Am. J. of Pol. Sci. 1982 26(2): 388-390.* There was a consistency in Supreme Court voting patterns during 1946-56 and 1956-67. Fluidity, or change of vote, was not strong; in the majority of cases the justices voted the same way on the final vote as they had on an initial vote. Ref., 2 notes, table.
    N. A. Newhouse

750. Brenner, Saul. MINIMUM WINNING COALITIONS ON THE U.S. SUPREME COURT: A COMPARISON OF THE ORIGINAL VOTE ON THE MERIT WITH THE OPINION VOTE. *Am. Pol. Q. 1979 7(3): 384-392.* It has been claimed that in nonthreat situations, opinions of the Court tend to receive a minimum winning vote. Using the private papers of Justice Burton, the size of the original vote on the merits was compared with the size of the opinion vote. No support was found for the minimum winning thesis except that smaller than minimum winning coalitions at the original vote tended to become minimum winning at the opinion stage. This finding, however, can be explained as a consequence of the desire of the opinion writer to secure an authoritative opinion of the Court. 3 tables, biblio.   J

751. Brenner, Saul. THE NEW CERTIORARI GAME. *J. of Pol. 1979 41(2): 649-655.* To assess support for certiorari on the Supreme Court, 213 votes and 87 cases with four votes for cert and 361 votes and 129 cases with more than four votes were studied from the terms of 1946, 1947, 1949, 1950, 1954 and 1955. When there were four cert votes, justices who wanted the Court to affirm lower court rulings were more successful than those who sought reversal. In addition, justices who voted for cert when there were four such votes were more successful than those who voted when there were more than four votes but no group controlled the final vote on the merits of the case. Table, 8 notes.   A. W. Novitsky

752. Brenner, Saul and Arrington, Theodore S. SOME EFFECTS OF IDE-OLOGY AND THREAT UPON THE SIZE OF OPINION COALITIONS ON THE UNITED STATES SUPREME COURT. *J. of Pol. Sci. 1980 8(1): 49-58.* Focuses on the number of justices who support the Supreme Court's opinions, to ascertain the extent to which opinion is determined by ideological

and nonideological variables. Only in racial discrimination cases do conditions suggest maximum winning votes as the predominant pattern. The mere existence of a threat is sufficient to produce a maximum winning vote. 2 tables, 20 notes.   T. P. Richardson

753. Brenner, Saul. STRATEGIC CHOICE AND OPINION ASSIGN-MENT ON THE U.S. SUPREME COURT: A REEXAMINATION. *Western Pol. Q. 1982 35(2): 204-211.* Inspects the original vote from the 1953-67 terms of the Supreme Court, and finds that in five-member original decision coalitions on the court the justices ideologically closer to the dissenters than to the other justices in the decision majority were assigned more opinions to write than could be expected by chance. Data was collected also concerning the consequences of assigning the opinion to these two justices and upon the possible motivations of the opinion assigner in selecting them.   J/S

754. Brenner, Saul and Arrington, Theodore. WILLIAM O. DOUGLAS: CONSISTENT CIVIL LIBERTARIAN OR PARABOLIC SUPPORTER? *J. of Pol. 1983 45(2): 490-496.* Challenges S. Sidney Ulmer's assertion that Supreme Court Justice William O. Douglas weakened in his support of civil liberties toward the end of his tenure and that a parabola depicts the pattern of his support. Ulmer's study concluded in 1971, although Douglas served through the 1974 term, and considered unanimous as well as nonunanimous decisions. There is no evidence of a decline in Douglas's support when only nonunanimous decisions are considered. 2 illus., table, biblio.
                                                                    A. W. Novitsky

755. Bretnor, Reginald. A PLEA FOR CENSORSHIP. *Modern Age 1966/67 11(1): 35-44.* Analyzes the factors involved in current definitions of "freedom of speech" and their application in practice as used by the "very curious leftist-liberal and quick-buck alliance." Examines the media's propagandizing of slaughter, violence, and law-breaking, especially television. Explores the nature and effect of pornography, sexual freedom, and advertising techniques that equate the sex pitch and the status pitch. Asserts that freedom of speech 1) should not "be absolute, unlimited, and subject neither to definition nor to limitation by law," 2) should not be equally enjoyed and exploited by all men, regardless of purposes, motives, methods, or obvious effects, and 3) should not include the right to advocate the destruction or nullification of the Constitution which guarantees our freedoms. Concludes that sane censorship would limit the license now enjoyed by the mass media.
                                                                    R. V. Ritter

756. Brisbin, Richard A., Jr. SEPARATION OF POWERS, THE RULE OF LAW, & THE STUDY OF POLITICAL INSTITUTIONS. *Polity 1982 15(1): 123-132.* Reviews Jesse H. Choper's *Judicial Review and the National Political Process: A Functional Reconsideration of the Role of the Supreme Court* (1980), Louis Fisher's *The Constitution between Friends: Congress, the President, and the Law* (1978), Michael A. Genovese's *The Supreme Court, the Constitution, and Presidential Power* (1980), Iredell Jenkins's *Social Order and the Limits of Law: A Theoretical Essay* (1980), and Henry J. Merry's *Five-Branch Government: The Full Measure of Constitutional Checks and Balances*

(1980) that discuss American political institutions including the three branches of national government, the rule of law, and the bureaucracy. 5 notes.

J. Powell

757.   Brisbin, Richard A., Jr. THE SUPREME COURT & THE POWER OF THE LEGAL PROFESSION. *Polity 1981 13(3): 505-523.* Lawyers have retained their traditional role in American legal institutions despite the twin threats of growing realism about lawyers and new stresses and demands on the profession resulting from changing litigation styles. During the past 30 years, Supreme Court cases involving the integrated bar, bar admissions, the ethics of legal practice, and legal income have enabled lawyers to retain their autonomy. Since *Powell v. Alabama* (US, 1931), the Supreme Court in right-to-counsel cases has subtly expanded the legal profession's role in civil matters, making lawyers more available to the public while at the same time freeing them from responsibility to their clients. By concentrating on procedural protections for rights in cases involving the role of the legal profession, the Supreme Court has protected and extended the substantive power of lawyers. Primary sources; 66 notes.

E. L. Keyser

758.   Brown, Thomas Elton. PATRIOTISM OR RELIGION. *Michigan Hist. 1980 64(4): 36-42.* In 1920 an attempt was made to force compulsory education upon Michigan children. The proposed state amendment in fact attempted to stem the power of the Catholic Church. Although Lutherans, Seventh Day Adventists, and other congregations rallied against the proposal, the Catholic Church spearheaded the opposition. Defeated in 1920, the issue resurfaced in 1924. This time Catholics abandoned the interdenominational approach and concentrated on their own vote. They succeeded in defeating the amendment. On 1 June 1925 the US Supreme Court declared a similar statute in Oregon unconstitutional, thus ending further agitation in Michigan on this issue. The politicization of Michigan Catholics presaged "the growing political maturity of American Catholics." It subsequently benefited the Democratic Party in Michigan. 7 photos, 62 notes.

L. E. Ziewacz

759.   Buenker, John D. THE RATIFICATION OF THE FEDERAL IN-COME TAX AMENDMENT. *Cato J. 1981 1(1): 183-223.* Discusses the process of ratification of the 16th Amendment to the Constitution between 1909 and 1913.

760.   Busch, D. Carolyn and Hartman, Lee Edward, Jr. JEFFERSON V. HACKNEY: CHARTING THE DIRECTION OF THE NIXON COURT. *Public Welfare 1973 31(2): 55-63.*

761.   Caldeira, Gregory A. THE UNITED STATES SUPREME COURT AND CRIMINAL CASES, 1935-1976: ALTERNATIVE MODELS OF AGENDA BUILDING. *British J. of Pol. Sci. [Great Britain] 1981 11(4): 449-470.* Discusses how the US Supreme Court decided what sort of issues should be brought before it in the field of criminal law.

762.   Canon, Bradley C. REACTIONS OF STATE SUPREME COURTS TO A U.S. SUPREME COURT CIVIL LIBERTIES DECISION. *Law and*

Soc. R. 1973 8(1): 109-134. Examines state supreme court reactions to the US Supreme Court decision in *Mapp* v. *Ohio* (US, 1961) which imposed rules on admissible evidence in criminal trials.   S

763.   Canon, Bradley C. TESTING THE EFFECTIVENESS OF CIVIL LIBERTIES POLICIES AT THE STATE AND FEDERAL LEVELS: THE CASE OF THE EXCLUSIONARY RULE. *Am. Pol. Q. 1977 5(1): 57-82.* Measures changes in the behavior of law enforcement officials in response to the exclusionary rule, judicially created after the *Mapp* v. *Ohio* (US, 1961) case, which prohibits the admission in criminal trials of evidence seized in violation of the Fourth Amendment. The relative efficacy of this Warren Court decision is compared with the efficacy of similar decisions made by state supreme courts.   P. Travis

764.   Carlson, Rick J. THE STATE OF THE LAW. *Center Mag. 1973 6(3): 20-35.* Discusses the First Amendment and its connection with the Federal Communications Commission; one of six articles in this issue on "Broadcasting and the First Amendment."   S

765.   Carmen, Ira H. THE CONSTITUTION IN THE LABORATORY: RECOMBINANT DNA RESEARCH AS "FREE EXPRESSION." *J. of Pol. 1981 43(3): 737-762.* A new science using fetal materials and indulging in psychosurgery has revived debate over the ethical and legal justifications for experiments. Scientific investigation is protected by the First Amendment, and the Recombinant DNA research of the late 1970's must be considered in that context. Regulation of such research has occurred through both local ordinances and National Institutes of Health grant procedures. Emotional arguments concerning the safety of recombinant DNA research has infringed on scientific investigators' free expression. 78 notes.   A. W. Novitsky

766.   Carr, Robert K. CONSTITUTIONAL AND STATUTORY LIMITATIONS ON CONGRESSIONAL INVESTIGATIONS. *Capitol Studies 1977 5(2): 11-40.* Examines constitutional and statutory rulings concerning Congressional investigations, focusing on cases which have been prosecuted under Section 192 of Title 2 of the US Code concerning withholding of evidence, 1950's-60's.

767.   Carroll, Berenice A. DIRECT ACTION AND CONSTITUTIONAL RIGHTS: THE CASE OF THE ERA. *OAH Newsletter 1983 11(2): 18-21.* The Equal Rights Amendment failed to pass because its supporters did not use sufficiently militant tactics to mobilize public opinion and support.

768.   Carrott, M. Browning. PREJUDICE GOES TO COURT—THE JAPANESE AND THE SUPREME COURT IN THE 1920S. *California History 1983 62(2): 122-138.* Traces the anti-Japanese decisions of the Supreme Court in the 1920's. The Supreme Court reflected the same prejudice against Japanese as was shown by racist journalists and politicians, upholding lower-court decisions to deny citizenship to Japanese aliens and sustaining state laws that denied or restricted the right of Japanese aliens to purchase or lease land. Only in the area of Japanese-language private schools did the Supreme Court

prohibit state restrictions. As a result of these conservative court decisions, the Japanese presence in agriculture, particularly in California, had declined by 1930. 8 photos, table, 50 notes.   A. Hoffman

769.   Carson, Gerald. THE INCOME TAX AND HOW IT GREW... AND GREW, AND GREW, AND GREW.... *Am. Heritage 1973 25(1): 4-9, 79-88.*

770.   Carter, Newman et al. EDWARD D. WHITE IN PERSONAL RET-ROSPECT. *Supreme Court Hist. Soc. Y. 1979: 5-7.* A review of the life and works of Chief Justice Edward Douglass White (1844-1921). White was born in Louisiana of a family involved in politics and law, served briefly in the Confederate Army, and entered state politics. Elected to the US Senate, he served only part of his term before being appointed to the Supreme Court in 1894 as a consequence of President Grover Cleveland's quarrel with New York Democrats. White was elevated to Chief Justice in 1910 by President William Taft. He achieved his most enduring fame in antitrust, arguing that prosperous, healthy corporations should be divided rather than dissolved, a principle that still stands. 3 photos.   V. L. Human

771.   Champagne, Anthony M. THE SEGREGATION ACADEMY AND THE LAW. *J. of Negro Educ. 1973 42(1): 58-66.* Studies Smallville Academy in Louisiana to see what a segregation academy is, how it operates, and its relation to the community, and how the possible use of the 13th Amendment would bring about desegregation of such schools.   S

772.   Cohan, A. S. OBSTACLES TO EQUALITY: GOVERNMENT RE-SPONSES TO THE GAY RIGHTS MOVEMENT IN THE UNITED STATES. *Pol. Studies [Great Britain] 1982 30(1): 59-76.* In the United States, action by the courts generally opens the door to concessions by the legislatures. The Gay Rights movement has not progressed as its adherents hoped for four reasons: the unpopularity of homosexuals; the disjointed nature of US govern-ment; the lack of cohesiveness of the movement itself; and the unwillingness of the Supreme Court to accord to homosexuals the same rights it has extended to other minorities, thereby giving a lead to legislatures. 20 notes.
                                                                 D. J. Nicholls

773.   Cohen, Michaele. WORLD WAR I: WOMEN. *Mankind 1977 5(11): 24-27.* The traditional view that American women benefited overall as a result of World War I is only partially correct. It is true that the 19th Amendment accompanied the events of the conflict, but the period also witnessed an end to reform, the collapse of the women's movement, a lack of meaningful economic gains for women, and a postwar conservative reaction against feminist reforms.
                                                                 N. Lederer

774.   Coleman, Stuart H. ACT OF STATE DOCTRINE HELD INAPPLI-CABLE TO FOREIGN SEIZURES WHEN THE PROPERTY AT THE TIME OF THE EXPROPRIATION IS LOCATED WITHIN THE UNITED STATES: UNITED BANK LTD. V. COSMIC INT'L. INC. *New York U. J. of Int. Law and Pol. 1977 9(3): 515-541.* Suggests that the Second Circuit's

blanket rule of territorial limitations is incompatible with the Supreme Court's controlling views using *United Bank Ltd.* v. *Cosmic Int'l, Inc* (US, 1976). Discusses points of divergence, and territorial versus extraterritorial expropriations. Concludes by suggesting that the Second Circuit should attempt a balancing of interests. "There are few if any issues in international law on which opinion seems to be so divided as the limitations on a state's power to expropriate the property of aliens." Decisions concerning international politics should be left to the foreign affairs power of the Executive." In "the dispute between Pakistan and Bangladesh, the court could not have turned to the Executive for an overall solution because there were no United States negotiations concerning the matter." 100 notes.   E. P. Stickney

775. Coode, Thomas H. TENNESSEE CONGRESSMEN AND THE NEW DEAL, 1933-1938. *West Tennessee Hist. Soc. Papers 1977 31: 132-158.* Examines the biographies, political attitudes, and voting records of US Senators and Representatives from Tennessee during the first six years of the New Deal. While there was some opposition to Franklin D. Roosevelt's initial programs, as the years passed the Tennessee delegation, with the exception of the two Republican representatives, became enamored of the Administration. The Tennessee Valley Authority (TVA) legislation of 1933 was supported unanimously; however, opposition to packing the Supreme Court was very strong. By 1940 only two of the 1933 Tennessee congressional delegation remained in office, death having claimed several. Based on personal papers and the *Congressional Record;* 7 illus., 62 notes.   H. M. Parker, Jr.

776. Cook, Beverly B. THE FIRST WOMAN CANDIDATE FOR THE SUPREME COURT—FLORENCE E. ALLEN. *Supreme Court Hist. Soc. Y. 1981: 19-35.* Discusses the legal career of Florence Ellinwood Allen from 1914, when she received her law degree, to her death in 1966. During her career, Allen served most importantly as a member of the Ohio Supreme Court and as judge of the US Court of Appeals for the 6th Circuit. In the 1930's and 1940's, under Roosevelt and Truman, she was the first woman candidate for the US Supreme Court, largely due to the impetus supplied by the women's suffrage and reform movements. Explains the role of public opinion, politics, and the wishes of the sitting justices in her failure to be nominated. Relies on the papers of Allen, Roosevelt, and Truman, and Gallup polls; 4 photos, 122 notes.
                G. V. Wasson

777. Cortner, Richard C. THE WOBBLIES AND *FISKE* V. *KANSAS:* VICTORY AMID DISINTEGRATION. *Kansas Hist. 1981 4(1): 30-38.* Attacks on the Industrial Workers of the World (IWW) after World War I led to arrests, trials and several precedent-setting appeals. Harold B. Fiske's conviction in 1923 for violating Kansas's Criminal Syndicalism law was reviewed by the US Supreme Court in 1927. The court's unanimous decision in his favor contributed to the contemporary efforts to establish freedom of speech as a right protected against state interference under the 14th amendment. The IWW's Legal Defense Committee could not capitalize on this victory, because many Wobblies believed their organization should concentrate on economic rather than political and judicial tactics. US Reports, Kansas

Reports, ACLU Archives, Princeton University, newspapers; illus., 46 notes.

W. F. Zornow

778. Cott, Nancy F. FEMINIST POLITICS IN THE 1920S: THE NA-
TIONAL WOMAN'S PARTY. *J. of Am. Hist. 1984 71(1): 43-68.*
Analyzes the efforts by the National Woman's Party (NWP) to achieve an equal rights
amendment to the Constitution during the 1920's and the influence of Alice
Paul and Alva Belmont in the party. For the NWP, an equal rights
amendment became the panacea for women's subjection in American society,
instead of the first step to end legal discrimination against women. The NWP
regarded such an amendment as the logical sequel to female suffrage, achieved
in 1920, but its single-mindedness alienated labor and the Left. 48 notes.

T. P. Linkfield

779. Coulson, David C. ANTITRUST LAW AND THE MEDIA: MAK-
ING THE NEWSPAPERS SAFE FOR DEMOCRACY. *Journalism Q. 1980
57(1): 79-85.* Ownership concentration in the news media poses a threat to the
public's right to the free flow of information as much as does an attack on
reporters' First Amendment rights. A 1946 Supreme Court ruling affirmed the
government's right to enforce antitrust laws to prevent ownership combinations
that create monopolies. However, the Justice Department has not been
vigorous in asserting its enforcement powers. Based on court rulings and
secondary sources; 42 notes.

J. S. Coleman

780. Cowdrey, Albert E. PIONEERING ENVIRONMENTAL LAW: THE
ARMY CORPS OF ENGINEERS AND THE REFUSE ACT. *Pacific Hist.
R. 1975 44(3): 331-349.* The legislative history of the Refuse Act (1899) can be
traced to a bill introduced into Congress in 1876 at the instigation of the New
York Chamber of Commerce and supported by the Army Corps of Engineers.
The Corps worked with sympathetic Congressmen during the 1880's in
successful attempts to pass waterways regulatory measures, culminating in a
comprehensive antiobstruction measure in 1890. The 1890 act proved to be
poorly drafted and difficult to enforce, leading the Corps to propose a new bill,
which was passed in 1899. The new bill was more sweeping than any earlier
legislation, containing no express limitations on its purposes. But the Corps'
enforcement policies and judicial rulings soon nullified its potential as an
antipollution measure and limited its purposes to keeping the waterways open
for shipping. After 1960, the act began to function as an antipollution measure
when the US Supreme Court interpreted it more broadly. Based on documents
in National Archives and on published government documents; 35 notes.

W. K. Hobson

781. Cox, Archibald. THE NEW DIMENSIONS OF CONSTITUTIONAL
ADJUDICATION. *Massachusetts Hist. Soc. Pro. 1976 88: 60-79.* In the past
25 years, the courts have moved into new areas of activity: constitutional
adjudication has been increasingly used as a means of reform, there have been
many procedural changes, and the courts have imposed affirmative duties on
the other branches of government. These developments lead one to ask, "What
is the source of judicial power to command acceptance—for decrees which
have no basis in popular consent?" The answer seems to lie in the Supreme

Court's perception of the common will and its understanding of the general consensus. Based on Supreme Court cases; 30 notes, index.   G. W. R. Ward

782.   Cutts, John A., III. PROCEDURAL DUE PROCESS: A HAVEN FOR JUDGES. Am. Bar Assoc. J. 1968 54(12): 1199-1208. Since the Supreme Court clearly has, and takes advantage of, the power to legislate, how can we make the Court responsible to the will of the people?   J

783.   Daniels, Jack L. and Lawson, C. Robert. PROCEDURAL DUE PROCESS IN HIGHER EDUCATION: A PROTECTION OF STUDENTS' RIGHTS. Southern Q. 1974 12(3): 217-223. Examines the evolution of the protection of students' rights in state-supported units of higher education. Four rules of jurisprudence receive attention: in loco parentis, contractual, educational purpose, and custom or legislation. Primary focus is on the period since 1960. Several Supreme Court cases and decisions are reviewed. 18 notes.
R. W. Dubay

784.   Davis, Paul B. THE RESULTS AND IMPLICATIONS OF THE ENACTMENT OF THE TWENTY-SECOND AMENDMENT. Presidential Studies Q. 1979 9(3): 289-303. Discusses the results and future implications of the 22d Amendment which limits a president's terms to two and was passed during Harry Truman's administration in 1950, and presents the views of Presidents Truman through Carter on the amendment.

785.   Davis, Sue. JUSTICE REHNQUIST'S JUDICIAL PHILOSOPHY: DEMOCRACY V. EQUALITY. Polity 1984 17(1): 88-117. How judges interpret the law may result, among other things, from their varying perspectives on their own mission, their different values, and their different understandings of the nature and purposes of our polity. Together these values, outlooks, and understandings may be said to constitute a judge's philosophy. Our knowledge of it is likely to enhance our understanding of how he or she views and decides certain types of cases. Examines the ingredients of William H. Rehnquist's judicial philosophy as these emerge from his opinions in cases involving the Fourteenth Amendment's equal protection clause.   J/S

786.   Deloria, Vine, Jr. LEGISLATION AND LITIGATION CONCERNING AMERICAN INDIANS. Ann. of the Am. Acad. of Pol. and Social Sci. 1978 436: 86-96. The period 1957-77 witnessed an increasing tendency to include Indians in programs and legislation that affected all Americans, particularly in the field of social welfare and development. Indians, as a whole, made good use of their eligibility for these new opportunities, and entered the mainstream of public social concern. Legislation dealing specifically with Indian rights and legal status was generally trivial because no administration made more than a perfunctory effort to define the larger philosophical issues that might have clarified and modernized the Indian legal status. In litigation Indians were unusually successful in some of their efforts, although, again, truly definitive cases that might have proved a fertile ground for long-term gains in the development of contemporary understanding were sparse. Generally, those cases which might have produced landmark theories or doctrines, the Supreme Court refused to take and the decisions, remaining on the federal

circuit level, are not sufficiently strong or clear to provide a basis for further development. The era ended with a state of benign confusion, in which Indians seemed more concerned with funding programs than sketching out in broader and more comprehensive terms the ideologies and theories that are necessary for sustained growth. It was, basically, an undistinguished era, but one of maturing and awareness.   J

787. Dennis, Everette E. PURLOINED INFORMATION AS PROPERTY: A NEW FIRST AMENDMENT CHALLENGE. *Journalism Q. 1973 50(3): 456-462, 474.* Discusses court cases, especially *Pearson* v. *Dodd* (US, 1965), to show the legal ramifications of defining government documents as property.
                                                                                 S

788. Dershowitz, Alan M. WIRETAPS AND NATIONAL SECURITY. *Commentary 1972 53(1): 56-61.* Uses the "Pun" Plamondon Supreme Court case as an example of the need to question the constitutionality of political surveillance for national security.   S

789. Diamond, Martin. THE ELECTORAL COLLEGE AND THE IDEA OF FEDERAL DEMOCRACY. *Publius 1978 8(1): 63-77.* Presents the author's testimony (given on the last morning of his life, 22 July 1977) before the Constitutional Subcommittee of the Senate Judiciary Commmittee, on a proposed constitutional amendment providing for direct election of the President. Diamond presents an opening statement and then is questioned by the amendment's sponsor, Senator Birch Bayh. The rhetoric of many academic opponents of the electoral college, Diamond asserts, reveals an aversion to it based to an absurd extent on its mere antiquity. The other major objection to it, that the possibility of the college electing a candidate who fails to receive a popular plurality represents "a loaded pistol to our heads" (the phrase is Estes Kefauver's), is equally absurd—the pistol having gone off, without discernible damage, in 1888. Diamond warns also that the proposed amendment will encourage splinter parties.   L. W. Van Wyk

790. Dillon, Conley. AMERICAN CONSTITUTIONAL REVIEW: ARE WE PREPARING FOR THE 21ST CENTURY? *World Affairs 1977 140(1): 5-24.* Presents recent proposed constitutional changes (such as redefining the use of presidential power in foreign relations), but suggests that major revisions in fundamental law will not be forthcoming in the near future, due to lack of public support.

791. Dixon, Robert G., Jr. THE CONSTITUTION IS SHIELD ENOUGH FOR NEWSMEN. *Am. Bar. Assoc. J. 1974 60(6): 707-710.* "Granting newsmen an absolute privilege against disclosure through judicial processes would upset a delicate constitutional balance."   J

792. Dorsen, Norman. THE COURT OF SOME RESORT. *Civil Liberties R. 1974 1(2): 82-104.* "The Burger Court is unlike the Warren Court, whose innovative opinions broke new ground; it is different as well from the pre-1937 Court, which distrusted almost all attempts to fashion new legislative remedies for economic and social ills."   J

793. Douglas, Cathleen H. WILLIAM O. DOUGLAS: THE MAN. *Supreme Court Hist. Soc. Y. 1981: 6-9.* Discusses the life and career of William O. Douglas (1898-1980), associate justice of the US Supreme Court, focusing on aspects of his early life in Yakima, Washington, and later personal experiences that profoundly affected the development of his legal philosophy. Throughout his career on the bench, Douglas stressed the practical side of legal problems and the need to assess the social impact of individual laws. Based on the personal remembrances of Douglas's widow; photo.

G. V. Wasson

794. Douglas, Charles G., III. THE NEW ROLE FOR STATE COURTS AND BILLS OF RIGHTS. *J. of Social and Pol. Studies 1978 3(2): 181-199.* Traces the changing roles of state and federal court systems in the protection of citizens' constitutional rights since the founding of the Republic, emphasizing the years since 1930, and discusses recent retrenchments of federal jurisdiction by the Burger court which require federal courts to defer more to the role of state courts in this area.

795. Dunbar, Leslie W. MEIKLEJOHN'S COMMITMENT TO FREEDOM. *Democracy 1983 3(4): 128-138.* Reviews *Alexander Meiklejohn: Teacher of Freedom* (1981), edited by Cynthia Stokes Brown, an anthology of Professor Alexander Meiklejohn's writings on the 1st Amendment, the need for a new world order, and the evils of capitalism.

796. Duram, James C. CONSTITUTIONAL CONSERVATISM: THE KANSAS PRESS AND THE NEW DEAL ERA AS A CASE STUDY. *Kansas Hist. Q. 1977 43(4): 432-447.* Analyzes the editorial treatment of constitutional law issues of the New Deal in 46 Kansas newspapers in 1934-35. The editorial response of the Kansas press to the New Deal was the product of the Republican backgrounds and probusiness attitudes of the editors. Many editorials excoriated the New Deal for excessive regulation of business, wild spending, socialistic concepts, dangerous experimentation, and hastily drawn legislation. Most of the Kansas papers welcomed the Supreme Court's decisions on legislation, and criticized some decisions for not being more conservative than they were. Primary sources; 2 tables, 46 notes.

A. W. Howell

797. Duram, James C. THE SHAPING OF CONSTITUTIONAL CONSERVATISM: THE MICHIGAN PRESS AND THE NEW DEAL ERA AS A CASE STUDY. *Michigan Hist. 1972 56(3): 247-268.* Examination of editorials published in 53 Michigan newspapers during 1934-36 permits reconstruction of the conservative constitutional critique of the New Deal. Opportunism, not principle, guided the editors, for they advocated flexibility when applauding the Minnesota Moratorium decision, but counseled restraint when business opposition to Roosevelt crystallized. From the Holt Oil Cases onward, they consistently labeled the New Deal un-American, unconstitutional, and dangerous; stressed the nonpolitical nature of the judicial process; used technical discussions of points at law to accentuate constitutional shortcomings of federal statutes; called the Constitution fundamental and unchanging; and identified sound constitutional government with freedom from regulation.

Based upon newspaper editorials and secondary sources; 2 tables, 71 notes.

D. W. Johnson

798. Dyer, Brainerd. ONE HUNDRED YEARS OF NEGRO SUFFRAGE. *Pacific Hist. R. 1968 37(1): 1-20.* Reviews the legislative and judicial history of Black suffrage movement from the Civil War through the Supreme Court decision *South Carolina* v. *Katzenbach* (US, 1966) which upheld the Voting Rights Act (1965). Concludes that winning the suffrage battle through legislation and the courts has not brought Blacks into full partnership in all phases of society. Other battles will require continuous effort by white and black citizens alike. 57 notes.

D. L. Smith

799. Dykhovichnaia, M. Iu. and Kochetkov, G. B. BANKI DANNYKH: NASTUPLENIE NA GRAZHDANSKIE PRAVA V SSHA [Data banks: infringement of constitutional rights in the USA]. *Sovetskoe Gosudarstvo i Pravo [USSR] 1977 (6): 97-101.* Describes the compilation and use of data banks, and discusses the legality of federal and private data acquisition and processing. Legal questions raised by the project of creating a National Data Bank are still being debated by the specially set up Subcommittee on Constitutional Rights of the Senate Committee on the Judiciary. Only the Communist Party of the USA has consistently opposed the establishment of such an "invisible government" controlled by the CIA and the FBI. 9 notes.

N. Frenkley

800. Dymally, Mervyn M. THE SUPREME COURT AND CIVIL RIGHTS: TEN CASES. *Black Politician 1971 3(1): 96-100.* Reviews ten cases from *Dred Scott* v. *Sanford* (1857) to *Powell* v. *McCormick* (1969), noting the changing position of the Supreme Court in its position toward Civil Rights.

L. Grothaus

801. Earle, Valerie A. and Earle, Chester B. THE SUPREME COURT AND THE ELECTORAL PROCESS. *World Affairs 1977 140(1): 25-40.* The Supreme Court has extended the power of Congress to enforce the 14th and 15th Amendments in a series of court cases stemming from the Voting Rights Act (1965) and the Federal Election Campaign Acts (1971, 1974).

802. Easterbrook, Frank H. ANTITRUST AND THE ECONOMICS OF FEDERALISM. *J. of Law & Econ. 1983 26(1): 23-50.* Discusses the Supreme Court's accommodation since 1975 between federal antitrust law, which is designed to increase business competition, and state regulations that tend to reduce competition.

803. Easterling, Larry J. SEN. JOSEPH L. BRISTOW AND THE SEVEN-TEENTH AMENDMENT. *Kansas Hist. Q. 1975 41(4): 488-511.* Senator William Borah of Idaho deserves major credit for getting the resolution out of committee and guiding it through senatorial debate, but Bristow of Kansas is also important because he authored the resolution, introduced it in the Senate, and insisted upon the particular wording that the amendment embodied. Details Bristow's role. Writers have insisted that the Progressives worked for political reforms in order to enact more important social reforms and that in

their efforts to gain senatorial support for the amendment they were willing to bargain away a potential means of protecting the voting rights of southern blacks. Examines both of these topics with reference to Bristow. Based on primary and secondary sources; illus., 74 notes.   W. F. Zornow

804.   Edelman, Marian Wright. SOUTHERN SCHOOLS DESEGREGA-TION, 1954-1973: A JUDICIAL-POLITICAL OVERVIEW. *Ann. of the Am. Acad. of Pol. and Social Sci. 1973 (407): 32-42.* "Following the *Brown* decisions of 1954 and 1955, the Supreme Court refrained from ordering immediate dismantlement of the dual school system, leaving formulation of specific orders with regard to school desegregation in the hands of district courts. Obstruction and delay resulted, with massive southern resistance and a weak federal response. It was not until passage of the Civil Rights Act of 1964, when federal desegregation standards were adopted, that substantial desegregation could begin. Soon both the Department of Health, Education, and Welfare and the federal courts took a unified stand behind the law, attacking 'free choice' and southern delay. Progress finally seemed at hand. However, under the Nixon administration, federal enforcement efforts have been undercut. Major responsibility for enforcing school desegregation has been shifted from HEW to the slower judicial efforts of the Justice Department. Negative executive leadership has set a tone of national retreat. The current issue of busing and neighborhood schools threatens to erase desegregation progress already made in the South as well as to defeat efforts at making *Brown* a nationally applied policy. However, strong national and local leadership could maintain desegregation progress."   J

805.   Eglit, Howard; Waldman, Lois; and Levine, Naomi. IS COMPULSO-RY RETIREMENT CONSTITUTIONAL? *Civil Liberties R. 1974 1(4): 87-105.* The authors debate the constitutionality of compulsory retirement in the 1970's.   S

806.   Ekirch, Arthur A., Jr. THE SIXTEENTH AMENDMENT: THE HISTORICAL BACKGROUND. *Cato J. 1981 1(1): 161-182.* Discusses the factors leading to the enactment of the 16th Amendment to the Constitution, approved by Congress in July 1909, and operational in February 1913, better known as the income tax amendment.

807.   Ellis, L. Ethan. CHARLES EVANS HUGHES: A PROFILE. *Am. Hist. Illus. 1968 3(6): 28-37.* Discusses the varied public career of Charles Evans Hughes, including his successful private practice as a lawyer in New York City in the early 1900's, his election and tenure as governor of New York (1906-10), his appointment as Associate Justice of the Supreme Court in 1910, his unsuccessful bid for the Presidency in 1916, his term as Secretary of State during the Harding administration, and his final career as Chief Justice of the Supreme Court, 1930-41. "His contributions to the law, to politics, to foreign policy, and to the bench make him, surely, one of the most distinguished statesmen of his generation." Based on secondary sources; 7 photos.
M. J. McBaine

808.   Emerson, Thomas I. SOUTHERN JUSTICE IN THE THIRTIES. *Civil Liberties Rev. 1977 4(1): 70-74.* Uses Charles H. Martin's *The Angelo Herndon Case and Southern Justice* (Baton Rouge: Louisiana State U. Pr., 1976) to chronicle the 1932 Atlanta, Georgia case against a young black Communist who organized a protest regarding depletion of county relief funds, was arrested and convicted under the Georgia Insurrection Law, was defended by the largely Communist International Labor Defense of New York, and was freed from an 18-to-20-year sentence by the US Supreme Court in 1937.

809.   Erskine, Hazel and Siegel, Richard L. CIVIL LIBERTIES AND THE AMERICAN PUBLIC. *J. of Social Issues 1975 31(2): 13-29.* Important new survey findings show the American public's restrictive approach to the First Amendment rights of people who express deviant views to be moderating over the last two decades. This mellowing is backed up by parallel findings of major liberalizing of the consensus in other areas, notably equality and sexual freedom. Liberalization has been limited in such areas as criminal justice and separation of church and state. Post-McCarthy and post-Watergate developments are credited, along with educational progress, with much of the advance. Reduced value consensus and a growing sense of self-interest in civil liberties seem to have contributed to the trends in support of civil liberties.

810.   Everett, Dianna. THE WETTEST DROUGHT IN THE HISTORY OF TEXAS: A SURVEY OF THE ENFORCEMENT OF THE EIGH-TEENTH AMENDMENT AND THE DEAN ACT, 1920-1933. *Panhandle-Plains Hist. Rev. 1979 52: 39-61.* Efforts to end liquor production and consumption in Texas paralleled the development of a national prohibition movement during the early 20th century. Texas joined a growing list of states when in 1918 it enacted a prohibition law, but problems of constitutionality and enforcement undercut its effectiveness. In 1919, Texas legislators passed the Dean Act to supplement the national Volstead Act and insure greater enforcement of prohibition. Too few agents, too many bootleggers, and too much public demand for alcohol forced a repeal of the 18th Amendment in 1933. Based on newspapers and government reports; 101 notes.   M. L. Tate

811.   Fair, Daryl R. REMOTE FROM THE SCHOOLHOUSE: THE PAS-SAGE OF THE NEW JERSEY PAROCHIAL SCHOOL BUS BILL. *New Jersey Hist. 1981 99(1-2): 49-65.* During 1937-41, a school busing law came before the New Jersey legislature. Finally passed into law and scheduled to go into effect on 1 July 1941, the legislation provided transportation to nonprofit, church schools. Groups such as the New Jersey State Board of Education, the New Jersey Education Association, the American Association of University Women, and the New Jersey League of Women Voters were opponents. The Catholic Daughters of America, New Jersey Young Republicans, and the Newark City Commission, and organized labor supported it. After passage, the legislation was challenged in the courts as a violation of the separation of church and state. The US Supreme Court upheld the law. Based on records of court cases, newspaper accounts, state and city records, and secondary sources; illus., 2 photos, 36 notes.   E. R. McKinstry

812. Feerick, John D. AMENDING THE CONSTITUTION THROUGH A CONVENTION. *Am. Bar Assoc. J. 1974 60(3): 285-288.* "Amending the Constitution by the convention procedure presents many problems. Now is the time to begin solving them."   J

813. Feigert, Frank B. COMPONENTS OF ABSENTEE VOTING. *Polity 1972 4(4): 491-511.* Analyzes the factors involved in the increase in absentee voting from 3.6 percent in 1960 to 4.6 percent in 1968. One possibility is a greater educational effort on the part of election officials or party workers. Other possibilities are the perceived efficacy of the vote and a sense of civic duty. Questions what effect the 26th Amendment and the 1970 Voting Rights Act will have. 3 tables, 18 notes.   E. P. Stickney

814. Ferster, Herbert V. THE DEVELOPMENT OF THE AMISH SCHOOL SYSTEM. *Pennsylvania Mennonite Heritage 1983 6(2): 7-14.* Since 1925, Amish and Mennonites have operated one-room parochial schools to pass on their religious traditions; until the US Supreme Court case of *Wisconsin* vs. *Yoder* (1972), ruled in their favor, they had to fight compulsory education laws to keep their children out of public schools.

815. Finkelstein, Zane E. *THE BRETHREN* AT LAW AND AT WAR: AN ESSAY. *Parameters 1980 10(2): 79-83.* Reviews Bob Woodward and Scott Armstrong's *The Brethren: Inside the Supreme Court* (1979), "a chronological narrative dealing with the docket of the U.S. Supreme Court from October 1969 through July 1976." Criticizes the book for lack of scholarship.   J. Powell

816. Flowers, Ronald B. FREEDOM OF RELIGION VERSUS CIVIL AUTHORITY IN MATTERS OF HEALTH. *Ann. of the Am. Acad. of Pol. and Social Sci. 1979 (446): 149-161.* Decisions of the United States Supreme Court in 1963 and 1972 expanded the scope of the free exercise clause of the First Amendment beyond any previous interpretation of that clause in American judicial history. Although it is still understood that government may prohibit religiously motivated behavior which represents harm to individuals or to the public welfare, civil authorities now may intervene only when the religious activity threatens a compelling state interest. The possibilities of religious activity are abundant, and government intervention is limited to only the gravest offenses of the public order. This article examines some of the areas of health, broadly defined, in which religious attitudes have conflicted with state interests: the handling of poisonous snakes and drinking of poison in religious worship, the use of prohibited drugs in worship, compulsory blood transfusions for those who have theological objections to them, and the application of public health laws to those whose theology rejects medicine altogether. In the light of these cases, as much as the American constitutional system exalts religious liberty, it can never be unfettered. But, even in this area, it is imperative that our governmental units make religious liberty the rule and its curtailment the exception.   J

817. Flowers, Ronald B. THE SUPREME COURT'S INTERPRETATION OF THE FREE EXERCISE CLAUSE. *Religion in Life 1980 49(3): 322-335.*

Examines the Supreme Court's interpretation of the free exercise clause of the First Amendment from *Reynolds* v. *United States* (US, 1878), in which polygamy even if practiced in the name of religion was banned because it was harmful to society, to *McDaniel* v. *Paty* (US, 1978), declared unconstitutional a Tennessee constitutional provision prohibiting ministers from holding office in the state legislature.

818. Flowers, Ronald B. THE SUPREME COURT'S THREE TESTS OF THE ESTABLISHMENT CLAUSE. *Religion in Life 1976 45(1): 41-52.* According to Supreme Court rulings, 1963-70, the separation of church and state is maintained when enactments have a "secular legislative purpose," when they "neither advance nor inhibit religion," and when there is not "excessive entanglement" between the government and religious institutions.

819. Fox, Russell H. ACHEIVING FAIR REPRESENTATION: THE ROME AND MOBILE DECISIONS. *Natl. Civic Rev. 1980 69(10): 555-565.* The US Supreme Court decisions in *City of Rome* v. *United States* (US, 1980) and *City of Mobile* v. *Bolden* (US, 1980) weigh heavily on the freedom with which state and local governments may change their form or district lines. The two cases leave the law somewhat unclear in the field of voting rights, and voters seeking to challenge the electoral system must adopt differing approaches to litigation depending on the grounds on which they choose to argue.   J

820. Franck, Michael. THE MYTH OF *SPEVACK V. KLEIN. Am. Bar Assoc. J. 1968 54(10): 970-974.* Bar discipline remains intact despite the Supreme Court's assumption that the state has less interest in the integrity of its attorneys than in that of its employees.   J

821. Francome, Colin. ABORTION POLITICS IN THE UNITED STATES. *Pol. Studies [Great Britain] 1980 28(4): 613-621.* Discusses the legalization of abortions and opposition to it in the United States since 1959. The reasons for the success of those seeking to repeal antiabortion laws included a cultural preference for repeal rather than reform, the constitutional power of the courts; the attitude of the medical profession, and divisions within the opposition. Since ca. 1973, however, popular opposition has increased, especially in the Midwest and South. The political move to the Right has also contributed. The Right to Life movement, adopting an extreme position and concentrating on this single issue, has used a variety of methods to try to produce changes. 26 notes.   D. J. Nicholls

822. Frank, Thomas M. AFTER THE FALL: THE NEW PROCEDURAL FRAMEWORK FOR CONGRESSIONAL CONTROL OVER THE WAR POWER. *Am. J. of Int. Law 1977 71(4): 605-641.* Reviews the war power in historical perspective. Considers the fight (1969-73) for congressional control over warmaking. Examines the War Powers Resolution (1973) in practice with reference to the presidential duty to consult and to report. Treats the presidential perspective on the effect of the War Powers Resolution on "inherent" presidential powers. Ponders the legislative perspective of the War Powers Resolution's effect on inherent powers of the commander-in-chief.

Challenges the constitutionality of the congressional veto in the War Powers context. Discusses treaty commitments. Suggests reforms for the War Powers Resolution. Concludes that the War Powers Resolution "weakens the congressional power to prevent military action by conceding, without effectively limiting or defining it, a presidential power to start wars while only marginally strengthening the power of Congress to terminate them."   R. J. Jirran

823.   Franzen, Don Erik. AMERICAN INQUISITION: THE FDA'S PERSECUTION OF WILHELM REICH. *Reason 1980 11(9): 30-34.* As the actions of the Food and Drug Administration in suppressing the research activities of Wilhelm Reich into the curative power of orgone energy reveal, the administration is violating the 1st Amendment right to free speech by passing judgment on the validity of scientific experiments.

824.   Fredman, Howard S. THE OFFENSES CLAUSE: CONGRESS' INTERNATIONAL PENAL POWER. *Columbia J. of Transnatl. Law 1969 8(2): 279-309.* Discusses Congress' constitutional authority to punish offenses against the Law of Nations.   S

825.   Freund, Paul A. DIRECT ELECTION OF THE PRESIDENT: ISSUES AND ANSWERS. *Am. Bar Assoc. J. 1970 56(8): 773-775.* In dwelling on the imponderables of a constitutional amendment to provide for the direct election of the president, we obscure the real dangers of the present system.   J

826.   Freund, Paul A. JUSTICE BRANDEIS: A LAW CLERK'S REMEMBRANCE. *Am. Jewish Hist. 1978 68(1): 7-18.* The author who served as Supreme Court justice Louis D. Brandeis's law clerk in 1932-33, calls him a working justice, incisive moralist, observant host, and ardent Zionist. Brandeis' power derived from a harmonious fusion of biblical moral responsibility, classical restraint and proportion, and the common law tradition of rubbing against the hard face of experience.   F. Rosenthal

827.   Freyer, Tony A. POLITICS AND LAW IN THE LITTLE ROCK CRISIS, 1954-1957. *Arkansas Hist. Q. 1981 40(3): 195-219.* Discussion of the effects of legal and political entwinement on the integration plans of the Little Rock, Arkansas, School Board. A more comprehensive plan, developed after the Supreme Court's ruling on *Brown* v. *Board of Education of Topeka* (1954), was reduced to only the token integration of Little Rock Central High in Superintendent Virgil Blossom's plan because of vagueness in what the court required. Even this was opposed by segregationists who invoked the states' rights doctrine of "interposition." Based on interviews, case files, and other primary and secondary sources; 35 notes.   G. R. Schroeder

828.   Friendly, Fred W. CENSORSHIP AND JOURNALISTS' PRIVILEGE: THE CASE OF NEAR *VERSUS* MINNESOTA—A HALF CENTURY LATER. *Minnesota Hist. 1978 46(4): 147-151.* The Supreme Court decision in *Near* v. *Minnesota* (US, 1931) stated that the due process clause of the Constitution protects newspapers against arbitrary state action in regard to censorship. Recent court cases, such as the Farber case in New Jersey, indicate

that a reappraisal of this decision by the legal machinery of the nation may be taking place. Acrimonious disputes over the issue cannot serve the causes of fair trials or freedom of the press. N. Lederer

829. Friendly, Henry J. THE DARTMOUTH COLLEGE CASE AND THE PUBLIC-PRIVATE PENUMBRA. *Texas Q. 1969 12(2): 1-41.* Deals with "the extent to which the guarantees of the 14th Amendment apply to such 'private' institutions as universities, libraries, hospitals, and agencies for the care of the young and old." Argues that "the constitutional problems in this area are not susceptible of black and white solutions; much depends on the extent of government involvement, on the seriousness of the particular social and political values at stake, and on the precise guarantee invoked." Seeks to define the limits of application of the 14th Amendment by citing judicial opinions and discusses the appropriateness of judicial or legislative action in such areas. A lecture delivered 10 March 1968 at Dartmouth College in honor of the sesquicentennial of Daniel Webster's famous argument before the Supreme Court in *Dartmouth College v. Woodward* (US, 1819). Based on primary sources; 140 notes. R. V. Ritter

830. Funston, Richard. PORNOGRAPHY AND POLITICS: THE COURT, THE CONSTITUTION, AND THE COMMISSION. *Western Pol. Q. 1971 24(4): 635-652.* Examines the Supreme Court's position on pornography and censorship and its interpretation of the Constitution (1970-71). S

831. Funston, Richard Y. JUDICIALIZATION OF THE ADMINISTRATIVE PROCESS. *Am. Pol. Q. 1974 2(1): 38-60.* Discusses the accountability of administrative agencies to the law of due process. S

832. Gallagher, Robert S. "I WAS ARRESTED, OF COURSE." *Am. Heritage 1974 25(2): 16-24, 92-94.* Interview with Alice Paul (b. 1885) on her role in the women's suffrage movement, the ratification of the 21st amendment, and the early beginnings of the Equal Rights Amendment. S

833. Gándara, Arturo. CHICANOS Y EXTRANJERSO ILEGALES: LA CONJUNCIÓN DE SUS DERECHOS CONSTITUCIONALES FRENTE AL ESTADO NORTEAMERICANO [Chicanos and illegal immigrants: the convergence of their constitutional rights before the North American state]. *Foro Int. [Mexico] 1978 18(3): 480-493.* Surveys the legal impact of the US attempt to contain illegal Mexican immigration on the rights of Mexican Americans, and concludes that the constitutional and civil rights of Mexican Americans have been adversely affected. Based on court cases and secondary sources; 19 notes. D. A. Franz

834. Garvey, Edward R. FROM CHATTEL TO EMPLOYEE: THE ATHLETE'S QUEST FOR FREEDOM AND DIGNITY. *Ann. of the Am. Acad. of Pol. and Social Sci. 1979 (445): 91-101.* Sports owners in America have always played by different rules than other corporate entities. Gives examples of exemptions provided by Congress and various practices to enable them. The US Supreme Court has ruled that such practices are exempt from federal antitrust laws. The professional athlete has had no choice but to accept the

system imposed by management. However, the courts have started to change and athletes now have unions to help them gain dignity and freedom from the reserve system. Questions whether the athletes will continue to make progress in the 1980's.   J/S

835. Geller, Henry and Young, Gregg. FAMILY VIEWING: AN FCC TUMBLE FROM THE TIGHTROPE? *J. of Communication 1977 27(2): 193-201.* Discusses the legal problems springing from the National Association of Broadcasters' 1975 decision regarding television prime time programming and the ensuing case challenging the FCC's authority and activities as violating the Federal Communications Act and the First Amendment.

836.   Giles, Michael W. LAWYERS AND SUPREME COURT: A COMPARATIVE LOOK AT SOME ATTITUDINAL LINKAGES. *J. of Pol. 1973 35(2): 480-486.* Examines the attitude of lawyers toward the Supreme Court by comparing attitudes of practicing lawyers with those of law students and the general public. Concludes that the "bulwark of support for the Supreme Court" is provided by lawyers, with the strongest support coming from the younger members of the profession. As lawyers grow older their reasons for support of the Court tend to change and lessen in many cases. Based on data gathered in Kentucky. 2 tables, 14 notes.   A. R. Stoesen

837.   Gillers, Stephen. ORGANIZING TO BEAT THE LAWYERS. *Civil Liberties R. 1974 1(4): 121-124.* Discusses the right to legal representation during the 1970's, including Supreme Court opinions.   S

838.   Gillespie, J. David and Mitchell, Michael L. *BAKKE, WEBER,* AND RACE IN EMPLOYMENT. *Policy Studies J. 1979 8(3): 383-391.* Applies quantitative methodology to informed public opinion to determine the linkage between the *Bakke* decision (1978) and the discretionary use of race in private employment, noting the legal parallel of Title 6 of the Civil Rights Act (US, 1964) as applied to *Bakke* and Title 7 as used in the *Weber* decision (1979) and other cases.

839.   Gillette, Michael L. BLACKS CHALLENGE THE WHITE UNIVERSITY. *Southwestern Hist. Q. 1982 86(2): 321-344.* The University of Texas inadvertently admitted its first black student in October 1938. Although the student was soon forced to withdraw, the incident served as the first challenge to segregated higher education in Texas. Subsequently during the 1940's, the NAACP sought to desegregate the university's law, medical and graduate schools. The university was found unable to provide separate but equal facilities, and in 1950 was ordered by the US Supreme Court to admit students who could not find training at the black colleges in the state. Desegregation proceeded slowly, and blacks were not admitted to undergraduate study until 1956. Segregated dormitories existed until the 1960's. Based on university records at the Eugene C. Barker Texas History Center in Austin and NAACP records in Houston; 2 photos, 52 notes.   R. D. Hurt

840.   Gillmor, Donald M. FREE PRESS AND FAIR TRIAL: THE VOLCANO ERUPTS. *Current Hist. 1976 71(418): 19-22, 33.* The conflict between

the 1st and 6th Constitutional Amendments—freedom of the press and the right to a fair trial by a jury unprejudiced by pretrial press coverage—has generally been decided in favor of the press, 1971-76.

841. Gillmor, Donald M. JUSTICE WILLIAM BRENNAN AND THE FAILED "THEORY" OF ACTUAL MALICE. *Journalism Q. 1982 59(2): 249-255.* Supreme Court Justice William J. Brennan, an inveterate supporter of 1st Amendment rights, in his 1965 Alexander Meiklejohn lecture at Brown University "paid tribute to the philosopher's revolutionary idea that freedom of expression must be absolute in areas of public affairs." However, Brennan has failed in his search for a scale on which to weigh defamatory public speech against the constitutional dictates of the 1st Amendment, and his invocation of Meiklejohn's theory has been largely in vain. 33 notes.   L. J. Klass

842. Glazer, Nathan. IS BUSING NECESSARY? *Commentary 1972 53(3): 39-52.* Questions whether federal courts have the right to impose a school policy depriving local communities of power over their schools.   S

843. Glazer, Nathan. TOWARDS AN IMPERIAL JUDICIARY. *Public Interest 1975 (41): 104-123.* Assesses the Supreme Court since 1954, noting its increasing role in determining the law.   S

844. Gleicher, Jules. THE STRAYING OF THE CONSTITUTION: RAOUL BERGER AND THE PROBLEM OF LEGAL CONTINUITY. *Continuity 1980 (1): 99-123.* The 14th Amendment (1868) to the US Constitution has merited an especially large share of the country's constitutional litigation in the past few years. Raoul Berger, respected constitutional scholar, has written the definitive history of the original meaning of the 14th Amendment in his *Government by Judiciary* (1977) by carefully screening relevant data. In the first part, he finds that the original aim of the amendment was more political than ideological. The Republicans who controlled Congress at the time saw the amendment as a means to help maintain power. In the second part, he renders an essay on jurisprudence that takes aim at a variety of justices and several Supreme Courts (most notably the Warren Court) and accuses them of usurping power constitutionally vested in the legislature.
W. A. Wiegand

845. Goldstein, Leslie Friedman and Porter, Mary Cornelia. JUDICIAL POLICYMAKING & THE QUEST FOR ACCOUNTABILITY: RECENT VARIATIONS ON AN ANCIENT AIR. *Polity 1983 16(1): 165-176.* Reviews Frank M. Coffin's *The Ways of a Judge: Reflections from the Federal Appellate Bench* (1980), Phillip L. Dubois's *From Ballot to Bench: Judicial Elections and the Quest for Accountability* (1980), Richard Hodder-Williams's *The Politics of the Supreme Court* (1980), and *The Judiciary in a Democratic Society* (1979), edited by Leonard J. Theberge. These books address the judicial process, particularly in the higher courts, emphasizing the controversy over the appropriateness of judicial lawmaking and the accountability of the courts.   D. Powell

846.   Gordon, Nicole A. THE CONSTITUTIONAL RIGHT TO CANDI-DACY. *Pol. Sci. Q. 1976 91(3): 471-487.* Looks at the extent to which the rights of candidates for elective office have been found to be constitutionally protected. Traces the different theories courts have used to justify invalidation of laws hindering prospective candidates and suggests that the Supreme Court recognize cadidacy as a "fundamental" right.   J

847.   Gould, William B. RACIAL PROTEST AND SELF-HELP UNDER TAFT-HARTLEY: THE WESTERN ADDITION CASE. *Arbitration J. 1974 29(3): 161-175.* "Under federal labor law, a bargaining unit employee who, ignoring grievance and arbitration procedure available to him, engages in 'self-help' by a work stoppage or a refusal to obey reasonable orders, runs the risk of discharge or other forms of discipline. He thereby loses the protection of the Taft-Hartley law. But there is now pending before the U.S. Supreme Court a case involving employees who are arguing that, as the purpose of their self-help was to vindicate rights guaranteed by Title VII of the Civil Rights Act, they did not lose the protection of law by choosing not to stay within the limits prescribed by the collective agreement.... Suggests that courts must decide such cases in the light of the union's policies not only with respect to the particular grievance but of its total record with respect to minority races."   J

848.   Grabiner, Gene and Grabiner, Virginia E. "WHERE ARE YOUR PAPERS?": "OPERATION ZEBRA" AND CONSTITUTIONAL CIVIL LIBERTIES. *J. of Black Studies 1982 12(3): 333-350.* Although the 5th Amendment to the US Constitution outlaws official imposition of mass infamy ("social reprobation or disgrace"), US officials violated this constitutional prohibition several times in this century from the Palmer Raids to Operation Zebra—the stopping and questioning of over 500 young blacks in San Francisco, California, 17-25 April 1974. Operation Zebra made many whites suspicious of blacks. These incidents show the possibility and danger of massive repression in the United States. Based on Buffalo, New York, and San Francisco, California, newspapers; 3 notes, biblio.   R. G. Sherer

849.   Grant, Gerald. CHILDREN'S RIGHTS AND ADULT CONFU-SIONS. *Public Interest 1982 (69): 83-99.* America has long been confused about the appropriateness of certain parental behaviors. Shifting societal attitudes toward children are reflected in Supreme Court decisions defining children's rights. The elaboration of children's legal rights in the 1960's-70's weakened the authority of schools and parents and may have contributed to declining academic achievement. In some areas, child abuse reporting laws may be used to hamper the legitimate exercise of parental authority. Excessive attention to the procedural rights of children may diminish parents' rights. 11 notes.   J. M. Herrick

850.   Green, Justin J. JUDICIAL POLICY-MAKING, 1973-1974. *Western Pol. Q. 1975 28(1): 167-191.* The 1973-74 term of the US Supreme Court was characterized by major decisions in the areas of Federal Court jurisdiction, school desegregation, search and seizure law, and the rights of prisoners. Substantially reaffirmed were existing precedents which encouraged govern-

mental regulation of pornography, weakened the *Miranda* rule, expanded access to the ballot, and accepted a balancing approach to the right of a free press. The Court often divided along ideological lines in civil liberties cases. The Court seems to have passed through a period of hesitation following the Nixon appointments and now appears to be under the control of a conservative coalition. Documentation comes from published court opinions. 7 notes.

G. B. McKinney

851. Grigg, Susan. THE ALEXANDER M. BICKEL PAPERS. *Yale U. Lib. Gazette 1977 52(2): 66-69.* Alexander M. Bickel (1924-74) was a contributing editor to the *New Republic,* a constitutional and judicial authority, advisor to Democratic politicians, and professor at Yale University Law School. Bickel's papers were donated to Yale by his widow, Josephine Ann Bickel, and by his editor, Jeannette Hopkins. Note.   D. A. Yanchisin

852. Grofman, Bernard. ALTERNATIVES TO SINGLE-MEMBER PLURALITY DISTRICTS: LEGAL AND EMPIRICAL ISSUES. *Policy Studies J. 1980-81 9(6): 875-898.* Reviews the theoretical and empirical arguments against multimember districts and at-large elections and traces the Supreme Court's attempts in the 1970's to deal with the question of when nonsingle-member district elections violate "one person, one vote" standards.

853. Grothaus, Larry. "THE INEVITABLE MR. GAINES": THE LONG STRUGGLE TO DESEGREGATE THE UNIVERSITY OF MISSOURI, 1936-1950. *Arizona and the West 1984 26(1): 21-42.* When the all-white University of Missouri at Columbia denied the 1936 petition of Lloyd L. Gaines for admission to its law school, the NAACP launched a campaign to desegregate the state's colleges and universities. Eventually, US Supreme Court decisions forced modified state laws and token desegregation. The first blacks were not admitted to the university until 1950. Missouri's slow and reluctant compliance was typical of higher education institutions throughout the South. 7 illus., 52 notes.   D. L. Smith

854. Gruhl, John. THE SUPREME COURT'S IMPACT ON THE LAW OF LIBEL: COMPLIANCE BY LOWER FEDERAL COURTS. *Western Pol. Q. 1980 33(4): 502-519.* Examines libel as treated in federal courts, to determine the extent to which the Supreme Court's series of libel decisions, beginning with *New York Times* v. *Sullivan* (US, 1964) and continuing through *Rosenbloom* v. *Metromedia* (US, 1971), was complied with by federal district and appellate courts. The study reaches the opposite conclusion of previous studies and finds overwhelming compliance. This suggests that the traditional hierarchical model used to explain the Court's relation to the lower courts retains some validity.   J/S

855. Grumm, John G. and Murphy, Russell D. DILLON'S RULE RECONSIDERED. *Ann. of the Am. Acad. of Pol. and Social Sci. 1974 416: 120-132.* "Dillon's Rule has been a guiding doctrine in the constitutional relations between state and local government for more than a century. Simply stated, it declares that local jurisdictions are the creatures of the state and may exercise only those powers expressly granted them by the state. Historically, this

doctrine represented a response to the revolutionary changes of the latter half of the nineteenth century and was part of the struggle to control and reconcile the often conflicting demands of the old and the new. Though not always at a steady pace, state centralization mounted during this period. Eventually a countermovement emerged, identified with the proponents of home rule. The latter, however, had only a minor impact in arresting the erosion of local autonomy. In the face of the overwhelming political, economic and social forces of the twentieth century fostering centralization, the constitutional controversy originating with Dillon's Rule became less relevant as a determinant of state-local relations. The kind of centralization that eventually emerged was one in which power was concentrated in functionally-defined bureaucracies which essentially transcended geographically-defined levels of government. The recognition of this development fostered new home rule movements aimed at weakening the grip of professional bureaucracies and returning greater discretionary authority to the *political* officials at the local level. Such programs as the war on poverty, model cities and revenue sharing represent the attempts to diminish the influence of bureaucracies on local policy."   J

856. Grunbaum, Werner F. A QUANTITATIVE ANALYSIS OF THE "PRESIDENTIAL BALLOT" CASE. *J. of Pol. 1972 34(1): 223-239.* Analyzes the voting behavior of justices in *Williams v. Rhodes* (US, 1968) utilizing the St. Louis Supreme Court Dictionary and based on computer content-analysis. "While previous studies emphasized either fact or attitude variables, the present study indicates that both types of variables help determine a Justice's vote. The facts in judicial decisions appear to position the decision on a Justice's attitudinal scale and it is that position that determines his vote." 4 tables, 30 notes.   A. R. Stoesen

857. Guthertz, Judith Paulette. THE CAMPAIGN, THE VOTE AND THE DEFEAT: A REVIEW AND ANALYSIS OF THE 1979 REFERENDUN ON THE PROPOSED CONSTITUTION OF THE UNITED STATES TERRITORY OF GUAM. *Pol. Sci. [New Zealand] 1982 34(1): 111-136.* Analyzes the liberal, reformist, "intellectual," constitution of 1977-79, its ratification campaign, and its defeat in the public referendum.

858. Haiman, Franklyn S. HOW MUCH OF OUR SPEECH IS FREE? *Civil Liberties Rev. 1975 2(1): 111-137.* Examines First Amendment rights as they are applied to nonverbal communication, obscenity, vituperative or inciteful language, commercial enterprises, and the visual arts, 1970's.

859. Haiman, Franklyn S. NONVERBAL COMMUNICATION AND THE FIRST AMENDMENT: THE RHETORIC OF THE STREETS REVISITED. *Q. J. of Speech 1982 68(4): 371-383.* Developments of the last fifteen years in the relationship of free speech theory to nonverbal communication lead to the conclusion that many purely symbolic, emotive and victimless modes of nonverbal expression have won a firm place under the umbrella of First Amendment protection but that some nonverbal forms of communication, such as flag and draft card burnings, economic boycotts, and coercive persuasion generally, are still viewed as raising troublesome First Amendment questions.   J

860.   Hall, David. THE REAL ISSUE: NEED FOR TAX REFORM. *Compact 1973 7(2): 24-26.* Discussion of the need for reform in tax laws, public school financing, and education, sparked by the Supreme Court decision in *Rodriguez v. San Antonio Independent School District* (US, 1973).   S

861.   Halperin, Morton H. NATIONAL SECURITY AND CIVIL LIBER-TIES. *Foreign Policy 1975 (21): 125-167.* Contradicts prowiretappers who claim that such surveillance helps national security. Bugging and similar activities undermine constitutional rights, particularly those guaranteed by the First and Fourth Amendments. Wiretapping has a chilling effect on free speech, and the Fourth Amendment prohibits unreasonable searches and seizures. From the viewpoint of gathering information of value to national security, generally wiretapped information has had limited value. For dubious values, intelligence agencies are destroying constitutional rights.

R. F. Kugler

862.   Hamilton, Edward K. ON NONCONSTITUTIONAL MANAGE-MENT OF A CONSTITUTIONAL PROBLEM. *Daedalus 1978 107(1): 111-128.* Discusses the transformation and growth of government and the question of government accountability; this transformation has been effected without any fundamental change to the Constitution and with only two major shifts in judicial interpretation.

863.   Hamowy, Ronald. THE IRS AND CIVIL LIBERTIES: POWERS OF SEARCH AND SEIZURE. *Cato J. 1981 1(1): 225-275.* Summarizes the investigatory powers of the Internal Revenue Service, especially as these conflict with the rights and privileges of individuals under the Constitution and the courts, and indicates that these powers pose a grave threat to personal liberty within a free society.

864.   Handberg, Roger B., Jr. THE 1974 TERM OF THE UNITED STATES SUPREME COURT. *Western Pol. Q. 1976 29(2): 299-312.* The 1974 term was basically a period of marginal change. Significant policy decisions (such as the death penalty) were delayed due to Justice Douglas' illness. In environmental-natural resource cases, the Court made environmental litigation more difficult by not allowing the awarding of attorneys' fees. Also control of the Continental Shelf was resolved in favor of the federal govern-ment. A bar association's minimum fee schedule was struck down as violating the Sherman Act. Sex discrimination was struck down in jury selection procedures, social security benefits for widowers, and child support payments. Sexual classifications were upheld in military promotion policies. State support of religious schools was upheld as regards textbooks but not for auxiliary services. The press was allowed to publish material available in public records while abortion clinic ads came under First Amendment guarantees. Criminal defendants found the Court hostile to such claims. Using Elementary Linkage Analysis, a bloc analysis of the Court is presented both generally and in terms of economic and political issues.   J

865.   Harris, J. John, III. EDUCATION, SOCIETY, AND THE BROWN DECISION: HISTORICAL PRINCIPLES VERSUS LEGAL MANDATES.

J. of Black Studies 1982 13(2): 141-154. Surveys Supreme Court decisions affecting the education of blacks from *Roverts* v. *City of Boston* (US, 1850) to *Brown* v. *Board of Education* (US, 1954) and presents a brief discussion of the impact of the latter decision on attitudes and laws to 1975. Based on court decisions; biblio.   R. G. Sherer

866. Harrison, Stanley L. CONGRESS AND PRESIDENT: NATO TROOP-REDUCTION CONFLICT. *Military R. 1971 51(9): 13-24.* Argues that questions of how US forces in Europe will be pared relates to a fundamental controversy involving the Constitution. Basically, the conflict involves Congress and the President, but the ramifications have an impact on foreign relations and on the role of NATO. Traces the problem of American troop reductions in Europe, from the Mansfield amendment of February 1971 to the June 1971 NATO Foreign Ministers meeting in Lisbon, concluding that the outcome of this struggle will be felt for some time to come.   G. E. Snow

867. Hart, Jack R. THE RIGHT OF NEUTRAL REPORTAGE: ITS ORIGINS AND OUTLOOK. *Journalism Q. 1979 56(2): 227-234.* Traces the development of constitutional libel law from the US Supreme Court decision in *New York Times* v. *Sullivan* (US, 1964) to the Second Circuit Court of Appeals decision in *Edwards* v. *National Audobon Society* (US, 1977). *Sullivan* and later cases did not decide whether the press evinces malice by reporting libelous charges between public officials or prominent citizens. In the *Edwards* case, Judge Irving Kaufman settled the question in favor of the press, provided reporters extend the right of reply to those who are the objects of libelous charges. Based on federal court rulings and secondary sources; 51 notes.
                                                          R. P. Sindermann, Jr.

868. Hastie, William H. TOWARD AN EQUALITARIAN LEGAL OR-DER: 1930-1950. *Ann. of the Am. Acad. of Pol. and Social Sci. 1973 (407): 18-31.* "Though the post-Civil War amendments to the Constitution promised black Americans that thereafter their rights and opportunities would not be demeaned because of race, the ensuing fifty years witnessed the comprehensive institutionalization of racial segregation and subordination by force of law. During the first quarter of this century the racist legal order was so firmly established, with the support or acquiescence of most whites, that struggle against it seemed futile. But beginning about 1930, under the leadership of the National Association for the Advancement of Colored People, a nationwide legal campaign was planned and undertaken with an equalitarian legal order as its goal. Early lawsuits served to arouse public interest and support as well as to win significant peripheral changes in the segregated legal order. Social scientists and educators were persuaded to reexamine the segregated order critically. The federal government moved from a posture of neutrality to forthright assertion that laws requiring racial segregation could not be squared with the Constitution. Responding case by case, the Supreme Court progres-sively eroded antecedent constitutional doctrine that sanctioned American apartheid until, by 1950, the Court appeared ready to strike down all statutes and all other governmental action that imposed racial segregation or discrimi-nation."   J

869. Hatcher, John Henry. FRED VINSON: BOYHOOD AND EDUCA-TION IN THE BIG SANDY VALLEY. *Register of the Kentucky Hist. Soc.* *1974 72(3): 243-261.* Sketches the early life of Frederick Moore Vinson, mentioning his romantic and provincial heritage and education. His two early interests were reading and baseball. Involvement in local law and politics whetted his appetite for a later career in Congress, the Court of Appeals, wartime economic stabilization and mobilization programs, and to appointments as Secretary of the Treasury and Chief Justice of the Supreme Court. 33 notes.

J. F. Paul

870. Hazard, William R. COURT INTERVENTION IN PUPIL DISCI-PLINE: IMPLICATIONS AND COMMENT. *Am. Behavioral Scientist 1979 23(2): 169-205.* Examines court cases of the 1970's and determines that judicial scrutiny of schools to protect students' rights under the 14th Amendment has eroded the doctrine of *in loco parentis.*

871. Heberle, Klaus H. FROM GITLOW TO NEAR: JUDICIAL "AMENDMENT" BY ABSENT-MINDED INCREMENTALISM. *J. of Pol.* *1972 34(2): 458-483.* Studies the Supreme Court's "application of the First Amendment protections of speech and press to the states," from *Gitlow* v. *New York* (1925) through *Near* v. *Minnesota* (1931). "The court as a whole did not... address itself to the problem of the relation between the federal courts and state governments, did not discuss it, and did not evince any particular awareness that the problem was involved." Thus, a "major constitutional shift was affected without a coherent discussion of its merits" because the justices did not discuss "incorporation" of the first eight amendments into the 14th. They merely based their decisions on the 14th Amendment. Once freedom of speech had been "incorporated" in this fashion it became "difficult... to resist the incorporation of the First Amendment as well as other provisions of the 'Bill of Rights.' " Table, 86 notes. A. R. Stoesen

872. Heck, Edward V. and Hall, Melinda Gann. BLOC VOTING AND THE FRESHMAN JUSTICE REVISITED. *J. of Pol. 1981 43(3): 852-860.* Earlier studies concerning the freshman effect on Supreme Court decisions do not apply to the Warren and Berger eras, when the norm of individual responsibility for one's votes and opinions has muted group influences. Freshman justices are as politically and ideologically committed as their seniors. With the single exception of John Paul Stevens, Gerald Ford's sole appointee, freshmen formed close alliances with other justices during their first natural court. Some aligned with a sitting member whose views they shared; others joined large, moderately cohesive blocs while still others associated with several interlocking blocs. 2 tables, 22 notes. A. W. Novitsky

873. Heck, Edward V. CIVIL LIBERTIES VOTING PATTERNS IN THE BURGER COURT, 1975-78. *Western Pol. Q. 1981 34(2): 193-202.* Evaluations of the civil liberties record of the Warren E. Burger Supreme Court have often been based on analysis of the outcome of selected cases rather than on an entire set of civil liberties cases. This paper focuses on the voting record of individual justices and the Court as whole between the appointment of Justice Stevens and the end of the 1977-78 term. Despite a few libertarian advances,

this Court was markedly hostile to libertarian claims and the prospects for change via the appointment process are far from realization. J/S

874. Heffron, Paul T. PROFILE OF A PUBLIC MAN. *Supreme Court Hist. Soc. Y. 1980: 30-37, 48.* William Henry Moody was educated at the Phillips Academy in Andover, Massachusetts, and at Harvard College. After a brief term of study at Harvard Law School and an apprenticeship in the law office of Richard Henry Dana, Moody was admitted to the Massachusetts bar in 1878. He distinguished himself in private practice and local public offices, including that of Essex County district attorney. Moody, a Republican, was elected to the House of Representatives in 1895. President Theodore Roosevelt appointed Moody Secretary of the Navy in 1902, attorney general in 1904, and justice of the Supreme Court in 1906. Illness forced Moody's resignation from the court in 1910. His jurisprudence was marked by adherence to judicial restraint, a liberal view of federal power in the regulation of commerce, and deference to state power when exercised in the community interest. Based on the Theodore Roosevelt Papers, court records, and other primary and secondary sources; 2 illus., 47 notes. S

875. Henschen, Beth. STATUTORY INTERPRETATIONS OF THE SUPREME COURT: CONGRESSIONAL RESPONSE. *Am. Pol. Q. 1983 11(4): 441-458.* Examines Congress's response to the Supreme Court's interpretations of labor and antitrust statutes. Factors like the unanimity and direction of the Supreme Court's decision, which are often thought to have some bearing on the responses of other political actors, do not provide clear-cut explanations for congressional reaction to the Supreme Court's statutory decisions. J/S

876. Hentoff, Nat. ARE THERE ANY DEFENSES AGAINST A FREE, IRRESPONSIBLE PRESS? *Social Policy 1976 7(1): 50-53.* Discusses the American Civil Liberties Union's lawsuit on behalf of defendants William and Emily Harris in Los Angeles, California, on the basis that their right to a free trial had been denied by a prejudicial press. Considers freedom of speech issues in constitutional law and relations between law enforcement officials and journalists.

877. Hentoff, Nat. LIBRARIANS AND THE FIRST AMENDMENT AFTER NIXON. *Wilson Lib. Bull. 1974 48(9): 724-741.* Richard M. Nixon's administration was responsible for the censorship of libraries and other abuses of the First Amendment which restricted freedom of speech. S

878. Herbst, Robert L. THE LEGAL STRUGGLE TO INTEGRATE SCHOOLS IN THE NORTH. *Ann. of the Am. Acad. of Pol. and Social Sci. 1973 (407): 43-62.* "The struggle to integrate public schools in the North has been conducted largely in the federal courts. While the landmark case of *Brown v. Board of Education* and its progeny have clearly outlawed 'de jure' or state-imposed school segregation, the Supreme Court has not yet clarified whether its constitutional proscription extends to racial imbalance which results from the application of neighborhood school principles to racially imbalanced residential areas—so-called 'de facto' segregation. In the early phase of northern litigation, the NAACP (National Association for the

Advancement of Colored People) lawyers who led the legal struggle sought, largely unsuccessfully, to vindicate their theory that racial imbalance in the public schools, whether caused directly by state officials or not, unconstitutionally deprived black children of equal educational opportunity. Recently, the NAACP has changed its strategy and has attempted to prove in every case that school officials have taken at least some intentionally discriminatory actions which have helped isolate black children in black schools, and its lawyers have managed to convince a more sympathetic judiciary to grant comprehensive integration relief." J

879. Hill, Ann Corinne. PROTECTION OF WOMEN WORKERS AND THE COURTS: A LEGAL CASE HISTORY. *Feminist Studies 1979 5(2):* 247-273. History of labor law pertaining to women's job protection in the United States, focusing on four periods: from 1876 (when the Massachusetts Supreme Court upheld the first piece of protective legislation for women workers) until 1923; from 1935 to 1948, when unemployment during the Depression and women working at traditionally male-held jobs during World War II raised contradictory questions in the courts about equality in the work force; from 1964 to 1971, when women challenged labor laws; and from 1974 to 1979, characterized by more Supreme Court cases on discrimination against women in the labor force than in any other period in American labor history. Examines specific court cases and legislation.   G. Smith

880. Hill, Herbert. THE POSTPONEMENT OF ECONOMIC EQUALITY. *Black Scholar 1977 9(1): 18-23.* Despite the NAACP's struggle during 1964-77 to force adherence to the Civil Rights Act (US, 1964), a Supreme Court ruling which let stand seniority systems in effect before 1965 (systems which traditionally exclude women and blacks) has blocked economic equality.

881. Hine, Darlene Clark. BLACKS AND THE DESTRUCTION OF THE DEMOCRATIC WHITE PRIMARY 1935-1944. *J. of Negro Hist. 1977 62(1): 43-59.* The adoption of the white primary by southern states in the 1890's became the most effective subterfuge to disenfranchise blacks. A 25-year legal struggle by the National Association for the Advancement of Colored People (NAACP) resulted in the victory of the Supreme Court decision in the case of *Smith* v. *Allwright* (US, 1944). 72 notes.   P. J. Taylorson

882. Hine, Darlene Clark. THE ELUSIVE BALLOT: THE BLACK STRUGGLE AGAINST THE TEXAS DEMOCRATIC WHITE PRIMARY, 1932-1945. *Southwestern Hist. Q. 1978 81(4): 371-392.* After the Texas white primary law was ruled unconstitutional in *Nixon* v. *Herndon* (1927), the Texas Democratic Party tried every conceivable way of avoiding black voting in primaries. The state NAACP fought a losing battle against exclusion, as the Supreme Court allowed the party, but not the state, to impose a white primary: *Grovey* v. *Townshend* (1935). Nine years later the Court finally did outlaw a white primary under any pretext, in *Smith* v. *Allwright* (1944). Through this entire controversy, the state and national NAACP had led the campaign for black participation in Democratic politics. Primary and secondary sources; 49 notes.   J. H. Broussard

883.   Hirshon, Arnold. RECENT DEVELOPMENTS IN THE ACCESSI-
BILITY OF PRESIDENTIAL PAPERS AND OTHER PRESIDENTIAL
HISTORICAL MATERIALS. *Government Publ. Rev. 1979 6(2): 343-357.*
Access to presidential papers and related historical documents has been
advanced by the Freedom of Information Act (and its amendments), Supreme
Court rulings on Watergate materials, and the Presidential Records Act of
1978.

884.   Hodder-Williams, Richard. THE WORKLOAD OF THE SUPREME
COURT: A COMMENT ON THE FREUND REPORT. *J. of Am. Studies
[Great Britain] 1976 10(2): 215-239.* Criticizes a 1972 proposal by a committee
of lawyers of which Paul Freund was chairman. The committee, noting heavy
workloads burdening the Supreme Court, recommended the establishment of a
National Court of Appeals. The proposal is challenged on constitutional
grounds, and there are many pragmatic reasons for viewing it skeptically.
Based on legal writings, judicial decisions, and secondary sources; 74 notes.
H. T. Lovin

885.   Hoffecker, Carol E. DELAWARE'S WOMAN SUFFRAGE CAM-
PAIGN. *Delaware Hist. 1983 20(3): 149-167.* The campaign for woman's
suffrage in Delaware attracted national attention, but the state legislature failed
to ratify the 19th Amendment because of internecine political warfare among
the state's Republicans; effective antisuffrage lobbying by women; and the
perceived association of suffrage with other reforms, some of which were
unpopular in the state. Discusses the work of suffragists Mabel Vernon and
Florence Bayard Hilles and the Congressional Union's activities in the state,
and describes the antisuffrage contributions of Mary Wilson Thompson and
Emily P. Bissell. 7 illus., 42 notes.   R. M. Miller

886.   Hoffer, Thomas W. and Butterfield, Gerald A. THE RIGHT TO
REPLY: A FLORIDA FIRST AMENDMENT ABERRATION. *Journalism
Q. 1976 53(1): 111-116.* The US Supreme Court declared the Florida right to
reply statute unconstitutional in 1974. Part of an overall reform attempt, it was
passed in 1913. It required newspapers to print a candidate's reply without cost
if the newspaper attacked him. It was judged to interfere with the editorial
function of the press. Based on primary and secondary sources; 29 notes.
K. J. Puffer

887.   Holzer, Phyllis Tate and Holzer, Henry Mark. LIBERTY AND
EQUALITY? *Modern Age 1964 8(2): 134-142.* Contends that the US Supreme Court's decision in *Shelby* v. *Kraemer* (1947) destroyed the right of
private discrimination, one of the most fundamental rights of man in a free
society. Argues that to limit the use to which a man may put his property and
deprive him of the ability to make it available on a restrictive basis is to make
ownership a privilege, not a right. This is contrary to natural law and without
legal or constitutional justification. Details the application of the 14th Amendment from its adoption in 1868, the *Civil Rights Case* of 1884, the first legal
test of 1892, and *Buchanan* v. *Warley* (1917). Concludes that property and
contract rights have been dealt a crippling blow from which they may never
recover. Secondary sources; 3 notes.   P. T. Herman

888. Houseman, Gerald L. THE RIGHTS OF MOVEMENT. *Society 1977 14(5): 16-19.* Discusses the right of mobility related to antiautomobile literature, mobility as a natural right, and the possibility of a Constitutional amendment in order to guarantee this right.

889. Huffman, John L. and Trauth, Denise M. AFTER *GINSBERG* AND *TINKER:* BOOK BANNING AND MINORS' FIRST AMENDMENT RIGHTS. *Journalism Q. 1981 58(3): 434-438, 443.* During the past decade, judicial opinion on book banning in the schools has generally been divided. One view holds that, once a book is acquired by a school, it gains a sort of constitutional protection and cannot be removed without violating the First Amendment. The other, contrary opinion contends that removing a book is not unconstitutional, provided a sort of due process is observed in carrying out the removal. Until the Supreme Court rules in this area, it seems likely that the courts will continue to hand down inconsistent rulings. Based on judicial documents; 40 notes.   J. S. Coleman

890. Hull, Elizabeth. RESIDENT ALIENS, PUBLIC EMPLOYMENT AND THE POLITICAL COMMUNITY DOCTRINE. *Western Pol. Q. 1983 36(2): 221-240.* In 1971, the Supreme Court held that state laws penalizing resident aliens would hereafter survive challenge only if they served compelling interests. The court has recently invoked the so-called "political community" doctrine, however, in order to restrict its earlier decision. According to this doctrine, as originally articulated, a state retains the right to protect the "character and needs of its political community," and thus might consider only citizens for governmental positions that involve the formation or execution of high-level policy. The court has subsequently expanded this doctrine, however, and since 1978 it has sanctioned state regulations that disqualify aliens from a number of occupations unrelated to the creation or implementation of official policy. The expansion of the political community doctrine vests the status of citizenship with a significance that is at variance with constitutional tradition.
                                                       J/S

891. Hunter, Howard O. THE CONSTITUTIONAL STATUS OF ACADEMIC FREEDOM IN THE UNITED STATES. *Minerva [Great Britain] 1981 19(4): 519-568.* Constitutional 1st Amendment guarantees of academic freedom have been largely upheld.

892. Hurst, James Willard. THE FUNCTIONS OF COURTS IN THE UNITED STATES, 1950-1980. *Law & Soc. Rev. 1980-81 15(3-4): 401-471.* Case volume has grown, but court dispositions account for a small part of all dispute resolutions. Most matters which reach disposition in court end at some stage of trial court proceedings. Judges also continue to be makers of general public policy. Common law growth has dwindled. But courts contribute much to the content of public policy through their interpretation of statutes and their review of executive and administrative action. Judicial review of the constitutionality of legislation has declined sharply in fields centered on the economy, while expanding in areas of civil liberties.   J

893.   Hurst, James Willard. LEGAL ELEMENTS IN UNITED STATES HISTORY. *Perspectives in Am. Hist. 1971 5: 3-92.* Law is intricately bound up in the social structure and yet is little understood because of a dearth of historical legal literature. More legal research is needed to comprehend the "constitutional ideal." Cites five limitations in the existing literature: 1) an overemphasis of the importance of the Supreme Court and a neglect of state courts; 2) an exaggeration of the importance of "judge-made constitutional law"; 3) a narrow approach to legal history; 4) an emphasis on identifying the history of public policy with regulation; and 5) a tendency to concentrate on highly visible areas of controversy. In discussing available but previously unused source materials in legal history, the author mentions several subjects worthy of further scholarly research. 124 notes.   W. A. Wiegand

894.   Hurst, Willard. LAWYERS AS STRATEGISTS AND TACTICIANS. *Rev. in Am. Hist. 1983 11(1): 112-117.* Reviews Peter H. Irons's *The New Deal Lawyers* (1982), which details the roles of lawyers in three US Supreme Court cases of the middle 1930's.

895.   Hutchins, Robert M. ENVIRONMENT AND CIVIL RIGHTS. *Center Mag. 1975 8(6): 2-5.* Discusses potential conflicts between the environmental groups and civil rights movements during the 1970's, including the position of the US Supreme Court on housing and zoning issues.

896.   Hutchins, Robert M. TWO FATEFUL DECISIONS. *Center Mag. 1975 8(1): 7-13.* Two court decisions which allegedly denied disadvantaged school children equal protection in the law.   S

897.   Hynes, Terry. A CONVERSATION WITH LEONARD LEVY. *Journalism Hist. 1980 7(3-4): 96-103.* Interview with Leonard W. Levy on the First and Fifth Amendments, including remarks on historians and experiences which have influenced his thinking; 1940-80.

898.   Ichioka, Yuji. THE EARLY JAPANESE IMMIGRANT QUEST FOR CITIZENSHIP: THE BACKGROUND OF THE 1922 OZAWA CASE. *Amerasia J. 1977 4(2): 1-22.* Barred by law from citizenship and facing legal discriminations based upon that ineligibility, early Japanese immigrants to the United States sought naturalization rights through diplomatic, legislative, and judicial means. Anti-Japanese public opinion doomed any hope of legislative relief. The Japanese government applied diplomatic pressures, but refused to press the matter, according the immigrants' welfare a lower priority than "diplomatic necessity." Despite Tokyo's opposition, the immigrants supported Ozawa Takao's suit for citizenship as a test case, but the US Supreme Court's unfavorable decision in 1922 checked their efforts. 77 notes.
                                                                      T. L. Powers

899.   Isaac, Amos. THE ISSUE IS NOT BUSING BUT THE FOURTEENTH AMENDMENT: STRATEGIES FOR EVASION. *Educ. and Urban Soc. 1977 9(3): 259-276.* Reviews efforts to escape federally mandated forced busing since *Brown* v. *Board of Education* (US, 1954). Outlines the Southern response and the Northern response, using Chicago as an example.

Concludes that: resistance comes primarily from the majority community whose special resources are threatened; low income whites tend to be the "victims" of such efforts; the rewards for merely being white remain significant enough to prevent meaningful cooperation between poor whites and blacks; and when traditional sources of power and leadersh1p in a community support desegregation it is successful. The general benefits of American society are not available to the impoverished and the media tends to emphasize opposition to desegregation rather than successful school integration. 8 tables, note, 15 ref.

C. D'Aniello

900. Israel, Fred L. MILITARY JUSTICE IN HAWAII, 1941-1944. *Pacific Hist. R. 1967 36(3): 243-267.* Since military intelligence reports questioned the allegiance of Japanese Americans in Hawaii and was convinced that Japanese strategy envisioned invasion of the islands, a scheme for martial law was completed several months before attack came. Martial law was proclaimed with the attack on Pearl Harbor. Constitutional safeguards enunciated in the Civil War case of *Ex parte Milligan* were dismissed because of the "national interest" circumstances involved in Hawaii. Harold L. Ickes and his Department of the Interior, normally in administrative control of the territorial government of Hawaii, relentlessly fought martial law. Some modification was achieved in 1943 and formally terminated by presidential proclamation in October 1944. 98 notes.

D. L. Smith

901. Ives, C. P. A CASE OF CONTINUING ENCROACHMENTS. *Modern Age 1981 25(3): 249-254.* Louis Lusky, as clerk for the chief justice of the US Supreme Court for the 1937-38 term, authored a portentous footnote in the case of *United States* v. *Carolene Products Co.* Until this time, the classic rule for the court was that legislation, resting upon some rational basis, was presumed to be constitutional. A principle was expressed in this footnote, however, that this presumption may operate within a narrower scope when legislation appears to be within a specific prohibition of the Constitution. Lusky himself feels that the theme of the footnote merely defines an implied power in the court to prompt as well as to police legislation. The theme has been absolutized, however, into a doctrine of preferred freedoms, with property rights demeaned in favor of human rights. The result has been "juro-legislation" in civil rights. Based on the writings of Louis Lusky, Supreme Court decisions, and secondary sources; note.

R. D. Rahmes

902. Jackson, Donald W. A NEW VISION OF EQUALITY: TESTING THE EFFECTS OF GATE-KEEPING CRITERIA. *Policy Studies J. 1975 4(2): 122-126.* Discusses the Supreme Court's interpretation of Title VII of the Civil Rights Act of 1964 and the related Economic Opportunity Commission Guidelines which permit employers to use professionally developed ability tests to screen prospective employees so long as the tests are not designed, used, or intended to discriminate contrary to the provisions of the act.

903. Jacobsohn, Gary J. THE "PRAGMATIC DOGMA" OF THE POLITICAL THICKET: THE JURISPRUDENTIAL PARADOX OF "ONE MAN, ONE VOTE." *Polity 1977 9(3): 279-301.* The compatibility or contradiction of pragmatism and dogmatism has presented a problem to students of

American jurisprudence. With seeming inconsistency both critics and supporters of the Warren Court have stressed the pragmatic nature of its decisions
despite the dogmatic quality of some of its major guiding norms. The author
analyzes the apparent contradiction in the context of the reapportionment
issue. He finds that the judicial logic of the Warren Court can accommodate
both principles and concludes that pragmatism provides no reliable guarantee
against the pitfalls of dogmatism.   J

904. Jakoubek, Robert E. A JEFFERSONIAN'S DISSENT: JOHN W.
DAVIS AND THE CAMPAIGN OF 1936. West Virginia Hist. 1974 35(2):
145-153. John W. Davis, the 1924 Democratic presidential nominee, believed
in a limited federal government. He supported Franklin D. Roosevelt in 1932
but feared the liberalism of the first Hundred Days. He helped form the anti-
New Deal American Liberty League and as a constitutional lawyer argued
many cases against New Deal measures. Although Davis distrusted the
Republican Party, he decided finally to openly oppose Roosevelt's re-election
in 1936. Afterward, he stood apart from both parties. Based on Davis' private
papers; 45 notes.   J. H. Broussard

905. James, Dorothy Buckton. ROLE THEORY AND THE SUPREME
COURT. J. of Pol. 1968 30(1): 160-186. The role attributes of Supreme Court
justices can be classified as pivotal, relevant, and peripheral. The first is closely
related to the structure of the court, allows "zero tolerance," and includes such
activities as supervision of the federal court system. The second is highly
flexible and is closely connected with the background of the justice. It includes
adherence to precedent, the court's relationship to the federal system, and
"judicial self-restraint." The third involves matters which are optional or tend
to allow alternatives. Applies this theory to the careers of William O. Douglas
and Robert H. Jackson. Jackson exercised restraint while Douglas favored
judicial activism. The reason for these differences can be seen in the justices'
backgrounds and personalities. The most basic difference could be found in
their philosophy of the law. Law was only a part of Douglas's highly active
life, while it constituted virtually all of Jackson's life. 87 notes.
                                                              A. R. Stoesen

906. Johansen, Robin B. and Rosen, Sanford Jay. STATE AND LOCAL
REGULATION OF RELIGIOUS SOLICITATION OF FUNDS: A CON-
STITUTIONAL PERSPECTIVE. Ann. of the Am. Acad. of Pol. and Social
Sci. 1979 (446): 116-135. State and local governments, to regulate solicitation
on behalf of religious groups, are using existing laws and also enacting new
laws in a growing effort by government to regulate and monitor the actions of
all religious groups. Implicit in this growing trend is the arrogation by state
and local officials and lawmakers of the authority to decide what is "religion"
and therefore exempt from regulation. The increased regulation of religious
solicitation touches a longstanding tension in American life involving the
separation of church and state, and invokes three central themes: our money,
our privacy, and our faith. Most laws and regulations currently used to
regulate religious solicitation are constitutionally infirm. They are either too
vague to protect against arbitrary or capricious enforcement by public officials,
or they place officials in the position of deciding what is religious and what is

secular activity. The use of traditional time, place, and manner regulations—and sparing use of the existing criminal fraud law—are better means of curbing abuse in religious solicitation, and will prevent dangerous blurring of the boundary between church and state.   J/S

907. Johnson, Dorothy E. ORGANIZED WOMEN AS LOBBYISTS IN THE 1920'S. *Capitol Studies 1972 1(1): 41-58.* With the ratification of the 19th Amendment in 1920, 21 women's organizations unified under the Women's Joint Congressional Committee, which served as a clearing house for the legislative efforts of its members.   S

908. Johnson, Niel M. THE MISSOURI SYNOD LUTHERANS AND THE WAR AGAINST THE GERMAN LANGUAGE. *Nebraska Hist. 1975 56(1): 137-156.* Examines the attack on the Missouri Synod Lutherans for teaching German in church schools. The Nebraska Council of Defense charged them with disloyalty, but in 1923, the US Supreme Court overturned a decision by the Nebraska Supreme Court, and held that laws designed to make English the mother tongue of all children reared in the state were unconstitutional.
R. Lowitt

909. Johnson, Ralph H. and Altman, Michael. COMMUNISTS IN THE PRESS: A SENATE WITCH-HUNT OF THE 1950S REVISITED. *Journalism Q. 1978 55(3): 487-493.* In the mid-1950's the US Senate Internal Security Subcommittee conducted investigative hearings on the alleged influence of Communists in the press. Although the hearings were without legislative purpose, they raised issues regarding the rights of congressional witnesses. During the period, the US Supreme Court ruled on those rights, especially in *Watkins* v. *United States* (US, 1957) and *Barenblatt* v. *United States* (US, 1959), and usually decided against persons accused of being Communists. Newspaper publishers often fired employees for associating with Communists and in general were slow to recognize and debate the threat to constitutional rights posed by the hearings and court decisions. 38 notes.
R. P. Sindermann, Jr.

910. Johnson, Whittington B. THE VINSON COURT AND RACIAL SEGREGATION, 1946-1953. *J. of Negro Hist. 1979 63(3): 220-230.* Decisions of the Supreme Court under the leadership of Frederick M. Vinson made the state action concept the bulwark of protection of civil rights for blacks and rendered the separate-but-equal doctrine invalid, 1946-53.

911. Jones, Bartlett C. NULLIFICATION AND PROHIBITION, 1920-1933. *Southwestern Social Sci. Q. 1964 44(4): 389-398.* They never explicitly prescribed nullification of federal law (in this case, the 18th amendment), but pronullification forces advocated cooperative action between Congress and the states, passive resistance of states, and aggressive resistance by individuals, to secure the repeal of Prohibition, 1920-33.

912. Jones, Benjamin. PUBLIC EMPLOYEE LABOR ARBITRATION AND THE DELEGATION OF GOVERNMENTAL POWERS. *State Government 1978 51(2): 109-114.* Discusses the use of arbitration, the legal

concept of the delegation of powers (in compulsory arbitration), its judicial application, and the statutory and constitutional options for state governments; 1960's-70's.

913. Jones, Calvin P. KENTUCKY'S IRASCIBLE CONSERVATIVE: SU-PREME COURT JUSTICE JAMES CLARK MCREYNOLDS. *Filson Club Hist. Q. 1983 57(1): 20-30.* Studies Supreme Court Justice James Clark McReynolds and traces his career as a law professor at Vanderbilt School of Law, Assistant Attorney General under Theodore Roosevelt, and Attorney General for Woodrow Wilson. After Wilson appointed McReynolds to the Supreme Court in 1914, he made an early reputation as a liberal. After 1920, McReynolds became increasingly conservative and was an outspoken opponent of the New Deal. Secondary sources; 29 notes, 2 photos.   G. B. McKinney

914. Jones, Nathaniel R. THE *BROWN* DECISION: 25 YEARS LATER. *Crisis 1979 86(6): 211-214.* There is irony in that on the 25th anniversary of *Brown v. Board of Education* (US, 1954), the NAACP once again is compelled to argue before the Supreme Court the continuing validity of its original holding. Northern and western school segregation has hidden behind the "neighborhood school" concept while official policies and practices have created segregated education. The new NAACP cases have cataloged the devices by which black Americans have been denied rights recognized in 1954.
A. G. Belles

915. Jones, Oliver, Jr. THE BLACK MUSLIM MOVEMENT AND THE AMERICAN CONSTITUTIONAL SYSTEM. *J. of Black Studies 1983 13(4): 417-438.* Social, economic, and political factors shaped Black Muslim ideology in the 1930's. As the Black Muslims developed a complex institutional organization, they sought acceptance as a religion protected by the 1st Amendment, particularly with respect to taxation. They also abandoned some of their controversial, radical political philosophy, and complied with social norms of quietness, accommodation, and placidity. Based on court cases; table, fig., biblio.   R. G. Sherer

916. Katz, Ellis. APPORTIONMENT AND MAJORITY RULE. *Publius 1971 1(1): 141-161.* The evaluation of the American political structure by the Supreme Court indicates that the government is controlled by a minority of the nation's population. A close examination of the American political process, using Pennsylvania as a case study, proves that the process functioned democratically, as defined by the court, before reapportionment, despite the fact that the political structure appeared undemocratic vis-à-vis the court's model. Studies indicate that there never was a threat to majoritarianism in the form of a majority of legislators representing a minority of the population and controlling legislation. The Court rulings based on static structural models do not accurately reflect the actual dynamics of political processes. Based on secondary sources, published court cases, and voting records of legislature; graph, 8 tables.   M. R. Deaderick

917. Katz, Ellis. PRISONER'S RIGHTS, STATE'S RIGHTS, AND THE BAYH-KASTENMEIER "INSTITUTIONS BILL." *Publius 1978 8(1):*

179-198. In *Monroe* v. *Pape* (US, 1961), the US Supreme Court resurrected an 1871 civil rights act (42 U.S.C.A. 1983) enabling institutionalized persons to seek relief in federal courts for violations of their rights. In *Holt* v. *Sarver* (US, 1970), District Court Judge J. Smith Henley issued the first of a number of recent injunctions requiring that specific steps be taken to improve conditions at specific institutions. However, in *Solomon* v. *Mattson* (US, 1976), the authority of the US Attorney General to initiate prisoners' rights lawsuits without mandate from Congress was denied, whence the 1977 introduction by Senator Birch Bayh (Dem.-Indiana) and Representative Robert W. Kastenmeier (Dem.-Wisc.) of a bill to provide the Attorney General with such a mandate. Questions this approach, both in its tendency to perpetuate an adversary model in prison reform efforts, and in its tendency to undermine the state-federal balance in this area. 14 notes.   L. W. Van Wyk

918. Kaus, Robert M. HOW THE SUPREME COURT SABOTAGED CIVIL SERVICE REFORM. *Washington Monthly 1978 10(9): 38-44.* President Jimmy Carter was forced to change a proposal for civil service reform, due to the threat of its unconstitutionality.

919. Kearnes, John. UTAH, SEXTON OF PROHIBITION. *Utah Hist. Q. 1979 47(1): 5-21.* Utah, whose Mormon majority espoused abstinence, was the 36th state to ratify the 21st amendment, which repealed the 18th (Prohibition) amendment. Urban majorities prevailed over rural prohibitionists in spite of concerted efforts of secular and religious leaders. Wets pointed to disrespect for law created by Prohibition. They argued that additional revenue repeal would provide toward recovery from the depression, and made Prohibition a political, not a religious, issue. Drys rejected the economic appeal, pointed out evils rampant before Prohibition, and made prohibition a moral and religious obligation. Covers 1932-33. 8 illus., 59 notes.   J. L. Hazelton

920. Kendall, Willmoore. AMERICAN CONSERVATISM AND THE "PRAYER" DECISIONS. *Modern Age 1964 8(3): 245-259.* In 1963, following the Supreme Court's decision that the requirement of prayer in public schools was unconstitutional, the school board of North Brookfield, Massachusetts, voted to defy the Supreme Court and continue to obey the 137-year-old state law. Details the crisis in North Brookfield and suggests that conservatives must stop wasting their energies in argument with the Supreme Court, seeking solutions either by relenting or by striking at the whole business of judicial review. Conservatives must learn to distinguish between the 'legality' of a decision and the 'prudence' of such a decision. Suggests restoring the *status quo ante* and calls for the amendment of the 14th Amendment. Secondary sources; 13 notes.   T. Z. Herman

921. Kennedy, Edward M. THE NEED FOR GUN CONTROL LEGISLATION. *Current Hist. 1976 71(418): 26-28, 31.* Counters common arguments against gun control, including the 2nd Amendment, and cites international gun murder rates, 1970's.

922. Killenberg, George M. *BRANZBURG* REVISITED: THE STRUGGLE TO DEFINE NEWSMAN'S PRIVILEGE GOES ON. *Journalism Q.*

1978 55(4): 703-710. In *Branzburg* v. *Hayes* (US, 1972), the Supreme Court ruled 5-4 that journalists must respond to grand jury subpoenas and answer questions relevant to criminal investigations. Since then, rulings from federal and state courts regarding journalists' withholding of confidential information in court have conflicted with each other, in light of the vagueness and diversity of views expressed in the Supreme Court's majority and dissenting opinions. The pattern of rulings indicates, however, that no court is likely to recognize the withholding of information as a journalist's unqualified right under the First Amendment. 48 notes.   R. P. Sindermann, Jr.

923.   Kinoy, Arthur. THE MAKING OF A PEOPLE'S LAWYER. *Sci. & Soc. 1981 45(3): 324-334.* Shows how the authors, a life-long labor lawyer and civil rights activist, through a legal confrontation with the House Education and Labor Committee during a 1948 Evansville, Indiana, United Electrical, Radio, and Machine Workers of America strike helped bring about the recognition that the act of instituting a lawsuit to vindicate the fundamental constitutional rights of the people is itself a political expression, an activity protected by the 1st Amendment to the Constitution.   L. V. Eid

924.   Kirp, David L. THE BOUNDED POLITICS OF SCHOOL DESEG-REGATION LITIGATION. *Harvard Educ. Rev. 1981 51(3): 395-414.* Examines the evolution of Supreme Court doctrine since the *Brown* decision of 1954, showing that the decisionmaking process in contemporary US school integration cases is both a political and a constitutional event.

925.   Kirp, David L. SCHOOL DESEGREGATION AND THE LIMITS OF LEGALISM. *Public Interest 1977 (47): 101-128.* During the mid-1960's, Congress, the executive branch, and the courts acted in concert in the implementation of school desegregation in the South and provided extraordinary leadership. With the Supreme Court's expansion of the constitutional meaning of *de jure* segregation and the subsequent actions required of school districts, this joint effort began to collapse. When an interpretation of Title VI of the 1964 Civil Rights Act made desegregation nationwide, busing became an issue. The executive branch and Congress first withdrew and then attempted to undermine what had become an almost exclusively judicial effort. Today, the courts are opposed by the executive branch and Congress, and the vigor of the judiciary's rulings has outstripped its principles. The successes of the Johnson Administration will only be realized again when the effort is shared by the three branches of government and not just the courts. On the national level, Washington can distribute money, establish minimum standards, and encourage state and local educators who are the ones best able to select the means of resolving the questions of race and schooling in their locales.   S. Harrow

926.   Kitch, Edmund W. THE YELLOW CAB ANTITRUST CASE. *J. of Law and Econ. 1972 15(2): 327-336.* The Supreme Court Yellow Cab opinion (1949) has been considered the major effort by the court to apply a rule to vertical acquisitions. The various Yellow Cab decisions made during 1947-49 indicate that veteran operators had been removed "not by restrictive licensing laws but by competition," aided by the "post war replacement of the private automobile fleet." Primary and secondary sources; 50 notes.   C. A. Gallacci

927. Korenev, A. P. and Solovei, Iu. P. DISKRETSIONNYE POLNO-
MOCHIIA POLITSII SSHA [The discretionary powers of the US police].
Sovetskoe Gosudarstvo i Pravo [USSR] 1982 (4): 94-97. Examines increased
police power deemed necessary to defend the bourgeois state and control
complaints systems, emphasizing individual discretion versus constitutional
guarantees.

928. Kovaleff, Theodore P. DIVORCE AMERICAN-STYLE: THE DU
PONT-GENERAL MOTORS CASE. *Delaware Hist. 1978 18(1): 28-42.* In
1948 the US government brought a civil suit against the Du Pont Company to
force the company's complete divestiture of its stock in General Motors Corp.
and its control of General Motors. The case dragged on through three
presidential administrations, eventually leading to a government victory handed down by the Supreme Court. The prosecution of the case by the Eisenhower
administration, after the government lost its original suits, demonstrated the
administration's commitment to upholding and using the nation's antitrust
laws. Based on Antitrust Papers in the Department of Justice Records,
Records of the Du Pont Company, and secondary accounts; 66 notes.
R. M. Miller

929. Kramer, Daniel C. and Riga, Robert. THE NEW YORK COURT OF
APPEALS AND THE UNITED STATES SUPREME COURT, 1960-76.
Publius 1978 8(4): 75-111. Enumerates eight ways "... in which a state court
can bridle Supreme Court liberalism or spurn Supreme Court conservativ-
ism..." Examines decisions of the New York Court of Appeals in the
constitutional areas of obscenity, search and seizure, right to assigned counsel,
and the Miranda warnings. Shows the complexity of the relationship existing
between the US Supreme Court and a state court, and the dangers inherent in
oversimplifying, while indicating the interdependence of the two. Discusses the
composition and philosophy of the individual judges on the New York Court
of Appeals. Concludes that scholars should be more precise in describing the
relationship between a state court and the US Supreme Court in human rights
cases. 172 notes.
R. S. Barnard

930. Kupferberg, Seth. DON'T BLAME THE COURT. *Washington
Monthly 1977 9(8): 40-43.* Examines the change in attitude toward minorities,
women, civil rights, and generally-considered liberal causes following the
inclusion of Nixon administration appointees to the Supreme Court, 1968-77.

931. Kutler, Stanley I. THE JUDICIARY AND SOCIAL POLICY: USUR-
PATION OR ACQUIESCENCE? *Rev. in Am. Hist. 1978 6(2): 263-271.*
Review article prompted by Raoul Berger's *Government by Judiciary: The
Transformation of the Fourteenth Amendment* (Cambridge, Mass.: Harvard U.
Pr., 1977) which comments on the excessive powers of the judiciary, and
specifically, criticizes the goals of the framers of the Fourteenth Amendment;
covers 1866-1970's.

932. Kyvig, David E. AMENDING THE U.S. CONSTITUTION: RATIFI-
CATION CONTROVERSIES, 1917-1971. *Ohio Hist. 1974 83(3): 156-169.*
Discusses whether the people of state legislatures should have the final

approval of constitutional amendments, considering that in the 20th century many incidents of legislative votes against the popular will have occurred. Reviews the controversy surrounding the passing of the 18th Amendment in 1919, and describes the subsequent efforts of antiprohibitionists to repeal the 18th Amendment using the state convention method. Though the state convention method succeeded in 1933, it has not been employed in subsequent constitutional amendments. Based on government publications on the ratification of amendments, published court cases, journals, newspapers, and secondary works; 52 notes.   J. B. Street

933.   Kyvig, David E. RASKOB, ROOSEVELT, AND REPEAL. *Historian 1975 37(3): 469-487.* A prohibition repeal advocate, John J. Raskob exploited his chairmanship (1928-32) of the Democratic National Committee to secure repeal of the 18th Amendment. In so doing he collided with the presidential course of Franklin D. Roosevelt who mistakenly questioned the political wisdom of making any party commitment to repeal. However, Raskob was successful, first at the Democratic National Convention of 1932 with passage of a strong anti-prohibition plank to which Roosevelt gave opportunistic endorsement, and finally with the actual repeal on 5 December 1933. 83 notes.

934.   Ladenson, Robert F. FREEDOM OF THE PRESS: A JURISPRUDENTIAL INQUIRY. *Social Theory and Practice 1980 6(2): 163-185.* Develops a constitutional theory of freedom of the press, especially as it relates to freedom of speech.

935.   LaMarche, Gara. AFTER SKOKIE: NEW DIRECTIONS FOR CIVIL LIBERTIES. *New York Affairs 1980 6(3): 84-91.* Major trends of the civil liberties movement in the 1970's included a broadening scope, aggressiveness, and a shift in emphasis from litigation to legislation, due to the Warren E. Burger Supreme Court's lack of response to civil liberties concerns.

936.   Lamb, Charles M. LEGAL FOUNDATIONS OF CIVIL RIGHTS AND PLURALISM IN AMERICA. *Ann. of the Am. Acad. of Pol. and Social Sci. 1981 (454): 13-25.* Addresses the question of legal protections for minorities in the context of the transformation of the concept of equal protection since *Plessy* v. *Ferguson* (1896). Certainly the legal metamorphosis from the "separate but equal" doctrine to the current status of minority rights is profound. Particularly important in recent years is the issue of affirmative action. Traces the progression of the equal protection principle with emphasis on the three most recent affirmative action decisions announced by the Court: *University of California Regents* v. *Bakke* (1978), *United Steelworkers of America* v. *Weber* (1979), and *Fullilove* v. *Klutznick* (1980).   J/S

937.   Lang, Harold W. THE FOURTEENTH AMENDMENT, ITS EQUAL PROTECTION CLAUSE AND PUBLIC ACCOMMODATIONS. *Negro Hist. Bull. 1968 31(2): 6-13.* Discusses the equal protection clause of the 14th Amendment from a historical perspective of state action and litigation, showing its effects on black civil rights.   S

938. Laska, Lewis L. MR. JUSTICE SANFORD AND THE FOUR-TEENTH AMENDMENT. *Tennessee Hist. Q. 1974 33(2): 210-227.* Edward Terry Sanford (1865-1930) was one of Tennessee's most distinguished jurists. Born in Knoxville of Unionist parents, he graduated from the University of Tennessee and later Harvard Law School, was a strong supporter of higher education, and an outstanding public speaker. After a successful law practice, Sanford was appointed to the US Supreme Court where his most famous decision was his defense of civil liberties in *Gitlow v. New York* (US, 1925). Primary and secondary sources; 52 notes.   M. B. Lucas

939. Lau, Estelle Pau-on. CALIFORNIA'S CONTRIBUTION TO BILIN-GUAL EDUCATION: LAU VS. NICHOLS. *Pacific Hist. 1980 24(1): 45-54.* Using the 1974 Supreme Court decision *Lau v. Nichols* (US, 1974), as a base, discusses recent developments in bilingual bicultural education. This decision stated that students who do not understand English are denied a meaningful opportunity to obtain an education. The Court ruled that to deny instruction to students in their own language violated the Civil Rights Act (US, 1964). California enacted the Chacone-Moscone Bilingual Bicultural Education Act (1976), which requires bilingual learning opportunities for all students with limited facility in English. US and California Codes, Statutes, and court decisions; 41 notes.   G. L. Lake

940. Leavy, Edward N. and Raps, Eric Alan. THE JUDICIAL DOUBLE STANDARD FOR STATE AID TO CHURCH-AFFILIATED EDUCA-TIONAL INSTITUTIONS. *J. of Church and State 1979 21(2): 209-222.* The US Supreme Court has ruled that state and federal governments may provide financial support for private colleges and schools for the construction of secular facilities. Based on *Lemon v. Kurtzman* (US, 1971), laws providing funding are constitutional if they have a secular purpose, if the primary effect neither advances nor inhibits religion, and if the statute does not foster an excessive government entanglement with religion. In *Roemer v. Board of Public Works of Maryland* (US, 1976), a double standard was established: aid to church-related colleges receives less scrutiny than does aid to parochial schools.   S

941. Ledbetter, Cal, Jr. THE ANTIEVOLUTION LAW: CHURCH AND STATE IN ARKANSAS. *Arkansas Hist. Q. 1979 38(4): 299-327.* Discusses the history of the Arkansas Antievolution Law (1928) from preliminary legislative attempts to pass such an act, through the 1927 popular campaign which initiated the act and voted it into effect. The court cases involving Mrs. Susan Epperson, a Little Rock biology teacher, which resulted in the Supreme Court declaring the Arkansas law unconstitutional in 1968, are also described. 148 notes.   G. R. Schroeder

942. Lee, Eugene C. THE INITIATIVE AND REFERENDUM: HOW CALIFORNIA HAS FARED. *Natl. Civic Rev. 1979 68(2): 69-76, 84.* California has had the constitutional and direct statutory initiative since 1911. What is it? Who uses it? Why? What kinds of measures pass? Is California likely to abandon it? No.

943. Leech, Noyes. REPORT ON COMMITTEE IV. *Ann. of the Am. Acad. of Pol. and Social Sci. 1976 426: 204-212.* Professor [Covey T.] Oliver [in this issue of *AAAPSS*] observed that the current expression of Congress' will to participate in foreign policy and the unrelieved separation of powers impose serious impediments on the ability of the Executive branch to enter into reliable, immediate foreign commitments. The committee appeared to recognize that the crisis in the exercise of our foreign relations power existed and was in some measure created by congressional will to participate and complicated by our separation of powers; but it did not agree that the U.S. was unduly hampered in its power to carry on foreign relations effectively. The committee dealt with the relationship between the Executive and Congress as one of continuing political balance that could be accommodated within our present Constitution. It considered how certain problems of congressional-Executive branch organization related to international agreements might be approached. In looking to the future, the committee projected that the U.S. would want to join international organizations of an increasingly sophisticated type. The view was expressed that constitutional problems arising from joining such organizations, if the matter were approached without amendments, could be quite complex. [A report on Committee IV of the AAPSS Bicentennial Constitutional Conference, 1976]. J

944. Lessard, Suzannah. REHNQUIST, POWELL AND THE CULT OF THE PRO. *Washington Monthly 1972 3(12): 48-56.* Focusing on the Senate debate on Nixon Supreme Court appointees William Rehnquist and Lewis Powell, the author investigates the motives of those Senators in opposition. He finds that their distaste for the nominees centered on philosophical differences, but as liberals they could not admit a firm philosophical position. As a result, Clement Haynsworth and G. Harold Carswell were rejected while Rehnquist, who shared their philosophical position, was accepted. In conclusion, the author speculates on the basis for Senate debate on Court appointees, finding it based less on philosophy than on a "pro ethic": an impression that one who has achieved distinction in the law profession should be accepted if nominated. Haynsworth and Carswell had not achieved distinction—Powell and Rehnquist had.   S. R. Duguid

945. LeVar, C. Jeddy. THE NIXON COURT: A STUDY IN LEADERSHIP. *Western Pol. Q. 1977 30(4): 484-492.* Identifies eight voting bloc formations within the Supreme Court of the Nixon administration and finds that intrabloc leadership accounts for greater unity in questions of civil liberty, liberal economic regulation, and judicial self-restraint than in nationalism, judicial activism, and conservative economic regulation, 1968-74.

946. Lewan, Kenneth M. STAATLICHER ZWANG ZUR EINSCHRÄNKUNG DER UNGLEICHBEHANDLUNG IN DEN USA [State compulsion to reduce discrimination in the USA]. *Zeitschrift für Politik [West Germany] 1971 18(2): 160-176.* Examines three classes of actions to prohibit discrimination in employment, housing, use of public facilities, and admission to schools, universities, and labor and professional organizations. The first class discussed is the expansion of common law. In this class the principle of equality before the law could be employed. This approach is seldom used, and

where it has been used, applies only in individual states. The second class is federal legislation, which has been used to remove discrimination in employment practices, in purchase and rental of housing, and in admission to public facilities. The third class, based on the 14th Amendment to the Constitution, has been used in the purchase of housing and in admission to schools and universities. Although legal bases exist in some cases, little or nothing has been done to assure admission to cultural, sports, or professional organizations; to extend nondiscrimination to homosexuals or communists; to assure Negroes or women admission to private schools; to assure nondiscrimination by charitable organizations and foundations; or to guarantee expression for opposing views in newspapers and advertising. 52 notes.   E. F. Ziemke

947. Lewis, John D., Jr. AMERICAN GESTAPO: HOW THE BATF IS RIDING ROUGHSHOD OVER CIVIL LIBERTIES. *Reason 1980 11(12): 24-28, 44.* The federal Bureau of Alcohol, Tobacco, and Firearms (BATF), faced with less to enforce after moonshining declined in the 1970's, has stepped up its violations of the civil liberties and the Second Amendment rights of legal firearms owners and dealers through paramilitary-style raids, unjustified confiscations of legal firearms, entrapment, and use of untrustworthy informants.

948. Lewis, Robert. GISSEL PACKING: WAS THE SUPREME COURT RIGHT? *Am. Bar Assoc. J. 1970 56(9): 877-880.* The law of labor relations was significantly changed with the Court's approval of the use of authorization cards by unions for establishing representative status.   J

949. Lindholm, Richard W. THE CONSTITUTIONALITY OF A FEDERAL NET WEALTH TAX: A SOCIOECONOMIC ANALYSIS OF A STRATEGY AIMED AT ENDING THE UNDER-TAXATION OF LAND. *Am. J. of Econ. and Sociol. 1984 43(4): 451-454.* Examines the taxation powers of the federal government specified in the Constitution and traces Supreme Court decisions on the subject. Although the federal government has been prohibited from taxing the value of land, a net wealth tax on all other assets would probably be possible, leaving taxation of land to state governments.   J/S

950. Lipton, Paul P. CONSTITUTIONAL ISSUES IN TAX FRAUD CASES. *Am. Bar Assoc. J. 1969 55(8): 731-735.* How much longer will the IRS [Internal Revenue Service] be permitted to take advantage of the taxpayer's inclination to believe that when it pays a visit its concern is money, not crime?   J

951. Littlefield, Daniel F., Jr. and Underhill, Lonnie E. DIVORCE SEEKER'S PARADISE: OKLAHOMA TERRITORY, 1890-1897. *Arizona and the West 1975 17(1): 21-34.* Soon after Oklahoma gained territorial status in 1890, the "divorce mill" came into being. A short residency requirement, confusion as to which court had jurisdiction in matters of divorce, and the publicity furnished by lawyers and hotel and boarding house owners made Oklahoma the "divorce center" of the nation. Many lawyers became wealthy and Oklahoma towns prospered from the spending of temporary, divorce-

seeking residents. The campaign of a territorial judge, the veto of legislation by the governor, a federal law lengthening residency requirements for divorce in territories, and a 1906 US Supreme Court decision ended Oklahoma's notorious divorce business. 4 illus., 25 notes.   D. L. Smith

952.   Lofgren, Charles A. MR. TRUMAN'S WAR: A DEBATE AND ITS AFTERMATH. *R. of Pol.* 1969 31(2): 223-241. Discusses the debate over the legal basis of President Harry S. Truman's commitment of US military forces in Korea, 27 June 1950. Truman, Secretary of State Dean Acheson, and their supporters seemed to intimate that the President derived at least some authority from UN Security Council resolutions on the Korean fighting. Republican Senators Robert Alphonso Taft, Karl Earl Mundt, Arthur V. Watkins, and others argued that even under UN provisions, Congress would have to approve US participation in UN wars. Taft further held that even the President's status as Commander-in-Chief did not allow him to "precipitate any open warfare" without a declaration of war (at least after the fact) by Congress. The debate later affected the actions of President Dwight David Eisenhower over the Pescadores and the Middle East, and of President Lyndon Baines Johnson over the Vietnam War. 33 notes.   S

953.   Lowenfeld, Andreas F. ACT OF STATE AND DEPARTMENT OF STATE: *FIRST NATIONAL CITY BANK V. BANCO NACIONAL DE CUBA. Am. J. of Internat. Law* 1972 66(5): 795-814. Discusses "whether courts of one nation should sit in judgment on the acts of other nations with respect to foreign held property...." The US Supreme Court in *Banco Nacional de Cuba vs. Sabbatino* upheld and reaffirmed the "act of state" doctrine. The State Department argued "... that when it perceives no objection to adjudication on foreign policy grounds, the courts should judge the validity of the foreign nation's acts under international law standards—at least as to counterclaims." Such a ruling was made in *First National Bank* v. *Banco Nacional de Cuba* (1972). 73 notes.   D. D. Cameron

954.   Lynch, Thomas D. FEDERAL BUDGETARY MADNESS. *Society* 1983 20(4): 27-31. Discusses the current state of fiscal responsibility in reference to the federal budget process and evaluates methods of correcting through constitutional amendment or legislation.

955.   Mabbutt, Fred R. THE CONSTITUTION AND THE NIXON COURT. *Colorado Q.* 1973 22(2): 149-165. The Supreme Court has been disavowed by Presidents ever since Thomas Jefferson. Richard Milhous Nixon has said that the Court is "weakening the peace forces as against the criminal forces in our society...." The argument has often been that the Court, full of lifetime appointees, is neither dependent upon nor responsive to the will of the people, and it is therefore undemocratic. One of the key arguments is that the Court's use of judicial review is antidemocratic. On the other hand, it is pointed out that the Founding Fathers purposively built in judicial restraints on the majority in the belief that they were neither necessarily right nor necessarily reasonable. Many remedies to make the Court more democratic are available, e.g., amendment of the Constitution, control through the Senate confirmation process, simple congressional legislation on such matters as

jurisdiction and duties, and abolition of judicial review through constitutional amendment. Explores the Miranda decision and the judicial thinking behind it. The Court is turning away from the Warren Court's defense of civil liberties. 5 notes.   B. A. Storey

956. Maddox, Robert. THE WAR AGAINST DEMON RUM: PART 1. *Am. Hist. Illus. 1979 14(3): 10-18.* Describes the attempts to enforce Prohibition in the United States from the passing of the Volstead Act (1919) to the repeal of Prohibition in 1933 with the ratification of the 21st Amendment.

957. Maidment, R. A. THE US SUPREME COURT AND AFFIRMATIVE ACTION: THE CASES OF BAKKE, WEBER AND FULLILOVE. *J. of Am. Studies [Great Britain] 1981 15(3): 341-356.* Challenges to affirmative action laws and discriminatory procedures which favored minorities reached the Supreme Court during the 1970's. Important cases before the court included: *Regents of the University of California v. Bakke; United Steelworkers of America v. Weber;* and *Fullilove v. Klutznick.* In these cases, jurists were forced to confront problems raised by their desire to uphold affirmative action procedures and sanction discrimination on behalf of minorities, although the court's own 1954 dicta in *Brown v. Board of Education* required nondiscrimination. 35 notes.   H. T. Lovin

958. Maidment, Richard A. POLICY IN SEARCH OF LAW: THE WARREN COURT FROM *BROWN* TO *MIRANDA. J. of Am. Studies [Great Britain] 1975 9(3): 301-320.* Reviews notable decisions of the US Supreme Court during the tenure of Earl Warren as Chief Justice (1953-69). The Warren court rejected much of the "mechanistic jurisprudence" which dominated American law and court proceedings during the 19th and early 20th centuries. Decisions by the Warren Court reflected the doctrines and conceptions of American "Legal Realists." Realists depended heavily upon the thinking and writings of Oliver Wendell Holmes (1841-1935) and Benjamin Cardozo (1870-1938). Based on Supreme Court decisions and professional legal commentaries; 40 notes.   H. T. Lovin

959. Mambretti, Catherine Cole. THE BURDEN OF THE BALLOT. *Am. Heritage 1978 30(1): 24-25.* The arguments of those opposed to ratification of the woman suffrage (19th) amendment included the breaking up of the family, the emotional nature of women, nativism, the right of states to make such decisions, and the electoral problems which would follow ratification. Efforts were coordinated by a National Association Opposed to the Extension of Suffrage to Women. Illus.   J. F. Paul

960. Marfin, Gary C. and Hanus, Jerome J. SUPREME COURT RESTRAINTS ON STATE AND LOCAL OFFICIALS. *Natl. Civic Rev. 1981 70(2): 83-89.* The US Supreme Court's decision in *State of Maine, et al. v. Thiboutot* (US, 1980) marks a radical change in the law governing the personal liability of state and local officials in the administration of public programs. As a result of *Thiboutot,* individuals may seek relief whenever they believe they have been injured in the administration of any federal-state cooperative program.   J

961.   Marr, Warren, ed. HISTORY OF THE FIVE SCHOOL CASES. *Crisis 1979 86(6): 189-194.* The constitutional power to segregate black and white students in separate schools was challenged by attorneys of the NAACP in cases initiated in 1950 and which resulted in the Supreme Court decision *Brown* v. *Board of Education* (US, 1954). Based on the history of the 14th Amendment, on recent judicial precedents, and on current scholarly research, the Supreme Court ruled that segregation was unconstitutional.

A. G. Belles

962.   Marsh, James M. THE GENIAL JUSTICE: ROBERT H. JACKSON. *Am. Bar Assoc. J. 1974 60(3): 306-309.* A former law clerk recalls the distinguished Supreme Court justice.   S

963.   Marshall, Thurgood and Wilkins, Roy. INTERPRETATION OF SUPREME COURT DECISION AND THE NAACP PROGRAM. *Crisis 1979 86(6): 205-209.* The Supreme Court in *Brown* v. *Board of Education* (US, 1954) has provided the legal machinery required to end segregation. All school segregation laws are invalid and school authorities must eliminate all obstacles promptly to begin full compliance. The constitutional principles cannot yield simply because of disagreement with them. Compliance should come without legal action, but the tools are now available if school authorities resist.

A. G. Belles

964.   Marshall, Thurgood. JUSTICE THURGOOD MARSHALL'S OPINION IN THE *BAKKE* CASE. *Crisis 1979 86(2): 45-50.* Marshall agrees with the judgment of the Supreme Court only insofar as it permits universities to consider race in making admissions decisons. He does not agree that the *Bakke* case violates the Constitution. The history of the black man in America demonstrates pervasive institutional racism that has on many occasions been promoted by decisions of the Supreme Court. The 14th Amendment can be used by universities to remedy the cumulative effect of society's discrimination. Race-based remedies should be as valid as the policies that discriminated on the basis of race.   A. G. Belles

965.   Martineau, Robert J., Jr. INTERPRETING THE CONSTITUTION: THE USE OF INTERNATIONAL HUMAN RIGHTS NORMS. *Human Rights Q. 1983 5(1): 87-107.* Discusses the implications of *Rodriguez-Fernandez* v. *Wilkinson* (US, 1980), in which international human rights law was incorporated into domestic law, for domestic enforcement of human rights.

966.   Marx, Gary. UNDERCOVER COPS: CREATIVE POLICING OR CONSTITUTIONAL THREAT? *Civil Liberties Rev. 1977 4(2): 34-44.* Explores the necessity of restriction and close regulation of undercover police activities to avoid violation of constitutional rights, 1970's.

967.   Mathias, Charles McC., Jr. NATIONAL EMERGENCIES AND THE CONSTITUTION. *Congressional Studies 1979 7(1): 5-9.* Discusses the perennial power struggle between the legislative and executive branches of government, 1933-78, and notes the importance of President Gerald Ford's decision

to sign the National Emergencies Act on 14 September 1976 as a move to restore power to the Congress.

968. Mathias, Charles McC., Jr. STATE OF EMERGENCY. *Civil Liberties R. 1974 1(2): 75-81.* "States of emergency provide the president with extraordinary powers: to seize property, control the means of production, and institute martial law. And it is all legal, all with the acquiescence of Congress, all constitutional."   J

969. McCleskey, Clifton. PARTIES AT THE BAR: EQUAL PROTECTION, FREEDOM OF ASSOCIATION, AND THE RIGHTS OF POLITICAL ORGANIZATIONS. *J. of Pol. 1984 46(2): 346-368.* Since the 1960's, the role of political parties in the constitutional system has been fundamentally altered by the judiciary. No longer are parties accorded the status of other nonpublic associations regulated only in pursuit of a legitimate governmental objective. The most numerous and significant cases have eased requirements for access to the ballot for independent candidates and minority parties. Other cases permitting increased participation in primary elections have altered the doctrine of freedom of association as applied to party structures and processes. Only in *Elrod* v. *Burns* (US, 1976), despite a long tradition of laws and administrative orders limiting patronage, did the Supreme Court determine that the 1st Amendment prohibits the dismissal of public employees for partisan reasons. 51 notes, biblio.   A. W. Novitsky

970. McCluskey, Neil G. AID TO NONPUBLIC SCHOOLS: HISTORICAL AND SOCIAL PERSPECTIVES. *Current Hist. 1972 62(370): 302-304, 306, 310.* Discusses issues in constitutional law regarding federal aid to education for Catholic elementary schools in the 1960's and 70's.

971. McCoy, Candace. NEW FEDERALISM, OLD REMEDIES, AND CORRECTIONS POLICYMAKING. *Policy Studies Rev. 1982 2(2): 271-278.* Analyzes Burger Supreme Court decisions regarding prison reform; they seek to reduce the federal role in prison regulation, and give more autonomy to state prison administrators, but there is no attempt to cut back on the protection of prisoners' rights.

972. McCree, Wade, Jr. and Copelon, Rhonda. TEXT OF U.S. SUPREME COURT DECISION: *HARRIS V. MCRAE. J. of Church and State 1980 22(3): 575-595.* This Supreme Court case, *Harris* v. *McRae* (US, 1980), concerns whether the First and Fifth Amendments are violated by the Hyde Amendment (1976) in the case of abortions paid for by the Medicaid Program. The Supreme Court upheld the Hyde Amendment and held that neither federal nor state governments are constitutionally required to pay for abortions. 28 notes.   E. E. Eminhizer

973. McFeeley, Neil D. A CHANGE OF DIRECTION: HABEAS CORPUS FROM WARREN TO BURGER. *Western Pol. Q. 1979 32(2): 174-188.* Studies some differences between the Supreme Court of the United States under Chief Justice Warren and that Court today. The Warren Court was primarily concerned with individual liberty while the Burger Court is more

concerned with the institutional consequences of its decisions. The paper explores the Burger Court's decisions on cases in the areas of civil rights, voting rights, individual freedoms and criminal justice and then compares the two Courts' decisions on the writ of habeas corpus. The Warren Court utilized that writ to protect the due process rights of state defendants while the Burger Court has retracted the scope of the writ. The recent decisions in *Stone* v. *Powell* and *Wolff* v. *Rice* indicate the Burger Court's primary concern with institutional relationships in derogation of protection of individual liberties.

J

974.   McFeeley, Neil D. THE SUPREME COURT AND THE FEDERAL SYSTEM: FEDERALISM FROM WARREN TO BURGER. *Publius 1978 8(4): 5-36.* Compares the Warren Court with the Burger Court. Discusses the changes that took place in Supreme Court decisions after 1968. The Warren Court is portrayed as ignoring institutional questions in their effort to protect individual rights. The Burger Court, however, stressed the preservation of certain traditional principles, especially federalism, and was willing to sacrifice individual claims for these principles. Examples of the strong points of each court are given. Their views on specific substantive issues is contrasted. 134 notes.

R. S. Barnard

975.   McGaffey, Ruth. GROUP LIBEL REVISITED. *Q. J. of Speech 1979 65(2): 157-170.* Recent activities of neo-Nazi groups have rekindled interest in group libel laws. Several significant court cases have not yet clearly determined the constitutional status of such laws. In a free society, however, the wisdom of these laws seem questionable. Primary and secondary sources; 91 notes.

E. Bailey

976.   McGurn, Barrett. LAW CLERKS: A PROFESSIONAL ELITE. *Supreme Court Hist. Soc. Y. 1980: 98-101.* Law clerks became part of the Supreme Court staff in 1885. The clerks, often drawn from the top of their law school classes, act as researchers and legal assistants for the justices. Harvard and Yale law schools have traditionally supplied most of the Supreme Court's law clerks, although in recent years other law schools have provided a large proportion of the young lawyers who fill these prestigious positions.   S

977.   McKay, Pamela R. PRESIDENTIAL PAPERS: A PROPERTY ISSUE. *Lib. Q. 1982 52(1): 21-40.* The dramatic change which occurred in the ownership of presidential papers due to litigation surrounding former President Nixon's papers is the underlying theme in this discussion of the property aspects of presidential papers from George Washington to the present. The paper begins with the Supreme Court case *Nixon* v. *Administrator of General Services* (US 1977). Additional topics include a description of presidential papers, a survey of past practice and law regarding the ownership and control of presidential papers, and the pro and con arguments of presidential ownership.   J/S

978.   McKay, Robert B. RACIAL DISCRIMINATION IN THE ELECTORAL PROCESS. *Ann. of the Am. Acad. of Pol. and Social Sci. 1973 (407): 102-118.* "Nearly a century ago the Supreme Court of the United States

acknowledged that the right to vote is 'a fundamental political right, because preservative of all rights.' A Court thus armed with lofty ideals might have been expected to apply the Fourteenth and Fifteenth Amendments to strike down racially discriminatory restrictions on the franchise that were adopted by many states after the Reconstruction period ended with the Hayes-Tilden Compromise of 1876. However, the Supreme Court largely confined its efforts to rhetoric and for many decades closed its eyes to the use of the white primary, literacy tests, the poll tax, and other devices to deny black citizens the vote. The white primary was at last outlawed in 1944, but Congress did not act until 1957. The Civil Rights Acts of 1957, 1960, and 1964 were well intended but not very effective. The Voting Rights Act of 1965, as amended in 1970, is now the principal vehicle for protection of the franchise against racial discrimination. It forbids literacy tests and other discriminatory tests and devices and requires federal approval of any changes in voting qualifications or procedures in states with a history of voting discrimination."   J

979. McLean, Deckle. JUSTICE WHITE AND THE FIRST AMEND-MENT. *Journalism Q. 1979 56(2): 305-310.* Assesses the views of US Supreme Court Justice Byron R. White on the freedom of the press as they appear in his court opinions. White has occupied a middle ground: on the one hand he has defended rights of individuals against the established media in cases such as *Branzburg v. Hayes* (US, 1972) and *Gertz v. Welch* (US, 1974), and on the other hand he has expressed the fear in cases such as *Miami Herald Publishing Co. v. Tornillo* (US, 1974) and *Nebraska Press Association v. Stuart* (US, 1976) that limits on the rights of the press signal a slide toward totalitarianism. 38 notes.   R. P. Sindermann, Jr.

980. McMorris, S. Carter. CAN WE PUNISH FOR THE ACTS OF ADDICTION? *Am. Bar Assoc. J. 1968 54(11): 1081-1085.* It is logically inconsistent to punish the acts and "derivative crimes" of addiction when the Supreme Court has held that the status of addiction cannot be penalized.   J

981. Mead, Walter B. MANAGING PROFLIGACY. *Society 1983 20(4): 16-19.* Describes the proposed amendment to the Constitution, Senate Joint Resolution 58, and its provisions mandating a balanced budget, requiring that taxes in any year not increase more than the previous year's national income increase, and forbidding an increase in the federal accumulated debt.

982. Melton, Gary B. CHILD WITNESSES AND THE FIRST AMEND-MENT: A PSYCHOLEGAL DILEMMA. *J. of Social Issues 1984 40(2): 109-123.* There have been a number of recent proposals for procedural reforms to protect child victims in their role as witnesses. The Supreme Court's decision in *Globe Newspaper Co. v. Superior Court* suggests both the constitutional limits of these reforms and some circumstances in which social-science evidence is unlikely to be given weight by the judiciary. *Globe* is particularly interesting with respect to the latter issue because its judgment appeared to turn on perceptions of empirical data. The Court's use of these data is analyzed, and suggestions are made for future research about children's involvement as witnesses.   J/S

983. Mendelson, Wallace. FROM WARREN TO BURGER: THE RISE AND DECLINE OF SUBSTANTIVE EQUAL PROTECTION. *Am. Pol. Sci. R. 1972 66(4): 1226-1233.* Substantive due process is the classic, if temporary, achievement of judicial activism. The Roosevelt Court destroyed it out of respect for the democratic processes. Mr. Justice Black's "incorporation" ploy was calculated to forestall backsliding by equating the Fourteenth Amendment with the Bill of Rights. But the Bill of Rights, after all, is quite old fashioned. It does not cover many matters deemed crucial in our day, e.g., poverty. To fill this "gap" the Warren Court used "equal protection" as "actively" as the pre-Roosevelt Court had used "due process." Obviously inspired by the Black incorporation principle, the early Burger Court is doing to substantive equal protection what the Roosevelt Court did to substantive due process. A generation ago we called it a "return to the Constitution," now it is called strict construction. If in time the full Nixon Court succumbs to the magic of power and imposes *its* ideals upon the nation, some of us may find embarrassment in our quondam efforts to convince ourselves that judicial activism (it used to be called judicial supremacy) is a proper handmaiden of democracy.   J

984. Mendelson, Wallace. HUGO BLACK AND JUDICIAL DISCRETION. *Pol. Sci. Q. 1970 85(1): 17-39.* Supreme Court Justice Hugo Black embraced a philosophy contemptuous of judicial discretion and natural law, preferring to rely on vague absolutes. But absolutes tend to conflict with each other as much as do cautious discretions. Black would support one absolute in one case and another in the next. In his final years, Justice Black tended to reverse many of his earlier positions, a situation perhaps resulting from changes in the judicial composition of the court rather than an abrupt alteration of basic philosophy. Based on secondary sources; 79 notes.

V. L. Human

985. Meyer, Howard N. MOORFIELD STOREY AND THE FOURTEENTH AMENDMENT. *Crisis 1973 80(9): 299-302.* Offers a biography of Moorfield Storey (1845-1929), detailing his work with the National Association for the Advancement of Colored People to secure civil rights for blacks.   S

986. Miller, Ben R. THE PRESIDENCY AND SEPARATION OF POWERS. *Am. Bar Assoc. J. 1974 60(2): 195-197.* "President Nixon's assertion of executive privilege in the Watergate Tapes case is constitutionally sound."
                                                                                    J

987. Miller, Harry L. THE "RIGHT TO TREATMENT": CAN THE COURTS REHABILITATE AND CURE? *Public Interest 1977 (46): 96-118.* A constitutional "right to treatment" was enunciated in 1966 by Judge David Bazelon in *Rouse v. Cameron.* In the 10 years following this decision legal actions have been brought against state hospitals and youth facilities on the grounds that they offered only confinement and not therapeutic treatment. Advocates of right to treatment claim that state commitment laws implictly promise treatment as an exchange for liberty. Some judges have confined themselves to the specific issues before them, while others have taken a broad view and assumed effective control of state facilities. This broad interpretation

is unfortunate because lawyers and judges are often naive concerning medical matters. Their ability to make independent judgments from masses of data is questionable. Most of them are ignorant of the managerial problems of state institutions. Few of them are able to make sensible accommodations between the law and institutional reality.   S. Harrow

988. Moens, Gabriel. DIE FORMEN DES INNERSTAATLICHEN MIN-DERHEITENSCHUTZES [Forms of domestic minority guarantees]. *Europa Ethnica [Austria] 1975 32(1): 2-8.* US Supreme Court decisions on minority cases from 1886 to 1972 differ in their legal interpretation, either prohibiting discrimination on individual grounds or on the basis of the rights of groups to preserve their ethnological characteristics.

989. Monroe, Charles P. ADDRESSING TERRORISM IN THE UNITED STATES. *Ann. of the Am. Acad. of Pol. and Social Sci. 1982 (463): 141-148.* Terrorism presents a serious threat to democratic governments that must protect themselves without trampling individual rights. Federal Bureau of Investigation successes have shown that the US government can effectively deal with this threat while protecting the constitutional rights of citizens.   J

990. Montero, Anne M. FARADAY WOOD—THE REDS OR THE BLACKS? *New York Affairs 1975 2(3): 42-49.* "The Soviet Mission to the UN is about to move into new buildings constructed on a Riverdale site that in 1967 was part of the city's plans for scatter-site housing, killed by community opposition. The subsequent, unsuccessful challenge in federal court has grave implications for both housing policy and the 14th Amendment."   J

991. Moran, Felix F. FREE SPEECH, THE MILITARY, AND THE NATIONAL INTEREST. *Air U. Rev. 1980 31(4): 106-113.* Examines military application of First Amendment rights, maintaining that though they are the same as civilian rights, they are not absolute and cannot be used to endanger a service person's immediate unit or the national interest; 1950-80.

992. Morris, Jeffrey B. WHAT HEAVEN MUST BE LIKE: WILLIAM HOWARD TAFT AS CHIEF JUSTICE, 1921-30. *Supreme Court Hist. Soc. Y. 1983: 80-101.* William Howard Taft served as chief justice of the Supreme Court during 1921-30. In his career, Taft was president, state and federal judge, law professor at the University of Cincinnati and at Yale, governor of the Philippines, secretary of war, and several other public positions. The chief justiceship was the one job he wanted more than any other. While Taft is not the most respected of the chief justices, his vision of the position's duties set a precedent that still exists. 131 notes, 11 illus.   G. B. Childress

993. Moss, Larry E. FEDERAL WATER DEVELOPMENT: IMPERIAL EDICT OR FEDERAL-STATE PARTNERSHIP? *Publius 1979 9(1): 127-140.* Studies conditions in California, especially the balancing of wildlife, agricultural, recreational, and industrial needs for fresh water, which have made important the *California v. United States* (US, 1978) Supreme Court decision. This decision mandated a significant role to the states in the management of all water projects built or operated under the authority of the

Reclamation Act (US, 1902) and its amendments. Cooperative federalism has now been put in force, and the secretary of the interior must lead the Bureau of Reclamation into compliance. 16 notes.   R. V. Ritter

994.   Mounts, Gregory J. LABOR AND THE SUPREME COURT: SIG-NIFICANT DECISIONS OF 1977-78. *Monthly Labor Rev. 1979 102(1): 51-57.*

995.   Mounts, Gregory J. LABOR AND THE SUPREME COURT: SIG-NIFICANT DECISIONS OF 1979-80. *Monthly Labor Rev. 1981 104(4): 13-22.* Views recent Supreme Court decisions as a return to private sector emphasis insofar as a series of cases expanded the flexibility of private sector employers and unions while limiting that of public sector employers.

996.   Mounts, Gregory J. LABOR AND THE SUPREME COURT: SIG-NIFICANT DECISIONS OF 1978-79. *Monthly Labor Rev. 1980 103(1): 14-21.* Surveys the decisions of the term, emphasizing the Supreme Court's approval of voluntary efforts to eliminate the effects of discrimination, its rejection of NLRB attempts at balancing conflicting interests, and its strengthening of public employers' rights.

997.   Moynihan, Daniel Patrick. SOCIAL SCIENCE AND THE COURTS. *Public Interest 1979 54: 12-31.* At the beginning of the century, American legal scholars and jurists began to speak of the "science of law," and gradually social science has become prominent in American court proceedings and decisions. The usefulness of social science in the judicial process is limited because social science is basically concerned with predicting events, whereas law attempts to order these events, and social scientists are frequently caught up in politics and are rarely dispassionate. Also, the reliability of social science is shaky, as is the way it is used by judges. In the Supreme Court case of *Tilton* v. *Richardson* (US, 1971), which is the controlling decision concerning federal aid to church-related schools, the Court committed a number of "bloopers," because its efforts to base its decision on social science argument were "rigorous, but not rigorous enough."   S. Harrow

998.   Moynihan, Daniel Patrick. WHAT DO YOU DO WHEN THE SU-PREME COURT IS WRONG? *Public Interest 1979 (57): 3-24.* Often, the Supreme Court has been wrong about major constitutional issues. Two examples that are treated in detail are *Everson* v. *Board of Education* (US, 1947), which prohibits state aid to nonpublic schools, and *Gannett* v. *DePasqual* (US, 1979), which denies the public an independent constitutional right of access to pretrial judicial proceedings. Evidence shows how *Everson,* a wrong Supreme Court decision, has been undone by a "hierarchy of responses": debate, litigation, and legislation. The "predictive power" of the author's analysis (the "hierarchy of responses") will be tested by the *Gannett* case.   S. Harrow

999.   Murphy, Thomas P. RACE-BASE ACCOUNTING: ASSIGNING THE COSTS AND BENEFITS OF A RACIALLY MOTIVATED ANNEX-ATION. *Urban Affairs Q. 1978 14(2): 169-194.* To prevent black control in

1970, Richmond's city council annexed 23 square miles. Since 97% of the area's 50,000 residents were white, the city's black population declined from 52% to 42%. Notwithstanding the charge that Richmond had violated the 15th Amendment and the 1965 Voting Rights Act, the Supreme Court only used economic criteria in ruling against deannexation petitions. Criticizes the Court for using only quantifiable factors, permitting both sides to use suspect data and ignoring the economic interests of those annexed. Notes that the annexation resulted in blacks controlling a larger city when they came to power in 1977. 3 tables, fig., biblio.   L. N. Beecher

1000. Nathanson, Nathaniel L. THE COURT, THE CONSTITUTION, AND THE CHANGING OF THE GUARD. *Social Sci. 1973 48(2): 97-106.* A study of the changes of stance on constitutional questions as exhibited in US Supreme Court decisions, especially as they affect civil rights. Argues that the great decisions of the Warren Court "were revolutionary not because they created new values or denigrated old ones, but because they threatened to upset elements of our established order which persisted in defiance of our professed values." The present Court may be expected to present a very mixed profile in view of such cases.   R. V. Ritter

1001. Neier, Aryeh. THE FIRST AMENDMENT: FIRST IN IMPOR-TANCE. *Crisis 1975 82(9): 356-359.* Of all the constitutional rights, First Amendment rights are first in importance. Freedom of speech, press, worship, and assembly allow those who suffer grievances to call attention to their plight, to share their experiences with others, to organize, and to demand correction. There are foes on the right and the left but the civil rights movement of the 1960's demonstrated the effectiveness of the First Amendment.
                                                            A. G. Belles

1002. Neighbor, Howard D. THE CASE AGAINST NONPARTISAN-SHIP: A CHALLENGE FROM THE COURTS. *Natl. Civic Rev. 1977 66(9): 447-452.* Recent Supreme Court and lower court decisions on dilution of voting strength, and earlier rulings opening political parties to minority representation, challenged nonpartisanship reform in city government.   J/S

1003. Nicholson, Jeanne Bell and Stewart, Debra W. THE SUPREME COURT, ABORTION, AND STATE RESPONSE. *Publius 1978 8(1): 159-178.* In three separate decisions on 20 June 1977, the US Supreme Court established that nontherapeutic abortions are not a "fundamental right," and that state governments are not obliged to finance such abortions through taxation. These decisions opened the way, at the national level, for Health, Education, and Welfare Secretary Joseph Califano's implementation (4 August) of the Hyde Amendment—passed by Congress in 1976—which allows federal abortions funding only "if the life of the mother would be endangered if the fetus were carried to term." By autumn, 35 states were funding only such abortions; 12 states and the District of Columbia were paying for all abortions where financial need existed; and three states were paying for "medically necessary" abortions, a term equivalent in practice to elective abortions. Studies the results to date, and those foreseeable, of the shift of the abortion battle's focus from the courts to the political-legislative arena. Based on data from the Louis Harris Data Center, Chapel Hill, N.C., plus secondary sources; table, 2 fig., 23 notes.   L. W. Van Wyk

1004. Nikiforov, B. S. VERKHOVNYI SUD SShA: SMESHCHENIE VPRAVO? [The Supreme Court of the USA: A move to the right?]. *Sovetskoe Gosudarstvo i Pravo [USSR] 1978 (5): 107-113.* Describes the liberal period of the US Supreme Court (E. Warren's court, 1953-69), analyzes several Supreme Court decisions (in Burger's court), and shows that the Supreme Court has become more conservative. Discusses the constitutionality of capital punishment and the Supreme Court's decision concerning it in 1972 and civil rights of the accused and the rights of the police. Cites an article from the *Saturday Review* in which the editor concludes that a narrowing of constitutional guarantees has occurred and that each American now has less freedom. In essence, "Burger's Court" is aiding the displacement to the right of the political situation in America. Primary sources; 20 notes.   L. Kalinowski

1005. Noragon, Jack. CONGRESSIONAL REDISTRICTING AND POP-ULATION COMPOSITION, 1964-1970. *Midwest J. of Pol. Sci. 1972 16(2): 295-302.* By comparing the congressional districts of the 88th Congress (1963-64) with the districts of the 91st Congress (1969-70) in respect to the composition of their population, seeks to assess the effect of the "one man, one vote" rule of the Supreme Court. Evidence indicates that changes were not great and that more urban than suburban districts were created. 4 tables, 12 notes.   J. W. Thacker, Jr.

1006. Oakes, Jeannie. TRACKING AND ABILITY GROUPING IN AMERICAN SCHOOLS: SOME CONSTITUTIONAL QUESTIONS. *Teachers Coll. Record 1983 84(4): 801-819.* Because the practice of tracking or ability grouping tends to provide different educational experiences for different students and is relatively permanent and frequently haphazardly administered, it may be subject to legal challenge based on either the due process or equal protection clauses of the 14th Amendment. A court determination that tracking infringes on a fundamental interest or creates a suspect classification would require the government to prove a compelling need to maintain it. So far, however, the only successful challenges have been in cases where tracking produced racially identifiable groups in areas with a history of segregation. Based on court cases and secondary sources; 60 notes.   E. C. Bailey, Jr.

1007. O'Connor, Karen and Epstein, Lee. AMICUS CURIAE PARTICI-PATION IN U.S. SUPREME COURT LITIGATION: AN APPRAISAL OF HAKMAN'S "FOLKLORE." *Law & Soc. Rev. 1981-82 16(2): 311-320.* Discusses the use of *amicus curiae* in Supreme Court litigation by special interest groups since 1928. Nathan Hakman stated that contrary to belief the use of *amicus curiae* was not "a form of political action." However, a majority of the briefs involving use of the friend of the court approach are filed by groups such as minorities, women, and those representing such perennial issues as the death penalty, separation of church and state, and school desegregation and busing. These indicate a politically-oriented usage. Based on US Supreme Court records and other primary sources; 8 notes, 3 tables, appendix, ref.
                                                                N. A. Newhouse

1008. O'Connor, Karen and Epstein, Lee. THE RISE OF CONSERVA-
TIVE INTEREST GROUP LITIGATION. *J. of Pol. 1983 45(2): 479-489.*
While liberal participation in Supreme Court cases remained constant at 40%
of the cases, conservative participation tripled by 1980 from 9% in 1969. While
liberals sponsored 39% of the cases in which they participated, conservatives
sponsored only 2% and clearly preferred the *amicus curiae* role. Liberals
concentrated on civil rights and civil liberties issues; conservatives on economic
liberalism issues, manifesting interest in civil liberties cases only since 1976.
Criminal issues were not of great importance to either group. Conservatives
may have been motivated by the presence of conservative Justices Rehnquist
and Powell as well as greater general acceptance of conservatism. 4 illus., 4
notes, biblio.   A. W. Novitsky

1009. O'Connor, Karen and Epstein, Lee. SEX AND THE SUPREME
COURT: AN ANALYSIS OF JUDICIAL SUPPORT FOR GENDER-
BASED CLAIMS. *Social Sci. Q. 1983 64(2): 327-331.* Examines the voting
records of Supreme Court justices in cases in which litigants made claims of
sex discrimination; the court supported plaintiffs in sex discrimination cases
more often than plaintiffs in race discrimination cases.

1010. Oleszek, Walter J. HOUSE-SENATE RELATIONSHIPS: COMITY
AND CONFLICT. *Ann. of the Am. Acad. of Pol. and Social Sci. 1974 411:*
75-86. "Although equal in power, the national House and Senate differ in
more ways than they are similar. They differ in size, rules and procedures,
policy biases, customs and traditions, terms of office, constitutional responsibilities, constituencies and in numerous other ways. Moreover, each chamber is
jealous of its powers and prerogatives and generally suspicious of the other
body. Despite their differences, the two houses must still work together if
policy recommendations are to be enacted into law. Two principal legislative
devices serve to join senators and representatives together on matters of
common concern: conference committees and joint committees. In this analysis, two important aspects of conference procedure are explored: the conferee
selection process and the question of who wins in conference, the House or the
Senate. Joint committees, although used since the First Congress, are viewed
negatively by many members. Given both the variety and uses of joint
committees, it is worth identifying some of the factors which facilitate their
creation. Finally, two principal suggestions are offered to better facilitate
interhouse cooperation—more contact between respective party leaders of each
house and the development of parallel committee jurisdictions. Of course, the
goal of interhouse cooperation needs to be balanced against the requirement
that each house present and defend different and conflicting points of view on
the issues of the day."   J

1011. Oliver, Covey T. THE UNITED STATES AND THE WORLD.
Ann. of the Am. Acad. of Pol. and Social Sci. 1976 426: 166-197. Most experts
on America's dealings with other nations would agree that we have a unique,
complicated, energy-depleting system of law for allocating authority to govern
our official conduct offshore. The U.S. state and federal constitutions incorpo-
rate some version of separation of powers with checks and balances, requiring
the interrelated independence of 3 branches of government. At the constitu-

tional level, this system allocates action and commitment ability related to foreign affairs between the Executive and Legislative branches, but so far the courts have not ventured far into resolution of conflicts between them. The Constitution says the president has executive power and Congress does not have express, general power to legislate or manage in foreign affairs. It does not resolve the question of who is master in foreign policy. A number of problem cases influencing the shaping of our external relations are military policy, control of expenditures, and arms control and disarmament. The possibility of a transnational government, citizen participation in policy decisions, America's good faith in international agreements, and the constitutional revision for foreign affairs are also important questions concerning America and the world. And in this complex it may be that for the first time in the nation's history the people have to live with unrelieved separation of powers, while Congress increasingly asserts a will to participate in foreign affairs.   J

1012. O'Neil, Robert M. CREATIONISM, CURRICULUM, AND THE CONSTITUTION. *Acad.: Bull. of the AAUP 1982 68(2): 21-26.* There is legal difficulty in resolving the equal time issue as equal time laws are vulnerable on two broader grounds: 1)the possible breach of separation of church and state and 2)the possible stifling of free expression in the classroom.

1013. O'Neill, Timothy J. THE LANGUAGE OF EQUALITY IN A CONSTITUTIONAL ORDER. *Am. Pol. Sci. Rev. 1981 75(3): 626-635.* Like all languages, the language of American law can liberate or confine thinking. Its confining power is illustrated by the absence of the radical "group rights" claim in the *Bakke* litigation despite the prominence of that argument in the popular debate over affirmative discrimination. This absence establishes the limitations of the metaphor developed to give meaning to the concept "persons" in the equal protection context. While capable of investing the corporation with many of the attributes of "personhood" as defined by the 14th Amendment, the metaphor makes absurd the claim of a racial group to exercise rights or privileges distinct from those of its members. The restricted range of metaphorical thinking in law weakens the law's capacity to mediate struggles over social goals.   J/S

1014. O'Reilly, Kenneth. THE STAMLER CHALLENGE: CONGRESSIONAL INVESTIGATIVE POWER AND THE FIRST AMENDMENT. *Congressional Studies 1979 7(1): 57-72.* Starting in 1965, Dr. Jeremiah Stamler legally challenged the authority of the House Committee on Un-American Activities to subpoena him as a witness; reluctant witnesses before investigating committees must rely on personal interpretations of the Constitution rather than statutory guidelines to determine the extent of their First Amendment rights.

1015. Pace, David. LENOIR CHAMBERS OPPOSES MASSIVE RESISTANCE: AN EDITOR AGAINST VIRGINIA'S DEMOCRATIC ORGANIZATION, 1955-1959. *Virginia Mag. of Hist. and Biog. 1974 82(4): 415-429.* The Supreme Court's 1954 decision outlawing racial segregation in public schools led to a campaign in Virginia to prevent implementation of the decision. Lenoir Chambers, editor of the *Norfolk Virginian-Pilot,* waged an editorial struggle against the plan backed by Senator Harry F. Byrd to close schools before accepting integration. Chambers' position resulted not from racial liberalism but from a traditional respect for law and order. Based on primary sources; photo, 34 notes.   R. F. Oaks

1016.   Pacheco, Donald N. ALL THE CONSTITUTIONAL PROTECTION YOU CAN BUY. *J. of Intergroup Relations 1974 3(3): 31-35.* Equal justice for ethnic minorities and low-income groups does not currently exist in America.   S

1017.   Packer, Herbert L. THE PORNOGRAPHY CAPER. *Commentary 1971 51(2): 72-77.* A critical assessment of behavioral studies supporting the *President's Commission Report on Obscenity and Pornography* (New York: Random House, 1971).   S

1018.   Padgett, George E. THE VOTING RECORD OF JUSTICE STEWART ON FIRST AMENDMENT CASES. *Journalism Q. 1982 59(4): 554-559.* Retired Supreme Court Justice Potter Stewart was one of the stronger judicial supporters of First Amendment rights on the high court and consistently voted to protect the freedom of the press. Originally appointed to the Supreme Court by President Eisenhower in 1958, Stewart more often than not sided on First Amendment questions with the more liberal members of the court. He believed strongly in the special status of the press as protected by the Constitution, supported the rights of libeled individuals to seek compensation for damages, and believed that only hard-core pornography exceeded the normal bounds of free expression and could be limited. Primary sources; 27 notes.   L. J. Klass

1019.   Pei, Mario. THE CASE FOR A CONSTITUTIONAL CONVEN-TION. *Modern Age 1967/68 12(1): 8-13.* Argues from a conservative view-point the need for a national constitutional convention that would alter the US Constitution in a manner suitable to a modern age society. Contends that current dilemmas in areas ranging from education to taxation stem from basic constitutional flaws and subsequent interpretations. Finds fault with such a mechanism as the electoral college and the method of selecting US Supreme Court justices. Constitutional amendments have not proven satisfactory, yet state conventions have worked relatively well. Suggests that a never-attempted national convention is the only logical way to allow the United States to move forward more efficiently and more democratically. He urges that the conven-tion delegates be chosen directly by each state's voters to insure that the people's voice will be heard. Concludes by suggesting that a political party sponsor such a gathering in the interests of democracy.   M. J. Barach

1020.   Pember, Don R. THE "PENTAGON PAPERS" DECISION: MORE QUESTIONS THAN ANSWERS. *Journalism Q. 1971 48(3): 403-411.* The *New York Times Company* v. *United States* and *United States* v. *The Washington Post Company* (both US, 1971) developed when articles based on "top secret" documents were published. The newspapers argued that prior restraint is prohibited by the First Amendment. An earlier Supreme Court had declared in *Near* v. *Minnesota* (1931) that prior restraint protection was not absolute. The legal and political impact must be determined in the future. Primary and secondary sources; 57 notes.   K. J. Puffer

1021. Peterson, Walfred H. CONFUSION CONFOUNDED: GOVERN-MENT AID TO PRIVATE EDUCATION IN THE BURGER COURT. *Christian Scholar's Rev. 1980 9(3): 195-214.* Examines conflicting interpretations of Supreme Court justices on the meaning of the First Amendment when they have considered public aid to private schools with religious affiliations; 1970's.

1022. Peterson, Walfred H. THE THWARTED OPPORTUNITY FOR JUDICIAL ACTIVISM IN CHURCH-STATE RELATIONS: SEPARATION AND ACCOMMODATION IN PRECARIOUS BALANCE. *J. of Church and State 1980 22(3): 437-458.* Judicial activism on the part of the Supreme Court members *can* be a part of an activist effort to alter long-established constitutional policy. The Burger court's opinions on federal and state aid to church-related schools and colleges show how this occurs; 1965-75. Based on court decisions; 3 charts, 43 notes.   E. E. Eminhizer

1023. Pfeffer, Leo. THE CURRENT STATE OF THE LAW IN THE UNITED STATES AND THE SEPARATIONIST AGENDA. *Ann. of the Am. Acad. of Pol. and Social Sci. 1979 (446): 1-9.* The Religion Clauses of the First Amendment are aimed at securing both religious freedom and the separation of church and state. The former forbids limitation not shown to be justified by a compelling government interest; the latter prohibits laws failing to meet the purpose-effect-entanglement test. On the whole the Supreme Court has been faithful to the mandate imposed by the clauses and interpreted and applied by the judiciary. Although it has been urged that there are or may be instances in which freedom might demand what church-state separation forbids or vice versa, the Court has not yet been faced with any case requiring it to make a choice. While not fully satisfied with the Court's resolution of conflicts between church and state, particularly in the area of financing religious school operations or refusing to finance abortions for the economically underprivileged, the separationist agenda is basically the defense of present constitutional principles and the assurance of their faithful application by the executive and legislative branches of government.   J

1024. Pfeffer, Leo. UNEASY TRINITY: CHURCH, STATE, AND CONSTITUTION. *Civil Liberties Rev. 1975 2(1): 138-161.* Overview of the debate over the separation of church and state and constitutional issues brought into play, 1930's-70's; discusses tax write-offs for parochial schools, prayer in the classroom, educational requirements for parochial schools, and religious freedom.

1025. Pickering, John W. A BEHAVIORAL ANALYSIS OF THE 1965 TERM OF THE UNITED STATES SUPREME COURT. *Southern Q. 1969 7(3): 323.* Examines the blocs formed by the individual attitudes of the justices of the 1965 term of the Earl Warren court in cases involving civil liberties and economics. Furthers understanding of legal methodology of behavioralism.

Members of the court are categorized in terms of typal or voting blocs and an index is provided to determine the rate of individual power of the justices by means of a cases won and lost ratio. Results are inconclusive. 24 notes.

R. W. Dubay

1026. Pilling, Arnold R. NATIVE AMERICAN RELIGIOUS RIGHTS: CONSTITUTIONAL CONSIDERATIONS. *Indian Hist. 1979 12(1): 13-19.* General overview of Supreme Court rulings on religious liberty (under the 1st amendment) is applied to the case of the Eight Mile-Blue Creek land of California containing Indians' sacred areas, where the US Forest Service proposed road construction and logging, 1975.

1027. Pilpel, Harriet F. and Parsons, Marjorie T. DIRTY BUSINESS IN COURT. *Civil Liberties R. 1974 1(4): 30-41.* "The real target is not obscenity at all, but unpopular, dissident, irreverent, or satirical expression unsettling to current complacencies." J

1028. Pollock, Paul K. THE POLITICAL SCIENTIST AND SUPREME COURT HISTORY. *Polity 1972 5(2): 260-267.* A review article of Robert J. Steamer's *The Supreme Court in Crisis* (Amherst: U. of Massachusetts Press, 1971) and Gerald Garvey's *Constitutional Bricolage* (Princeton: Princeton U. Press, 1971). The two books are very dissimilar in structure, scope, and approach. Steamer's is a conventional narrative of the Supreme Court's history. Garvey's is not strictly a judicial history; rather he has "employed interdisciplinary tools to construct a grand theory of law and society," applying his theory to the Court's history. 6 notes. E. P. Stickney

1029. Potts, Margaret H. JUSTICE FRANK MURPHY: A REEXAMINATION. *Supreme Court Hist. Soc. Y. 1982: 57-65.* Frank Murphy served on the Supreme Court during 1940-49 and was considered by his admirers as the "Conscience of the Court." Yet others have criticized his unorthodox approach to law and contended that he knew nothing of legal analysis. Four of his opinions dispel these allegations and demonstrate that Murphy relied on legal precedent and solid reasoning. He had a flair for language, which appealed to emotion, and delivered careful decisions. Based primarily on Murphy's Supreme Court decisions; 41 notes, 3 illus. G. B. Childress

1030. Prettyman, E. Barrett, Jr. *FIKES V. ALABAMA:* THE UNCONSTITUTIONAL CONVICTION OF "BABY." *Supreme Court Hist. Soc. Y. 1978: 68-76.* In *Fikes* v. *Alabama,* the Supreme Court in 1957 reversed William Earl Fikes's burglary conviction on the grounds that his confession of the 1953 burglary in Selma, Alabama, was obtained unconstitutionally; in 1975 Fikes was released from prison after serving 22 years on a rape conviction to which he had also confessed.

1031. Priddy, Laurance L. "SAVE OUR NEIGHBORHOOD SCHOOLS!!" *Crisis 1975 82(4): 115-117.* A community group of parents met to discuss busing. The pastor of the church in which they were meeting prayed that busing was an "unworkable, immoral, and satanic scheme" to destroy neighborhood schools. Some parents called for a boycott of the schools, while others advocated impromptu private schools. Everyone supported a Constitutional amendment against busing. All of these tactics were considered justified in order to preserve the neighborhood school. The parents involved denied that they were racist.   A. G. Belles

1032. Pritchett, C. Herman. CONGRESS AND ARTICLE 5 CONVEN-TIONS. *Western Pol. Q. 1982 35(2): 222-227.* Deals with the role and powers of Congress in connection with amendment of the Constitution by the convention process under Article 5. The original intention of the Framers of the Constitution is difficult or impossible to determine, and there is no reason to interpret Article 5 as excluding Congress from the exercise of discretion in setting up conventions to the request of two-thirds of the state legislatures. Legislation which Congress has considered, though not adopted, assumes that Congress can control the calling of conventions and limit the proposals they can consider, thus preventing the possibility of a "runaway" convention.
                                                                                                  J/S

1033. Pritchett, C. Herman. [SUPREME COURT VOTING]. *Social Sci. Q. 1970 50(4): 972-984.*
TEN YEARS OF SUPREME COURT VOTING, *pp. 972-982.* Describes in quantitative terms the voting behavior of the justices of the Supreme Court, 1931-40, usually termed "bloc analysis." Each justice can be located on a continuum ranging from the extreme left to the extreme right of the court, with relatively fixed positions on this continuum and a high rate of agreement with the justices closest to him. The Court was more homogeneous in the first half of the decade than in the latter half. Reprinted from *Southwestern Social Sci. Q.* 1943 24(1); 13 tables, 6 notes.
"TEN YEARS OF SUPREME COURT VOTING": A COMMENT IN RETROSPECT, *pp. 983-984.* The significance is in "the basic conception of the judiciary as a participant in the political process, subject to study within the same frame of reference as other governmental institutions, and thus in helping to restore public law... to a meaningful place in the discipline."   R. V. Ritter

1034. Rabkin, Jeremy. THE CHARISMATIC CONSTITUTION. *Public Interest 1983 (73): 142-147.* Reviews Aryeh Neier's *Only Judgment: The Limits of Litigation in Social Change* (1982), Arthur Selwyn Miller's *Toward Increased Judicial Activism: The Political Role of the Supreme Court* (1982), Philip Bobbitt's *Constitutional Fate: Theory of the Constitution* (1982), and Michael J. Perry's *The Constitution, the Courts, and Human Rights: An Inquiry into the Legitimacy of Constitutional Policymaking by the Judiciary* (1982). These books chronicle the judicial arrogance of the late 20th century that ignores the Constitution in favor of programs of social change.
                                                                                                  R. Grove

1035. Ragsdale, J. Donald. LAST TANGO IN PARIS, ET AL. V. THE SUPREME COURT: THE CURRENT STATE OF OBSCENITY LAW. *Q. J. of Speech 1975 61(3): 279-289.* The Supreme Court has so far failed to define obscenity and pornography and to let pass laws that would lead to censorship of X-rated films (1970's).

1036. Rathjen, Gregory J. and Spaeth, Harold J. DENIAL OF ACCESS AND IDEOLOGICAL PREFERENCES: AN ANALYSIS OF THE VOTING BEHAVIOR OF THE BURGER COURT JUSTICES, 1969-1976. *Western Pol. Q. 1983 36(1): 71-87.* Previous research by the authors delineated the policy considerations that caused the individual members of the Burger Court to vote to open and close access to the federal courts. An additional question—whether the denial of access produces a liberal or conservative effect on the merits of the underlying controversy—is investigated by analyzing cases in which the court denied the plaintiff access. Access outcomes are a function of the ideological preferences of the individual justices.   J/S

1037. Raymond, John M. and Frischholz, Barbara J. LAWYERS WHO ESTABLISHED INTERNATIONAL LAW IN THE UNITED STATES, 1776-1914. *Am. J. of Int. Law 1982 76(4): 802-829.* American lawyers from all areas of the law made invaluable contributions to the sound foundation of international law and a Supreme Court decision declared that international law be a part of our law; the 20th century has seen the publication of many articles, books, and textbooks on the subject as well as the founding of the American Society of International Law.

1038. Reardan, Nancy B. REVERSAL OF HISTORICAL DISCRIMINATION: IS IT CONSTITUTIONAL? *Crisis 1977 84(10): 459-462.* Charges that programs of affirmative action and preferential treatment are unconstitutional acts of reverse discrimination rest on assumptions which fail to analyze the past and present situations which require remedial treatment. The effects of centuries of discrimination against blacks, women, and minorities cannot be corrected by declarations, court decisions, and laws which have been in effect for less than 25 years. Whites are not excluded or barred simply because blacks or women are given boosts. Affirmative action certainly is not a program designed to establish or perpetuate discrimination, prejudice, or racism.
A. G. Belles

1039. Regan, Richard J. SUPREME COURT ROUNDUP: 1980 TERM. *Thought 1981 56(223): 491-502.* Reviews 1980 Supreme Court decisions, focusing on two areas of civil liberties: religion and abortion, and criminal law. In cases concerning claims to freedom of religious exercise, the court decided that legality refers to the honesty of the conviction, not the quality of the reasoning process leading to such conviction. Where public law does not prohibit specific options of exercising religious freedom, according preference to religious believers fulfills the government's obligation to be neutral in the face of religious differences. After deciding last term that federal funds for abortions can be restricted, the court this term upheld a statute requiring physicians to notify parents before performing abortions on minors. In the area of criminal justice, decisions split evenly favoring government and defendants regarding the constitutionality of searches and seizures. Based on published Supreme Court decisions; 59 notes, table.   R. D. Rahmes

1040. Reid, Herbert O., Sr. and Foster-Davis, Frankie. STATE OF THE ART: THE LAW AND EDUCATION SINCE 1954. *J. of Negro Educ. 1983 52(3): 234-249.* During 1954-71, the Supreme Court supported school desegregation and ordered broad remedies to end segregation, but since 1973 its emphasis on the intent rather than the result of school-board policies, as well as the court's limited remedies to segregation, have slowed progress. Despite passage of the Civil Rights Act of 1964, since 1974 Congress has limited desegregation efforts, although it has refused to pass extreme segregationist proposals. The executive branch worked for desegregation in the 1960's, slowed its activities in the 1970's, and since 1981 has opposed desegregation. Based on Supreme Court decisions; 81 notes.   R. G. Sherer

1041.   Reitman, Alan. FREEDOM OF INFORMATION AND PRIVACY: THE CIVIL LIBERTARIAN'S DILEMMA. *Am. Archivist 1975 38(4): 501-508.* Describes some of the conflicts between the need for freedom of information, and protection of privacy, constitutional rights which are protected by the Freedom of Information Act (1966) and the Privacy Act (1974). Enumerates four problem areas noted by the American Civil Liberties Union in its efforts to protect civil liberties, and postulates guidelines for resolving the conflicts. Note.   J. A. Benson

1042.   Relyea, Harold C. EXTENDING THE FREEDOM OF INFORMA-TION CONCEPT. *Presidential Studies Q. 1978 8(1): 96-98.* Discusses the necessity of protecting "the people's right to know" in light of recent Watergate disclosures. The concept of an informed citizenry is confirmed by the First Amendment and the Freedom of Information Act (US, 1974). Current safeguards are inadequate to ensure access to documents of public officials. Suggests needed legislation and describes a new role for the National Archives and Records Service as manager of all Federal Government information policy.   S. C. Strom

1043.   Rigaux, François. L'ÉLABORATION D'UN "RIGHT OF PRIVA-CY" PAR LA JURISPRUDENCE AMÉRICAINE [The elaboration of a right of privacy by American case law]. *Rev. Int. de Droit Comparé [France] 1980 32(4): 701-730.* A comprehensive study of the right of privacy in US law through an analysis of legal doctrine and US Supreme Court decisions; 1886-1980.

1044.   Rioch, Margaret J. IN MEMORIAM: ABE FORTAS. *Psychiatry 1983 46(1): 83-86.* Eulogizes former Supreme Court Associate Justice Abe Fortas (d. 1982) and celebrates his abilities to merge the fields of psychiatry and law, as well as his role as trustee of the William Alanson White Psychiatric Foundation, publisher of *Psychiatry* journal.

1045.   Robbins, J. C. DECIDING FIRST AMENDMENT CASES. *Journal-ism Q. 1972 49(2): 263-270.* Discusses the current inadequacy of definition of the First Amendment to the US Constitution, particularly as it pertains to freedom of the press issues (1963-66).

1046.   Roberts, Sylvia. EQUALITY OF OPPORTUNITY IN HIGHER EDUCATION: IMPACT OF CONTRACT COMPLIANCE AND THE EQUAL RIGHTS AMENDMENT. *Liberal Educ. 1973 59(2): 202-217.* Summarizes evidence of discrimination against women, especially in hiring, by institutions of higher education, the development of legal precedents and legislation, and the constitutional amendment aimed at correcting these abuses. Argues the advantages for institutions and plaintiffs alike in reform through voluntary compliance. Primary and secondary sources; 19 notes.

W. H. Ahern

1047. Robinson, D. L. PRESIDENTIAL AUTOCRACY AND THE RULE OF LAW. *Worldview 1973 16(3): 5-12.* Argues the existence of autocracy in the formulation of foreign policy in the presidency and Executive Branch in the 1970's, including issues in Constitutional law.

1048. Rodgers, Harrell R., Jr. CENSORSHIP CAMPAIGNS IN EIGHTEEN CITIES: AN IMPACT ANALYSIS. *Am. Pol. Q. 1974 2(4): 371-392.* Primarily examines the impact of urban censorship campaigns during 1967-68 on the effectiveness of US Supreme Court decisions on obscenity laws which protected the "right of newsdealers to sell and the public to buy certain types of publications."

S

1049. Rodgers, Raymond S. ABSOLUTISM AND NATURAL LAW ARGUMENT: WILLIAM O. DOUGLAS ON FREEDOM OF EXPRESSION. *Southern Speech Communication J. 1982 48(1): 22-37.* William O. Douglas's 1st Amendment opinions show that, although Douglas has been characterized as an "absolutist," his policy positions provided something less than absolute freedom to communicate but did reveal an absolutism that was a reliance on "absolute philosophies and immutable canons" for rhetorical means to generalized policy orientations.

1050. Rogers, Raymond S. and Lujan, Phillip. NATURAL LAW, SANTA CLARA, AND THE SUPREME COURT. *J. of Ethnic Studies 1981 9(3): 71-77.* The case of *Santa Clara Pueblo* v. *Martinez* (US, 1977), focusing on a 1939 Pueblo tribal ordinance barring tribal membership to children of female members who married nonmembers brought into conflict two fundamental theories of self-evident natural law: that of a sovereign tribe to determine its own membership, and the 14th-Amendment guarantee of equal protection of the law embodied in the Indian Civil Rights Act (US, 1968). Consideration of Hans Kelsen's distinction between two normative systems, the static and the dynamic, shows that Native Americans, despite the trappings of a positive legal order, see their own normative system as static. The Supreme Court's upholding of the Pueblo ordinance gives rise to meaningful implications for the future of the Bill of Rights. Based on court briefs of the litigants and amici curiae; 21 notes.

G. J. Bobango

1051. Rogge, O. John. THE RIGHT TO KNOW. *Am. Scholar 1972 41(4): 643-659.* Traces the current status of the right to know, as guaranteed under the First Amendment of the US Constitution. "Despite the victories of the *New York Times* and the *Washington Post* in the Supreme Court for First Amendment freedom of the press, and despite the gains, such as they are, under the Freedom of Information Act, we, the people, still have far to go for enough information to make up our minds and to vote intelligently on the larger issues that confront our country."

F. F. Harling

1052. Romero, Patricia. A LOOK AT SUPREME COURT JUSTICE WILLIAM O. DOUGLAS. *Negro Hist. Bull. 1966 29(6): 129-130, 137.* Discusses William O. Douglas' career on the Supreme Court beginning in 1939, and his role in upholding civil rights, especially as they pertain to blacks.   S

1053. Rooks, James E., Jr. "THE GREAT AND INESTIMABLE PRIVILEGE": THE AMERICAN CRIMINAL JURY. *Current Hist. 1976 70(417): 261-264, 274.* Discusses the constitutional basis for juries (5th, 6th, 7th Constitutional Amendments), the nature of juries, and the 7.4% of crimes that have gone to jury trial since 1945.

1054. Roper, Robert T. THE GAG ORDER: ASPHYXIATING THE FIRST AMENDMENT. *Western Pol. Q. 1981 34(3): 372-388.* Discusses the historic US Supreme Court decision that prohibits the enforcement of Gag Orders, except as a last resort then tests some of the Court's assumptions in that decision through a quasi-experimental research design. After considering and rejecting various research approaches used by others to study jury decisionmaking, jury-simulation was determined to be the most effective way to test these hypotheses. The findings indicate that where conventional safeguards are ineffective at precluding any impact of pretrial publicity, the prejudicial effect that most people anticipate of low-level pretrial publicity does not materialize.   J/S

1055. Rosenthal, Albert J. THE CONSTITUTION AND CAMPAIGN FINANCE REGULATION AFTER BUCKLEY V. VALEO. *Ann. of the Am. Acad. of Pol. and Social Sci. 1976 425: 124-133.* In a decision virtually unprecedented in scope, the Supreme Court, in *Buckley* v. *Valeo*, decided January 30, 1976, has ruled on a wide range of constitutional questions generated by federal campaign finance reform legislation. In brief, limitations on contributions, reporting and disclosure requirements, and public financing of campaigns have been upheld as at least constitutional on their face, although the door is still open to attacks based on specific evidentiary showings of unconstitutional effects in particular situations. Limitations on expenditures— independently made on behalf of candidates, by candidates themselves out of their own funds, or in the course of the candidates' campaigns—have all been held unconstitutional, as infringing upon rights under the First Amendment. The choices available for future legislative action, both federal and state, are henceforth likely to be limited in the light of the constraints to be found in the holdings and implications of this case.   J

1056. Ross, James F. A NATURAL RIGHTS BASIS FOR SUBSTANTIVE DUE PROCESS OF LAW IN U.S. JURISPRUDENCE. *Universal Human Rights 1980 2(2): 61-79.* Citing many cases, uses a mirror image of traditional due process analysis to demonstrate the place of natural basic moral liberty in constitutional law.

1057. Rossum, Ralph A. AMELIORATIVE RACIAL PREFERENCE AND THE FOURTEENTH AMENDMENT: SOME CONSTITUTIONAL PROBLEMS. *J. of Pol. 1976 38(2): 346-366.* Analyzes the problem of ameliorative racial preference. Uses the *DeFunis* v. *Odegaard* preferential admission case to explore the issues related to the Equal Protection Clause of the 14th Amendment. 82 notes.   R. V. Ritter

1058. Rotfeld, Herbert J. REGULATION OF THE FREE: ADVERTIS-ING AND THE FIRST AMENDMENT. *Policy Studies Rev. 1983 2(3):* 474-483. Discusses the relationships between advertising and mass communications and the ramifications of Supreme Court rulings since 1942 regarding regulation of certain types of advertising.

1059. Rothman, David J. DECARCERATING PRISONERS AND PA-TIENTS. *Civil Liberties R. 1973 1(1): 8-30.* The efforts of prisoners'-rights and right-to-treatment advocates are at last bearing fruit. But their strategies for securing the basic constitutional rights of inmates can carry some unintended consequences: paradoxically, reforming the institutions may block genuine rehabilitation.   J

1060. Rowland, C. K. and Carp, Robert A. A LONGITUDINAL STUDY OF PARTY EFFECTS ON FEDERAL DISTRICT COURT POLICY PROPENSITIES. *Am. J. of Pol. Sci. 1980 24(2): 291-305.* Comparison with the effects of party differences on congressional voting suggests that party-related liberalism or conservatism on the federal district courts may vary over time. The proposition that partisan differences in district courts will increase during periods of Supreme Court ambiguity is tested by correlating party preference to civil liberalism for each year from 1960 to 1976. The finding that party effects increased dramatically after 1968 offers some support for the ambiguity proposition. However, the pattern of increased party-related differences suggests that these differences may also be influenced by issue evolution and by change in presidential party. Future research is needed to clarify the relative effects of presidential party change, issue evolution, and Supreme Court ambiguity on the expression of federal district judges' partisan differences. 2 fig., biblio., appendix.   J

1061. Rusco, Elmer R. THE ORGANIZATION OF THE TE-MOAK BANDS OF WESTERN SHOSHONE. *Nevada Hist. Soc. Q. 1982 25(3):* 175-196. Primarily because of insistence from Commissioner John Collier, of the Bureau of Indian Affairs, New Deal policymakers of the 1930's broke new ground in federal relations with Indians. Collier also initiated policies leading to greater recognition and authority for Indian tribal governments. Among the Te-Moak bands of the Western Shoshoni, tribal governance was revived; this new lease on life resulted from power vested in the native government by a constitution and by-laws that were federally approved in 1938. Based on US National Archives material, principally RG 75 files, and secondary works; 53 notes.   H. T. Lovin

1062. Sanders, Wayne. THE FIRST AMENDMENT AND THE GOV-ERNMENT WORKPLACE: HAS THE CONSTITUTION FALLEN DOWN ON THE JOB? *Western J. of Speech Communication 1983 47(3):* 253-276. Examines the changes in 1st Amendment protection of free speech among public employees after the landmark Supreme Court decision in

Pickering v. *Board of Education* (US, 1968) and the assumptions about organizational communication that support those changes.

1063. Sanders, Wayne. FREE SPEECH FOR THE PRIVATE EMPLOY-EE: WILL STATE ACTION RULINGS BRING THE CONSTITUTION TO THE WORKPLACE? *Southern Speech Communication J. 1981 46(4): 397-410.* Discusses whether or not private sector employees should have First Amendment free speech protections at the workplace by presenting "a rationale for free speech in private organizations, a review of free speech cases argued on state action grounds, and an assessment of the effectiveness of the state action strategy in seeking free speech protection"; 1968-80.

1064. Sarat, Austin. CONSTITUTIONALISM AND AMERICAN POLITICS. *Polity 1979 11(4): 588-603.* A review of: Alexander Bickel, *The Morality of Consent* (New Haven: Yale U. Pr., 1975), Stephen Wasby, *Continuity and Change: From the Warren Court to the Burger Court* (Pacific Palisades, Calif.: Goodyear, 1976), Frank Sorauf, *The Wall of Separation* (Princeton: Princeton U. Pr., 1976), and Howard Ball, *The Vision and the Dream of Justice Hugo L. Black* (University, Alabama: U. of Alabama Pr., 1975). These titles explore the implications of the Constitution for American life. The problem becomes complex when one realizes the polarities which may arise by examining different interpretations of the meaning and nature of constitutionalism. 15 notes.   R. V. Ritter

1065. Schaefer, David L. FEDERALISM AND THE FIRST AMENDMENT. *Publius 1973 3(1): 31-55.* Discusses political scientist George Anastaplo's legal attitudes toward the relationship between federalism, freedom of speech, civil liberties, and states' rights implied in the First Amendment of the Constitution, 1971.

1066. Schey, Peter A. UNNAMED WITNESS NUMBER 1: NOW ATTENDING THE TEXAS PUBLIC SCHOOLS. *Migration Today 1982 10(5): 22-27.* The Supreme Court on 15 June 1982 ruled that the Texas statute limiting school admission to legal residents violated the Equal Protection Clause of the 14th Amendment; the decision was the result of the consolidated cases of *Plyler* v. *Doe* and *Texas* v. *Certain Named and Unnamed Alien Undocumented Children.*

1067. Schlafly, Phyllis. ELECTION "REFORM" AND YOUR RIGHT TO VOTE. *Daughters of the Am. Revolution Mag. 1977 111(10): 1000-1003.* Questions 1) a proposed constitutional amendment to abolish the electoral college and substitute direct popular election of the President and Vice President; 2) an instant voter registration plan; 3) government financing of Congressional elections; and 4) repeal of the Hatch Act.

1068. Schlup, Leonard. PHILOSOPHICAL CONSERVATIVE: PORTER JAMES MC CUMBER AND POLITICAL REFORM. *North Dakota Hist. 1978 45(3): 16-21.* A conservative Republican senator from North Dakota, Porter James McCumber was the product of the political machine of Alexander John McKenzie. Serving in the US Senate during 1898-1922, McCumber, despite his conservative beliefs and those of his Party, voted for such reforms as women's suffrage and the direct election of senators. He deeply believed in voting according to the desires of his constituents even if taking their position violated his own convictions. McCumber was a loyal party stalwart, supporting the "Old Guard" of the GOP during the factional battles with Theodore Roosevelt and the "Bull Moosers." He bitterly attacked Roosevelt for the latter's defection from Republican Party ranks. In his political philosophy McCumber favored gradual change in accordance with the Constitution.

N. Lederer

1069. Schlup, Leonard. PRESIDENTIAL DISABILITY: THE CASE OF CLEVELAND AND STEVENSON. *Presidential Studies Q. 1979 9(3): 303-310.* Discusses the lack of a systematic means for the transfer of power from president to vice-president in emergencies until the 25th Amendment was passed in 1967, using President Grover Cleveland and his Vice-President Adlai E. Stevenson in 1893 as an example.

1070. Scott, John Anthony. *LOEWEN V. TURNIPSEED:* A LANDMARK CASE. *AHA Newsletter 1980 18(7): 7-8.* Provides the background to *Loewen v. Turnipseed* (US, 1980), in which a federal district court ruled in favor of the plaintiffs who argued that James W. Loewen and Charles Sallis's *Mississippi: Conflict and Change,* a ninth-grade history text, should be placed on the state-approved list of textbooks, based on the 14th Amendment, after being rejected as too controversial and racially oriented by a white majority State Purchasing Board in 1974.

1071. Seddig, Robert G. TOWARD A POLITICAL JURISPRUDENCE: RECENT WRITING IN PUBLIC LAW. *Am. J. of Pol. Sci. 1973 17(2): 441-456.* Reviews six books dealing with political jurisprudence: David F. Forte's *The Supreme Court in American Politics: Judicial Activism vs. Judicial Restraint* (1972), Sheldon Goldman and Thomas P. Jahnige's *The Federal Courts as a Political System* (1971), Walter F. Murphy and Joseph Tananhaus' *The Study of Public Law* (1972), John R. Schmidhauser and Larry L. Berg's *The Supreme Court and Congress: Conflict and Interaction, 1945-1968* (1972), Robert Scigliano's *The Supreme Court and the Presidency* (1971), and Robert J. Steamer's *The Supreme Court in Crisis: A History of Conflict* (1971). These books explore the concern of political scientists with judges and the courts which participate so powerfully in political processes. 67 notes.

V. L. Human

1072. Segal, Jeffrey A. PREDICTING SUPREME COURT CASES PRO-BABILISTICALLY: THE SEARCH AND SEIZURE CASES, 1962-1981. *Am. Pol. Sci. Rev. 1984 78(4): 891-900.* The overwhelming consensus of 4th Amendment scholars is that the Supreme Court's search and seizure cases are a mess. The confusion arises from the manner in which the cases were studied, not from the decisions themselves. A legal model with variables that measure the prior justification of the search, the nature of the intrusion, and a few mitigating circumstances is used to explain the court's decisions on the reasonableness of a given search or seizure. The parameters are estimated through probit. The results show that the search and seizure cases are much more ordered than has commonly been believed. Virtually all of the estimates are as expected. Additionally, the court is shown to act more favorably toward the federal government than toward the states. Preliminary analysis suggests that the model has predictive as well as explanatory value.   J

1073. Semerjian, Evan Y. THE RIGHT OF CONFRONTATION. Am. Bar Assoc. J. 1969 55(2): 152-156. A 1957 Supreme Court decision gives strong indication that it is unconstitutional to deny an accused access to prior statements of witnesses who testify against him.   J

1074. Shanks, Hershel. EQUAL EDUCATION AND THE LAW. Am. Scholar 1970 39(2): 255-269. Studies the legal issues involved in the application of the Fourteenth Amendment's "equal opportunity" clause to public education. In the McInnis v. Ogilvie (US, 1969) case filed in the Federal District Court in Chicago, the variations in per student expenditures in different school districts was challenged as being in violation of the "equal opportunity" clause. The court found sufficient justification to satisfy constitutional requirements. Although the decision was upheld by the US Supreme Court, there is evidence that a less broadly applied case might get a different decision. The question still remains unanswered, whether the state has an obligation to provide an equal education to its children.   R. V. Ritter

1075. Shapiro, Herbert. THE BAKKE DECISION: ILLUSION AND RE-ALITY IN THE SUPREME COURT. Crisis 1979 86(2): 62-66. The Supreme Court has returned to the spirit behind the Plessy decision. The opinion of Justice Lewis F. Powell in the Bakke case epitomizes an unreal view of American life and law. Blacks can no longer look to the 14th Amendment to guarantee their struggle for equality. Segregation, ghettos, unemployment, poverty, and unequal opportunity must be solved in a passive manner since the Court has viewed positive remedies as violations of the Constitution. The decision lacks social responsibility and an accurate view of life in America today.   A. G. Belles

1076. Sharp, Allen. SOCIAL SECURITY DISABILITY CASES. Am. Bar Assoc. J. 1969 55(2): 141-143. The Supreme Court's 1968 opinion in Hopkins v. Cohen shows the need for competent counsel for claimants who apply for disability benefits under Social Security.   J

1077. Shattuck, John. NATIONAL SECURITY A DECADE AFTER WATERGATE. Democracy 1983 3(1): 56-71. Chronicles the erosion of constitutional rights for reasons of national security since 1945, focusing on the period 1972-82.

1078. Shenfield, Arthur. MR. JUSTICE STEVENS AND THE ZEIT-GEIST. Modern Age 1979 23(2): 130-139. On 26 June 1976 the Supreme Court decided in favor of the claimants in the consolidated cases of McCary and Gonzales v. Runyon and the Fairfax-Brewster School. Wholly private and commercially operated, these schools refused to admit the claimants solely because they were Negroes. John Paul Stevens joined the majority only because he believed their decision conformed to the mores of the time, not because he believed their analysis of the case had merit. Contends that though discrimination is wrong, the courts are not legislative bodies and change in a stable society must come through Rule of Law. Social engineering by a guilt-ridden nation to cure the prejudice of centuries will result in backlash as the majority encounters racially inspired limits to its freedom. Stevens should have dissented; law changes to fit the times, but in a stable society it remains in structure the same. 2 notes.   C. D'Aniello

1079. Shepherd, William. LEGAL PROTECTION FOR FREEDOM OF RELIGION. *Center Mag. 1982 15(2): 30-33.* Discusses constitutional conflicts between 1st Amendment religious protections and individuals and legitimate interests of government in protecting public welfare, emphasizing the recent cases concerning religious cults; interference with the rights of nonconforming religious believers is constitutionally illegal and violates moral principles on which the Constitution is based.

1080. Siegan, Bernard H. THE TAKING ISSUE. *Freeman 1974 24(8): 464-466.* The Environmental Protection Agency wants to alter the last clause of the Fifth Amendment, which protects private property from confiscation by the federal government.   S

1081. Siegel, David D. THE FEDERAL RULES IN DIVERSITY CASES: *ERIE* IMPLEMENTED, NOT RETARDED. *Am. Bar Assoc. J. 1968 54(2): 172-176.* According to "The Federal Rules in Diversity Cases: *Erie* in Retreat," an article which appeared in an earlier issue of the *Journal,* the Supreme Court decision in *Hanna* v. *Plumer* heralded the end of *Erie's* applicability to any item whose subject matter is treated in a federal statute or rule. In response, Mr. Siegel contends that *Hanna* merely sets forth another, though perhaps firmer, guideline for making the distinction between "substantive" and "procedural" law necessitated by the *Erie* decision [*Erie Railroad Company* v. *Tompkins* (US, 1938)].   J

1082. Silber, Jerome S. BROADCAST REGULATION AND THE FIRST AMENDMENT. *Journalism Monographs 1980 (70): 1-28.* Entire journal devoted to study of court decisions since the late 1920's that indicate that the radio and television broadcast industry, "despite federal regulation, deserves a fuller measure of the First Amendment protection enjoyed by other media."

1083. Simon, Rita James. THE AMERICAN JURY: INSTRUMENT OF JUSTICE OR OF PREJUDICE AND CONFORMITY? *Sociol. Inquiry [Canada] 1977 47(3-4): 254-293.* Examines jury decisions concerning First Amendment rights, 1940's-75, to assess whether juries truly block oppressive government and whether they reflect prejudice and ignorance.

1084. Singer, Richard. THE AFTERMATH OF AN INSANITY ACQUIT-TAL: THE SUPREME COURT'S RECENT DECISION IN *JONES* V. *UNITED STATES. Ann. of the Am. Acad. of Pol. and Social Sci. 1985 (477): 114-124.* The disposition of persons acquitted on insanity grounds has always cast a shadow on the insanity debate. Recently, the Supreme Court of the United States decided that these persons could constitutionally be given fewer procedural and substantive protections against indeterminate confinement than other persons confined for mental illness. The Court's opinion dealt with questions not directly raised by the case and may have been prompted by a general unease about the insanity defense itself. The opinion is likely to discourage many from entering such a plea in the future.   J

1085. Skotzko, Eugene. SIGNIFICANT DECISIONS IN LABOR CASES. *Monthly Labor R. 1969 92(4): 71-74.* Recent federal and state Supreme Court decisions on labor-related issues.   S

1086. Slonim,   Solomon. CONGRESSIONAL-EXECUTIVE   AGREE-MENTS. *Columbia J. of Transnat. Law 1975 14(3): 434-450.* Discusses principles of constitutional law involved in agreements between Congress and the executive branch regarding control of US foreign policy and treatymaking powers, 1969-74.

1087. Smith, C. Calvin. THE POLITICS OF EVASION: ARKANSAS' REACTION TO *SMITH* V. *ALLWRIGHT,* 1944. *J. of Negro Hist. 1982 67(1): 40-51.* Immediately after the Supreme Court ruled the all-white Democratic primary unconstitutional in Texas, changes began to take place in Arkansas; blacks began to vote and whites began to preserve their all-white system. The Democratic Party of Arkansas created the double primary in order to keep the party and the South white, but the complications, expense, and law eventually changed the situation.   A. G. Belles

1088. Smith, Donald L. ZECHARIAH CHAFEE JR. AND THE POSITIVE VIEW OF PRESS FREEDOM. *Journalism Hist. 1978 5(3): 86-92.* Summarizes Harvard Law School professor Zechariah Chafee, Jr.'s, theory of a free press and analyzes his balancing-of-interests approach to First Amendment questions; covers 1921-57.

1089. Smith, F. Leslie. SELLING OF THE PENTAGON AND THE FIRST AMENDMENT. *Journalism Hist. 1975 2(1): 2-5, 14.* Examines Congress's clash with the Columbia Broadcasting System (CBS) in 1971 over the television special, *The Selling of the Pentagon,* and whether the incident advanced the cause of broadcast journalism in the context of the First Amendment.

1090. Soley, Mary. CONTROVERSIAL ISSUES AS VIEWED BY SOCIAL STUDIES TEACHERS. *Social Educ. 1981 45(6): 412-417.* Discusses the results of a recent survey of social studies teachers' views on a variety of controversial issues such as busing, the draft, the Equal Rights Amendment, a constitutional amendment to prohibit abortion, and sex education; their opinions mirror those of the general public, and age, sex, religion, and years of teaching experience do not influence their opinions.

1091. Spitz, David. BLACK RIGHTS AND JUDICIAL WRONGS. *Dissent 1979 26(2): 194-203.* Discusses the role of the courts in human rights issues since the Civil Rights Act (US, 1866), in a review article prompted by

Raoul Berger's *Government by Judiciary: The Transformation of the Four-teenth Amendment* (Cambridge, Mass.: Harvard U. Pr., 1977).

1092. Steamer, Robert J. CONTEMPORARY SUPREME COURT DI-RECTIONS IN CIVIL LIBERTIES. *Pol. Sci. Q. 1977 92(3): 425-442.* Current literature is concerned with measuring erosion to civil liberties since the Warren years, but the Burger Court is in fact more like than unlike the Warren Court. The Burger Court is skewed toward a "conservative-restraint" position, but it has not yet broken out of old Warren pathways. Where the two courts differ, the Burger Court has often taken a sensible position. There are indications that the Court is moving away from expanded judicial review in some areas, recognizing that judges cannot become administrators or budget-makers without eroding their political immunity. Based on Burger Court decisions and on secondary sources; 100 notes.   W. R. Hively

1093. Stempel, Guido H., III. A GUTTMAN SCALE ANALYSIS OF THE BURGER COURT'S PRESS DECISIONS. *Journalism Q. 1982 59(2): 256-259.* An analysis of the overall record of the Supreme Court on press cases during 1971-81 shows a consistent pattern of response by the justices on a wide variety of press-related situations. Although there has been much speculation about possible trends in Supreme Court decisions relative to the press, it is difficult to suggest an overriding factor or to prove the existence of a liberal-conservative continuum. Nonetheless, it is possible that the high court is practicing politics rather than jurisprudence. Primary sources; table, 7 notes.
                                                              L. J. Klass

1094. Stern, Ralph D. THE LAW AND PUBLIC EDUCATION: PROJEC-TIONS FOR THE 1980S. *Educ. and Urban Soc. 1982 14(2): 211-234.* Examines major Supreme Court decisions of the past decade affecting public education, demonstrating how these decisions will affect management and control of public schools in the future.

1095. Stevenson, Janet. ROSA PARKS WOULDN'T BUDGE. *Am. Heri-tage 1972 23(2): 56-64, 85.* Rosa Parks' refusal to give up her bus seat to a white man on 1 December 1955 was the spark which united Montgomery Alabama Negroes behind a challenge of the constitutionality of state law which decreed segregated buses. The black community, led by the newly-formed Montgomery Improvement Association and its president, Martin Luther King, Jr., organized a successful bus boycott. The buses were integrated a year later after the Supreme Court affirmed a special three-judge federal court decision declaring segregated seating on buses to be unconstitutional. 5 illus.
                                                              J. F. Paul

1096. Stone, Lauson H. HARLAN F. STONE: MY FATHER THE CHIEF JUSTICE. *Supreme Court Hist. Soc. Y. 1978: 7-17.* Recollections on Harlan F. Stone's career of practicing and teaching law, serving as dean at the Columbia University Law School, and serving as a member of the Supreme Court; covers 1905-46.

1097. Stonecipher, Harry W. and Trager, Robert. THE IMPACT OF *GERTZ* ON THE LAW OF LIBEL. *Journalism Q. 1976 53(4): 609-618.* The Supreme Court's decision in *Gertz* v. *Robert Welch, Inc.* (US, 1974) has been cited in more than 80 libel cases in at least 23 states, but interpretations have differed on public figure criteria and liaility standards for private persons.

1098. Stonecipher, Harry W. PROTECTION FOR THE EDITORIAL FUNCTION: IS FIRST AMENDMENT RIGHT BEING ERODED? *Journalism Q. 1981 58(3): 363-370.* Recent Supreme Court rulings have seemed to chip away at editorial freedom. However, rather than legitimize prior restraint in cases involving editorial privilege, the rulings have called attention to the means by which those who feel aggrieved can seek redress. Courts have ruled consistently, as in the *Branzburg* decision, that a reporter has no more right to enter closed proceedings or closed institutions than does any other citizen. Generally, it seems that the Burger Court has extended First Amendment rights in the dissemination of news, while restricting them in cases involving the gathering of news. Based on judicial documents and secondary sources; 68 notes.   J. S. Coleman

1099. Strom, Sharon Hartman. LEADERSHIP AND TACTICS IN THE AMERICAN WOMAN SUFFRAGE MOVEMENT: A NEW PERSPECTIVE FROM MASSACHUSETTS. *J. of Am. Hist. 1975 62(2): 296-315.* Describes the role of the rank and file, large and small state organizations, the reformist climate of the Progressive era, and militant English suffragist tactics in rejuvenating the Massachusetts suffrage movement after 1900. These forces played a larger part in winning passage of the 19th Amendment in 1919 in Massachusetts than better-known leaders of the women's movement. Based on reports of suffrage organizations, newspapers, journals, and secondary works; 69 notes.   J. B. Street

1100. Sukenik, Moshe M. TESTIMONY INCRIMINATING UNDER THE LAWS OF A FOREIGN COUNTRY: IS THERE A RIGHT TO REMAIN SILENT? *New York U. J. of Int. Law and Pol. 1978 11(2): 359-385.* The Fifth Amendment may protect a witness from incrimination under laws of foreign countries on a case-by-case basis, 1960's-70's.

1101. Swanson, Roger F. CANADA AND THE UNITED STATES: THE RANGE OF DIRECT RELATIONS BETWEEN STATES AND PROVINCES. *Int. Perspectives [Canada] 1976 (2): 18-23.* Discusses the US State Department's research into types of arrangements between American states and Canadian provinces in the 1970's; findings indicated that most arrangements involved licensing procedures at borders and occasional issues in constitutional law.

1102. Swartz, Barbara J. DENATURALIZATION OF NAZI WAR CRIMINALS AFTER *FEDORENKO*. *New York U. J. of Int. Law and Pol. 1982 15(1): 169-194.* Discusses the ramifications for immigration law and the denaturalization of accused Nazi war criminals of the Supreme Court decision in *Fedorenko* v. *US* (1981).

1103. Swinton, Katherine. JUDICIAL POLICY MAKING: AMERICAN AND CANADIAN PERSPECTIVES. *Can. Rev. of Am. Studies [Canada] 1979 10(1): 89-94.* In *Constitutional Counter-Revolution? The Warren Court and the Burger Court: Judicial Policy Making in Modern America* (New York: Shenkman, 1977), Richard Funston compared policymaking by the US Supreme Court during the tenures of Chief Justices Earl Warren and Warren E. Burger since 1953. The Burger Court, more than the Warren Court, deferred to the will of legislatures and agencies of the executive branch of the government. However, the Burger Court has not reversed Warren Court decisions in most civil rights matters. 22 notes.   H. T. Lovin

1104. Tanenhaus, Joseph and Murphy, Walter F. PATTERNS OF PUBLIC SUPPORT FOR THE SUPREME COURT: A PANEL STUDY. *J. of Pol. 1981 43(1): 24-39.* While the level of diffuse popular support for the Supreme Court declined moderately in 1975 from that recorded in 1966, it still remained favorable. While the level of specific support had increased during that period, popular reaction to specific court decisions remained strongly unfavorable. In both years, decisions concerning civil rights, school prayer, and the rights of criminal defendants were highly visible. While the court's handling of the Watergate Affair substantially enhanced specific support in 1975, its decisions concerning abortion had the opposite effect. Illus., 4 tables, 18 notes.
A. W. Novitsky

1105. Tench, Richard. WHOSE SIDE ARE THE LAWYERS ON? *Antioch Rev. 1975 33(1): 53-65.* Examines aspects and issues of constitutional law in light of contemporary legal education, concluding that such education is actually training lawyers away from constitutionally guaranteed civil rights.

1106. Terchek, Ronald J. POLITICAL PARTICIPATION AND POLITICAL STRUCTURES: THE VOTING RIGHTS ACT OF 1965. *Phylon 1980 41(1): 25-35.* The 24th Amendment (1964) abolished the poll tax as a prerequisite for voting, but hardly affected voter registration. The Voting Rights Act (US, 1965) did precipitate the anticipated increase. 4 tables, 29 notes.   N. G. Sapper

1107. Thatcher, Terence L. THE BRICKER AMENDMENT: 1952-54. *Northwest Ohio Q. 1977 49(3): 107-120.* In 1952 Senator John W. Bricker (R.-Ohio) proposed a constitutional amendment to limit executive power, particularly in conducting foreign policy; traces the origin of the Bricker amendment to the American Bar Association arguments in 1948 opposing several treaties proposed at the UN.

1108. Theoharis, Athan G. FBI SURVEILLANCE DURING THE COLD WAR YEARS: A CONSTITUTIONAL CRISIS. *Public Hist. 1981 3(1): 4-14.* Describes Federal Bureau of Investigation surveillance of supposed dissident political activities from 1940 to 1980, but focuses on the Cold War years, confirming a distinct pattern of indifference to the law and to the constitutional system of checks and balances, though full public knowledge of these activities did not exist until the 1970's.

1109. Thomson, Harry C. THE WAR POWERS RESOLUTION OF 1973: CAN CONGRESS MAKE IT STICK? *World Affairs 1976 139(1): 3-9.* Discusses the constitutional implications for the presidency and the executive branch of Congress' passing of the War Powers Resolution (1973).

1110. Tomatsu, Hidenori. BYOTOHOGO TO SHIHOSHINSA [Equal protection and judicial review (4)]. *Kokkagakkai Zasshi [Japan] 1978 91(7-8): 27-55.* Continued from a previous article. The judicature plays a decisive role in connection with the equal protection clause of the 14th Amendment.

1111. Tomberlin, Joseph A. FLORIDA AND THE SCHOOL DESEGREGATION ISSUE, 1954-1959: A SUMMARY VIEW. *J. of Negro Educ. 1974 43(4): 457-467.* By 1959 Florida had not fully adhered to the 1954 Supreme Court ruling on desegregation in schools, and it was not until the Civil Rights Act of 1964 that desegregation was stepped-up appreciably.

1112. Trauth, Denise M. and Huffman, John L. NEW U.S. SUPREME COURT PHILOSOPHY ON ADVERTISING FACES OPPOSITION. *Journalism Q. 1979 56(3): 540-545.* With its decisions in the cases of *Bigelow* v. *Virginia* (US, 1975) and *Virginia State Board of Pharmacy* v. *Virginia Consumer Council* (US, 1976), the US Supreme Court placed commercial advertisements in both print and broadcast media within the scope of the First Amendment's guarantee of free speech rights. But state legislatures, federal regulatory agencies, and public interest groups have moved in the opposite direction, seeking restrictions on certain kinds of advertising. Based on Supreme Court decisions and secondary sources; 22 notes.
                                                                    R. P. Sindermann, Jr.

1113. Tribe, Laurence H. and Remes, David H. SOME REFLECTIONS ON *THE PROGRESSIVE CASE:* PUBLISH *AND* PERISH? *Bull. of the Atomic Sci. 1980 36(3): 20-24.* The imposition of a restraining order on Howard Morland's 1979 article in *The Progressive* on nuclear arms raises questions about 1st Amendment freedom of the press issues.

1114. Tugwell, Rexford G. REFLECTIONS ON THE WARREN COURT. *Center Mag. 1973 6(1): 59-63.*

1115. Tugwell, Rexford Guy. HOW RESPONSIBLE IS THE PRESS: HOW "FREE" SHOULD IT BE? *Center Report 1973 6(1): 10-12.* The author, one of Franklin D. Roosevelt's top advisors, draws a distinction between the constitutional guarantee of the "public's right to know" and the demand of the press for "free access" and the right to publish whatever it likes, whenever it likes.   S

1116. Tyrmand, Leopold. THE MEDIA SHANGRI-LA. *Am. Scholar 1975/76 45(1): 752-775.* Views the First Amendment as a marvelous and wonderful institution, but raises questions about its applications in mass media communications. Sees grave dangers in the absolutism, monopoly, and transcending power of the mass media and wonders if the free press is being corrupted by its enormous growth of power.   F. F. Harling

1117. Ulmer, S. Sidney. PARABOLIC SUPPORT OF CIVIL LIBERTY CLAIMS: THE CASE OF WILLIAM O. DOUGLAS. *J. of Pol. 1979 41(2): 634-639.* Support for civil liberties claims offered by Justice William O. Douglas across 34 Supreme Court terms varied in the same parabolic fashion depicted earlier for Hugo L. Black by A. E. Howard. Both justices were less liberal early and late in their judicial careers, and most liberal in the middle years. Fig., 12 notes.   A. W. Novitsky

1118. Ulmer, S. Sidney. SELECTING CASES FOR SUPREME COURT REVIEW: AN UNDERDOG MODEL. *Am. Pol. Sci. Rev. 1978 72(3): 902-910.* In making review decisions, Supreme Court justices are predisposed to support underdogs and upperdogs disproportionately but, also, are motivated to hide any "bias" that may be at work in determining votes. In balancing these two values, justices may be expected to vote their "bias" more frequently 1)when that vote will determine outcome, and 2)when the "bias" will be harder to detect. The latter goal may be served by voting the "bias" more frequently in close cases and less frequently otherwise. In an analysis of the voting patterns of five justices in the decade 1947-56, I found that two liberal and two conservative justices conformed to these expectations. A fifth, or control justice, defined as neither liberal nor conservative, did not pattern his votes in the manner predicted for liberals and conservatives. This relationship held when four projected intervening variables were controlled individually and collectively.   J

1119. Ulmer, S. Sidney. SOCIAL BACKGROUND AS AN INDICATOR TO THE VOTES OF SUPREME COURT JUSTICES IN CRIMINAL CASES: 1947-1956 TERMS. *Am. J. of Pol. Sci. 1973 17(3): 622-630.* Considers the role of social background as an influencing factor in Supreme Court criminal decisions. 12 social background variables were selected which explained over 91 percent of all decisions during the period 1947-56. Researchers who have reached opposite conclusions probably erred in variable selection, had different objectives, or worked with different courts. Nevertheless, the justices' decisionmaking process is complicated; an intimate knowledge of the social backgrounds of justices probably will never permit precise prediction of decisions. 3 tables, 14 notes.   V. L. Human

1120. Ulmer, S. Sidney. SUPREME COURT JUSTICES AS STRICT AND NOT-SO-STRICT CONSTRUCTIONISTS: SOME IMPLICATIONS. *Law and Soc. R. 1973 8(1): 13-32.* Examines how the individual attitudes of Supreme Court justices toward government authority influenced their decisions during 1947-56 in criminal law and on requests for review of lower court cases.   S

1121. Urofsky, Melvin I. THE "OUTRAGEOUS" BRANDEIS NOMINATION. *Supreme Court Hist. Soc. Y. 1979: 8-19.* The confirmation fight resulting from the nomination of Louis D. Brandeis to the Supreme Court in 1916 was essentially a battle between liberals and conservatives. Religion played a minor role. Brandeis had built a career and reputation by siding with small interests against the large concerns. This was the core of the battle, but political considerations also weighed heavily in the outcome, costing support here and gaining it there. Opponents of the nomination marshalled massive resources, but it eventually became clear that many of the opposition were simply persons and organizations likely to be damaged by Brandeis's "radical" outlook. By a vote of 10-8 the Senate committee approved the nomination, and the full Senate soon followed suit. 4 photos.   V. L. Human

1122. Van Alstyne, William W. THE SPECIFIC THEORY OF ACADEM-IC FREEDOM AND THE GENERAL ISSUE OF CIVIL LIBERTIES. *Ann. of the Am. Acad. of Pol. and Social Sci. 1972 (404): 140-156.* "Academic freedom has been blurred in law and in popular usage. Its clarification should enable the Supreme Court to grant it explicit protection under the Constitution as an identifiable subset of First Amendment freedoms. Its identification with the professional endeavors of faculty members, moreover, should reduce the tendency of institutions to intrude upon the aprofessional personal liberties of the faculty even while adequately protecting the extramural professional pursuits of the faculty and assuring them of equal protection in their interests as private citizens. Adjustments of standards by the American Association of University Professors, more definitely distinguishing the special accountability of faculty members for the integrity of their professional endeavors from their roles as private citizens, is long overdue."   J

1123. Varkey, Ouseph. CRISIS SITUATIONS AND FEDERAL SYS-TEMS: A COMPARATIVE STUDY OF AMERICA AND INDIA. *Indian J. of Am. Studies [India] 1979 9(1): 65-79.* Studies two comparable situations where state governments challenged federal governments. Details of the American 1957 segregation crisis in Little Rock, Arkansas, are contrasted with the 1968 conflict between the central Indian government and the united front anti-Congress coalition in Kerala. The American president, with fewer explicit constitutional powers, intervened successfully; the Indian federal executive, with many more explicit constitutional powers, retreated. Constitutions and laws do not by themselves determine the nature of federal-state relations. 73 notes.   L. V. Eid

1124. Vasicko, Sally Jo. JOHN MARSHALL HARLAN: NEGLECTED ADVOCATE OF FEDERALISM. *Modern Age 1980 24(4): 387-395.* John Marshall Harlan served as Associate Justice on the Supreme Court of the United States, 1955-71. His term was characterized by sound judicial logic, especially in the area of due process. During an era of emotionalism concerning the definition and expansion of constitutional rights, Harlan called for a limited role for the judiciary through adherence to basic constitutional principles of federalism. 36 notes.   J. Powell

1125. Vasicko, Sally Jo. JUSTICE HARLAN AND THE EQUAL PRO-TECTION CLAUSE. *Supreme Court Hist. Soc. Y. 1982: 46-56.* John Marshall Harlan was on the Supreme Court during a period when the equal protection clause of the Constitution was widely interpreted. During this time Harlan wrote many dissenting opinions in the areas of reapportionment, voting rights, race relations, defendant rights, and welfare rights as they were affected by the equal protection clause. He insisted the Court use prudence and not emotion when deciding such cases and had a deep commitment to maintaining the balance between the states and the federal government. Based primarily on Harlan's dissenting opinions; 72 notes, 3 illus.   G. B. Childress

1126. Vaughn, Stephen. FIRST AMENDMENT LIBERTIES AND THE COMMITTEE ON PUBLIC INFORMATION. *Am. J. of Legal Hist. 1979 23(2): 95-119.* The Committee on Public Information, created on 13 April 1917 to create propaganda for the federal government during World War I, became involved with censorship. Topics include the work of publicist Arthur Bullard, who was responsible for its creation, cabinet discussions and congressional debates, the role of its executive head, George Creel, and his relationship with the Wilson administration and the press, the problem of liberalism, and conflicting historiographical interpretations. 84 notes.   L. A. Knafla

1127. Vose, Clement E. WHEN DISTRICT OF COLUMBIA REPRESEN-TATION COLLIDES WITH THE CONSTITUTIONAL AMENDMENT INSTITUTION. *Publius 1979 9(1): 105-126.* A study of the constitutional amendment process by analyzing the procedures being followed to promote an amendment granting congressional representation to the District of Columbia. Another approach would be statehood, but this seems inappropriate. By comparison with the ratification of the 23d Amendment which provided electoral votes for the District of Columbia, determines some of the favorable methods which may be used as well as some of the obstacles faced by virtue of the amendment process itself. 9 notes. Covers 1930-78.   R. V. Ritter

1128. Wall, Joseph Frazier. SOCIAL DARWINISM AND CONSTITU-TIONAL LAW WITH SPECIAL REFERENCE TO *LOCHNER V. NEW YORK. Ann. of Sci. [Great Britain] 1976 33(5): 465-476.* American historians have generally accepted Richard Hofstadter's thesis that the scientism of Social Darwinism, or more appropriately, Spencerianism, dominated American thought in the late nineteenth and early twentieth century, and nowhere more enthusiastically or more purposively than within the conservative business community, which used Herbert Spencer's scientism to justify corporate business practices and to rewrite American constitutional law to protect property interets against governmental regulations. The author examines in detail the validity of the Hofstadter thesis as applied to the notorious *Lochner v. New York* Supreme Court opinion of 1905. The conclusions drawn from this analysis are offered as a repudiation of the generally accepted belief that it was the conservative activists on the Court who were guilty of Spencerian scientism. On the contrary, the argument is presented that it was Justice Holmes and the liberal reformers who found the evolutionary doctrines of Spencer congenial to their efforts of identifying needed reinterpretations of the American Constitution with biological evolution. [Commentary by David A. Hollinger, who states:] "Wall is convincing on the Fuller court, but less so on Holmes, who may have understood Spencer's *Social statics* as a laissez faire rather than as a Darwinist document."   J

1129. Wallace, David. DESEGREGATION IN HOXIE, ARKANSAS: "RIGHT IN THE SIGHT OF GOD." *Southern Studies 1981 20(3): 311-325.* As a result of the Supreme Court decision of 1954 against public school segregation, the school board of Hoxie, Arkansas, in northeastern Arkansas voted to desegregate its school, citing in their decision that it was "right in the sight of God." Although eastern Arkansas had a higher percentage of blacks and a stronger tradition of slavery than the western part of the state, Hoxie had only a few blacks. Although at first there was no resistance or reaction, within two months segregationist sentiment within a small group, who attracted help and attention from larger communities in the state, appeared and attempted to apply pressure on the board in various ways. The problem was taken to the courts, where it was settled, and desegregation took place peacefully; there were no conflicts on the school grounds or in the classrooms. Primary sources; 39 notes.   J. J. Buschen

1130. Ward, Alan. FREEDOM OF THE PRESS AND CONTEMPT OF COURT: A COMPARISON OF THE ENGLISH AND U.S. LAW. *J. of Media Law and Practice [Great Britain] 1982 3(2): 175-196.* Compares English and American law concerning freedom of the press versus the judicial control of information in legal proceedings; the US Supreme Court has given greater freedom to the press in this area than is granted the English press.

1131. Warheit, George J.; Swanson, Edith; and Schwab, John J. A STUDY OF RACIAL ATTITUDES IN A SOUTHEASTERN COUNTY: A CONFIRMATION OF NATIONAL TRENDS. *Phylon 1975 36(4): 395-406.* Reviews earlier research on social distance and racial attitudes in the United States and corroborates with recent findings changes toward a growing inclusiveness of racial attitudes among whites over the last 50 years. However, the study recognizes that a change in attitudes does not necessarily mean behavior will change. Attitudinal changes occurred following the historic 1954 Supreme Court decision and a decade of Civil Rights legislation. The political climate today is different inasmuch as "forced busing" has become an explosive political issue and may signal a reemergence of more exclusive racial attitudes on the part of white Americans. Based on primary research and secondary sources; 7 tables, 16 notes.   K. C. Snow

1132. Warren, Earl, Jr. MY FATHER THE CHIEF JUSTICE. *Supreme Court Hist. Soc. Y. 1982: 6-9.* Earl Warren was chief justice of the United States, governor of California, state district attorney, and attorney general as well as a vice-presidential candidate. Despite all of the public attention Warren lived with, his family life was not different from that of a normal American family. His children grew up in a setting that included blacks, Hispanics, Asians, and Jews. Religious tolerance was another trait of the Warren family. Earl Warren's rise to national prominence had little effect on the basic values of his family structure. Illus.   G. B. Childress

1133. Wasby, Stephen L.; D'Amato, Anthony A.; and Metrailer, Rosemary. THE FUNCTIONS OF ORAL ARGUMENT IN THE U.S. SUPREME COURT. *Q. J. of Speech 1976 62(4): 410-422.* Uses primarily race relations cases during 1954-69 to examine the role of the oral argument, an aspect of Supreme Court deliberations whose importance has not been widely recognized. The oral argument permits the lawyer to focus on the most important points in his case while also allowing justices to obtain further information and clarification and to communicate with each other. It also helps the justices to consider the methods and effects of implementing a decision. Based on court records and secondary sources; 55 notes.   E. C. Bailey

1134. Watkins, John J. NEWSGATHERING AND THE FIRST AMEND-MENT. *Journalism Q. 1976 53(3): 406-416, 493.* Examines the question, "Is news gathering constitutionally protected?" Although the constitutional guarantee of freedom of the press seems to be meaningless without the right to gather information, there has been no definitive court decision equating the two. As government at all levels becomes more complex, the people's right to access to information becomes increasingly difficult to fulfill. Only a press guaranteed the right to obtain information as the people's agent can insure good government. Court decisions and secondary sources; 99 notes.
E. Gibson

1135. Watkins, John J. PRIVATE PROPERTY VS. REPORTER RIGHTS: A PROBLEM IN NEWSGATHERING. *Journalism Q. 1977 54(4): 690-696.* Deals with federal court cases on trespass law and the freedom of the press and proposes a limited constitutional privilege for news gathering. In light of such cases as *Dietemann* v. *Time, Inc.* (1971) and *Galella* v. *Onassis* (1973), judicial standards protecting press freedom must be established for trespass law as they have been for libel and privacy law. The constitutional privilege to gather news requires the weighing of the public interest in certain information against the nature of the trespass. Based on court reports and secondary sources; 45 notes.
R. P. Sindermann, Jr.

1136. Watson, Denton L. CIVIL RIGHTS LAW: CONCEPT TO REALITY. *Crisis 1979 86(6): 233-239.* The justices on the US Supreme Court used sociological jurisprudence in *Brown* v. *Board of Education* (US, 1954). In reaching the conclusion that segregation denied blacks equal protection, the Court relied on educators, sociologists, psychologists, psychiatrists, and anthropologists as much as on historians and lawyers. One of the lawyers for the NAACP, Thurgood Marshall, believed that the law and Constitution can respond to social change, reaffirm principles, and initiate change. Marshall based his argument on the history of civil rights law in the United States since the Civil War.   A. G. Belles

1137. Watson, Denton L. IN THE WAKE OF BAKKE. *Crisis 1979 86(2): 51-61.* The Supreme Court's decision on the *Regents of the University of California* v. *Allan Bakke* (US, 1978) case led to a symposium sponsored by the NAACP. It was held in Detroit in July 1978. Participants gathered to assess the ruling. The consensus was that there has been and will be a strong trend in anti-affirmative action strategies. The *Bakke* case has had a chilling effect and resulted in the scaling down of civil rights programs. The six separate opinions handed down provide a variety of arguments to strike down many progressive activities. Members at the symposium issued a manifesto declaring war on every attempt to weaken affirmative action and civil rights.
A. G. Belles

1138. Way, G. Darryl. JAPANESE EMPLOYERS AND TITLE VII: *SUMITOMO SHOJI AMERICA, INC. V AVAGLIANO. New York U. J. of Int.*

Law and Pol. 1983 15(3): 653-695. Discusses the Supreme Court's determination that foreign-owned businesses in the United States are subject to the Civil Rights Act of 1964, regardless of the existence of other, contradictory agreements.

1139. Way, H. Frank. THE STUDY OF JUDICIAL ATTITUDES: THE CASE OF MR. JUSTICE DOUGLAS. *Western Pol. Q. 1971 24(1): 12-27.* "The conclusions about judicial attitudes frequently derived from voting records can be more sharply focused by additional reference to attitudinal statements contained in the opinions of a justice."   S

1140. Weaver, Robert C. THE EVOLUTION AND SIGNIFICANCE OF THE PROPOSED FAIR HOUSING AMENDMENTS ACT OF 1979. *Crisis 1979 86(10): 422-424.* The struggle for effective fair housing legislation began in the late 1930's, gained momentum during World War II, achieved a breakthrough in 1948 with the US Supreme Court decision *Shelley* v. *Kraemer,* and became a national issue in the 1960 presidential campaign of John F. Kennedy. Lyndon Johnson pushed Congress to enact Title VIII (1968) of the Civil Rights Act (1964) which authorized programs to increase supply of low-income housing and subsidies to support demand. Restrictions and weaknesses could be eliminated by the Fair Housing Amendments Act of 1979, providing the federal government with realistic authority for enforcement.
                                                                A. G. Belles

1141. Weaver, Warren. DISCRIMINATION IN REVERSE?: NOW THAT MARCO DE FUNIS HAS HIS LAW DEGREE.... *Compact 1974 8(4): 5-8.* Discusses the legal implications of the Supreme Court's ruling [*DeFunis* v. *Odegaard* (US, 1974)] regarding possible reverse discrimination toward whites in affirmative action programs in professional schools.

1142. Weber, Paul J. THE FIRST AMENDMENT AND THE MILITARY CHAPLAINCY: THE PROCESS OF REFORM. *J. of Church and State 1980 22(3): 459-474.* Discusses the history of military chaplaincy and its First Amendment application and reviews the present system of allocation of positions and possible reforms to this system. Secondary sources; 47 notes.
                                                                E. E. Eminhizer

1143. Wechsler, Herbert. THE NATIONALIZATION OF CIVIL LIBERTIES AND CIVIL RIGHTS. *Texas Q. 1969 12(2): 1-61.* Discusses the process by which civil liberties and civil rights, which in the recent past were thought to derive mainly from state law, have come to be delineated by decisions of the Supreme Court and by acts of Congress. Defines, and illustrates through judicial opinions, elements in this change: the interpretation of the due process clause of the Fourteenth Amendment to forbid encroachment by the states upon First Amendment freedoms, safeguards, and rights; the increasingly expansive reading of the "equal protection of the laws" against a state's classification or discrimination based on race or poverty; the articulation of a new and broader concept of the power of Congress to protect equality and liberty under the enforcement clauses of the Civil War Amendments. The Oliver Wendell Holmes Devise Lecture for 1967 delivered at the

University of South Dakota on 4 May and at the University of North Dakota on 6 May as part of the commemoration of Law Day at both. 154 notes, appendix.   R. V. Ritter

1144. Weinberg, Lee S. ASKEW V. AMERICAN WATERWAY OPERA-TORS, INC.: THE EMERGING NEW FEDERALISM. *Publius 1978 8(4): 37-53.* In this case the Supreme Court has attempted to define the extent of state regulations concerning oil spills. The court's philosophy advocates both the strengthening of states ability to defend themselves, while upholding laws "... which will save the environment from unnecessary, costly and far reaching devastation." The opinion upholds a 1973 Florida Act which took effect three months after the Federal Water Quality Improvement Act. This decision reveals the court's view of federalism in environmental problems. It permitted Florida to enforce its oil pollution statutes while permitting "... the court to step in if the states attempt to legislate in a fashion which hinders interstate maritime commerce." 81 notes.   R. S. Barnard

1145. Welch, Charles E., III. THE REGULATION OF AMERICAN FER-TILITY: FACTS AND MISCONCEPTIONS. *Int. J. of Women's Studies [Canada] 1984 7(3): 273-281.* Reviews the *Roe* v. *Wade* (US, 1973) Supreme Court decision on women's sexual privacy rights in the matter of abortion and examines the legal implications of fertility regulation, stressing that the state does not have the right to interfere in what is the prospective mother's legal domain.

1146. West, E. G. AN ECONOMIC ANALYSIS OF THE LAW AND POLITICS OF NON-PUBLIC SCHOOL "AID." *J. of Law and Econ. 1976 19(1): 79-101.* Examines the economic and constitutional problems of public aid to nonpublic schools. "User taxes" are a possible solution to the problem. Primary and secondary sources; 29 notes.   J. Reed

1147. West, Ellis M. JUSTICE TOM CLARK AND AMERICAN CHURCH-STATE LAW. *J. of Presbyterian Hist. 1976 54(4): 387-404.* Tom Clark (1899-) was an Associate Justice of the US Supreme Court, 1949-67. While on the Court he wrote major opinions in the areas of civil rights, separation of powers, antitrust, national security and church-state relations. His opinions in the cases of *US* v. *Seeger* and *Abington School District* v. *Schemp* were historic in church-state relations and of far reaching conse-quences. The latter struck down officially prescribed prayer and Bible-reading in the public schools. Points out that Clark, a very dedicated Presbyterian layman, was a constructive moderate who argued for the essential autonomy of religion and government but refused to support their complete separation. Based largely on Supreme Court decisions and Clark's writings; illus., 90 notes.
                                                                  H. M. Parker, Jr.

1148. Westin, Alan F. and Mahoney, Barry. MARTIN LUTHER KING, JR., AND THE SUPREME COURT: ON PROTEST AND THE FIRST AMENDMENT. *Civil Liberties Rev. 1976/1977 3(6): 9-46.* Discusses King's 1963 Birmingham desegregation campaign and analyzes the effects of the ensuing US Supreme Court decision, *Walker* v. *City of Birmingham* (US, 1967), on First Amendment rights.

1149. Wheeler, Harvey. THE MULTI-MEDIA HOME. *Center Mag. 1973 6(3): 47-51.* Examines the First Amendment and cable television as a positive force toward more democratic thought; one of six articles in this issue on "Broadcasting and the First Amendment."   S

1150. White, G. Edward. TAKING A FLYER: LEONARD LEVY ON THE NIXON COURT. *Rev. in Am. Hist. 1975 3(3): 394-398.* Review article prompted by Leonard W. Levy's *Against the Law: The Nixon Court and Criminal Justice* (New York: Harper & Row, 1974). Compares the book with earlier works by Levy; notes the book's provocative and personal nature, summarizes its portraits of the Supreme Court justices, and assesses the book's major thesis that the Nixon appointees' control of the Supreme Court in the area of criminal justice began to significantly change constitutional law.

1151. White, Larry. THE RETURN OF THE THIEF: THE REPEAL OF PROHIBITION AND THE ADVENTIST RESPONSE. *Adventist Heritage 1978 5(2): 34-47.* Discusses the response (1932-34) of Seventh-Day Adventists to the campaign for repeal of Prohibition and its aftermath.

1152. Wilber, Leon A. DEVELOPMENT OF CRIMINAL LAW IN THE SUPREME COURT, 1966 TO 1971. *Southern Q. 1973 11(2): 121-145.* Examines Supreme Court cases 1966-71 which pertain to the fifth, sixth, eighth, and 14th amendments to the Constitution. Discusses such issues as the right to a speedy trial, the right to be confronted by an accuser, the right of testimony, freedom from cruel and unusual punishment, due process of law, and equal protection under the law. 60 notes.   R. W. Dubay

1153. Wilber, Leon A. DEVELOPMENT OF CONSTITUTIONAL LAW IN THE SUPREME COURT, 1966 to 1971: CIVIL ASPECTS. *Southern Q. 1973 11(3): 221-240, (4): 315-344.* Part I. Investigates issues and cases involving the First Amendment, especially civil decisions 1966-71. Focuses on religious freedom, political campaigns and practices, obscenity, and the rights of assembly and dissent. 51 notes. Part II. Analyzes cases concerning the fifth, seventh, 13th, and 14th Amendments. Focuses on due process of law, equal protection of the laws, state jurisdiction and federal supremacy, and congressional powers from the commerce clause. Studies additional problems such as eminent domain, welfare payments, garnishment of wages, desegregation, rights of illegitimate children, loss of citizenship, and congressional immunity. 76 notes.   R. W. Dubay

1154. Williams, Richard L. [THE SUPREME COURT: HOW IT WORKS]. THE SUPREME COURT OF THE UNITED STATES: THE STAFF THAT KEEPS IT OPERATING. *Smithsonian 1977 7(10): 39-49.* Summarizes the responsibilities of Chief Justice Warren E. Burger and the job descriptions of the Officers of the Court, Clerk of the Court, Supreme Court Marshall, Reporter of Decisions, and Librarian. Secondary sources; 19 illus.

JUSTICES RUN "9 LITTLE LAW FIRMS" AT SUPREME COURT. *Smithsonian 1977 7(11): 84-93.* Examines how Supreme Court justices function. They have conferences which afford them their principal opportunity for discussion, debate, and group deliberation and at which they determine what cases to hear. Aside from the conferences and actual court session, the justices operate independently. All nine justices share the burden of overseeing one or more of the 11 US Judicial Circuits and their Courts of Appeal. The number of cases filed with the Supreme Court is large and Congress has tried periodically to solve the problem. In 1891 the creation of the Circuit Courts of Appeal helped winnow out hundreds of cases. The 1925 Judiciary Act gave the Supreme Court discretionary power to reject some petitions. A current proposal would create a national court of appeals to settle differing results on the same points of law in various circuits. Secondary sources; 11 illus.   K. A. Harvey

1155. Wilson, W. Cody. PORNOGRAPHY: THE EMERGENCE OF A SOCIAL ISSUE AND THE BEGINNING OF PSYCHOLOGICAL STUDY. *J. of Social Issues 1973 29(3): 7-18.* "Pornography has not always been a social issue. Indeed societal concern about it has waxed and waned several times in the past 200 years, and this concern seems to have been a function of accessibility, religious influences, and social manners. The emergence of pornography as a current social issue is associated with a series of Supreme Court cases beginning in the late 1950s, posing the question as to whether or not legal prohibition of obscenity violates the First Amendment guarantees of freedom of speech and freedom of the press. The ensuing discussion was based primarily on fear and speculation because there were few empirical facts to inform the discussion. In 1967 Congress declared that obscenity and pornography were matters of national concern, raised questions about the effects of these materials, called for a thorough study, and authorized the use of funds for the collection of relevant scientific data. Thus the beginning of extensive 'scientific' analysis of the social issue of pornography."   J

1156. Wirth, Clifford. SPEAKER BANS ON COLLEGE CAMPUSES: THEIR SUBSTANCE AND THE JUDICIAL ATTITUDE TOWARD THEM. *New Scholar 1971 3(2): 195-207.* After reviewing several cases of speakers bans and their judicial consequences, concludes that Supreme Court review is necessary for the protection of first amendment rights of speech. Believes that Supreme Court review is not an unwarranted intrusion of federal policymaking into university life and policy.   D. K. Pickens

1157. Wolf, Robert A. ELECTRONIC SURVEILLANCE: FOREIGN INTELLIGENCE-WIRETAPPING OF AN ALIEN SPY FOR FOREIGN INTELLIGENCE PURPOSES DOES NOT VIOLATE COMMUNICATIONS ACT OF 1934 OR FOURTH AMENDMENT. *New York U. J. of Int. Law and Pol. 1976 8(3): 479-520.* Examines the problem of electronic eavesdropping and its possible conflicts with the "individual's right to privacy, free speech and related freedoms." In *United States* v. *Butenko* (US, 1974) the Supreme Court "upheld the power of the President to install a warrantless wiretap for intelligence purposes on the telephone of a foreign agent operating within the United States. Concludes that the courts should use a test to decide the constitutionality of warrantless eavesdropping. The fundamental question for the courts is: "do the needs of the Government so outweigh the constitutional interests of the individual as to justify the installation of the surveillance without a judicial warrant." Primary and secondary sources; 205 notes.   M. L. Frey

1158. Wolfinger, Raymond E. and Greenstein, Fred I. THE REPEAL OF FAIR HOUSING IN CALIFORNIA: AN ANALYSIS OF REFERENDUM VOTING. *Am. Pol. Sci. R. 1968 62(3): 753-769.* In November 1964 Californians voted two to one to repeal the Rumford Act and prevent the state or any locality within it from adopting any fair housing legislation. This action was declared unconstitutional by the US Supreme Court in 1967. Analyzes the voting decision as illustrative of problems of political behavior, including the role of campaigns in clarifying choices, the adequacy of "direct democracy" devices such as referenda, the degree to which whites are willing to support black aspirations for equality, and the ways in which civil rights attitudes and voting behavior differ among various population groups. The referendum technique appears to have serious weaknesses compared to the more flexible legislative approach, and is less likely to take into account negative results on other desirable goals. 10 tables, 44 notes.   R. V. Ritter

1159. Wolters, Raymond. CIVIL RIGHTS SINCE 1964: FROM OPPORTUNITY TO ALMS. *Rev. in Am. Hist. 1979 7(2): 262-272.* Review article prompted by Lino A. Graglia's *Disaster by Decree: The Supreme Court Decisions on Race and the Schools* (Ithaca, N.Y.: Cornell U. Pr., 1976), James C. Harvey's *Black Civil Rights During the Johnson Administration* (Jackson: U. and Coll. Pr. of Mississippi, 1973), Ray C. Rist's *The Invisible Children: School Integration in American Society* (Cambridge, Mass.: Harvard U. Pr., 1978), and Ray C. Rist's *The Urban School: A Factory for Failure* (Cambridge: Massachusetts Institute of Technology, 1973).

1160. Wood, James E., Jr. RELIGION AND EDUCATION: A CONTINUING DILEMMA. *Ann. of the Am. Acad. of Pol. and Social Sci. 1979 (446): 63-77.* Discusses the role of religion in the public schools and the use of public funds for religious schools. Reviews religion and education in the context of US church-state relations and several decades of judicial interpretations based on the Establishment Clause of the First Amendment. Even with tuition tax-credit legislation, however, the eligibility for such funds may require that church schools maintain an essentially secular character and thereby lose their religious identity and church-relatedness.   J/S

1161. Wright, Steve. THE FIRST AMENDMENT UNDER SIEGE. *Reason 1978 10(5): 25-27, 36.* Examines the philosophical bases for recent legal actions against the press and broadcast media.

1162. Yellin, Carol Lynn. COUNTDOWN IN TENNESSEE, 1920. *Am. Heritage 1978 30(1): 12-23, 26-35.* The story of the ratification of the 19th amendment (woman suffrage) by the Tennessee legislature in 1920. Both pro- and antiamendment forces put full effort into this state, because 35 of the required 36 states had already ratified. After an intense struggle, Tennessee became number 36. 15 illus.   J. F. Paul

1163. Yellin, Jean Fagan. DUBOIS' *CRISIS* AND WOMEN'S SUF-FRAGE. *Massachusetts R. 1973 14(2): 365-375.* William Edward Burghardt DuBois' attitudes toward women's rights were expressed in the *Crisis*, the magazine of the National Association for the Advancement of Colored People (NAACP) which he edited 1910-34. DuBois consistently sided with suffrag-ettes, even after exposing the racism predominant in the feminist movement. He hoped to unite the women's movement with the black movement, because both groups were traditionally victims in American society. As the 19th Amendment neared ratification, DuBois urged black women to exercise their future voter's rights to the best interests of black people in general. While the amendment brought white women the franchise, it did little to uplift the status of black women. Because feminist groups continued to ignore this glaring inequity throughout the 1920's, DuBois realized that there could be no "women-Negro" alliance. 11 notes.   W. A. Wiegand

1164. Zahniser, Marvin R., ed. JOHN W. BRICKER REFLECTS UPON THE FIGHT FOR THE BRICKER AMENDMENT. *Ohio Hist. 1978 87(3): 322-333.* Discusses the 1954 Senate Joint Resolution 102 (the Bricker Amend-ment) and includes Bricker's explanation and defense of that proposed constitutional amendment in the form of an after-dinner speech to a convention of foreign policy historians in 1976. Bricker argued that the amendment, which was intended to limit the president's abilities to negotiate treaties and executive agreements, to limit the widening powers of the Supreme Court, and to halt interference from the UN and One Worlders, was undermined by the opposition of John J. McCloy and John Foster Dulles of the Eisenhower administration. It lost in the Senate, by one vote. Based on the Bricker Amendment, the Congressional Record, and the Journal of the Senate; photo, 13 notes.   L. A. Russell

1165. —. AND WHAT MUST BE DONE FOR 1980: A CONVERSA-TION WITH JOEL GORA. *Civil Liberties Rev. 1977 4(3): 20-26.* Joel Gora, who represented the American Civil Liberties Union in the *Buckley* vs. *Valeo* case before the Supreme Court, discusses the court's ruling on political campaign finances as it affected the 1976 election.

1166. —. [CIVIL RIGHTS SINCE *BROWN*]. *Center Mag. 1984 17(5): 2-40.*
Weinstein, Allen et al. PART 1. CIVIL RIGHTS SINCE *BROWN:* 1954-1984, *pp. 2-10.* Presents, from a banquet commemorating the 1954 *Brown* v. *Board of Education* Supreme Court decision, excerpts of speeches on the decision and the progress of the civil rights movement.
Weinstein, Allen et al. PART 2. CIVIL RIGHTS TODAY: DEFINITIONS AND SOLUTIONS, *pp. 11-40.* Group discussion on the status of civil rights today.

1167. —. THE DEFENSE OF LIBERTY: THE CONSTITUTIONAL GUARANTEES ARE NOT SELF-EXECUTING. *Center Mag. 1979 12(6):*

41-50. Interview with American Civil Liberties Union attorney John H. F. Shattuck, who discusses constitutional liberties in the United States and the ACLU's role in defending them; 1970's.

1168. —. INSIDE THE GREAT CAMPAIGN FINANCES CASE OF 1976: A CONVERSATION WITH IRA GLASSER. *Civil Liberties Rev. 1977 4(3): 8-19.* Analyzes the Federal Election Campaign Act of 1971 and its 1974 amendments which ended in the *Buckley* vs. *Valeo* case focusing on the rights of Congress, given First Amendment rights to limit the amount of money given to support a political campaign, as well as the right to nondisclosure of campaign contributions.

1169. —. THE LEGAL PROGRAM AND THE NAACP DILEMMA. *Crisis 1979 86(6): 221-222, (9): 379-386.* Part I. During 1940-56, the Legal Defense Fund and the NAACP had interlocking boards and staffs and functioned as a cooperative single entity with the control coming from the NAACP and the financing coming from the LDF. After the legal separation in 1957, the Legal and Educational Defense Fund no longer was subject to or accountable to the NAACP board. In effect, the NAACP lost control over its legal instrumentality and lost financing for legal activities. Part II. The separation in 1957 undermined the NAACP's legal activities and morale, and created complex problems in staffing, fund raising, and publicity. Worse than the public's confusion over the identity of the two bodies was the LDF's claiming credit that the NAACP deserved for the Supreme Court's *Brown* decision in 1954. Finally, in June 1979, the NAACP board forbade the LDF to use the NAACP initials any more.   A. G. Belles

1170. —. [THE MEDIA'S CONFLICT OF INTEREST].
McDonald, Donald. THE MEDIA'S CONFLICT OF INTEREST. *Center Mag. 1976 9(6): 15-35.* Discusses the importance of mass communication (via the press and broadcasting systems) in a free society and the extent to which the mass media have become a controlling power in American society during the 1960's-70's; mentions first Amendment issues.
Knoll, Erwin et al. FOLLOW-UP: THE MEDIA'S CONFLICT OF INTEREST. *Center Mag. 1977 10(1): 63-67.* Presents the opinions of leaders in the mass media regarding possible conflicts of interest between the media's role as a private business and as a guarantor of the public interest, 1970's; responds to McDonald's article, examining possible violations of the First Amendment.

1171. —. [MIRANDA'S FATE IN THE BURGER COURT]. *Center Mag. 1980 13(5): 43-52.*
Collins, Ronald K. and Welsh, Robert. *MIRANDA'S* FATE IN THE BURGER COURT, *pp. 43-45.* Examines the impact of the Supreme Court's *Rhode Island* v. *Innis* (US, 1975) decision on the viability of the landmark *Miranda* v. *Arizona* (US, 1966) decision concerning rights of suspects in criminal cases.
—. DISCUSSION, *pp. 45-52.* A panel, including the authors, considers the issues discussed above.

1172. —. [MONETARY POLICY IMPLEMENTATION]. *Cato J. 1983 3(1): 121-146.*
Christ, Carl. RULES VS. DISCRETION IN MONETARY POLICY, *pp. 121-141.* Advocates a policy of limited federal discretion in regulating the money supply.
Buchanan, James M. MONETARY RESEARCH, MONETARY RULES, AND MONETARY REGIMES, *pp. 143-146.* Discusses the potential use of a constitutional amendment to achieve monetary stability.

1173. —. [MORMONS AND WATERGATE]. *Dialogue 1974 9(2): 9-24.*
England, Eugene. HANGING BY A THREAD: MORMONS AND WA-TERGATE, *pp. 9-18.* Mormon theology posits natural laws of political justice and liberty which are described and guaranteed by the Declaration of Independence and the Constitution. Mormons were wrong to have given unquestioning loyalty to Nixon.
Rushforth, Brent N. WATERGATE: A PERSONAL EXPERIENCE, *pp. 19-24.* In contributing to the Committee to Re-elect the President in illegal ways, the business community revealed moral laxity. The author, in helping to prosecute the Northrop case, rediscovered the value of the gospels in shaping ethics.   D. L. Rowe

1174. —. ON THE DISREGARD OF THE CONSTITUTIONAL ROLE OF THE HOUSE OF REPRESENTATIVES IN THE DISPOSITION OF PROPERTY OF THE UNITED STATES. *Inter-American Econ. Affairs 1979 33(1): 91-94.* Sets forth the role of the House of Representatives in disposition of property of the United States, in answer to a contention that action by the House was unnecessary in the case of the Panama Canal Treaty of 1978.

1175. —. OUR LITIGIOUS SCHOOLS: A CONTROVERSY. *Public Affairs 1982 (67): 131-139.*
Menacker, Julius. THE COURTS ARE NOT KILLING OUR CHILDREN, *pp. 131-136.* Wynne's argument that liberal Supreme Court decisions have substantially increased youth self-destructiveness cannot be logically and empirically supported. Societal events, such as the Vietnam War, seem correlated with upsurges in youth self-destructiveness. Not all recent court decisions support students, and if student victories in court decisions inspire more lawsuits, that is the price the nation must pay for a better society.
Wynne, Edward A. COURTS, SCHOOLS, AND FAMILY CHOICE, *pp. 136-139.* Resolution of public school problems should not be left solely to the cumbersome efforts of the courts.   J. M. Herrick

1176. —. PREFERENTIAL ADMISSION IN HIGHER EDUCATION: SHOULD WE SUPPORT OR CONDEMN IT? *Civil Liberties R. 1975 2(2): 95-116.*
Askin, Frank. ELIMINATING RACIAL INEQUALITY IN A RACIST WORLD, *pp. 96-105, 114-115.*
Cohen, Carl. HONORABLE ENDS, UNSAVORY MEANS, *pp. 107-114, 115-116.* A few years ago the University of Washington Law School, one

of many troubled by the small number of blacks in the legal profession, began to give preference to black applicants who had met the basic requirements for admission and were competing for places against whites who had passed that same initial hurdle. In 1971 Marco DeFunis, Jr., a white applicant who had been turned down in two successive years, sued the law school, alleging that the school had discriminated against him: while his grades and aptitude test scores were high, he said, other candidates with qualifications and credentials inferior to his had been admitted. A lower court in the state agreed with DeFunis's contention and ordered the school to admit him. The school did so. It then appealed to the Supreme Court of the State of Washington, which decided in favor of the school's right to exercise its preferential admission policy. DeFunis's attorney appealed to the U.S. Supreme Court. By the time the high court heard the case, DeFunis, who had been permitted to remain in school, was about to receive his law degree. In April 1974 the Supreme Court, by a 5-to-4 majority, declared the case to be without practical significance and rendered no decision on the issues involved. The issues raised by the DeFunis case—"reverse discrimination," quota systems, the application of the equal protection of the laws doctrine of the Constitution—aroused so much interest and concern that the Court received 30 "friend-of-the-court" briefs on both sides of the case from such diverse quarters as organized labor, business groups, educational associations, Jewish organizations, black organizations, chicano organizations, the American Bar Association, and the American Civil Liberties Union. Though Marco DeFunis's own case had to do with preference for blacks in admission to law school, its implications are broader: they concern all disadvantaged groups seeking access to better education and better jobs. How blacks, other racial minorities, and women can be enabled to catch up to the rest of a society that hs discriminated against them for centuries, and to do so in a way that is fair and constitutional. In the absence of an easy answer, it is not surprising that the issue of preferential treatment is once again before the courts in a number of cases. To shed more light on the civil liberties aspects of preferential treatment, we invited two civil libertarians who took opposing positions on *DeFunis* to join in debate in our pages. Each debater states his case at length, and then each briefly rebuts the other.   J

1177.   —. SCHOOL DESEGREGATION AND THE COURTS. *Social Policy 1976 6(4): 32-41.*
Taylor, William L.; Benjes, John E.; and Wright, Eric E. SCHOOL DESEGREGATION AND THE COURTS, *pp. 32-35.*
Gittell, Marilyn. [SCHOOL DESEGREGATION AND THE COURTS], *pp. 36-41.*
Discusses the social and legal implications of court-ordered school desegregation in the 1960's and 70's, emphasizing the Supreme Court's *Milliken* v. *Bradley* (US, 1974) decision.

1178.   —. TEXT OF U.S. SUPREME COURT DECISION: MUELLER V. ALLEN. *J. of Church and State 1984 26(1): 171-184.* Reprints the Supreme Court's majority and dissenting opinions in the case *Mueller* v. *Allen* (US,

1982), which concerned state-tax deductions for expenses of private, primary and secondary education. The majority upheld the constitutionality of such deductions. 16 notes.   E. E. Eminhizer

1179. —. [THE TRIUMPH OF WATERGATE]. *Am. Heritage 1984 35(4): 22-35.*
—. THE TRIUMPH OF WATERGATE, *pp. 22-23.* Reviews the events of the Watergate scandal and its impact.
Karp, Walter. THE HOUR OF THE FOUNDERS, *pp. 24-30.* Recounts the day to day events of the final months of Richard Nixon's presidency, as the constitutional crisis reached its conclusion.
Bourjaily, Vance. THE FINAL ACT, *pp. 31-35.* A self-described "Nixon hater" tells how his delight over Nixon's fall has given way to larger feelings of sadness over the tragedy as the years have passed. 11 photos.
                                                                          J. F. Paul

1180. —. [WILLIAM O. DOUGLAS AND JUDICIAL ACTIVISM].
Mendelson, Wallace. MR. JUSTICE DOUGLAS AND GOVERNMENT BY THE JUDICIARY. *J. of Pol. 1976 38(4): 918-937.* Studies developments within the federal judicial process that illustrate why new liberals seem inclined to look to the judiciary for help. Their great victories have been won in court, hence it is not strange that a major element of modern activism is an effort to open more widely the gateway to the federal judiciary. Mr. Justice Douglas was a leading spokesman for this approach, and champion of the issue of access to the courts. "The old liberalism resented government by judges; neo-liberalism embraces it. Mr. Justice Douglas started out in the one camp and ended up in the other." 86 notes.
Goldman, Sheldon. IN DEFENSE OF JUSTICE: SOME THOUGHTS ON READING PROFESSOR MENDELSON'S "MR. JUSTICE DOUG-LAS AND GOVERNMENT BY THE JUDICIARY." *J. of Pol. 1977 39(1): 148-158.* Questions Mendelson's characterization of Douglas as a "leading spokesman" for "neo-liberal" modern judicial activism on the Supreme Court. Douglas' decisions on certiorari, standing to sue, judicial ripeness, mootness, political questions, and substantive law consistently supported civil rights and liberties. Based on primary and secondary sources; 20 notes.
Mendelson, Wallace. A RESPONSE TO PROFESSOR GOLDMAN. *J. of Pol. 1977 (1): 159-165.* William O. Douglas emphasized his philosophy of justice over constitutional and legal standards and procedures, raising the spectre of government by an elite—the justices of the Supreme Court unaccountable to political or other judicial authority. Based on primary and secondary sources; 9 notes.   R. V. Ritter/A. W. Novitsky

Books

1182. Ackerman, Bruce A. *Private Property and the Constitution.* New Haven: Yale U. Pr., 1977. 303 pp.

1183.   Anderson, Douglas A. A "Washington Merry-Go-Round" of Libel Actions. Chicago: Nelson-Hall, 1980. 351 pp.

1184.   Ashmore, Harry S. Fear in the Air: Broadcasting and the First Amendment: The Anatomy of a Constitutional Crisis. New York: Norton, 1973. 180 pp.

1185.   Baer, Judith A. Equality under the Constitution: Reclaiming the Fourteenth Amendment. Ithaca, N.Y.: Cornell U. Pr., 1983. 308 pp.

1186.   Baum, Lawrence. The Supreme Court. Washington: Congressional Q., 1981. 248 pp.

1187.   Berger, Raoul. Death Penalties: The Supreme Court's Obstacle Course. Cambridge, Mass.: Harvard U. Pr., 1982. 242 pp.

1188.   Blasi, Vincent, ed. The Burger Court: The Counter-Revolution that Wasn't. New Haven: Yale U. Pr., 1983. 326 pp.

1189.   Bonomi, Patricia; Burns, James MacGregor; and Ranney, Austin, ed. The American Constitutional System under Strong and Weak Parties. New York: Praeger, 1981. 142 pp.

1190.   Bowers, William J. Legal Homicide: Death as Punishment in America, 1864-1982. Boston: Northeastern U. Pr., 1984. 614 pp.

1191.   Chamberlin, Bill F. and Brown, Charlene J., ed. The First Amendment Reconsidered. New York: Longman, 1982. 218 pp.

1192.   Chief Justice Earl Warren Conference on Advocacy in the United States. The First Amendment and the News Media. Cambridge, Mass.: Roscoe Pound-Am. Trial Lawyers Foundation, 1973. 88 pp.

1193.   Choper, Jesse H. Judicial Review and the National Political Process: A Functional Reconsideration of the Role of the Supreme Court. Chicago: U. of Chicago Pr., 1980. 494 pp.

1194.   Cortner, Richard C. The Supreme Court and the Second Bill of Rights: The Fourteenth Amendment and the Nationalization of Civil Liberties. Madison: U. of Wisconsin Pr., 1981. 360 pp.

1195.   Corwin, Edward S. The Constitution and What It Means Today. 13th ed., Princeton: Princeton U. Pr., 1973. 601 pp.

1196.   Cowan, Geoffrey. See No Evil: The Backstage Battle over Sex and Violence in Television. New York: Simon and Schuster, 1979. 323 pp.

1197. Cox, Archibald. *Freedom of Expression.* Original publ. in *Harvard Law Review* (November 1980). Cambridge, Mass.: Harvard U. Pr., 1981. 89 pp.

1198. Dennis, Everette E.; Gillmor, Donald M.; and Grey, David L., ed. *Justice Hugo Black and the First Amendment.* Ames: Iowa State U. Pr., 1978. 204 pp.

1199. Elliott, Ward E. Y. *The Rise of Guardian Democracy: The Supreme Court's Role in Voting Rights Disputes, 1845-1969.* (Harvard Political Studies.) Cambridge, Mass.: Harvard U. Pr., 1975. 391 pp.

1200. Fein, Bruce E. *Significant Decisions of the Supreme Court, 1978-1979 Term.* Washington: Am. Enterprise Inst. for Public Policy Res., 1980. 199 pp.

1201. Fellman, David. *The Defendant's Rights Today.* Madison: U. of Wisconsin Pr., 1977. 446 pp.

1202. Freedman, Samuel S. and Naughton, Pamela J. *ERA: May the State Change Its Vote?* Detroit, Mich.: Wayne State U. Pr., 1978. 170 pp.

1203. Friendly, Fred W. *The Good Guys, the Bad Guys and the First Amendment: Free Speech vs. Fairness in Broadcasting.* New York: Random, 1976. 268 pp.

1204. Funston, Richard. *A Vital National Seminar: The Supreme Court in American Political Life.* Palo Alto, Calif.: Mayfield, 1978. 226 pp.

1205. Gabin, Sanford Byron. *Judicial Review and the Reasonable Doubt Test.* Port Washington, N.Y.: Kennikat, 1980. 125 pp.

1206. Georgetown Law Journal. *Media and the First Amendment in a Free Society.* Amherst: U. of Massachusetts Pr., 1973. 229 pp.

1207. Goldman, Alvin L. *The Supreme Court and Labor Management Relations Law.* Lexington, Mass.: Heath, 1976. 191 pp.

1208. Hamlin, David. *The Nazi/Skokie Conflict: A Civil Liberties Battle.* Boston: Beacon, 1981. 184 pp.

1209. Highsaw, Robert B. *Edward Douglass White: Defender of the Conservative Faith.* William J. Cooper, Jr., ed. Baton Rouge: Louisiana State U. Pr., 1981. 212 pp.

1210. Hirsch, H. N. *The Enigma of Felix Frankfurter.* New York: Basic Books, 1981. 253 pp.

1211. Hohenberg, John. *A Crisis for the American Press.* New York: Columbia, 1978. 316 pp.

1212.   Irons, Peter H. *Justice at War: The Story of the Japanese American Internment Cases.* New York: Oxford U. Pr., 1983. 407pp.

1213.   Jacobs, Clyde E. *The Eleventh Amendment and Sovereign Immunity.* Westport, Conn.: Greenwood Pr., 1972. 216pp.

1214.   Kelly, Alfred A.; Harbison, Winfred A.; and Belz, Herman. *The American Constitution, Its Origins and Development.* 6th ed. New York: Norton, 1982. 877pp.

1215.   Keynes, Edward. *Undeclared War: Twilight Zone of Constitutional Power.* University Park: Pennsylvania State U. Pr., 1982. 236pp.

1216.   Kluger, Richard. *Simple Justice: The History of* Brown v. Board of Education *and Black America's Struggle for Equality.* New York: Knopf, 1976. 823pp.

1217.   Konvitz, Milton R. *Bill of Rights Reader.* 1954. 5th ed. rev., Ithaca, N.Y.: Cornell U. Pr., 1973. 748 pp.

1218.   Kurland, Philip B., ed. *Church and State: The Supreme Court and the First Amendment.* Rev. ed., Chicago: U. of Chicago Pr., 1975. 272pp.

1219.   Kurland, Philip B., ed. *The Supreme Court Review, 1976.* Chicago: U. of Chicago Pr., 1977. 343pp.

1220.   Kutler, Stanley I. *The American Inquisition: Justice and Injustice in the Cold War.* New York: Hill and Wang, 1982. 285pp.

1221.   Kyvig, David E. *Repealing National Prohibition.* Chicago: U. of Chicago Pr., 1979. 274pp.

1222.   Lash, Joseph P. *From the Diaries of Felix Frankfurter (with a Biographical Essay and Notes).* New York: Norton, 1975. 366pp.

1223.   Levy, Leonard W. *Against the Law: The Nixon Court and Criminal Justice.* New York: Harper and Row, 1974. 506pp.

1224.   MacKinnon, Catharine A. *Sexual Harassment of Working Women: A Case of Sex Discrimination.* New Haven: Yale U. Pr., 1979. 312pp.

1225.   Magee, James J. *Mr. Justice Black: Absolutist on the Court.* (Virginia Legal Studies.) Charlottesville: U. Pr. of Virginia, 1980. 214pp.

1226.   McDowell, Gary L. *Equity and the Constitution: The Supreme Court, Equitable Relief, and Public Policy.* Chicago: U. of Chicago Pr., 1982. 180pp.

1227.   Merry, Henry J. *Five-Branch Government: The Full Measure of Constitutional Checks and Balances.* Urbana: U. of Illinois Pr., 1980. 278pp.

1228. Meyer, Howard N. *The Amendment That Refused to Die.* Radnor, Pa.: Chilton, 1973. 252 pp.

1229. Miller, Arthur Selwyn. *Social Change and Fundamental Law: America's Evolving Constitution.* (Contributions in American Studies, no. 41.) Westport, Conn.: Greenwood, 1979. 395 pp.

1230. Miller, Arthur Selwyn. *The Supreme Court: Myth and Reality.* (Contributions in American Studies, no. 38.) Westport, Conn.: Greenwood, 1978. 388 pp.

1231. Morgan, Richard E. *The Supreme Court and Religion.* New York: Free Pr., 1972. 216 pp.

1232. Murphy, Paul L. *The Meaning of Freedom of Speech: First Amendment Freedoms from Wilson to FDR.* (Contributions in American History.) Westport, Conn.: Greenwood, 1972.

1233. O'Brien, David M. *Privacy, Law, and Public Policy.* (Praeger Special Studies Series.) New York: Praeger, 1979. 262 pp.

1234. O'Brien, David M. *The Public's Right to Know: The Supreme Court and the First Amendment.* New York: Praeger, 1981. 205 pp.

1235. O'Connor, Karen. *Women's Organizations' Use of the Courts.* Lexington, Mass.: Lexington Books, 1980. 157 pp.

1236. Owen, Bruce M. *Economics and Freedom of Expression: Media Structure and the First Amendment.* Cambridge: Ballinger, 1975. 203 pp.

1237. Paper, Lewis J. *Brandeis: An Intimate Biography of One of America's Truly Great Supreme Court Justices.* Englewood Cliffs, N.J.: Prentice-Hall, 1983. 442 pp.

1238. Perry, Michael J. *The Constitution, the Courts, and Human Rights: An Inquiry into the Legitimacy of Constitutional Policymaking by the Judiciary.* New Haven: Yale U. Pr., 1982. 241 pp.

1239. Reams, Bernard D., Jr. and Wilson, Paul E., eds. *Segregation and the Fourteenth Amendment in the States: A Survey of State Segregation Laws, 1865-1953.* Prepared for United States Supreme Court in re: *Brown vs. Board of Education of Topeka.* Buffalo, N.Y.: Hein, 1976. 761 pp.

1240. Rubin, Eva R. *Abortion, Politics, and the Courts:* Roe v. Wade *and Its Aftermath.* Westport, Conn.: Greenwood, 1982. 211 pp.

1241. Russell, Peter et al. *The Court and the Constitution: The Supreme Court Reference on Constitutional Amendment.* Kingston, Ont.: Inst. of Intergovernmental Relations, 1982. 81 pp.

1242. Schlesinger, Steven R. *Exclusionary Injustice: The Problem of Illegally Obtained Evidence.* (Political Science—Constitutional Law.) New York: Dekker, 1977. 116pp.

1243. Siegan, Bernard H. *Economic Liberties and the Constitution.* Chicago: U. of Chicago Pr., 1981. 383pp.

1244. Simon, James F. *Independent Journey: The Life of William O. Douglas.* New York: Harper & Row, 1980. 503pp.

1245. Spangler, Earl. *Presidential Tenure and Constitutional Limitation.* Washington: U. Pr. of America, 1977. 190pp.

1246. Spurrier, Robert L., Jr. *To Preserve These Rights: Remedies for the Victims of Constitutional Deprivations.* Port Washington, N.Y.: Kennikat, 1978.

1247. Stephan, Walter G. and Feagin, Joe R. *School Desegregation: Past, Present, and Future.* New York: Plenum, 1980. 357pp.

1248. Strum, Philippa. *The Supreme Court and "Political Questions:" A Study in Judicial Evasion.* University: U. of Alabama Pr., 1974. 188pp.

1249. Urofsky, Melvin I. *Louis D. Brandeis and the Progressive Tradition.* (Library of American Biography series.) Boston: Little, Brown, 1981. 183pp.

1250. Velvel, Lawrence R. *Undeclared War and Civil Disobedience: The American System in Crisis.* New York: Dunellen, 1970. 405pp.

1251. Westin, Alan F. and Mahoney, Barry. *The Trial of Martin Luther King.* New York: Crowell, 1975. 342pp.

1252. Wormuth, Francis D. *Essays on Law and Politics.* Dalmas H. Nelson and Richard L. Sklar, ed. Port Washington, N.Y.: Kennikat, 1978. 274pp.

1253. Yudoff, Mark G. *When Government Speaks: Politics, Law, and Government Expression in America.* Berkeley: U. of California Pr., 1983. 326pp.

Dissertations

1254. Bagby, Robert E. "Search and Seizure and the Fourth Amendment: Applicability to Student Rights." Miami U. 1976. 462 pp. *DAI 1977 37(7): 3999-A.*

1255. Barnett, Harold Thomas. "Credential Revocation, Dismissal, Non-Renewal and Suspension Based on Criminal Activities of Public School Teachers and Administrators: The Constitutional, Statutory, and Case Law." U. of Georgia 1983. 362 pp. *DAI 1983 44(5): 1255-A.* DA8320069

1256.   Bean, Robbie Lee Powell. "Legal Rights of Elementary School Age Children." U. of Colorado, Boulder 1979. 200 pp. *DAI 1979 40(4): 1761-A.*

1257.   Becker, Robert Myron. "Chief Justice Warren and Civil Liberties." New School for Social Res. 1974. 286 pp. *DAI 1975 35(8): 5471-A.*

1258.   Bigel, Alan Ira. "The Supreme Court on Presidential and Congressional Powers Relating to Foreign Affairs, War Powers, and Internal Security 1935-1980." New School for Social Res. 1984. 226 pp. *DAI 1984 45(4): 1196-A.* DA8414832

1259.   Blahna, Loretta J. "The Rhetoric of the Equal Rights Amendment." U. of Kansas 1973. 190 pp. *DAI 1974 34(12): 7909-A.*

1260.   Blount, Gary Lester. "Significant Legal and Constitutional Issues in Preferential Admissions (Racial) in Professional Schools." U. of Southern California 1978. *DAI 1978 38(12): 7164-A.*

1261.   Boggs, Timothy Jay. "An Analysis of the Opinions in the United States Supreme Court Decisions on Religion and Education from 1948 through 1972." U. of Colorado 1973. 899 pp. *DAI 1974 34(7): 3931-3932-A.*

1262.   Bokowski, Debrah. "Amending the Constitution: The Case of the Equal Rights Amendment." Ohio State U. 1984. 221 pp. *DAI 1985 45(8): 2635-A.* DA8426355

1263.   Bowers, Michael Wayne. "*Zurcher* v. *Stanford Daily:* The Supreme Court and the Limits of the First Amendment." U. of Arizona 1983. 193 pp. *DAI 1983 44(6): 1907-A.* DA8324449

1264.   Bowles, Dorothy Ann. "Newspaper Editorial Support for Freedom of Speech and Press, 1919-1969." U. of Wisconsin, Madison 1978. 183 pp. *DAI 1978 39(6): 3196-3197-A.*

1265.   Broadwater, Margaret Rogers. "Labor and the First Amendment: Thornhill to Logan Valley Plaza." Rutgers U. 1976. 395 pp. *DAI 1977 37(10): 6713-A.*

1266.   Brock, John Richard. "Constitutional Limits of Government Control and Regulation of Church Schools." Pepperdine U. 1984. 312 pp. *DAI 1985 45(7): 1930-1931-A.* DA8421611

1267.   Brockmeyer, Marta Anne. "The Warren Court First Amendment Decisions: Freedom of Expression Redefined for Students Enrolled in Public Institutions of Higher Education." Saint Louis U. 1982. 350 pp. *DAI 1984 44(7): 2054-A.* DA8325336

1268.   Cohen, Jeremy. "Schenck v. United States: A Clear and Present Danger to the First Amendment." U. of Washington 1983. 216 pp. *DAI 1984 44(8): 2279-A.* DA8326861

1269. Dalrymple, Candice. "Sexual Distinctions in the Law: Early Maximum Hour Decisions of the United States Supreme Court, 1905-1917." U. of Florida 1979. 337 pp. *DAI 1980 40(8): 4714-A.*

1270. Dalton, Thomas Carlyle. "The State Politics of Congressional and Judicial Reform: Implementing Criminal Records Policy." U. of Massachusetts 1984. 317 pp. *DAI 1984 45(1): 290-A.* DA8410276

1271. Daugherty, William James. "The Courts, the Constitution, and the War in Vietnam: A Legal Interpretation of Presidential War-Making." Claremont Grad. School 1979. 217 pp. *DAI 1979 39(11): 6934-6935-A.*

1272. Davidson, Philip Leon. "The Warren Court and Its Impact on the Fourth Amendment Rights of College and University Students." George Peabody Coll. 1981. 72 pp. *DAI 1981 42(4): 1393-A.* DA8121545

1274. Davis, Sue. "Balancing, Weighing, and Measuring: The Supreme Court, the Fourteenth Amendment, and the Concept of State Action." U. of California, Santa Barbara 1980. 316 pp. *DAI 1981 41(11): 4822-A.* DA8108360

1275. Dawson, Thomas A. "Women in Law Enforcement: *Fanchon Blake* v. *The City of Los Angeles.*" Claremont Grad. School 1984. 405 pp. *DAI 1984 44(8): 2589-A.* DA8328275

1276. Dean, Ronald Edward. "Obscenity Standards in Canada and the United States: A Comparative Study in Constitutional Law." U. of Tennessee 1974. 163 pp. *DAI 1975 35(11): 7361-A.*

1277. deBettencourt, Kathleen Bajorek. "Parent, Child, and State: The Family in American Constitutional Law." Catholic U. of Am. 1984. 189 pp. *DAI 1984 45(3): 930-931-A.* DA8414762

1278. Decker, James Thomas. "Historical Evolution of the Fourteenth Amendment Due Process of Law as it Relates to Students in Private Higher Educational Institutions." U. of Minnesota 1976. 161 pp. *DAI 1976 37(6): 3289-3290-A.*

1279. DeMontfort, Harold. "A Natural Law Interpretation of the Constitution of the United States." U. of Southern Mississippi 1973. 263 pp. *DAI 1974 34(9): 6062-6063-A.*

1280. Downs, Donald Alexander. "Freedom, Community, and the First Amendment: The Skokie Case and the Limits of Speech." U. of California, Berkeley 1983. 436 pp. *DAI 1984 45(3): 931-A.* DA8413367

1281. Drain, George Francis. "Individual School Board Member Liability Under 42 U.S.C., Section 1983 from 1871 to 1976." West Virginia U. 1979. 217 pp. *DAI 1979 39(11): 6424-A.*

1282. Drouin, Edmond G. "The United States Supreme Court and Religious Freedom in American Education in Its Decisions Affecting Church-Related Elementary and Secondary Schools During the First Three Quarters of the Twentieth Century." Catholic U. of Am. 1980. 502 pp. *DAI 1981 41(10): 4311-4312-A.* DA8107975

1283. Dunn, John Carah, Jr. "American Educational Jurisprudence: A Study of the Influence of State Statutes and Federal Courts on Public Schools and the Desegregation Process in the United States." Ohio State U. 1978. 214 pp. *DAI 1979 39(8): 4620-A.*

1285. Epperson, John Wallace Walker. "The Changing Legal Status of Political Parties in the United States." U. of Virginia 1980. 268 pp. *DAI 1980 41(4): 1747-1748-A.* DA8022954

1286. Farmer, Richard Franklin. "The Operational Relationship of the First Amendment Establishment and Free Exercise Clause to Public Education: An Analysis of Judicial Criteria Employed by Federal Courts." Southern Illinois U. 1973. 218 pp. *DAI 1974 34(9): 5523-A.*

1287. Fiscus, Ronald Jerry. "Before the Velvet Curtain: The Connecticut Contraceptive Cases as a Study in Constitutional Law and Supreme Court Behavior." U. of Wisconsin, Madison 1983. 578 pp. *DAI 1983 43(12): 4024-A.* DA8306671

1288. Fitzpatrick, Gerard Joseph. "The Role of the Judiciary in the Emerging Constitutional Rights of the Mentally Handicapped." U. of Virginia 1980. 804 pp. *DAI 1981 42(3): 1296-1297-A.* DA8117901

1289. Fleener-Marzec, Nickieann. "D. W. Griffith's *The Birth of a Nation:* Controversy, Suppression, and the First Amendment As It Applies to Filmic Expression, 1915-1973." U. of Wisconsin, Madison 1977. 577 pp. *DAI 1978 38(11): 6378-6379-A.*

1290. Gambill, Joel Thirlo. "Hugo Black: The First Amendment and the Mass Media." Southern Illinois U. 1973. 295 pp. *DAI 1974 34(9): 5895-A.*

1291. Gaston, Henry Victor. "An Analysis of Judicial Decisions Regarding Search and Seizure in Secondary Schools 1967-1978." Auburn U. 1980. 136 pp. *DAI 1980 40(12): 6088-A.* DA8013885

1292.   Gaugush, Bill Thomas. *"Griswold's* Legacy: The Ninth Amendment in the Federal Courts, 1965-1980." Southern Illinois U., Carbondale 1981. 249 pp. *DAI 1982 43(2): 542-A.* DA8215806

1293.   Geary, Thomas Alfred. "A Critical Analysis of the FCC's Fairness Doctrine and the Proposed Right to Access as Alternative Means of Serving the First Amendment in Broadcasting." Wayne State U. 1977. 339 pp. *DAI 1978 38(11): 6379-6380-A.*

1294.   Glenn, Charles Craig. "Citizenship Education and the First Amendment in Public Schools." U. of Illinois, Urbana-Champaign 1982. 195 pp. *DAI 1982 42(11): 4911-A.* DA8209574

1295.   Goldman, Edward Ehud. "Student Rights and the Disciplinary Process in Constitutional Law." U. of Nevada, Las Vegas 1982. 124 pp. *DAI 1983 43(7): 2179-2180-A.* DA8229755

1296.   Graham, Michael Allen. "Constitutional Rights and the Federal Grand Jury." U. of California, Santa Barbara 1982. 252 pp. *DAI 1982 43(6): 2080-A.* DA8224642

1297.   Greenfield, Steven L. "The Application of the First and Fourteenth Amendments to the United States Constitution to the Legal Rights of Students." Northwestern U. 1973. 149 pp. *DAI 1974 34(9): 5527-A.*

1298.   Gribbin, William G. "The So-Called Child Benefit Theory: Parochiaid and the Establishment Clause." Pennsylvania State U. 1977. 291 pp. *DAI 1978 38(10): 5822-A.*

1299.   Haltom, William Thomas. "The Judicial and Social Construction of Constitutionality: The Supreme Court and Newspaper Editorials." Int. U. 1984. *DAI 1984 45(6): 1857-A.*

1300.   Hine, Darlene Clark. "The NAACP and the Destruction of the Democratic White Primary, 1924-1944." Kent State U. 1975. 217 pp. *DAI 1975 36(3): 1722-1723-A.*

1301.   Hofeller, Thomas Brooks. "Mississippi Redistricting 1977-80." Claremont Grad. School 1979. 468 pp. *DAI 1981 41(8): 3705-A.* DA8103809

1302.   Hoffman, David Emerson. "The First Amendment Rights of High School Newspapers in Virginia." U. of North Carolina, Greensboro 1980. 151 pp. *DAI 1980 41(4): 1310-A.* DA8021775

1303.   Hogan, Leila Ann. "Jurisdiction over Foreign Merchant Vessels in American Waters and Ports: Territorial Jurisdiction and Law of the Flag in Selected Decisions of the United States Supreme Court, 1900-1970." U. of Maryland 1979. 234 pp. *DAI 1980 40(10): 5573-5574-A.*

1304.   Hughes, John Corcoran. "John Marshall Harlan, the Warren Court, and the Freedoms of Speech and Press." New School for Social Res. 1978. 386 pp. *DAI 1980 40(8) 4731-4732-A.*

1306.   Hull, Betty Cottrell. "A Legal Study of the Political Activities of Public School Employees: Their Candidacy for Public Offices and Their Campaigning for Other Political Candidates and Issues." U. of Georgia 1980. 326 pp. *DAI 1980 41(5): 1866-1867-A.* DA8023149

1307.   Ishimine, Keitetsu. "A Comparative Study of Judicial Review under American and Japanese Constitutional Law." Cornell U. 1974. 326 pp. *DAI 1974 35(2): 1132-A.*

1308.   Jennings, James Monroe, II. "The Press, the Courts, and the Regulation of Prejudicial Publicity: A Historical Analysis of Attempts to Balance First Amendment and Sixth Amendment Rights." Ohio U. 1983. 438 pp. *DAI 1983 44(4): 899-A.* DA8319002

1309.   Johnson, George Carl. "Special Privilege for an Autonomous Press: Justice Stewart's Structural Approach." Southern Illinois U., Carbondale 1984. 273 pp. *DAI 1985 45(8): 2288-2289-A.* DA8425128

1310.   Jones, Oliver, Jr. "The Constitutional Politics of the Black Muslim Movement in America." U. of Illinois at Urbana-Champaign 1978. 298 pp. *DAI 1979 40(1): 452-A.*

1311.   Jurow, Keith A. "The Bill of Rights, Due Process, and the States." New School for Social Res. 1973. 355 pp. *DAI 1974 35(3): 1720-A.*

1314.   King, Thomas Alfred. "An Analysis of the Jurisprudence of Cruel and Unusual Punishment." West Virginia U. 1982. 311 pp. *DAI 1983 43(11): 3696-A.* DA8306333

1315.   Kleiman, Howard Michael. "Public Broadcasting and Free Expression: An Examination of the Impact of the Government Nexus." U. of Oregon 1981. 413 pp. *DAI 1982 42(8): 3336-A.* DA8201844

1316.   Kornberg, Harvey Richard. "Charles Evans Hughes and the Supreme Court: A Study in Judicial Philosophy and Voting Behavior." Brown U. 1972. 218 pp. *DAI 1979 39(11): 6939-6940-A.*

1317.   Leff, Donna Rosene. "Journalists and Jurists: The Evolution of Reporter's Privilege after *Branzburg.*" U. of California, Berkeley 1982. 191 pp. *DAI 1983 43(8): 2480-A.* DA8300565

1318.   Levin-Epstein, Eve. "The Rhetoric of the Supreme Court: A Dramatistic Analysis of First Amendment Dissenting Opinions." Temple U. 1978. 188 pp. *DAI 1978 39(2): 539-540-A.*

1319.   Lorensen, Frederick Hamilton. "The Evolution and Implications of Tilton v. Richardson: The First United States Supreme Court Test of the Constitutionality of Federal Grants to Religious-Affiliated Colleges and Universities." U. of Connecticut 1979. 351 pp. *DAI 1980 40(8): 4434-A.*

1320.   Lutzker, Paul. "The Politics of Public Interest Groups: Common Cause in Action." Johns Hopkins U. 1973. 204 pp. *DAI 1974 34(11): 7297-A.*

1321.   MacLeod, Scott Roderick. "The Legal-Constitutional Aspects of Intelligence Related Matters in the American Military Justice System." Claremont Grad. School 1979. 187 pp. *DAI 1979 40(4): 2242-A.*

1322.   Magee, James Joseph. "Mr. Justice Black and the First Amendment: The Development and Dilemmas of an Absolutist." U. of Virginia 1976. 335 pp. *DAI 1976 36(7): 4735-A.*

1323.   Manion, Maureen Deborah. "The Impact of State Aid upon Church-Related Higher Education in the State of New York: The First Amendment Issues." State U. of New York, Albany 1982. 252 pp. *DAI 1982 43(2): 543-A.* DA8216395

1324.   Mauney, Connie Pat. "Mr. Justice Black and the First Amendment Freedoms: A Study in Constitutional Interpretation." U. of Tennessee 1975. 364 pp. *DAI 1976 36(8): 5516-5517-A.*

1325.   Mays, George Larry. "Supreme Court Disengagement from State Criminal Procedure: The Case of *Stone* v. *Powell.*" U. of Tennessee 1979. 185 pp. *DAI 1980 40(12): 6406-A.* DA8012477

1326.   McKeon, Thomas Joseph. "What Constitutes State Action in Private Higher Education?" Kent State U. 1983. 119 pp. *DAI 1983 44(5): 1351-1352-A.* DA8321151

1327.   Melder, Trent Osborn. "A Historical Study of the Court Cases That Have Affected the Constitutional and Statutory Provisions for Financing Education in Louisiana." U. of Wyoming 1980. 138 pp. *DAI 1981 41(10): 4239-A.* DA8106977

1328.   Melusky, Joseph Anthony. "Justice John Paul Stevens' Equal Protection Analysis." U. of Delaware 1983. 336 pp. *DAI 1984 45(6): 1858-A.* DA8420979

1329. Menke, Harold Francis. "What are the Legal Issues Confronting Religion in Schools." Southern Illinois U., Carbondale 1984. 186 pp. *DAI 1985 45(8): 2338-A.* DA8425136

1330. Mirabella, Peter Francis. "Justice Byron R. White and Fundamental Freedoms." New School for Social Res. 1980. 248 pp. *DAI 1980 41(5): 2275-A.* DA8025556

1331. Mize, Richard Leon. "The Legal Aspects of Religious Instruction in Public Schools." U. of North Carolina, Greensboro 1980. 208 pp. *DAI 1981 42(2): 486-A.* DA8114590

1332. Montoya, Solomon. "The Formulation and Ratification of the Twenty-sixth Amendment." New York U. 1973. 280 pp. *DAI 1974 34(12): 7841-7842-A.*

1333. Morris, Edward Alfred. "The Separation of Church and State Principle and the Use of Religious Music in the Public Schools." U. of Michigan 1979. 143 pp. *DAI 1979 40(2): 589-A.*

1334. Morrison, Farries Henry, Jr. "A Study of Prayer in the Public Schools, 1962-1980." Southern Illinois U., Carbondale 1983. 107 pp. *DAI 1983 44(5): 1277-1278-A.* DA8321452

1335. Nagy, Alex. "Federal Censorship of Communist Political Propaganda and the First Amendment: 1941-1961." U. of Wisconsin 1973. 394 pp. *DAI 1974 35(1): 490-491-A.*

1336. Nolen, Vance Nathan. "The Emergence and Refinement of the Constitutional Rights Doctrine in Respect to Student Disciplinary Proceedings in Public Higher Education: An Analysis of Doctrinal Change." U. of Southern California 1981. *DAI 1981 41(11): 4620-A.*

1337. O'Hara, Julie Underwood. "State Aid to Denominational Higher Education, a First Amendment Problem." U. of Florida 1984. 197 pp. *DAI 1985 45(7): 2007-A.* DA8421055

1338. Padgett, George Everett. "A Quantitative Analysis of United States Supreme Court Decision-making Relative to First Amendment Issues of Free Speech and Free Press." Ohio U. 1980. 137 pp. *DAI 1981 41(8): 3311-A.* DA8103039

1339. Palmer, Mack Redburn. "The Qualified Absolute: Alexander Meiklejohn and Freedom of Speech." U. of Wisconsin, Madison 1979. 454 pp. *DAI 1980 40(12): 6055-A.* DA8007567

1340. Peters, C. David. "The Demise of 'One Man, One Vote': Changes in Legislative Representation in the United States Since Baker v. Carr and Reynolds v. Sims." U. of Oklahoma 1977. 232 pp. *DAI 1978 39(3): 1812-A.*

1342. Racz, Ernest Bert. "Meiklejohn." Columbia U. Teachers Coll. 1979. 205 pp. *DAI 1981 41(9): 3916-A.* DA8105909

1343. Rentschler, Donald Richard. "The *Tinker* Test: An Analysis of the Judicial Interpretation of *Tinker* v. *Des Moines Independent Community School District.*" Duke U. 1981. 180 pp. *DAI 1982 42(7): 2958-A.* DA8129714

1344. Rodgers, Raymond Sinclair. "Justice William O. Douglas on the First Amendment: Rhetorical Genres in Judicial Opinions." U. of Oklahoma 1979. 271 pp. *DAI 1980 40(12): 6070-A.* DA8012292

1345. Romans, Clifford Scott. "State Regulation of Private Religious Schools: 'Compelling State Interest' and the First Amendment." Kent State U. 1981. 269 pp. *DAI 1982 42(11): 4780-A.* DA8209205

1346. Rothman, Jonathan Saul. "The Constitutional and Political Implications of Campaign Finance Reform." U. of California, Berkeley 1979. 407 pp. *DAI 1980 40(7): 4214-4215-A.*

1347. Schireson, Peter Leo. "The National Labor Relations Board's Faculty Bargaining Unit Decisions." Harvard U. 1980. 240 pp. *DAI 1981 41(9): 3911-A.* DA8100362

1348. Schwartz, David F. "The Thirteenth Amendment as a Basis for Judicial Protection of Individual Rights." Pennsylvania State U. 1975. 267 pp. *DAI 1976 36(7): 4737-A.*

1350. Schwartz, Frank. "The Changing Conception of Constitutional Culpability in School Desegregation Cases: A Search for Judicial Justification of Remedial Action, 1954-1977." U. of North Carolina, Chapel Hill 1979. 309 pp. *DAI 1979 40(5): 2874-A.*

1351. Schwartz, Thomas Alphonse. "A Reconceptualization of the First Amendment: The Burger Court and Freedom of the Press, 1969-1980." Southern Illinois U., Carbondale 1981. 303 pp. *DAI 1981 42(5): 1835-1836-A.* DA8122664

1352. Selvar, Drew K. "Legal Thinking in Six Selected Civil Liberties Decisions of the Warren Court." Southern Illinois U. 1973. 266 pp. *DAI 1974 34(9): 6007-6008-A.*

1353. Sharp, Sallie Martin. "The Evolution of the Invasion of Privacy Tort and Its Newsworthiness Limitations." U. of Texas, Austin 1981. 272 pp. *DAI 1981 42(3): 901-A.* DA8119371

1354. Simba, Malik. "The Black Laborer, the Black Legal Experience and the United States Supreme Court with Emphasis on the Neo-Concept of Equal Employment." U. of Minnesota 1977. 361 pp. *DAI 1978 39(1): 431-432-A.*

1355. Stacey, Charles Edward. "The Supreme Court and the Elevation of Education to the Status of a Fundamental Right." U. of Pittsburgh 1974. 333 pp. *DAI 1975 35(12): 7585-A.*

1356. Stewart, David Michael. "Supreme Court Appointments during the Harding and Coolidge Administrations: Influence, Critics, and Voting." Wayne State U. 1974. 220 pp. *DAI 1975 35(12): 7851-7852-A.*

1357. Stone, Ralph Thomas, Jr. "United States Supreme Court Directives on Corporate Mergers under the Antitrust Laws." U. of Tennessee 1975. 186 pp. *DAI 1975 36(3): 1780-1781-A.*

1358. Tananbaum, Duane Arden. "The Bricker Amendment Controversy: The Interaction between Domestic and Foreign Affairs." Columbia U. 1980. 683 pp. *DAI 1983 43(7): 2428-A.* DA8222494

1359. Tarpley, James Douglas. "Fair Use as Copyright Doctrine: Judicial and Statutory Interpretation." Southern Illinois U., Carbondale 1983. 199 pp. *DAI 1984 44(7): 1960-A.* DA8326571

1360. Thompson, John David, Jr. "Eroding the Fourth Amendment: The Burger Court and the Warrantless Search Exception: Some Post-1970 Developments." U. of Nebraska, Lincoln 1980. 379 pp. *DAI 1980 41(3): 1203-A.* DA8018673

1361. Tremper, Charles Robert. "Constitutionality of Policies Granting Parents of High School-Age Children Authority to Choose among Education Options." U. of California, Los Angeles 1983. 168 pp. *DAI 1983 44(5): 1288-A.* DA8322039

1362. Turman, Ira Nell. "United States Supreme Court Decisions Affecting Compulsory School Attendance Laws." East Texas State U. 1975. 92 pp. *DAI 1976 36(11): 7123-A.*

1363. Tyner, Beverly Bernard. "The Legal Aspects of Teacher Dress and Grooming in the United States." U. of North Carolina, Greensboro 1980. 175 pp. *DAI 1981 42(2): 497-A.* DA8115343

1364. Van Gerpen, Maurice Dale. "Privileged Communication and the Press." U. of California, Santa Barbara 1975. 461 pp. *DAI 1976 36(9): 6289-A.*

1365. Walden, Ruth Christine. "State Action and Media: Applicability of State Action Doctrine to Newspapers, Radio and Television." U. of Wisconsin, Madison 1981. 712 pp. *DAI 1982 42(7): 3279-A.* DA8124636

1366.   Watkins, Michael Charles. "United States Supreme Court Justice Lewis F. Powell: A Study of His Philosophy and Application of the Law in Education Cases." U. of Missouri, Columbia 1984. 201 pp. *DAI 1985 45(8): 2350-A.* DA8425603

1367.   West, Michael Anthony. "The Constitutional Rights of College Students: The Principles of the First, Fourth, and Fourteenth Amendments as They Apply to Higher Education." U. of Massachusetts, 1976. 569 pp. *DAI 1976 37(4): 2023-A.*

1368.   Wingerd, Harold Heindel, Jr. "The Application of the Equal Protection Clause of the Fourteenth Amendment to the Use of Academic Achievement, Exceptionality, Sex, School Fees, Marriage, and Pregnancy as Criteria for the Classification of Students Within a School." Temple U. 1980. 238 pp. *DAI 1980 41(5): 1849-A.* DA8025114

1369.   Wright, Claudia Frances Ayres. "Legitimation by the Supreme Courts of Canada and the United States: A Case Study of Japanese Exclusion." Claremont Grad. School 1973. 362 pp. *DAI 1974 34(7): 4358-A.*

1370.   Zobin, Joseph. "Gag Orders and the First Amendment: The Legal Path to *Nebraska Press Association* v. *Stuart* (1976)." U. of Wisconsin, Madison 1978. 276 pp. *DAI 1978 39(4): 1910-1911-A.*

USER'S GUIDE TO THE INDEXES

All titles in this series use ABC-CLIO's unique Subject Profile Index (ABC-SPIndex) and an author index. The following abstract is found in this volume:

Abstract

121. Shaffer, Thomas I. FIRST AMENDMENT: HISTORY AND THE COURTS. *Rev. of Pol. 1978 40(2): 271-279.* Review article prompted by Walter Berns's *The First Amendment and the Future of American Democracy* (New York: Basic Books, 1976), argues that the Supreme Court has "drifted intolerably far away from the principles and circumstances which caused the founding generation of free Americans to amend their written Constitution by limiting the government's control of religion, assembly, and speech." The Court can't be blamed for not following history as Berns states.   L. E. Ziewacz

In this Subject Index, each index entry is a complete profile of the abstract and consists of one or more subject, geographic, and biographic descriptors, followed by the dates covered in the article. These descriptors are rotated so that the complete subject profile is cited under each of the terms in alphabetical order. Thus, indexing for the abstract shown above is located in five different places in the index:

Subject Index

Berns, Walter (review article). Church and state. Supreme Court. 18c-20c. *121*

Church and state. Berns, Walter (review article). Supreme Court. 18c-20c. *121*

Supreme Court. Berns, Walter (review article). Church and state. 18c-20c. *121*

A dash replaces second and subsequent identical leading terms. Cross-references in the form of *See* and *See-also* references are provided. Refer also to the notes at the head of the Subject Index.

Negroes *See* Blacks

American Revolution *See also* Declaration of Independence

The separate Author Index lists the name of the author and abstract number.

Author Index

Semonche, John E. 670
Sernett, Milton C. 611
Shaffer, Thomas I. 121
Shalhope, Robert E. 309
Shanks, Hershel 1074

SUBJECT INDEX

Subject Profile Index (ABC-SPIndex) carries both generic and specific index terms. Begin a search at the general term but also look under more specific or related terms. This index includes selective cross-references.

Each string of index descriptors is intended to present a profile of a given article; however, no particular relationship between any two terms in the profile is implied. Terms within the profile are listed alphabetically after the leading term. The variety of punctuation and capitalization reflects production methods and has no intrinsic meaning; e.g., there is no difference in meaning between "History, study of" and "History (study of)."

Cities, towns, and counties are listed following their respective states or provinces; e.g., "Ohio (Columbus)." Terms beginning with an arabic numeral are listed after the letter Z. The chronology of the bibliographic entry follows the subject index descriptors. In the chronology, "c" stands for "century"; e.g., "19c" means "19th century."

Note that "United States" is not used as a leading index term; if no country is mentioned, the index entry refers to the United States alone. When an entry refers to both Canada and the United States, both "Canada" and "USA" appear in the string of index descriptors, but "USA" is not a leading term. When an entry refers to any other country and the United States, only the other country is indexed.

The last number in the index string, in italics, refers to the bibliographic entry number.

A

Ability tests. Civil Rights Act (US, 1964). Discrimination, Employment. Economic Opportunity Commission Guidelines. Supreme Court. 1975. *902*

Abolition movement. Amendments (15th). Blacks. Douglass, Frederick. Theology. 1825-86. *630*

—. *Amistad* (vessel). Blacks. Jocelyn, Simeon. Leavitt, Joshua. Supreme Court. Tappan, Lewis. 1839-50. *688*

—. Law. Wiecek, William M. (review article). 1760-1848. 1977. *555*

Abortion. Amendments (1st, 5th). *Harris v. McRae* (US, 1980). Hyde Amendment. Medicaid. Supreme Court. 1976-80. *972*

—. Blacks. Civil Rights. *Dred Scott v. Sandford* (US, 1857). Personhood. *Roe v. Wade* (US, 1973). Supreme Court. 1857. 1973. *611*

—. Civil Rights. Constitutional Law. Fertility. *Roe v. Wade* (US, 1973). Women. 1973-82. *1145*

—. Constitutional Law. *Roe v. Wade* (US, 1973). Women. 1950's-70's. *1240*

—. Criminal law. Religion. Supreme Court. 1980. *1039*

—. Hyde Amendment. State government. Supreme Court. Taxation. 1976-77. *1003*

—. Interest Groups. Law. Politics. 1959-80. *821*

Absentee voting. Amendments (26th). Voting Rights Act, 1970. 1960-72. *813*

Absolutism. Amendments (1st). Black, Hugo L. Literalism. Supreme Court. 1937-71. *1322*

Academic freedom. Amendments (1st). 1950's-82. *891*

—. American Association of University Professors. Civil liberties. 1972. *1122*

Academies, private. Amendments (13th). Louisiana. Segregation. Smallville Academy. 1963-70. *771*

Access. See Information Access.

Accountability. Coffin, Frank M. Dubois, Phillip L. Hodder-Williams, Richard. Judicial Process (review article). Theberge, Leonard J. 1979-80. *845*

—. Constitutional Law. Government. 1940-78. *862*

Acheson, Dean. Congress. Constitutional Law. Korean War. Truman, Harry S. War, declaration of. 1950-64. *952*

Act of state doctrine. Confiscations. Courts. Foreign Relations. International law. Property. *United Bank Ltd.* v. *Cosmic Int'l, Inc* (US, 1976). 1971-76. *774*

Active (vessel). American Revolution. Prize law. Supreme Court. 1778-1809. *393*

Adair, Douglass. *Federalist* No. 10. Hume, David. Madison, James. Political Theory. Republicanism. Wills, Garry. 1788. *392*

Adams, John. Amendments (1st). Jefferson, Thomas. Madison, James. Paine, Thomas. Religious Liberty. 1776-89. *274*

—. Constitutions, State. Massachusetts. 1780. *296*

—. Duane, William. Exiles. Great Britain. Journalists. Press. USA. 1790-1800. *370*

—. Federalism. Hamilton, Alexander. Jefferson, Thomas. Washington, George. 1775-90's. *239*

Addiction. Criminal Law. Drug Abuse. Supreme Court. 1962-68. *980*

Addison, Alexander. Constitutional Law. Federalists. Freedom of Speech. Pennsylvania. Sedition Act (US, 1798). 1792-98. *605*

Administrative Law. Due Process. Higher education. Students. Supreme Court. 1960-70. *783*

Admissions policy. Aliens (illegal). Amendments (14th). Public schools. Texas. 1980. *1066*

—. Colleges and Universities. *DeFunis* v. *Odegaard* (US, 1974). Discrimination. Supreme Court. Washington (University of, Law School). 1971-75. *1176*

—. Discrimination, Education. Law. Professional Schools. Quotas. 1977. *1260*

Adventists. Amendments (21st). Prohibition. 1932-34. *1151*

Advertising. Amendments (1st). Freedom of Speech. Government. Interest groups. Mass Media. Supreme Court. 1972-78. *1112*

—. Amendments (1st). Supreme Court. 1942-82. *1058*

—. Monopolies. Newspaper Preservation Act (US, 1970). Supreme Court. *Times-Picayune Publishing Co.* v. *United States* (US, 1953). 1953-78. *721*

241

—. Amendments. Federal Government. 1970's-82. *954*

—. Amendments. Senate Joint Resolution 58. 1983. *981*

—. Constitutional convention. 1787-1982. *43*

Bullard, Arthur. Amendments (1st). Censorship. Committee on Public Information. Creel, George. Press. Propaganda. World War I. 1917-20. *1126*

Burdick v. *United States* (US, 1915). Amendments (5th). New York *Tribune.* Newspapers. Pardons (refused). Supreme Court. 1913-15. *741*

Bureau of Alcohol, Tobacco, and Firearms. Amendments (2d). Civil Rights. 1970-80. *947*

Bureau of Indian Affairs. Collier, John. Federal Policy. Indians. Nevada. Shoshoni Indians. Tribal government. 1934-38. *1061*

Burger, Warren E. Amendments (1st). Church and state. Supreme Court. 1950-75. *743*

—. Amendments (1st). Freedom of Speech. Supreme Court. 1969-1981. *1197*

—. Amendments (1st). Freedom of the Press. Supreme Court. 1969-80. *1351*

—. Amendments (4th). Judicial Administration. *Pennsylvania* v. *Mimms. Schneckloth* v. *Bustamonte.* Supreme Court. 1971-79. *1360*

—. Civil liberties. Supreme Court. 1975-78. *873*

—. Civil Rights. Federalism. Supreme Court. Warren, Earl. 1953-78. *974*

—. Civil Rights. Habeas corpus. Institutions. Supreme Court. Warren, Earl. 1954-77. *973*

—. Civil Rights. Law Reform. Supreme Court. Warren, Earl. 1937-73. *792*

—. Civil Rights. Supreme Court. ca 1970-75. *1092*

—. Congress. Judges. Supreme Court. 1960's-70's. *1154*

—. Federal Policy. Funston, Richard (review article). Judicial Administration. Supreme Court. Warren, Earl. 1953-79. *1103*

—. Law and Society. Supreme Court. 1968-78. *723*

Burnside, Ambrose E. Amendments (1st). Civil War. Freedom of Speech. Lincoln, Abraham. North Central States. 1863. *697*

Burton, Harold. Attitudes. Decisionmaking. Supreme Court. 1945-58. *748*

Business. Amendments (1st). Freedom of the press. Mass media. 1789-1975. *89*

—. Amendments (1st). Mass Media. Public interest. 1960's-70's. *1170*

—. Amendments (5th, 14th). Labor law. 1868-1915. *596*

—. Antitrust. Supreme Court. *United States* v. *Yellow Cab Co.* (US, 1949). 1947-49. *926*

—. Civil rights. Constitutional Law (review article). Federal Government. Hyman, Harold M. Wiecek, William M. 1835-75. *512*

—. Civil Rights Act (US, 1964; Title VII). Foreign Investments. Japan. Law. *Sumitomo Shoji America, Inc.* v. *Avagliano* (US, 1982). Supreme Court. 1977-83. *1138*

—. Constitutional Law. Field, Stephen J. Government. Supreme Court. 1863-97. *578*

—. Ethics. Mormons. Theology. Watergate scandal. 1974. *1173*

Busing. Church and state. Church schools. Legislation. New Jersey. Supreme Court. 1937-41. *811*

—. Constitutional Law. Courts (federal). Public Schools. 1954-72. *842*

—. Race Relations. Schools. 1975. *1031*

Butler, Elizur. Cherokee Indians. Indian-White Relations. Marshall, John. Nullification crisis. Supreme Court. Worcester, Samuel A. *Worcester* v. *Georgia* (US, 1832). 1828-33. *586*

Butler, Pierce. Constitutional Convention. Documents. 1787. *409*

Byrd, Harry F. Chambers, Lenoir. Editors and Editing. School Integration. Supreme Court. Virginia. 1955-59. *1015*

C

Cabinet. Executive branch. 1776-1976. *32*

Calhoon, Robert McCluer. American Revolution. Bailyn, Bernard. Berkin, Carol. Great Britain. Loyalists (review article). Political Theory. 1760-83. *287*

California. Amendments. Initiatives. Legislation. Referendum. 1911-78. *942*

—. Bilingual education. Chacone-Moscone Bilingual Bicultural Education Act (1976). Civil Rights Act (US, 1964). *Lau* v. *Nichols* (US, 1974). Supreme Court. 1965-76. *939*

—. Boundaries. Congress. General Land Office. Legislation. Nevada. State Government. Supreme Court. 1850-1980. *556*

—. Campaign Finance. Constitutional Law. Federal Regulation. Political Reform. 1976. *1346*

—. Discrimination. Japanese Americans. Legislation. Supreme Court. 1920's. *768*

—. Fair housing. Housing. Referendum. Voting and Voting behavior. ca 1960-67. *1158*

—. Family. Governors. Judges. Law. Supreme Court. Warren, Earl. 1911-74. *1132*

—. Field, Stephen J. Law. Public lands. Supreme courts, state. 1850-66. *581*

California (Eight Mile, Blue Creek). Amendments (1st). Forest Service. Indians. Religious liberty. Supreme Court. 1975. *1026*

California (Fresno). Anti-Semitism. Foote, William D. Johnson, Grove L. Trials. 1893. *640*

California Irrigation District Law. California (Santa Margarita River, Fallbrook). Fallbrook Irrigation District Case (US, 1896). Water rights. 1886-99. *607*

California (Marysville). Field, Stephen J. Judges. Supreme Court. 1849-97. *625*

California (San Francisco). Amendments (5th). Blacks. Civil Rights. Law Enforcement. Operation Zebra. 1974. *848*

—. Field, Stephen J. Hill, Sarah Althea. Sharon, William. Terry, David S. 1884-89. *573*

California (Santa Margarita River, Fallbrook). California Irrigation District Law. Fallbrook Irrigation District Case (US, 1896). Water rights. 1886-99. *607*

California v. *United States* (US, 1978). Federalism. State Government. Supreme Court. Water Supply. 1978. *993*

Callender, James Thomson. Amendments (1st). Freedom of the press. Hay, George. Republican Party. Virginia. 1798-1803. *551*

Campaign finance. Amendments (1st). *Buckley* v. *Valeo* (US, 1976). Congress. Federal Election Campaign Act (US, 1971; amended 1974). Glasser, Ira (interview). 1971-74. *1168*

—. Amendments (1st). *Buckley* v. *Valeo* (US, 1976). Congress. Federal Election Commission. Gora, Joel (interview). 1974-76. *1165*

—. Amendments (1st). *Buckley* v. *Valeo* (US, 1976). Supreme Court. 1957-76. *1055*

—. California. Constitutional Law. Federal Regulation. Political Reform. 1976. *1346*

—. Citizen Lobbies. Common Cause. Constitutional Amendments (26th). Interest Groups. 1971. *1320*

—. Communist Party. Press. Senate Internal Security Subcommittee. Supreme Court. 1955-59. *909*
—. Confrontation. Criminal Law. Supreme Court. 1957-69. *1073*
—. Conscience, Private. Law. Public interest. Supreme Court. 19c-1972. *183*
—. Constitutional Amendments (14th). 1868-1973. *1228*
—. Constitutional Amendments (14th). *McInnis* v. *Ogilvie* (US, 1969). Public Schools. State Aid to Education. 1965-70. *1074*
—. Constitutional Law. Courts. Federal Government. State Government. 1776-1978. *794*
—. Constitutional Law. Douglas, William O. Judicial activism. Liberalism. Supreme Court. 1928-77. *1180*
—. Constitutional Law. Ideology. 1776-1976. *90*
—. Constitutional Law. Police, undercover. 1970's. *966*
—. Constitutional Law. Privacy. Supreme Court. 1886-1980. *1043*
—. Constitutional Law. Students. 1969-77. *1295*
—. Constitutional Law. Supreme Court. 1973. *1217*
—. Constitutional Law. Supreme Court. ca 1960-73. *1000*
—. Constitutional theory. Freedmen. Racism. Reconstruction. 1861-77. *667*
—. Constitutionalism. Emancipation. Politics. 1862-76. *642*
—. Courts. Handicapped. Mental Illness. 1970-79. *1288*
—. Crime and Criminals. Insanity. *Jones* v. *United States* (US, 1983). Mental Illness. Supreme Court. 1975-83. *1084*
—. Discrimination. Stevens, John Paul. Supreme Court. 1975-82. *1328*
—. Douglas, William O. Supreme Court. 1939-74. *754*
—. Economic Aid. *Everson* v. *Board of Education* (US, 1947). *Gannett* v. *DePasqual* (US, 1979). Judicial Process. State Government. Supreme Court. 1776-1979. *998*
—. Evidence (admissibility). *Mapp* v. *Ohio* (US, 1961). Supreme Court. Supreme courts, state (reactions to). 1960's. *762*
—. Federal Bureau of Investigation. Federal Government. Terrorism. 1977-82. *989*
—. Federalism. Prison Reform. Supreme Court. 1963-82. *971*
—. Freedom of Speech. Middle Classes. Privacy. Supreme Court. 1974-75. *726*
—. Government. Homosexuals. Supreme Court. 1960's-70's. *772*
—. Graglia, Lino A. Harvey, James C. Rist, Ray C. School Integration (review article). Supreme Court. 1954-78. *1159*
—. Handicapped. Supreme Court. 1970's-81. *719*
—. High Schools. Parents. Students. 1982. *1361*
—. Indian Civil Rights Act (US, 1968). Natural law. Pueblo Indians. *Santa Clara Pueblo* v. *Martinez* (US, 1977). Supreme Court. Tribal government. 1939-77. *1050*
—. Internal Revenue Service. 1920-80. *863*
—. Judicial Administration. Migration, internal. Supreme Court. 1780's-1977. *106*
—. Justice Department. Lawsuits. Prison reform. States' rights. Supreme Court. 1961-77. *917*
—. Legal information. Supreme Court. Warren, Earl. 1953-69. *1352*
—. Legal representation, right to. Supreme Court. 1970's. *837*
—. Legislation. Supreme Court. 1970-80. *935*
—. Lincoln, Abraham. War. 1861-65. *595*
—. Minorities. Supreme Court. 1886-1972. *988*

—. Mississippi. Redistricting. Supreme Court. *United States* v. *State of Mississippi* (US, 1980). 1965-80. *1301*
—. National security. 1945-82. *1077*
—. National security. Plamondon, "Pun". Supreme Court. Surveillance. Wiretaps. 1940-72. *788*
—. Pornography. Supreme Court. 1950's-73. *1155*
—. Prisons. Rehabilitation. 1900-72. *1059*
—. Reconstruction. South. 1865-77. *537*
—. Schools. Students. Supreme Court. 1950-81. *1175*
—. Segregation. Supreme Court. Vinson, Frederick Moore. 1946-53. *910*
—. Supreme Court. 1857-1969. *800*
—. Supreme Court. Warren, Earl. 1953-69. *1257*
Civil Rights Act (US, 1866). Amendments (14th, 15th). Blacks. Reconstruction. Republican Party. States' rights. ca 1865-77. *509*
Civil Rights Act (US, 1875). Amendments (13th, 14th). Blacks. Federal Government. 1875-83. *616*
—. Law Enforcement. Supreme Court. 1875-83. *538*
Civil Rights Act (US, 1964). Ability tests. Discrimination, Employment. Economic Opportunity Commission Guidelines. Supreme Court. 1975. *902*
—. Amendments (14th). Equal Protection. Labor. Sex Discrimination. Women. 1960's-70's. *1224*
—. Bilingual education. California. Chacone-Moscone Bilingual Bicultural Education Act (1976). *Lau* v. *Nichols* (US, 1974). Supreme Court. 1965-76. *939*
—. Employment. Equal opportunity. NAACP. Seniority. Supreme Court. 1964-77. *880*
—. Florida. School Integration. Supreme Court. 1954-64. *1111*
—. Judicial Administration. Public Schools. School Integration. South. State Legislatures. Supreme Court. 1954-78. *1283*
Civil Rights Act (US, 1964; Title VII). Business. Foreign Investments. Japan. Law. *Sumitomo Shoji America, Inc.* v. *Avagliano* (US, 1982). Supreme Court. 1977-83. *1138*
—. Courts. Labor Disputes. Taft-Hartley Act (US, 1947). 1968-71. *847*
Civil Rights Act (US, 1964; Titles VI, VII). Affirmative Action. Employment. *Kaiser Aluminum and Chemical Company* v. *Weber* (US, 1979). Race. *Regents of the University of California* v. *Allan Bakke* (US, 1978). Supreme Court. 1970's. *838*
Civil rights movement. Amendments (1st). 1960's-75. *1001*
—. Amendments (14th). Courts. Discipline. Higher Education. ca 1953-80. *1336*
—. Environment. Housing. Supreme Court. Zoning. 1970's. *895*
Civil service. Carter, Jimmy. Constitutional Law. Reform. Supreme Court. 1950's-70's. *918*
Civil War. 1861-77. *660*
—. Amendments. Blacks. Congress. Voting and Voting Behavior. 1838-69. *664*
—. Amendments. Fundamentalism. Lincoln, Abraham. National Fast Day. National Reform Association. 1863-1945. *513*
—. Amendments (1st). Burnside, Ambrose E. Freedom of Speech. Lincoln, Abraham. North Central States. 1863. *697*
—. Amendments (13th). Civil rights. Freedom. 1860-76. *684*
—. Amendments (13th). Emancipation. Lincoln, Abraham. Republicans, Radical. 1861-65. *589*
—. Amendments (13th). Emancipation. Ohio. 1857-66. *559*
—. Amendments (14th, 15th). Civil Rights. Slavery. Suffrage. Supreme Court. Women. 1863-75. *569*

—. New Deal. Political attitudes. Roosevelt, Franklin D. Tennessee. 1933-40. *775*
—. Political parties. Roll-call voting. 1789-1803. *550*
—. Political Reform. 1970-74. *1010*
—. Presidency. Separation of powers. Supreme Court. 1787-1978. *163*
—. Presidency. War powers. 1789-1820's. *672*
—. Presidency. War powers. 1797-1973. *208*
—. State Government. Suffrage. Supreme Court. Women. 1848-1920. *506*
Congressional investigations. Evidence. Law. 1950's-60's. *766*
Conkin, Paul K. (review article). Political Theory. 1760's-80's. 1974. *237*
Conkling, Roscoe. Amendments (14th). Supreme Court. 1882. *623*
Connecticut. Articles of Confederation. Boundaries. Courts. Pennsylvania. 1782-83. *314*
—. Bickel, Alexander M. Colleges and Universities. Documents. Yale University Law School. 1924-74. *851*
—. Constitutional Convention. Ellsworth, Oliver. 1787. *412*
—. Delaware. Georgia. New Jersey. Ratification. 1787-88. *488*
—. Ellsworth, Oliver. 1785-88. *423*
—. Ideology. Newspapers. Ratification. 1787. *460*
—. Johnson, William Samuel. Loyalists. Politics. 1727-1819. *211*
Connecticut Compromise. Congress. Constitutional Convention. Delegates. Political representation. Quantitative Methods. Roll-call voting. 1786-87. *417*
Conscience, Private. Civil Rights. Law. Public interest. Supreme Court. 19c-1972. *183*
Conscientious objection. Amendments (2d). Federal government. Madison, James. Military service. States' Rights. 1787-92. *445*
Conscription, military. American Revolution. Constitutional Law. 1775-89. *271*
Conservation of Natural Resources. Amendments (1st). Douglas, William O. Judicial Administration. Supreme Court. 1930-79. *1244*
Conservatism. Amendments (14th). Massachusetts (North Brookfield). Prayer. Public Schools. Supreme Court. 1963. *920*
—. American Revolution. Dickinson, John. Pennsylvania. 1757-1808. *164*
—. American Revolution. Political systems. Revolution. 1776-1976. *124*
—. Antiabolition sentiments. Clergy. Massachusetts (Boston). Missouri (St. Louis). Unitarianism. 1828-57. *619*
—. Antifederalists. Federalists. Government regulation. Liberalism. Liberty. 1787-1982. *113*
—. Capital punishment. Civil rights. Politics. Supreme Court. 1953-77. *1004*
—. Constitutional law. Kansas. New Deal. Newspapers. Supreme Court. 1934-35. *796*
—. Courts, District. Federal Government. Liberalism. Partisanship. Political Parties. Supreme Court. 1960-76. *1060*
—. Dorr Rebellion. Rhode Island. Social Change. Suffrage. 1835-55. *635*
—. Federalists. Local Government. Political conditions. Radicals and Radicalism. 1630-1789. *350*
—. Government. Liberalism. Politics. 1776-1976. *17*
—. Interest Groups. Supreme Court. 1969-80. *1008*
—. Judicial Review. Supreme Court. 1973-74. *850*
—. Liberalism. Political Theory. 1776-1973. *151*
—. Liberalism. Supreme Court. 1789-1973. *10*
—. McCumber, Porter James. McKenzie, Alexander John. North Dakota. Political reform. Republican Party. 1898-1933. *1068*
—. Michigan. New Deal. Press. 1934-36. *797*

Conspiracy. Assassination. Due process. Lincoln, Abraham. 1865-68. *566*
Constitutional Amendments. see also Amendments
Constitutional Amendments (1st). Democratic thought. Television. 1973. *1149*
—. Economics. Mass Media. 1975. *1236*
—. Federal Communications Commission. Radio. Television. 1973. *764*
Constitutional Amendments (12th). Political Parties. 1800-04. *628*
Constitutional Amendments, 14th. Citizenship. Indians. Law. ca 1776-1934. *567*
—. Civil Rights. 1868-1973. *1228*
—. Civil Rights. *McInnis* v. *Ogilvie* (US, 1969). Public Schools. State Aid to Education. 1965-70. *1074*
—. Housing, scatter-site. New York City (Faraday Wood). UN (Soviet Mission). 1967-75. *990*
—. *Jefferson* v. *Hackney* (US, 1972). Law. Public Welfare. Supreme Court. 1972. *760*
Constitutional Amendments (16th). Income tax. Tax loopholes. Treasury Department (Internal Revenue Service). 1873-1973. *769*
Constitutional Amendments (19th). American Antislavery Society. Anthony, Susan Brownell. Suffrage. Women. 1840's-1920. *604*
—. Blacks. *Crisis.* DuBois, William Edward Burghardt. Periodicals. Suffrage. Women. 1910-34. *1163*
Constitutional Amendments (21st). Equal Rights Amendment. Paul, Alice. Suffrage. Women. 1907-72. *832*
Constitutional Amendments (26th). Campaign Finance. Citizen Lobbies. Common Cause. Interest Groups. 1971. *1320*
Constitutional Convention. Amendments. 1789-1970. *432*
—. American Revolution. Bill of Rights. Declaration of Independence. Hamilton, Alexander. Inflation. Liberty. Washington, George. 1607-1800. *18*
—. Antifederalists. New York. Political Parties. Whigs, Radical. 1788. *499*
—. Arts. Founding Fathers. Humanities. 1780's. *319*
—. Beard, Charles A. Economic Conditions. Founding Fathers. Voting and Voting Behavior. 1775-89. 1913. *281*
—. Bill of Rights. Jefferson, Thomas. 1787. *457*
—. Budgets. 1787-1982. *43*
—. Butler, Pierce. Documents. 1787. *409*
—. Civic Virtue. Government. Republicanism. 1776-87. *220*
—. Clay, Henry. Madison, James. Political Theory. Virginia. 1788. *394*
—. Coalitions. 1787. *496*
—. Commerce. Politics. 1774-87. *326*
—. Congress. Connecticut Compromise. Delegates. Political representation. Quantitative Methods. Roll-call voting. 1786-87. *417*
—. Congress. Constitutions (Article 5). 1967-79. *1032*
—. Congress. Constitutions (Article 5). Supreme Court. 1787. *399*
—. Connecticut. Ellsworth, Oliver. 1787. *412*
—. Debates. Separation of powers. 1787. *389*
—. Decisionmaking. Presidency. 1787. *448*
—. Democracy. National Characteristics. Pennsylvania (Philadelphia). Superstition. Violence. 1787. *435*
—. Diamond, Martin (review article). Federalism. Republics. 1787. *475*
—. Dickinson, John. Documents. 1787. *408*
—. Documents. Editors and Editing. Genet, Edmond C. Lansing, John, Jr. Madison, James. Yates, Robert. 1787-1840. *406*
—. Electoral college. Founding Fathers. 1787. *467*
—. Electoral College. Founding Fathers. Political coalitions. Republicanism. 1787-1970's. *68*

—. *Federalist.* Government. Madison, James. Political Theory. 1783-90. *434*
—. Founding Fathers. Pennsylvania (Philadelphia). 1787. *440*
—. Founding Fathers. Political systems. 1783-1980. *62*
—. History. 1787. *498*
—. Ideology. Politics. 1787. *416*
—. Ideology. Presidency. 1776-87. *452*
—. Madison, James. 1787. *456*
—. Madison, James. Manuscripts. Virginia Plan. 1787. *405*
—. Madison, James. Political Representation. Virginia Plan. 1787. *414*
—. Military officers, retired. Pennsylvania (Philadelphia). Society of the Cincinnati. Washington, George. 1783-87. *473*
—. Pennsylvania (Philadelphia). Slavery. 1787. *495*
—. Pennsylvania (Philadelphia). Washington, George. 1787. *441*
—. Political Conventions. Supremacy Clause. 1787-89. *368*
—. Presidency. 1785-89. *259*
—. Presidency. 1787. 1974. *442*
—. Slave Trade Compromise. Voting and Voting Behavior. 1787. *413*
—. Voting and Voting Behavior. 1787. *415*
Constitutional Convention Implementation Bill. Constitutions (Article 5). 1787. 1981. *388*
Constitutional Convention (2d, proposed). 1787-1970's. *104*
—. 1967. *1019*
—. Antifederalists. Bill of Rights. 1788-89. *387*
Constitutional Law. Abortion. Civil Rights. Fertility. *Roe* v. *Wade* (US, 1973). Women. 1973-82. *1145*
—. Abortion. *Roe* v. *Wade* (US, 1973). Women. 1950's-70's. *1240*
—. Accountability. Government. 1940-78. *862*
—. Acheson, Dean. Congress. Korean War. Truman, Harry S. War, declaration of. 1950-64. *952*
—. Addison, Alexander. Federalists. Freedom of Speech. Pennsylvania. Sedition Act (US, 1798). 1792-98. *605*
—. Affirmative action. Discrimination. 1977. *1038*
—. Alabama (Selma). Crime and Criminals. *Fikes* v. *Alabama* (US, 1957). Fikes, William Earl. Supreme Court. 1948-75. *1030*
—. Aliens, illegal. Civil rights. Mexican Americans. 1970-77. *833*
—. Amendments (1st, 5th, 7th, 13th, 14th). Supreme Court. 1966-71. *1153*
—. Amendments (14th). Civil Rights. Nationalization. Supreme Court. 1873-1969. *1194*
—. American Civil Liberties Union. Civil Rights. Shattuck, John H. F. (interview). 1970's. *1167*
—. American Civil Liberties Union. Freedom of speech. Harris, Emily. Harris, William. Press. Trials. 1976. *876*
—. American Civil Liberties Union. Politics. 1921-71. *737*
—. American Revolution. Conscription, military. 1775-89. *271*
—. Anderson, Jack. Courts. Journalism. Libel. Pearson, Drew. 1949-74. *1183*
—. Antislavery Sentiments. Owens, Leslie Howard. Slavery (review article). South. Wiecek, William M. ca 1650-1977. *56*
—. Arkansas (Little Rock). Crises. Federal government. India (Kerala). Segregation. State government. 1957. 1968. *1123*
—. Attitudes. Legislation. 1760's-80's. *321*
—. Attitudes. Nixon, Richard M. Watergate scandal. 1973-82. *1179*
—. Attorneys General. Civil rights. Devens, Charles. 1877-81. *522*

—. Authority. Children. Civil Rights. Parents. Supreme Court. 1983. *1277*
—. Authority. Civil Rights. Editorials. Public Opinion. Supreme Court. ca 1960's-83. *1299*
—. Autocracy. Executive Branch. Foreign policy. Presidency. 1970's. *1047*
—. Bakke, Allan. Blacks. Equality. Morality. *Regents of the University of California* v. *Allan Bakke* (US, 1978). 18c-20c. *158*
—. Behavioral studies. Criminal Law. Pornography. President's Commission on Obscenity and Pornography. 1970-71. *1017*
—. Berger, Raoul (review article). Executive privilege. *United States* v. *Nixon* (US, 1974). 18c-1974. *19*
—. Bill of Rights. Citizens, Foreign-born. Deportation. Nixon, Richard M. Residency rights. 1798-1970's. *57*
—. *Branzburg* v. *Hayes* (US, 1972). Confidentiality. Reporters and Reporting. Supreme Court. 1972-82. *1317*
—. British North America Act (1867). Fulton-Favreau Formula. 1960-66. *706*
—. *Brown* v. *Board of Education* (US, 1954). Civil rights. Marshall, Thurgood. NAACP. Supreme Court. 1865-1954. *1136*
—. *Brown* v. *Board of Education* (US, 1954). Federal Policy. Judicial Administration. School Integration. 1954-77. *1350*
—. *Brown* v. *Board of Education* (US, 1954). NAACP. Public Schools. Segregation. Supreme Court. 1949-55. *961*
—. *Brown* v. *Board of Education* (US, 1954). NAACP. School Integration. Supreme Court. 1954. *963*
—. Business. Field, Stephen J. Government. Supreme Court. 1863-97. *578*
—. Busing. Courts (federal). Public Schools. 1954-72. *842*
—. California. Campaign Finance. Federal Regulation. Political Reform. 1976. *1346*
—. Campaign Finance. Elections. Supreme Court. 1976. *1219*
—. Canada. Licensing procedures. Provinces. States. USA. 1970's. *1101*
—. Canada. Obscenity. USA. 1950's-73. *1276*
—. Canada. Supreme Court. 1980-81. *1241*
—. Candidacy. Civil Rights. Supreme Court. 1960's-70's. *846*
—. Capital Punishment. 1790-1955. *37*
—. Capital punishment. 1864-1982. *1190*
—. Capital Punishment. Supreme Court. 1971-81. *1187*
—. Carter, Jimmy. Civil service. Reform. Supreme Court. 1950's-70's. *918*
—. Catholic Church. Church Schools. Elementary Education. Federal aid to education. 1960's-72. *970*
—. Catholic Church. Ireland. Irish Americans. O'Conor, Charles. O'Conor, Charles Owen. Political reform. Reconstruction. 1865-85. *531*
—. Censorship. Due process. *Near* v. *Minnesota* (US, 1931). Newspapers. Trials. 1931-78. *828*
—. Censorship. Pornography. Supreme Court. 1970-71. *830*
—. Central Intelligence Agency. Executive Power. Intelligence service. 1933-74. *745*
—. Chase, Salmon Portland. Supreme Court. Taney, Roger Brooke. 1857-71. *582*
—. Children. *Globe Newspaper* v. *Superior Court* (US, 1982). Social Sciences. Supreme Court. Witnesses. 1970's-82. *982*
—. Church and State. 1789-1980. *99*
—. Church and state. Church Schools. 1930's-70's. *1024*
—. Church and State. Church Schools. Government regulation. 1920-83. *1266*

Crèvecoeur, Michel Guillaume Jean de *(Letters from an American Farmer)*. American Revolution. Political Theory. Social Theory. 1782. *353*
Crime and Criminals. Alabama (Selma). Constitutional Law. *Fikes* v. *Alabama* (US, 1957). Fikes, William Earl. Supreme Court. 1948-75. *1030*
—. Amendments (2d). Gun control. 1975. *716*
—. Amendments (5th, 6th, 7th). Juries. 1945-75. *1053*
—. Civil Rights. Insanity. *Jones* v. *United States* (US, 1983). Mental Illness. Supreme Court. 1975-83. *1084*
—. Constitutional Law. Educational administrators. Teachers. 1982. *1255*
—. Constitutional Law. *Miranda* v. *Arizona* (US, 1966). *Rhode Island* v. *Innis* (US, 1975). Supreme Court. 1971-79. *1171*
—. Constitutional Law. Newspapers. Trials. 18c-20c. *218*
Criminal justice. Constitutional law. Levy, Leonard W. (review article). Nixon, Richard M. Supreme Court. 1968-74. *1150*
—. Nixon, Richard M. Supreme Court. 1969-72. *1223*
Criminal law. Abortion. Religion. Supreme Court. 1980. *1039*
—. Addiction. Drug Abuse. Supreme Court. 1962-68. *980*
—. Amendments. Supreme Court. 1966-71. *1152*
—. Amendments (4th). Courts, Appellate. Habeas corpus. *Stone* v. *Powell* (US, 1976). Supreme Court. 1976-79. *1325*
—. Behavioral studies. Constitutional Law. Pornography. President's Commission on Obscenity and Pornography. 1970-71. *1017*
—. Civil Rights. Confrontation. Supreme Court. 1957-69. *1073*
—. Congress. State Politics. Supreme Court. 1973-83. *1270*
—. Supreme Court. 1935-76. *761*
Criminal rights. Constitutional Law. Judicial Process. 1958-75. *1201*
Crises. Arkansas (Little Rock). Constitutional Law. Federal government. India (Kerala). Segregation. State government. 1957. 1968. *1123*
Crisis. Blacks. Constitutional Amendments (19th). DuBois, William Edward Burghardt. Periodicals. Suffrage. Women. 1910-34. *1163*
Croly, Herbert. Amendments (1st). Federal Regulation. Law. Political Parties. Ritchie, Thomas. ca 1850-1980. *1285*
Cuba. *Banco Nacional de Cuba* v. *Sabbatino* (US, 1964). *First National City Bank* v. *Banco Nacional de Cuba* (US, 1972). International law. State Department. Supreme Court. 1964-72. *953*
Cuban Americans. Bahamas Marine Patrol. Lobster. Maritime Law. 1978. *744*
Cue theory. Certiorari. Law. Supreme Court. 1940-81. *713*
Cults. Religious Liberty. 1970-81. *1079*
Cummings, John. Clergy. Constitutional Law. *Cummings* v. *Missouri* (US, 1867). Missouri (Louisiana). Oaths. Supreme Court. 1865-67. *600*
Cummings v. *Missouri* (US, 1867). Clergy. Constitutional Law. Cummings, John. Missouri (Louisiana). Oaths. Supreme Court. 1865-67. *600*
Current events. Colleges and Universities. Constitutional Law. Government. Textbooks. 1950's. 1970's. *58*

Curricula. Amendments (1st). Educators. Meiklejohn, Alexander. Political Reform. 1898-1964. *1342*
Customs law. Naval Office. State Government. Virginia. 1776-89. *226*
Cutters. Congress. Imports. Taxation. 1789-90. *469*

D

Dartmouth College v. *Woodward* (US, 1819). Amendments (14th). Institutions, private. Supreme Court. 1968-69. *829*
—. Corporations. Marshall, John. Virginia. 1801-19. *516*
—. New Hampshire. State Politics. Supreme Court. 1815-19. *674*
Data banks. Constitutional Law. Federal Government. Private sector. 1960's-70's. *799*
Davenport, George O. Blacks. Discrimination. Dovener, Blackburn B. Juries. Strauder, Taylor. *Strauder* v. *West Virginia* (US, 1880). West Virginia. 1872-81. *523*
Davis, John W. American Liberty League. New Deal. Political Campaigns. 1932-36. *904*
Day, Murray. Antifederalists (review article). Ratification. Storing, Herbert J. 1787-90. *419*
Dean Act (Texas, 1919). Amendments (18th). Prohibition. State Legislatures. Texas. 1917-33. *810*
Deane, Silas. American Revolution. Congress. Diplomacy. France. Gérard, Conrad. Lee, Arthur. 1779. *294*
Debates. Appointments to Office. Political Ethics. Powell, Lewis F. Rehnquist, William H. Senate. Supreme Court. 1969-70. *944*
—. Civil War. Confiscations. Congress. Constitutional Law. Reconstruction. 1861-65. *570*
—. Congress. Food Adulteration and Inspection. Oleomargarine. Taxation. Wiley, Harvey. 1886. *638*
—. Constitutional Convention. Separation of powers. 1787. *389*
—. Federalism. Government. New York State Ratifying Convention. 1788. *384*
—. Georgia. Newspapers. Ratification. State Politics. 1787-88. *420*
Debts. Amendments (10th). Congress. Hamilton, Alexander. Letters. Rutledge, Edward. Smith, William L. South Carolina. States. 1789-94. *454*
Decentralization. Federalism. Government. 1780's. 1880's. 1970's. *97*
Decisionmaking. Amendments (1st). Freedom of the Press. Political Attitudes. Supreme Court. 1930-79. *1338*
—. Amendments (1st). Gag Orders. Juries. 1931-80. *1054*
—. Amendments (1st). Juries. 1940's-75. *1083*
—. American Revolution. Bicentennial Celebrations. 1776-89. 1976. *286*
—. Attitudes. Authority. Government. Justices. Supreme Court. 1947-56. *1120*
—. Attitudes. Burton, Harold. Supreme Court. 1945-58. *748*
—. Behavior. Judicial Administration. Political Attitudes. Supreme Court. 1947-56. *1118*
—. Constitutional Convention. Presidency. 1787. *448*
—. Constitutional Law. Politics. School integration. Supreme Court. 1954-81. *924*
—. Judges. Supreme Court. 1803-1971. *210*

—. Jensen, Merrill (review article). Ratification. 1776-87. 1976. *451*
—. New Hampshire. Ratification. Toscan, Jean. 1788. *360*
—. Nixon v. *Administrator of General Services* (US, 1977). Ownership. Presidents. Supreme Court. 1791-1981. *977*
—. Pennsylvania. Political Conventions (state). Ratification. 1787. *487*
—. Political Commentary. 1787. *489*
—. Ratification. 1776-87. *332*
Dogmatism. Apportionment. Pragmatism. Supreme Court. Warren, Earl. 1962. *903*
Domestic Policy. Amendments. Bricker Amendment. Foreign Policy. UN. 1951. *1358*
—. Constitutional Law. School Integration. 1954-80. *1247*
Dorr Rebellion. Conservatism. Rhode Island. Social Change. Suffrage. 1835-55. *635*
—. Constitutional Law. Rhode Island. 1842-43. *529*
—. Election Laws. *Luther v. Borden* (US, 1849). Rhode Island. State government. Supreme Court. 1842-49. *528*
Douglas, William O. Amendments (1st). Conservation of Natural Resources. Judicial Administration. Supreme Court. 1930-79. *1244*
—. Amendments (1st). Freedom of Speech. 1950's-70's. *1049*
—. Amendments (1st). Judicial Opinions. Law. Rhetoric. Supreme Court. ca 1939-75. *1344*
—. Attitudes. Judges. Supreme Court. 1953-63. *1139*
—. Bill of Rights. Civil rights. Mill, John Stuart. Supreme Court. 18c-20c. *25*
—. Black, Hugo L. Civil Rights. Supreme Court. 1935-99. *1117*
—. Blacks. Civil rights. Supreme Court. 1939-66. *1052*
—. Civil rights. Constitutional Law. Judicial activism. Liberalism. Supreme Court. 1928-77. *1180*
—. Civil Rights. Supreme Court. 1939-74. *754*
—. Jackson, Robert H. Political Attitudes. Role theory. Supreme Court. 1939-68. *905*
—. Supreme Court. 1898-1980. *793*
Douglass, Frederick. Abolition movement. Amendments (15th). Blacks. Theology. 1825-86. *630*
Dovener, Blackburn B. Blacks. Davenport, George O. Discrimination. Juries. Strauder, Taylor. *Strauder v. West Virginia* (US, 1880). West Virginia. 1872-81. *523*
Dred Scott v. Sandford (US, 1857). Abortion. Blacks. Civil Rights. Personhood. *Roe v. Wade* (US, 1973). Supreme Court. 1857. 1973. *611*
—. Blacks. Citizenship. Supreme Court. 17c-19c. 1857. *162*
—. Blacks. Historiography. Slavery. Supreme Court. Taney, Roger Brooke. 1857. 19c-20c. *204*
—. Blacks. Supreme Court. Taney, Roger Brooke. 1836-57. *652*
—. Citizenship. Democratic Party. Fehrenbacher, Don E. (review article). Missouri Compromise. Slavery. 1857. 1978. *534*
—. Marshall, John. Slavery. Supreme Court. Taney, Roger Brooke. 1820-60. *636*
Dress codes. Amendments (1st). Law. Teachers. 1960-80. *1363*
Drug Abuse. Addiction. Criminal Law. Supreme Court. 1962-68. *980*
Dry, Murray. Antifederalism (review article). Constitutions (review article). Storing, Herbert J. 1776-1805. *428*
—. Antifederalists (review article). Documents. Storing, Herbert J. 1787-88. 1805. *438*

Duane, William. Adams, John. Exiles. Great Britain. Journalists. Press. USA. 1790-1800. *370*
Dubois, Phillip L. Accountability. Coffin, Frank M. Hodder-Williams, Richard. Judicial Process (review article). Theberge, Leonard J. 1979-80. *845*
DuBois, William Edward Burghardt. Blacks. Constitutional Amendments (19th). *Crisis.* Periodicals. Suffrage. Women. 1910-34. *1163*
Due Process. Administrative Law. Higher education. Students. Supreme Court. 1960-70. *783*
—. Aliens, Resident. Law. Supreme Court. 1788-1979. *59*
—. Amendments. Civil rights. Congress. Equal Protection. State Government. Supreme Court. 1866-1968. *1143*
—. Amendments (1st). Black, Hugo L. Judicial Administration. 1936-79. *730*
—. Amendments (14th). Colleges and Universities. Law. Students. 1960's-70's. *1278*
—. Assassination. Conspiracy. Lincoln, Abraham. 1865-68. *566*
—. Censorship. Constitutional Law. *Near v. Minnesota* (US, 1931). Newspapers. Trials. 1931-78. *828*
—. Constitutional law. Liberty. Morality. Natural rights. 1980. *1056*
—. Equal protection, substantive. Judicial activism. Supreme Court. 1930's-72. *983*
—. *Goldberg v. Kelly* (US, 1970). *Morrisey v. Brewer* (US, 1972). Public Administration (agencies). Supreme Court. 1969-74. *831*
Dulles, John Foster. Bricker Amendment. Bricker, John W. Executive agreements. McCloy, John J. Personal Narratives. Presidency. Senate. Treaties. 1951-54. 1976. *1164*
DuPont and Company. Antitrust. General Motors Corporation. Supreme Court. *United States* v. *E. I. Du Pont de Nemours and Company et al.* (US, 1957). 1948-65. *928*
Dupont, François Xavier. Letters. Social Conditions. Virginia (Petersburg). 1789. *437*
Dwight, Timothy. Christianity. Democracy. Federalism. Ideology. Morse, Jedidiah. Republicanism. 1790-1800. *614*

E

Economic Aid. Civil Rights. *Everson v. Board of Education* (US, 1947). *Gannett v. DePasqual* (US, 1979). Judicial cess. State Government. Supreme Court. 1776-1979. *998*
—. Press. State Government. 1791-1974. *51*
Economic Conditions. American Revolution. Articles of Confederation. 1782. *313*
—. Beard, Charles A. Constitutional Convention. Founding Fathers. Voting and Voting Behavior. 1775-89. 1913. *281*
—. Constitutional Law. Federal Government. Social Conditions. Transfer payments. 18c-20c. *142*
Economic development. Free market. Law. Natural rights. Supreme Court. 1776-1920. *84*
Economic Opportunity Commission Guidelines. Ability tests. Civil Rights Act (US, 1964). Discrimination, Employment. Supreme Court. 1975. *902*
Economic order. Constitutional law. Federalism. Historiography. Supreme Court. 1789-1910. *117*
Economic Policy. Great Britain. Public Finance. 1750-90's. *397*
Economic Regulations. Constitutional Law. Judicial Review. 1980. *1243*
Economics. Attitudes. Civil liberties. Judges. Supreme Court. 1965. *1025*

—. Constitutional Amendments (1st). Mass Media. 1975. *1236*

Editorials. Amendments (1st). Freedom of Speech. Newspapers. 1919-69. *1264*

—. Authority. Civil Rights. Constitutional Law. Public Opinion. Supreme Court. ca 1960's-83. *1299*

Editors and Editing. Amendments (1st). Reporters and Reporting. Supreme Court. 1970-78. *1098*

—. Byrd, Harry F. Chambers, Lenoir. School Integration. Supreme Court. Virginia. 1955-59. *1015*

—. Constitutional Convention. Documents. Genet, Edmond C. Lansing, John, Jr. Madison, James. Yates, Robert. 1787-1840. *406*

Education. *See also* Compulsory Education.

—. Amendments (1st). Citizenship. Public Schools. 1970's. *1294*

—. Amendments (1st). Freedom of Speech. Meiklejohn, Alexander. Social Theory. ca 1912-64. *1339*

—. Amendments (1st). Law. Religion in the Public Schools. 1941-79. *1331*

—. Amendments (1st, 14th). Students. 1830-1960. *203*

—. Amendments (1st, 14th). Students. 1830-1960. *1297*

—. Blacks. *Brown v. Board of Education* (US, 1954). Supreme Court. 1850-1975. *865*

—. Blacks. Census. Political representation. Racism. Revenue sharing. 1787-1980. *82*

—. Constitutional Law. Courts. Tracking. 1950-82. *1006*

—. Constitutional Law. Federal Government. Indians. 18c-20c. *199*

—. Constitutional Law. *San Antonio Independent School District v. Rodriguez* (US, 1973). Supreme Court. 20c. 1973. *1355*

—. Democracy. Human rights. *San Antonio Independent School District v. Rodriguez* (US, 1973). 1787-1980. *206*

—. Judges. Powell, Lewis F. Supreme Court. 1972-83. *1366*

—. Law and Society. Religion. Supreme Court. 1948-72. *1261*

Education Amendments Act (US, 1972; Title IX). Amendments (1st). Public Schools. Sexism. Textbooks. 1970's. *87*

Education, Finance. Amendments (1st). Church and State. Higher Education. Private Schools. State aid to education. 1982. *1337*

—. Amendments (1st). Church Schools. Religion in the public schools. 1950's-70's. *1160*

—. *Rodriguez v. San Antonio Independent School District* (US, 1973). Supreme Court. Tax reform. 1973. *860*

Educational administrators. Constitutional Law. Crime and Criminals. Teachers. 1982. *1255*

Educational Policy. Blacks. Federal Government. Law. School Integration. Supreme Court. 1954-82. *1040*

—. New England. Northwest Ordinance (1787). Ohio Company. Ordinance of 1785. 1785-87. *386*

Educators. Amendments (1st). Curricula. Meiklejohn, Alexander. Political Reform. 1898-1964. *1342*

Egalitarianism. Equality. Human rights. Ideas, History of. Law. 18c-1974. *126*

Ekirch, Roger. American Revolution (review article). Countryman, Edward. Reid, John Philip. 1729-90. *282*

Election districts. Political representation. Supreme Court. 1970-79. *852*

Election Laws. Apportionment. Attorneys General. Courts. Intergovernmental Relations. Voting Rights Act (US, 1965; Section 5). 1965-77. *734*

—. Dorr Rebellion. *Luther v. Borden* (US, 1849). Rhode Island. State government. Supreme Court. 1842-49. *528*

Elections. Amendments (14th, 15th). Congress. Federal Election Campaign Act (US, 1971; amended 1974). Supreme Court. Voting Rights Act (US, 1965). 1965-75. *801*

—. Antifederalists. Confederation. State Politics. 1787-88. *494*

—. *Buckley v. Valeo* (US, 1976). Democratic theory. Legislation. Reform. 1971-76. *709*

—. Campaign Finance. Constitutional Law. Supreme Court. 1976. *1219*

—. Judicial review. Partisan realignment. Supreme Court. 1800-1970. *49*

—. Political Reform. 1977. *1067*

—. Political Reform. Presidency. 1970. *825*

Elections, presidential. Nominations for office. Political parties. 1787-1978. *20*

Electoral college. Amendments. Bayh, Birch. Diamond, Martin. Senate Judiciary Committee (Constitutional Subcommittee). 1977. *789*

—. Constitutional Convention. Founding Fathers. 1787. *467*

—. Constitutional Convention. Founding Fathers. Political coalitions. Republicanism. 1787-1970's. *68*

Electoral process. Discrimination. Supreme Court. 1870's-1973. *978*

Electronic surveillance. Amendments (4th). Executive Power. Intelligence, foreign. Supreme Court. *United States v. Butenko* (US, 1974). 1974. *1157*

Elementary Education. Catholic Church. Church Schools. Constitutional law. Federal aid to education. 1960's-72. *970*

—. Children. Civil Rights. Supreme Court. 1920-78. *1256*

Elites. American Revolution. Leadership. Officeholding. Social Change. 1774-87. *303*

—. Democracy. 1787-1980. *168*

—. Diplomatics. Presidents. Supreme Court. 1861-1933. *647*

Ellsworth, Oliver. Connecticut. 1785-88. *423*

—. Connecticut. Constitutional Convention. 1787. *412*

Ely, John Hart. Constitutional Law. Democracy. Judicial Review (review article). 18c-1980. *91*

—. Constitutional Law. Judicial Power. Lincoln, Abraham. Political Theory. 1830's-65. *561*

Emancipation. Amendments (13th). Civil War. Lincoln, Abraham. Republicans, Radical. 1861-65. *589*

—. Amendments (13th). Civil War. Ohio. 1857-66. *559*

—. Civil Rights. Constitutionalism. Politics. 1862-76. *642*

Emergency, states of. Congress. Executive Power. Martial law. 1917-52. *968*

—. Executive power. Habeas corpus. Martial law. War. 1861-1944. *601*

Emigration. American Revolution. Books. Great Britain. Political Theory. 1776. *221*

Eminent domain. Courts, State. *Munn v. Illinois* (US, 1877). Public interest. Supreme Court. 1850-77. *608*

Employees. Amendments (1st). Law. Political Participation. Public Schools. 1867-1977. *1306*

Employers. Fuller, Melville. Liability. Progressivism. Supreme Court. 1888-1910. *701*

—. Congress. Constitutional law. Foreign policy. Treatymaking. 1969-74. *1086*
—. Congress. Constitutional Law. National Emergencies Act (US, 1976). Political power. Public Policy. 1933-78. *967*
—. Congress. Constitutional Law. Presidency. War Powers Resolution (1973). 1973. *1109*
—. Congress. Courts. School Integration. 1960's-70's. *925*
—. Congress. Foreign policy. Separation of powers. 1970's. *943*
—. Constitutional Law. Politics. 1979. *1227*
—. House of Representatives (investigations). Indian Wars. St. Clair, Arthur. 1791-93. *541*
Executive Power. *See also* Presidents, War Powers.
—. Amendments. American Bar Association. Bricker, John W. Foreign Policy. 1948-54. *1107*
—. Amendments (4th). Electronic surveillance. Intelligence, foreign. Supreme Court. *United States v. Butenko* (US, 1974). 1974. *1157*
—. Amendments (25th). Cleveland, Grover. Stevenson, Adlai E. (1835-1914). Vice-presidency. 1893-1967. *1069*
—. Central Intelligence Agency. Constitutional law. Intelligence service. 1933-74. *745*
—. Checks and balances. 1787-1975. *76*
—. Civil Disturbances. Military. 1789-1978. *105*
—. Civil War. Constitutional Law. Lincoln, Abraham. 1860-66. *558*
—. Congress. Constitutional Law. Foreign Policy. National Security. Supreme Court. War. 1935-80. *1258*
—. Congress. Constitutional Law. Foreign Policy. Vietnam War. War powers. 1960's-72. *1271*
—. Congress. Courts. Nixon, Richard M. Veto. 1787-1975. *41*
—. Congress. Emergency, states of. Martial law. 1917-52. *968*
—. Congress. Foreign policy. 1789-1972. *119*
—. Congress. Korean War. Vietnam War. War. 1776-1970. *251*
—. Congress. Police. War powers. 1776-1960. *14*
—. Congress. War Powers Resolution (1973). 1969-73. *822*
—. Constitutional Law. 18c-20c. *150*
—. Constitutional Law. Impoundment. 1776-1974. *2*
—. Constitutional Law. Marshall, John. Roosevelt, Theodore. Taft, William Howard. 19c-1913. *609*
—. Emergency, states of. Habeas corpus. Martial law. War. 1861-1944. *601*
—. Founding Fathers. 1787. *427*
—. Political systems. 1790-1976. *70*
Executive privilege. Berger, Raoul (review article). Constitutional law. *United States v. Nixon* (US, 1974). 18c-1974. *19*
—. Congress. Constitutional Law. Information (control). 1789-1974. *153*
—. Constitutional Law. Judicial review. 1789-1974. *146*
—. Constitutional Law. Nixon, Richard M. Watergate Tapes. 1973. *986*
—. Constitutional law. *United States v. Nixon* (US, 1974). ca 1700-1975. *8*
Exiles. Adams, John. Duane, William. Great Britain. Journalists. Press. USA. 1790-1800. *370*
Expatriation. *Afroyim v. Rusk* (US, 1967). Law. *Rogers v. Bellei* (US, 1971). Supreme Court. 1790-1973. *61*
Extradition. Constitutional Law. Supreme Court. 18c-20c. *217*

F

Fair housing. California. Housing. Referendum. Voting and Voting behavior. ca 1960-67. *1158*
Fair Housing Amendments Act (proposed). Federal government. Housing. 1930's-79. *1140*
Fairness Doctrine. Amendments (1st). Broadcasting. Federal Communications Commission. 1960's-73. *1293*
Fairness doctrine (disputes). Amendments (1st). Federal Communications Commission. Journalism. 1976. *1203*
Fallbrook Irrigation District Case (US, 1896). California Irrigation District Law. California (Santa Margarita River, Fallbrook). Water rights. 1886-99. *607*
Family. California. Governors. Judges. Law. Supreme Court. Warren, Earl. 1911-74. *1132*
Family viewing. Amendments (1st). Federal Communications Commission. National Association of Broadcasters. Programming, prime time. Television. 1975. *835*
Fanchon Blake v. City of Los Angeles (California). Constitutional Law. Law Enforcement. Women. 1960's-83. *1275*
Farmers. Populism. Railroads. State Government. Supreme Court. 1876-96. *632*
Farming. Articles of Confederation. Jefferson, Thomas. Landowning. Property. Republicanism. 1776-87. *263*
Federal Aid to Education. Amendments (1st). Church Schools. 1967. *708*
—. Catholic Church. Church Schools. Constitutional law. Elementary Education. 1960's-72. *970*
—. Constitutional Law. Private Schools. Taxation. 1970's. *1146*
—. Private schools. 1776-1978. *127*
Federal Bureau of Investigation. Civil Rights. Federal Government. Terrorism. 1977-82. *989*
—. Cold War. Political activism. Surveillance. 1940-80. *1108*
Federal Communications Commission. Amendments (1st). Broadcasting. Fairness Doctrine. 1960's-73. *1293*
—. Amendments (1st). Fairness doctrine (disputes). Journalism. 1976. *1203*
—. Amendments (1st). Family viewing. National Association of Broadcasters. Programming, prime time. Television. 1975. *835*
—. Amendments (1st). Freedom of Speech. Government regulation. Public Broadcasting Act (US, 1967). Television. 1967-81. *1315*
—. Constitutional Amendments (1st). Radio. Television. 1973. *764*
Federal Election Campaign Act (US, 1971; amended 1974). Amendments (1st). *Buckley v. Valeo* (US, 1976). Campaign finance. Congress. Glasser, Ira (interview). 1971-74. *1168*
—. Amendments (14th, 15th). Congress. Elections. Supreme Court. Voting Rights Act (US, 1965). 1965-75. *801*
Federal Election Commission. Amendments (1st). *Buckley v. Valeo* (US, 1976). Campaign finance. Congress. Gora, Joel (interview). 1974-76. *1165*
Federal Government. 1789-1820's. *677*
—. Amendments. Budgets. 1970's-82. *954*
—. Amendments (1st). Civil Rights. Freedom of the press. Right to know. 1972. *1051*
—. Amendments (2d). Conscientious objection. Madison, James. Military service. States' Rights. 1787-92. *445*
—. Amendments (11th). *Chisholm v. Georgia* (US, 1792). States' rights. 1792-98. *622*
—. Amendments (13th, 14th). Blacks. Civil Rights Act (US, 1875). 1875-83. *616*

—. Federal government. Sovereignty. States' rights. 1774-89. *269*
—. Federal Regulation. 1787-1970's. *137*
—. *Federalist.* Political theory. 1787-20c. *396*
—. Free states. Slaves (transport of). 1787-1861. *680*
—. Freedom. Government. Law. Public policy. 1790-1979. *118*
—. Government. 1787-1973. *47*
—. Intergovernmental Relations. 1787-1978. *110*
—. Jeffersonianism. 1789-1800. *671*
—. Jeffersonianism. Political Attitudes. Republicanism. Rush, Benjamin. 1776-1800. *267*
—. Latin America. Models. Political Theory. 1776-1830. *107*
—. Latin America. USA. 1776-89. 1825-50. *50*
—. Legislation. *National League of Cities* v. *Usery* (US, 1976). Supreme Court. 1792-1976. *69*
—. Madison, James. Political Theory. 1783-90. *222*
—. National Characteristics. Public Opinion. Social Organization. Values. 1787-1801. *359*
—. Political Attitudes. Ratification. Virginia. 1788-91. *450*
—. Presidency. Public administration. 1787-1979. *114*
—. Washington, George. 1789-96. *424*
Federalism (review article). Choper, Jesse H. Fisher, Louis. Genovese, Michael A. Jenkins, Iredell. Law. Merry, Henry J. 1978-80. *756*
Federalist. American Revolution. Declaration of Independence. Ideology. Rhetoric. 1776-89. *341*
—. Authorship. Hamilton, Alexander. Madison, James. 1788. *502*
—. Candor (concept). Conflict and Conflict Resolution. Hamilton, Alexander. Jay, John. Madison, James. 1787. *398*
—. Constitutional Convention. Government. Madison, James. Political Theory. 1783-90. *434*
—. Declaration of Independence. Diamond, Martin. Republicanism. Virtue. ca 1775-88. ca 1959-77. *305*
—. Democracy. Political Theory. 1787-88. *472*
—. Diamond, Martin. Hamilton, Alexander. Madison, James. Montesquieu, Charles de. 1748-88. 1961. *299*
—. Federal government. Founding Fathers. Political theory. 1780's. 1979. *232*
—. Federalism. Political theory. 1787-20c. *396*
—. Hamilton, Alexander. Jay, John. Madison, James. Political Theory. 1787-88. *361*
—. Hamilton, Alexander. Madison, James. Political Theory. 1787-88. *485*
—. Hamilton, Alexander. Madison, James. Political Theory. 1787-88. *486*
—. Hamilton, Alexander. Madison, James. Political theory. Republicanism. 1787-88. *378*
—. Hamilton, Alexander. Madison, James. Separation of powers. Veto. 1787-90. *367*
—. Madison, James. 1787-88. *493*
—. Madison, James. Political Theory. Public Welfare. 1787-92. *395*
—. Political offices. Republicanism. 1787. *443*
—. Political representation. 1776-87. *480*
—. Political Theory. 1788. *501*
—. Political Theory. Ratification. 1787-88. *465*
—. Political Theory. Representative Government. 1776-1976. *349*
—. Republicanism. Rhetoric. 1787. *503*
Federalist No. 10. Adair, Douglass. Hume, David. Madison, James. Political Theory. Republicanism. Wills, Garry. 1788. *392*
—. Democracy. Liberty. Madison, James. 1787. *356*
—. Enlightenment. Madison, James. Political theory. 1760-87. *235*
—. Government. Madison, James. Political Systems. Representative Government. 1740-88. *285*

—. Madison, James. Pluralist analysis. Political Theory. 1787-20c. *371*
—. Madison, James. Rousseau, Jean Jacques. 1787. *382*
Federalist No. 78. Hamilton, Alexander. Judicial review. Political Theory. Supreme Court. 1788-20c. *380*
Federalist Party. Ideology. Upper classes. 1789-1815. *615*
—. Republican Party. Rhetoric. 1789-1800. *678*
Federalist (review article). Enlightenment, Scottish. Hamilton, Alexander. Madison, James. Political Theory. Wills, Garry. 1787-88. *377*
Federalists. Addison, Alexander. Constitutional Law. Freedom of Speech. Pennsylvania. Sedition Act (US, 1798). 1792-98. *605*
—. Agrarian Republic. Antifederalists. Human Rights. 1780-88. *343*
—. American Revolution. Antifederalists. Public opinion. Rhetoric. 1787-88. *369*
—. Antifederalists. Conservatism. Government regulation. Liberalism. Liberty. 1787-1982. *113*
—. Antifederalists. Democracy. Enlightenment. Political Attitudes. Science. 1787-88. *497*
—. Antifederalists. Philosophy. 1787-89. *426*
—. Antifederalists. Religious liberty. 1776-92. *228*
—. Banning, Lance. Ideology. Jeffersonians. Political Parties (review articles). Zvesper, John. 1790's. 1977-78. *576*
—. Conservatism. Local Government. Political conditions. Radicals and Radicalism. 1630-1789. *350*
—. Democrats. Pennsylvania. Ratification. 1787. *357*
—. Federal Government. Political Attitudes. Publicity. Secrecy. 1800-12. *526*
—. French Revolution. Liberty. Republicans. USA. 1789-99. *364*
—. Hamilton, Alexander. Madison, James. Representative government. Republicanism. 1780's. *323*
—. Judges. Senate. 1776-87. *246*
—. Nullification movement. Political attitudes. South Carolina. 1788-1820's. *455*
—. Political Leadership. Values. Virtue. 1789-1800. *681*
—. Politics. Presidency. Washington, George. 1789-97. *418*
—. Sovereignty. State Government. 1787. *381*
Fedorenko v. *US* (US, 1981). Citizenship. Deportation. Supreme Court. War crimes. 1981. *1102*
Fehrenbacher, Don E. (review article). Citizenship. Democratic Party. *Dred Scott* v. *Sandford* (US, 1857). Missouri Compromise. Slavery. 1857. 1978. *534*
Feminism. Belmont, Alva. Equal rights amendment. National Woman's Party. Paul, Alice. Political Participation. 1919-28. *778*
—. Letters. Lockwood, Belva. Political Campaigns (presidential). 1884. *620*
Feminists. Amendments (19th). Pennsylvania. Suffrage. Women. 1837-1920. *598*
Ferries. Arkansas. Bridges. *Charles River Bridge* v. *Warren Bridge* (US, 1837). Supreme Court. ca 1837-1940. *530*
Fertility. Abortion. Civil Rights. Constitutional Law. *Roe* v. *Wade* (US, 1973). Women. 1973-82. *1145*
Field, Stephen J. Business. Constitutional Law. Government. Supreme Court. 1863-97. *578*
—. California. Law. Public lands. Supreme courts, state. 1850-66. *581*
—. California (Marysville). Judges. Supreme Court. 1849-97. *625*
—. California (San Francisco). Hill, Sarah Althea. Sharon, William. Terry, David S. 1884-89. *573*

—. Government. Information, access to. 1970's. *1134*
—. Great Britain. Information access. Judicial Process. Law. Press. 1973-83. *1130*
—. Howard Morland. Nuclear arms. Periodicals. *Progressive.* Supreme Court. 1979. *1113*
—. Libel. Supreme Court. 1798-1980. *663*
—. Privacy Protection Act (US, 1980). Supreme Court. *Zurcher* v. *Stanford Daily* (US, 1978). 1978-80. *718*
French and Indian War. Articles of Confederation. Indian-White relations. New York. Tiyanoga (Hendrick), Mohawk chief. 1700-55. 1776-77. *278*
French Revolution. Federalists. Liberty. Republicans. USA. 1789-99. *364*
Freund, Paul A. Brandeis, Louis D. Law. Personal Narratives. Supreme Court. 1932-33. *826*
—. National Court of Appeals (proposed). Supreme Court. 1972. *884*
Friends, Society of. American Revolution. Paine, Thomas. Political Attitudes. 1737-77. *262*
Fuller, Melville. Employers. Liability. Progressivism. Supreme Court. 1888-1910. *701*
Fullilove v. *Klutznick* (US, 1980). Affirmative action. Discrimination. Minorities. *Regents of the University of California* v. *Allan Bakke* (US, 1978). Supreme Court. *United Steelworkers of America* v. *Weber* (US, 1979). 1970's. *957*
—. *Kaiser Aluminum and Chemical Company* v. *Weber* (US, 1979). *Regents of the University of California* v. *Allan Bakke* (US, 1978). Supreme Court. 1977-80. *736*
Fulton-Favreau Formula. British North America Act (1867). Constitutional Law. 1960-66. *706*
Fund raising. Church and state. Constitutional Law. Local Government. Solicitation, religious. State Government. 1970's. *906*
Fundamentalism. Amendments. Civil War. Lincoln, Abraham. National Fast Day. National Reform Association. 1863-1945. *513*
Funston, Richard (review article). Burger, Warren E. Federal Policy. Judicial Administration. Supreme Court. Warren, Earl. 1953-79. *1103*

G

Gag Orders. Amendments (1st). Decisionmaking. Juries. 1931-80. *1054*
Gaines, Lloyd L. Blacks. Colleges and universities. Desegregation. Missouri, University of, Columbia. NAACP. Supreme Court. 1936-50. *853*
Gannett v. *DePasqual* (US, 1979). Civil Rights. Economic Aid. *Everson* v. *Board of Education* (US, 1947). Judicial Process. State Government. Supreme Court. 1776-1979. *998*
Garfield, James A. Lawyers. Rhetoric. Speeches. Supreme Court. 1860-80. *683*
Garfinkel, Herbert. Diamond, Martin. Fisk, Winston M. Political science. Textbooks. 1787. ca 1950-70. *52*
Garvey, Gerald (review article). Steamer, Robert J. (review article). Supreme Court. 1972. *1028*
General Advertiser. Aurora. Bache, Benjamin Franklin. Federalism. Newspapers. Pennsylvania (Philadelphia). Political Attitudes. 1790-98. *695*
General Land Office. Boundaries. California. Congress. Legislation. Nevada. State Government. Supreme Court. 1850-1980. *556*
General Motors Corporation. Antitrust. DuPont and Company. Supreme Court. *United States* v. *E. I. Du Pont de Nemours and Company et al.* (US, 1957). 1948-65. *928*

Genet, Edmond C. Constitutional Convention. Documents. Editors and Editing. Lansing, John, Jr. Madison, James. Yates, Robert. 1787-1840. *406*
Genovese, Michael A. Choper, Jesse H. Federalism (review article). Fisher, Louis. Jenkins, Iredell. Law. Merry, Henry J. 1978-80. *756*
Georgia. Connecticut. Delaware. New Jersey. Ratification. 1787-88. *488*
—. Debates. Newspapers. Ratification. State Politics. 1787-88. *420*
Georgia Insurrection Law. Communism. Demonstrations. *Herndon* v. *Lowry* (US, 1937). International Labor Defense. Martin, Charles H. (review article). Supreme Court. 1932-37. *808*
Gérard, Conrad. American Revolution. Congress. Deane, Silas. Diplomacy. France. Lee, Arthur. 1779. *294*
German language. Church Schools. Lutherans, Missouri Synod. Nebraska Council of Defense. Supreme Court. 1917-23. *908*
Germantown, Battle of. American Revolution. Letters. Rodney, Caesar. Washington, George. 1777-81. *256*
Germany. American Revolution. Diplomacy. Research. 1775-84. *40*
—. American Revolution. Enlightenment. Historians. 1775-87. *306*
Germany (Vormärz period). Liberals. 1787-1848. *4*
Gerrymandering. Apportionment. Common Cause. 1960's-70's. *705*
Gertz v. *Robert Welch, Inc.* (US, 1974). Law. Libel. Supreme Court. 1974-76. *1097*
Gettysburg Address. Declaration of Independence. Government. Preamble. 1776-1974. *140*
—. Lincoln, Abraham. Political Theory. 1865. *650*
Gibbons v. *Ogden* (US, 1824). Constitutional Law. Monopolies. Steamboats. Supreme Court. 1824. *641*
Giles, Benjamin. Founding Fathers. Libraries. New Hampshire. 1760's-87. *288*
Gilmore, Grant. Horwitz, Morton J. Horwitz, Robert H. Law (review article). Values. White, G. Edward. 1780-1980. *44*
Gitlow v. *New York* (US, 1925). Amendments (14th). Civil rights. Sanford, Edward Terry. Supreme Court. ca 1890-1930. *938*
Glasser, Ira (interview). Amendments (1st). *Buckley* v. *Valeo* (US, 1976). Campaign finance. Congress. Federal Election Campaign Act (US, 1971; amended 1974). 1971-74. *1168*
Globe Newspaper v. *Superior Court* (US, 1982). Children. Constitutional Law. Social Sciences. Supreme Court. Witnesses. 1970's-82. *982*
Goebel, Julius, Jr. Legal history. Supreme Court. 1789-1800. *524*
Goldberg v. *Kelly* (US, 1970). Due process. *Morrisey* v. *Brewer* (US, 1972). Public Administration (agencies). Supreme Court. 1969-74. *831*
Gora, Joel (interview). Amendments (1st). *Buckley* v. *Valeo* (US, 1976). Campaign finance. Congress. Federal Election Commission. 1974-76. *1165*
Government. *See also* Colonial Government; Representative Government.
—. 1789-20c. *166*
—. Accountability. Constitutional Law. 1940-78. *862*
—. Advertising. Amendments (1st). Freedom of Speech. Interest groups. Mass Media. Supreme Court. 1972-78. *1112*
—. Amendments (1st). Freedom of the press. Libel. Secrecy. 1793-1800. *553*
—. Amendments (1st). Information. Law. Politics. Propaganda. 1960's-82. *1253*

—. Depressions. Hughes, Charles Evans. New Deal. Supreme Court. 1930's. 1950's-60's. *98*
—. Morris, Thomas D. (review article). Politics. 1780-1861. 1974. *29*
History. Barlow, Joel. Federalism. Jefferson, Thomas. Political Systems. 1790-1815. *568*
—. Constitutional Convention. 1787. *498*
History Teaching. American History. Audiovisual materials. Higher Education. 1607-1789. 1976. *131*
—. Simulation and Games. Supreme Court. 1983. *78*
Hobbes, Thomas. Coleman, Frank. Liberalism. Political Theory. 1642-79. 1776-98. *258*
—. Great Britain. Political Theory. 17c-18c. *154*
Hodder-Williams, Richard. Accountability. Coffin, Frank M. Dubois, Phillip L. Judicial Process (review article). Theberge, Leonard J. 1979-80. *845*
Hofstadter, Richard. Constitutional law. *Lochner* v. *New York* (US, 1905). Reform. Social Darwinism. Spencer, Herbert. 1905. 1950's-70's. *1128*
Holmes, Oliver Wendell. Amendments (1st). Espionage Act (US, 1917). *Schenck* v. *United States* (US, 1917). Supreme Court. 1917. *1268*
—. Cardozo, Benjamin. Law. Supreme Court. Warren, Earl. 1953-69. *958*
Home rule movements. Constitutional Law. Dillon, John Forrest (Dillon's Rule). Local government. State centralization. 1868-1974. *855*
Homosexuals. Civil Rights. Government. Supreme Court. 1960's-70's. *772*
Hopkins v. *Cohen* (US, 1968). Disability. Law Reform. Social Security. Supreme Court. 1968-69. *1076*
Horwitz, Morton J. Gilmore, Grant. Horwitz, Robert H. Law (review article). Values. White, G. Edward. 1780-1980. *44*
Horwitz, Robert H. Gilmore, Grant. Horwitz, Morton J. Law (review article). Values. White, G. Edward. 1780-1980. *44*
Hospitals, state. Courts. Medicine and State. Treatment. Youth facilities. 1960's-70's. *987*
Hostages. Algeria. *Betsey* (vessel). Foreign relations. Morocco. *Polly* (vessel). Treaties. 1783-90. *320*
Hours of work. Constitutional Law. Sex Discrimination. Supreme Court. 1905-17. *1269*
House Committee on Un-American Activities. Amendments (1st). Lawsuits. Legislative Investigations. Stamler, Jeremiah. 1965-70's. *1014*
House Education and Labor Committee. Amendments (1st). Indiana (Evansville). Kinoy, Arthur. Personal Narratives. Strikes. United Electrical, Radio, and Machine Workers of America. 1948. *923*
House of Representatives. Amendments (13th). Ashley, James M. Montana Territory. Reconstruction. 1850's-70's. *658*
—. Amendments (13th). Ashley, James M. Nationalism. Ohio. Political Parties. 1848-65. *560*
—. Constitutional Law. Federal Government. Foreign Relations. Panama Canal Treaty. Property. 1978. *1174*
—. Documents. Marshall, John. Secretaries of state. Supreme Court. 1799-1800. *665*
—. Lawyers. Supreme Court. 1937-60. *746*
—. Moody, William Henry. Navies. Political Leadership. Supreme Court. 1895-1910. *689*
House of Representatives (investigations). Executive Branch. Indian Wars. St. Clair, Arthur. 1791-93. *541*
Housing. Amendments (14th). Discrimination. Employment. Law. 1940-70. *946*
—. California. Fair housing. Referendum. Voting and Voting behavior. ca 1960-67. *1158*

—. Civil rights movement. Environment. Supreme Court. Zoning. 1970's. *895*
—. Fair Housing Amendments Act (proposed). Federal government. 1930's-79. *1140*
Housing, scatter-site. Constitutional Amendments (14th). New York City (Faraday Wood). UN (Soviet Mission). 1967-75. *990*
Howard Morland. Freedom of the press. Nuclear arms. Periodicals. *Progressive*. Supreme Court. 1979. *1113*
Hughes, Charles Evans. Depressions. Historiography. New Deal. Supreme Court. 1930's. 1950's-60's. *98*
—. Judicial Administration. Political Attitudes. Supreme Court. 1930-37. *1316*
—. New York. Supreme Court. 1900-41. *807*
Hulton, Henry. American Revolution. Letters. Massachusetts (Boston). 1772-76. *231*
Human Rights. Agrarian Republic. Antifederalists. Federalists. 1780-88. *343*
—. Constitutional Law. Courts. Separation of powers. 1954-80. *1238*
—. Democracy. Education. *San Antonio Independent School District* v. *Rodriguez* (US, 1973). 1787-1980. *206*
—. Egalitarianism. Equality. Ideas, History of. Law. 18c-1974. *126*
—. Law Enforcement. *Rodriguez-Fernandez* v. *Wilkinson* (US, 1980). Supreme Court. 1980. *965*
Humanities. Arts. Constitutional Convention. Founding Fathers. 1780's. *319*
Hume, David. Adair, Douglass. *Federalist* No. 10. Madison, James. Political Theory. Republicanism. Wills, Garry. 1788. *392*
Hungary. American Revolution. Democracy. Independence movements. Models. Political corruption. 1776-1876. *71*
Hyde Amendment. Abortion. Amendments (1st, 5th). *Harris* v. *McRae* (US, 1980). Medicaid. Supreme Court. 1976-80. *972*
—. Abortion. State government. Supreme Court. Taxation. 1976-77. *1003*
Hyman, Harold M. Business. Review. Civil rights. Constitutional Law (review article). Federal Government. Wiecek, William M. 1835-75. *512*
—. Constitutional Law (review article). Government regulation. Industry. Wiecek, William M. 1835-75. *572*

I

Ickes, Harold L. Hawaii. Japanese Americans. Martial law. World War II. 1941-44. *900*
Ideas, History of. Egalitarianism. Equality. Human rights. Law. 18c-1974. *126*
Ideology. Amendments (1st). Black Muslims. 1932-79. *915*
—. American Revolution. 1776-87. *322*
—. American Revolution. Declaration of Independence. *Federalist*. Rhetoric. 1776-89. *341*
—. American Revolution. Political Theory. Social Organization. Wilson, James. 1770's-90's. *238*
—. American Revolution. Reid, John Philip. Shaw, Peter. Szatmary, David P. 1763-88. *268*
—. American Revolution (review article). Confederation. Loyalists. 1748-89. 1975. *257*
—. Antifederalists. Taxation. 1760-90. *310*
—. Banning, Lance. Federalists. Jeffersonians. Political Parties (review articles). Zvesper, John. 1790's. 1977-78. *576*
—. Christianity. Democracy. Dwight, Timothy. Federalism. Morse, Jedidiah. Republicanism. 1790-1800. *614*
—. Church and State. Congress. Constitutional Law. Supreme Court. 18c-20c. *156*

Insanity. Civil Rights. Crime and Criminals. *Jones v. United States* (US, 1983). Mental Illness. Supreme Court. 1975-83. *1084*
Institutions. Burger, Warren E. Civil Rights. Habeas corpus. Supreme Court. Warren, Earl. 1954-77. *973*
Institutions, private. Amendments (14th). *Dartmouth College* v. *Woodward* (US, 1819). Supreme Court. 1819. 1968-69. *829*
Integration. Litigation. NAACP. North. Public schools. 1954-73. *878*
Intelligence, foreign. Amendments (4th). Electronic surveillance. Executive Power. Supreme Court. *United States* v. *Butenko* (US, 1974). 1974. *1157*
Intelligence service. Central Intelligence Agency. Constitutional law. Executive Power. 1933-74. *745*
Interest Groups. Abortion. Law. Politics. 1959-80. *821*
—. Advertising. Amendments (1st). Freedom of Speech. Government. Mass Media. Supreme Court. 1972-78. *1112*
—. *Amicus curiae.* Hakman, Nathan. Law. Minorities. Supreme court. Women. 1928-80. *1007*
—. Campaign Finance. Citizen Lobbies. Common Cause. Constitutional Amendments (26th). 1971. *1320*
—. Conservatism. Supreme Court. 1969-80. *1008*
—. Madison, James. Pluralism. Political Theory. 1787-1836. *132*
Intergovernmental Relations. Antitrust. Federal Government. State Government. Supreme Court. 1975-82. *802*
—. Apportionment. Attorneys General. Courts. Election Laws. Voting Rights Act (US, 1965; Section 5). 1965-77. *734*
—. Constitutional Law. Federal Government. States. 1775-87. *336*
—. Federalism. 1787-1978. *110*
—. Political Theory. 1780's. *290*
Internal Revenue Service. Civil Rights. 1920-80. *863*
—. Constitutional Law. Tax fraud. 1960-69. *950*
International Labor Defense. Communism. Demonstrations. Georgia Insurrection Law. *Herndon* v. *Lowry* (US, 1937). Martin, Charles H. (review article). Supreme Court. 1932-37. *808*
International law. Act of state doctrine. Confiscations. Courts. Foreign Relations. Property. *United Bank Ltd.* v. *Cosmic Int'l, Inc* (US, 1976). 1971-76. *774*
—. American Society of International Law. Lawyers. Supreme Court. 1776-1914. *1037*
—. *Banco Nacional de Cuba* v. *Sabbatino* (US, 1964). Cuba. *First National City Bank* v. *Banco Nacional de Cuba* (US, 1972). State Department. Supreme Court. 1964-72. *953*
—. Congress. 1700-1969. *824*
—. Constitutional Law. Presidency. War. 1787-20c. *189*
International Organizations. USA. 1776-1976. *67*
Internationalism. American Revolution. Foreign policy. Historiography. Liberalism. Political Leadership. 1776-1801. *260*
Internment. Constitutional Law. Japanese Americans. Politics. Supreme Court. World War II. 1942-45. *1212*
Interpersonal Relations. Frankfurter, Felix. Harvard Law School. Law. Supreme Court. Zionism. 1894-1965. *1210*
Interstate Commerce. Industrial Relations. Jones and Laughlin Steel Corporation. Labor Law. 1824-1935. *649*
Intervention. Constitutional Law. Marines. Presidents. 1805-1959. *77*

Iredell, James. Constitutional law. Patriotism. Supreme Court. 1751-99. *459*
Ireland. Catholic Church. Constitutional Law. Irish Americans. O'Conor, Charles. O'Conor, Charles Owen. Political reform. Reconstruction. 1865-85. *531*
Irish Americans. Catholic Church. Constitutional Law. Ireland. O'Conor, Charles. O'Conor, Charles Owen. Political reform. Reconstruction. 1865-85. *531*
Irons, Peter H. Lawyers (review article). New Deal. Supreme Court. 1933-37. *894*
Iroquois Confederacy. Federal Policy. Indians. New York. 1783-98. *401*

J

Jackson, Howell Edmunds. Politics. Supreme Court. Tennessee. 1832-95. *548*
Jackson, Robert H. Douglas, William O. Political Attitudes. Role theory. Supreme Court. 1939-68. *905*
—. Supreme Court. 1947-49. *962*
Jacksonianism. Campbell, John Archibald. Lawyers. Supreme Court. 1829-89. *564*
Jacobsohn, Gary J. (review article). Constitutional Law. Supreme Court. 1789-1977. *108*
Japan. Business. Civil Rights Act (US, 1964; Title VII). Foreign Investments. Law. *Sumitomo Shoji America, Inc.* v. *Avagliano* (US, 1982). Supreme Court. 1977-83. *1138*
—. Citizenship. Immigration. Lawsuits. Ozawa Takao. Supreme Court. 1906-22. *898*
—. Constitutional Law. Judicial Review. USA. 1945-74. *1307*
Japanese Americans. California. Discrimination. Legislation. Supreme Court. 1920's. *768*
—. Constitutional Law. Internment. Politics. Supreme Court. World War II. 1942-45. *1212*
—. Hawaii. Ickes, Harold L. Martial law. World War II. 1941-44. *900*
Japanese Exclusion. Canada. Law and Society. Supreme Courts. USA. 1950-70's. *1369*
Jay, John. Candor (concept). Conflict and Conflict Resolution. *Federalist.* Hamilton, Alexander. Madison, James. 1787. *398*
—. *Federalist.* Hamilton, Alexander. Liberty. Madison, James. Political Theory. 1787-88. *361*
—. New York. Ratification. 1788. *436*
—. Political Attitudes. 1780-1800. *468*
Jay Treaty (1794). Newspapers. Nominations for Office. Political Factions. Rutledge, John. Supreme Court. 1794-95. *585*
Jefferson, Thomas. Adams, John. Amendments (1st). Madison, James. Paine, Thomas. Religious Liberty. 1776-89. *274*
—. Adams, John. Federalism. Hamilton, Alexander. Washington, George. 1775-90's. *239*
—. Articles of Confederation. Farming. Landowning. Property. Republicanism. 1776-87. *263*
—. Barlow, Joel. Federalism. History. Political Systems. 1790-1815. *568*
—. Bill of Rights. Constitutional Convention. 1787. *457*
—. Brazil. Letters. Maia, Jose Joaquim da. Natural history. Political Theory. Social Conditions. 1786-1819. *453*
—. Declaration of Independence. Enlightenment. Locke, John. Political Theory. Scotland. Wills, Garry (review article). 1690's-1776. 1970's. *255*
—. Federal Government. Foreign Relations. Ratification campaign. 1787. *429*
—. Liu Zhuochang. Political Theory. 1776-1820. *136*
—. Locke, John. Philosophy. Political theory. 1780-1826. *24*

K

Korean War. Acheson, Dean. Congress. Constitutional Law. Truman, Harry S. War, declaration of. 1950-64. *952*
—. Brainwashing. Communism. Morale. Prisoners of War. 1776-1955. *111*
—. Congress. Executive Power. Vietnam War. War. 1776-1970. *251*

L

Labor. *See also* Hours of Work.
—. Amendments (14th). Civil Rights Act (US, 1964). Equal Protection. Sex Discrimination. Women. 1960's-70's. *1224*
—. Blacks. Civil Rights. Employment. Novak, Daniel A. (review article). Reconstruction. 1865-1960's. *557*
Labor Disputes. Civil Rights Act (US, 1964; Title VII). Courts. Taft-Hartley Act (US, 1947). 1968-71. *847*
Labor law. Amendments (5th, 14th). Business. 1868-1915. *596*
—. Antitrust. Congress. Supreme Court. 1950-78. *875*
—. Colleges and Universities. National Labor Relations Board. Supreme Court. Teachers. Yeshiva University. 1970-80. *1347*
—. Courts. Discrimination, Employment. Women. 1876-1979. *879*
—. Discrimination, Employment. Public Employees. Supreme Court. 1969. *1085*
—. Industrial Relations. Interstate Commerce. Jones and Laughlin Steel Corporation. 1824-1935. *649*
—. Private sector. Supreme Court. 1979-80. *995*
—. Supreme Court. 1935-76. *1207*
—. Supreme Court. 1977-78. *994*
—. Supreme Court. 1978-79. *996*
Labor relations. Collective Bargaining. *National Labor Relations Board v. Gissel Packing* (US, 1969). Supreme Court. 1969. *948*
Labor Unions and Organizations. Amendments (1st). Picketing. Supreme Court. 1940's-76. *1265*
—. Amendments (14th). Fiske, Harold B. Freedom of speech. Industrial Workers of the World. Kansas. Supreme Court. Trials. 1923-27. *777*
—. Blacks. Civil Rights. Discrimination, Employment. Supreme Court. 19c-1978. *1354*
Land. Constitutional Law. Federal government. State government. Supreme Court. Taxation. 1909-83. *949*
Land (cessions, claims). Congress. Federalism. States' rights. Virginia. 1750-84. *289*
Land grants. Commons. Law. New Mexico. San Joaquín Grant. 1806-97. *532*
Landownership. *See also* Ownership.
—. Articles of Confederation. Farming. Jefferson, Thomas. Property. Republicanism. 1776-87. *263*
Language. Amendments (14th). Equality. Law. *Regents of the University of California v. Allan Bakke* (US, 1978). 1970's. *1013*
Lansing, John, Jr. Constitutional Convention. Documents. Editors and Editing. Genet, Edmond C. Madison, James. Yates, Robert. 1787-1840. *406*
Latin America. Federalism. Models. Political Theory. 1776-1830. *107*
—. Federalism. USA. 1776-89. 1825-50. *50*
Lau v. *Nichols* (US, 1974). Bilingual education. California. Chacone-Moscone Bilingual Bicultural Education Act (1976). Civil Rights Act (US, 1964). Supreme Court. 1965-76. *939*
Law. *See also* terms beginning with the word legal; Labor Law.

—. Abolition Movement. Wiecek, William M. (review article). 1760-1848. 1977. *555*
—. Abortion. Interest Groups. Politics. 1959-80. *821*
—. Admissions policy. Discrimination, Education. Professional Schools. Quotas. 1977. *1260*
—. *Afroyim* v. *Rusk* (US, 1967). Expatriation. *Rogers* v. *Bellei* (US, 1971). Supreme Court. 1790-1973. *61*
—. Aliens, Resident. Due process. Supreme Court. 1788-1979. *59*
—. Amendments (1st). Anastaplo, George. Freedom of Speech. Illinois Bar (admission controversy). 1787-1971. *141*
—. Amendments (1st). Croly, Herbert. Federal Regulation. Political Parties. Ritchie, Thomas. ca 1850-1980. *1285*
—. Amendments (1st). Douglas, William O. Judicial Opinions. Rhetoric. Supreme Court. ca 1939-75. *1344*
—. Amendments (1st). Dress codes. Teachers. 1960-80. *1363*
—. Amendments (1st). Education. Religion in the Public Schools. 1941-79. *1331*
—. Amendments (1st). Employees. Political Participation. Public Schools. 1867-1977. *1306*
—. Amendments (1st). Government. Information. Politics. Propaganda. 1960's-82. *1253*
—. Amendments (1st). Media. 1972-73. *1206*
—. Amendments (4th). Supreme Court. 18c-20c. *219*
—. Amendments (14th). Colleges and Universities. Due Process. Students. 1960's-70's. *1278*
—. Amendments (14th). Discrimination. Employment. Housing. 1940-70. *946*
—. Amendments (14th). Equality. Language. *Regents of the University of California v. Allan Bakke* (US, 1978). 1970's. *1013*
—. Amendments (14th). Equality. Public Policy. Students. 1954-76. *1368*
—. Amendments (14th). Public education. Segregation. States. 1865-1953. *1239*
—. American Revolution. Constitutionalism. Historiography. Politics. Religion. 1775-83. 1790-1950. *45*
—. American Revolution. Democracy. Lincoln, Abraham. 1775-83. 1850's-65. *591*
—. *Amicus curiae.* Hakman, Nathan. Interest groups. Minorities. Supreme court. Women. 1928-80. *1007*
—. Antitrust. Justice Department. Mass Media. Ownership. Supreme Court. 1946-76. *779*
—. Arbitration. Public Employees. State Government. 1960's-70's. *932*
—. Archival Catalogs and Inventories. Harvard Law School Library (Manuscript Division). 1861-1981. *21*
—. Arkansas (Little Rock). Politics. School Integration. 1954-57. *827*
—. Authoritarianism. Constitutionalism. Democracy. 1787-1976. *461*
—. Blacks. Educational Policy. Federal Government. School Integration. Supreme Court. 1954-82. *1040*
—. Brandeis, Louis D. Freund, Paul A. Personal Narratives. Supreme Court. 1932-33. *826*
—. Brandeis, Louis D. Reform. Supreme Court. Zionism. 1908-39. *1249*
—. Brandeis, Louis D. Supreme Court. 1890's-1941. *1237*
—. Business. Civil Rights Act (US, 1964; Title VII). Foreign Investments. Japan. *Sumitomo Shoji America, Inc. v. Avagliano* (US, 1982). Supreme Court. 1977-83. *1138*
—. California. Family. Governors. Judges. Supreme Court. Warren, Earl. 1911-74. *1132*

Lurton, Horace H. Courts (appellate). Harlan, John Marshall. Taft, William Howard. Tennessee. 1897. *594*

Lusky, Louis. Judicial review. Legislation. Supreme Court. 1937-81. *901*

Luther v. Borden (US, 1849). Dorr Rebellion. Election Laws. Rhode Island. State government. Supreme Court. 1842-49. *528*

Lutherans, Missouri Synod. Church Schools. German language. Nebraska Council of Defense. Supreme Court. 1917-23. *908*

M

Macbride Commission Report on a New World Communication Order. Communications. Constitutional Law. UNESCO. 1980. *710*

Machiavelli, Niccolo. Aristotle. Madison, James. Political Theory. Republics. 4c BC. 16c. 1780's-1830's. *354*

Maclay, William. Antifederalism. Congress. Diaries. New York. 1789-90. *358*

Madison, James. Adair, Douglass. *Federalist* No. 10. Hume, David. Political Theory. Republicanism. Wills, Garry. 1788. *392*

—. Adams, John. Amendments (1st). Jefferson, Thomas. Paine, Thomas. Religious Liberty. 1776-89. *274*

—. Amendments (1st). Political Attitudes. 1770-89. *241*

—. Amendments (2d). Conscientious objection. Federal government. Military service. States' Rights. 1787-92. *445*

—. American Revolution. Articles of Confederation. Documents. 1781-84. 1786-87. *333*

—. Aristotle. Machiavelli, Niccolo. Political Theory. Republics. 4c BC. 16c. 1780's-1830's. *354*

—. Articles of Confederation. Nationalism. 1780-83. *223*

—. Authority. Political Theory. 1780's. *284*

—. Authorship. *Federalist*. Hamilton, Alexander. 1788. *502*

—. Candor (concept). Conflict and Conflict Resolution. *Federalist*. Hamilton, Alexander. Jay, John. 1787. *398*

—. Clay, Henry. Constitutional convention. Political Theory. Virginia. 1788. *394*

—. Congress. Constitutional Law. Republicanism. State Legislatures. 1785-90. *404*

—. Constitutional Convention. 1787. *456*

—. Constitutional Convention. Documents. Editors and Editing. Genet, Edmond C. Lansing, John, Jr. Yates, Robert. 1787-1840. *406*

—. Constitutional Convention. *Federalist*. Government. Political Theory. 1783-90. *434*

—. Constitutional Convention. Manuscripts. Virginia Plan. 1787. *405*

—. Constitutional Convention. Political Representation. Virginia Plan. 1787. *414*

—. Democracy. *Federalist* No. 10. Liberty. 1787. *356*

—. Diamond, Martin. *Federalist*. Hamilton, Alexander. Montesquieu, Charles de. 1748-88. 1961. *299*

—. Enlightenment. *Federalist* No. 10. Political theory. 1760-87. *235*

—. Enlightenment, Scottish. *Federalist* (review article). Hamilton, Alexander. Political Theory. Wills, Garry. 1787-88. *377*

—. Federalism. Political Theory. 1783-90. *222*

—. *Federalist*. 1787-88. *493*

—. *Federalist*. Hamilton, Alexander. Jay, John. Liberty. Political Theory. 1787-88. *361*

—. *Federalist*. Hamilton, Alexander. Political Theory. 1787-88. *485*

—. *Federalist*. Hamilton, Alexander. Political Theory. 1787-88. *486*

—. *Federalist*. Hamilton, Alexander. Political theory. Republicanism. 1787-88. *378*

—. *Federalist*. Hamilton, Alexander. Separation of powers. Veto. 1787-90. *367*

—. *Federalist*. Political Theory. Public Welfare. 1787-92. *395*

—. *Federalist* No. 10. Government. Political Systems. Representative Government. 1740-88. *285*

—. *Federalist* No. 10. Pluralist analysis. Political Theory. 1787-20c. *371*

—. *Federalist* No. 10. Rousseau, Jean Jacques. 1787. *382*

—. Federalists. Hamilton, Alexander. Representative government. Republicanism. 1780's. *323*

—. Interest Groups. Pluralism. Political Theory. 1787-1836. *132*

—. Library of Congress. 1783-1815. *266*

—. Political Leadership. Political parties. Presidency. Republicanism. 1780-1820. *74*

—. Political Theory. Religious liberty. 1780-1830. *128*

—. Political Theory. Separation of powers. 1787-1836. *379*

—. Politics. ca 1775-89. *347*

Magna Carta. American Revolution. Great Britain. Locke, John. Political theory. 1215-1781. *298*

Maia, Jose Joaquim da. Brazil. Jefferson, Thomas. Letters. Natural history. Political Theory. Social Conditions. 1786-1819. *453*

Maier, Pauline (review article). Political Theory. Radicals and Radicalism. 1763-76. 1980. *236*

Mail (proscribed). Congress. Postal Service. Supreme Court. 18c-20c. *165*

Majority rule. Apportionment. Political systems. Supreme Court. 1965-68. *916*

Malice. Constitutional Law. Courts. Libel. Public figures. Reporters and Reporting. 1964-77. *867*

Management. Antitrust. Congress. Courts. Sports. Supreme Court. 1950's-70's. *834*

Manifest Destiny. American Revolution. Natural rights. 1776-1976. *38*

Manuscripts. Amendments (13th). Henry E. Huntington Library. Letters. Strohm, Isaac (daughters). 1864. 1896. *629*

—. Constitutional Convention. Madison, James. Virginia Plan. 1787. *405*

Mapp v. Ohio (US, 1961). Civil Rights. Evidence (admissibility). Supreme Court. Supreme courts, state (reactions to). 1960's. *762*

—. Evidence. Exclusionary rule. Law enforcement. Supreme Court. Trials. 1960's-70's. *763*

Marbury v. Madison (US, 1803). Jefferson, Thomas. Marshall, John. Supreme Court. 1789-1803. *651*

Marines. Constitutional Law. Intervention. Presidents. 1805-1959. *77*

Maritime Law. Bahamas Marine Patrol. Cuban Americans. Lobster. 1978. *744*

Marketing. Commercial Law. Corporations. 1875-90. *577*

Marriage. Equal Rights Amendment. Legal status. Sex discrimination. Women. 19c-1970's. *9*

Marshall, John. Butler, Elizur. Cherokee Indians. Indian-White Relations. Nullification crisis. Supreme Court. Worcester, Samuel A. *Worcester v. Georgia* (US, 1832). 1828-33. *586*

—. *Cohens* v. *Virginia* (US, 1821). Federalism. States' Rights. Supreme Court. Virginia. 1821. *687*

—. Constitutional law. 1775-1835. *130*

—. Constitutional Law. Executive Power. Roosevelt, Theodore. Taft, William Howard. 19c-1913. *609*

—. Constitutional Law. Supreme Court. 1801-15. *656*
—. Corporations. *Dartmouth College* v. *Woodward* (US, 1819). Virginia. 1801-19. *516*
—. Documentaries. Films. Supreme court. 1803-24. 1977. *639*
—. Documents. House of Representatives. Secretaries of state. Supreme Court. 1799-1800. *665*
—. *Dred Scott* v. *Sandford* (US, 1857). Slavery. Supreme Court. Taney, Roger Brooke. 1820-60. *636*
—. Jefferson, Thomas. *Marbury* v. *Madison* (US, 1803). Supreme Court. 1789-1803. *651*
—. Supreme Court. 1780-1835. *673*
—. Supreme Court. 1801-35. *675*
Marshall, Thurgood. *Brown* v. *Board of Education* (US, 1954). Civil rights. Constitutional Law. NAACP. Supreme Court. 1865-1954. *1136*
Martial law. Congress. Emergency, states of. Executive Power. 1917-52. *968*
—. Emergency, states of. Executive power. Habeas corpus. War. 1861-1944. *601*
—. Hawaii. Ickes, Harold L. Japanese Americans. World War II. 1941-44. *900*
Martin, Charles H. (review article). Communism. Demonstrations. Georgia Insurrection Law. *Herndon* v. *Lowry* (US, 1937). International Labor Defense. Supreme Court. 1932-37. *808*
Maryland. Carroll, Charles (of Carrollton). Chase, Samuel. 1787-88. *439*
—. Political Change. Sectionalism. Social Classes. 1776-89. *351*
Mason, George. Bill of Rights. Declaration of Rights. Virginia. 1776-91. *316*
Mass Media. Advertising. Amendments (1st). Freedom of Speech. Government. Interest groups. Supreme Court. 1972-78. *1112*
—. Amendments (1st). 1970's. *1116*
—. Amendments (1st). Black, Hugo L. Freedom of the Press. Supreme Court. 1937-71. *1290*
—. Amendments (1st). Business. Freedom of the press. 1789-1975. *89*
—. Amendments (1st). Business. Public interest. 1960's-70's. *1170*
—. Amendments (1st). Chief Justice Earl Warren Conference on Advocacy in the United States (recommendations). 1973. *1192*
—. Amendments (1st). Civil Rights. 1972. *1206*
—. Amendments (1st). Freedom of the Press. 1970's. *1161*
—. Amendments (1st). Information access. State action (concept). Supreme Court. 1365
—. Amendments (1st). Presidency. 18c-20c. *242*
—. Amendments (1st). Public Opinion. 1734-1981. *123*
—. Antitrust. Justice Department. Law. Ownership. Supreme Court. 1946-76. *779*
—. Censorship. Freedom of speech. 1966. *755*
—. Constitutional Amendments (1st). Economics. 1975. *1236*
Massachusetts. Adams, John. Constitutions, State. 1780. *296*
—. Amendments (4th). Legislation. Police. Privacy. Search and Seizure. Supreme Court. 1974. *714*
—. Amendments (19th). Suffrage. Women. 1900-19. *1099*
Massachusetts (Boston). Amendments (1st). Courts. Defamation. Freedom of the press. Newspapers. 1782-91. *363*
—. American Revolution. Hulton, Henry. Letters. 1772-76. *231*
—. Antiabolition sentiments. Clergy. Conservatism. Missouri (St. Louis). Unitarianism. 1828-57. *619*
—. Charles River Bridge Case (US, 1837). Law. Supreme Court. 1837. *662*

—. Chauncy, Charles. Political Theory. Theology. 1745-85. *331*
Massachusetts (Newburyport). *Essex Journal and New Hampshire Packet.* Newspapers. Propaganda. Ratification. 1787-88. *430*
Massachusetts (North Brookfield). Amendments (14th). Conservatism. Prayer. Public Schools. Supreme Court. 1963. *920*
McCloy, John J. Bricker Amendment. Bricker, John W. Dulles, John Foster. Executive agreements. Personal Narratives. Presidency. Senate. Treaties. 1951-54. *1164*
McCumber, Porter James. Conservatism. McKenzie, Alexander John. North Dakota. Political reform. Republican Party. 1898-1933. *1068*
McDaniel v. *Paty* (US, 1978). Amendments (1st). Free exercise clause. Polygamy. Religion. *Reynolds* v. *United States* (US, 1878). Supreme Court. 1878-1978. *817*
McInnis v. *Ogilvie* (US, 1969). Civil Rights. Constitutional Amendments (14th). Public Schools. State Aid to Education. 1965-70. *1074*
McKenzie, Alexander John. Conservatism. McCumber, Porter James. North Dakota. Political reform. Republican Party. 1898-1933. *1068*
McReynolds, James Clark. Congress. Longshoremen's and Harbor Worker's Compensation Act (US, 1927). Supreme Court. Workers' Compensation. 1917-27. *735*
—. Judges. Supreme Court. 1890's-1941. *692*
—. Law. Supreme Court. 1862-1946. *913*
Media. Amendments (1st). Law. 1972-73. *1068*
Medicaid. Abortion. Amendments (1st, 5th). *Harris* v. *McRae* (US, 1980). Hyde Amendment. Supreme Court. 1976-80. *972*
Medicine and State. Courts. Hospitals, state. Treatment. Youth facilities. 1960's-70's. *987*
Meiklejohn, Alexander. Amendments (1st). Curricula. Educators. Political Reform. 1898-1964. *1342*
—. Amendments (1st). Education. Freedom of Speech. Social Theory. ca 1912-64. *1339*
Meiklejohn, Alexander (review article). Amendments (1st). Brown, Cynthia Stokes. Capitalism. Foreign Relations. Political Theory. 1912-55. *795*
Mennonites. Amish. Church Schools. Compulsory education. Public schools. Supreme Court. *Wisconsin* vs. *Yoder* (US, 1972). 1925-82. *814*
Mental Illness. Civil Rights. Courts. Handicapped. 1970-79. *1288*
—. Civil Rights. Crime and Criminals. Insanity. *Jones* v. *United States* (US, 1983). Supreme Court. 1975-83. *1084*
Mergers, Corporate. Antitrust. Corporations. Supreme Court. ca 1900-75. *1357*
Merry, Henry J. Choper, Jesse H. Federalism (review article). Fisher, Louis. Genovese, Michael A. Jenkins, Iredell. Law. 1978-80. *756*
Methodology. Amendments (1st). Freedom of the press. Newspapers. Social Sciences. Virginia. 1785-89. *362*
—. Psychohistory. Psychology. Supreme Court. 18c-1979. *552*
Mexican Americans. Aliens, illegal. Civil rights. Constitutional Law. 1970-77. *833*
Michigan. Catholic Church. Church and State. Compulsory education. Politics. Supreme Court. 1920-25. *758*
—. Conservatism. New Deal. Press. 1934-36. *797*
Middle Classes. Civil Rights. Freedom of Speech. Privacy. Supreme Court. 1974-75. *726*
Migration, internal. Civil Rights. Judicial Administration. Supreme Court. 1780's-1977. *106*

Military. Amendments (1st). Freedom of Speech. 1950-80. *991*
—. Amendments (2d). Political Theory. 1656-1791. *383*
—. Civil Disturbances. Executive Power. 1789-1978. *105*
Military Intelligence. Amendments (6th). Courts Martial and Courts of Inquiry. Secrecy. 1970's. *1321*
Military Law. Constitutional Law. Supreme Court. Universal Code of Military Justice (general articles). 1775-1968. *129*
Military officers. American Revolution. Leadership. Political Theory. Washington, George. Whigs. 1775-83. *308*
Military officers, retired. Constitutional Convention. Pennsylvania (Philadelphia). Society of the Cincinnati. Washington, George. 1783-87. *473*
Military Service. Amendments (1st). Chaplains. 1607-1978. *1142*
—. Amendments (2d). Conscientious objection. Federal government. Madison, James. States' Rights. 1787-92. *445*
—. Blacks. Citizenship. Civil Rights. Reconstruction. 1861-68. *644*
Military Strategy. American Revolution. Public Policy. Washington, George. 1770's-90's. *88*
Militia. Amendments (2d). Civil Rights. 1774-89. *352*
Mill, John Stuart. Bill of Rights. Civil rights. Douglas, William O. Supreme Court. 18c-20c. *25*
Miller, Arthur Selwyn. Bobbitt, Philip. Constitutional Law (review article). Judges. Neier, Aryeh. Perry, Michael J. Policymaking. Social Policy. 1950's-83. *1034*
Milliken v. *Bradley* (US, 1974). Discrimination, Educational. *San Antonio Independent School District* v. *Rodriguez* (US, 1973). Supreme Court. 1974. *896*
—. Law. School desegregation. Supreme Court. 1960's-70's. *1177*
Minor v. *Happersett* (US, 1875). Amendments (14th). Missouri (St. Louis). Suffrage. Women. 1867-75. *618*
Minorities. Affirmative action. Discrimination. *Fullilove* v. *Klutznick* (US, 1980). *Regents of the University of California* v. *Allan Bakke* (US, 1978). Supreme Court. *United Steelworkers of America* v. *Weber* (US, 1979). 1970's. *957*
—. Amicus curiae. Hakman, Nathan. Interest groups. Law. Supreme court. Women. 1928-80. *1007*
—. Civil Rights. Supreme Court. 1886-1972. *988*
—. Constitutional law. Law and Society. Poor. 1960's-74. *1016*
Miranda v. *Arizona* (US, 1966). Constitutional Law. Crime and Criminals. *Rhode Island* v. *Innis* (US, 1975). Supreme Court. 1971-79. *1171*
Mishin, A. A. (views). Amendments. 1789-1972. *93*
Mississippi. Amendments (14th). *Loewen* v. *Turnipseed* (US, 1980). Textbooks. 1968-80. *1070*
—. Civil Rights. Redistricting. Supreme Court. *United States* v. *State of Mississippi* (US, 1980). 1965-80. *1301*
Missouri. Blacks. Indians. Lawsuits. Legal status. Scypion, Marie Jean (descendants). Slavery. Supreme Court. 1769-1838. *48*
Missouri Compromise. Citizenship. Democratic Party. *Dred Scott* v. *Sandford* (US, 1857). Fehrenbacher, Don E. (review article). Slavery. 1857. 1978. *534*
Missouri (Louisiana). Clergy. Constitutional Law. Cummings, John. *Cummings* v. *Missouri* (US, 1867). Oaths. Supreme Court. 1865-67. *600*

Missouri (St. Louis). Amendments (14th). *Minor* v. *Happersett* (US, 1875). Suffrage. Women. 1867-75. *618*
—. Antiabolition sentiments. Clergy. Conservatism. Massachusetts (Boston). Unitarianism. 1828-57. *619*
Missouri, University of, Columbia. Blacks. Colleges and universities. Desegregation. Gaines, Lloyd L. NAACP. Supreme Court. 1936-50. *853*
Mobility. Amendments. Automobiles. Civil Rights. 1977. *888*
Models. American Revolution. Democracy. Hungary. Independence movements. Political corruption. 1776-1876. *71*
—. Federalism. Latin America. Political Theory. 1776-1830. *107*
Monetary policy. Federal Government. 1948-82. *1172*
Monopolies. Advertising. Newspaper Preservation Act (US, 1970). Supreme Court. *Times-Picayune Publishing Co.* v. *United States* (US, 1953). 1953-78. *721*
—. Constitutional Law. *Gibbons* v. *Ogden* (US, 1824). Steamboats. Supreme Court. 1824. *641*
Monroe, James. Congress. Kentucky. Political Parties. ca 1781-89. *240*
Montana Territory. Amendments (13th). Ashley, James M. House of Representatives. Reconstruction. 1850's-70's. *658*
Montesquieu, Charles de. Diamond, Martin. *Federalist*. Hamilton, Alexander. Madison, James. 1748-88. 1961. *299*
—. Greece. Locke, John. Political Theory. Separation of powers. 5c-4c BC. 17c-1787. *390*
Montgomery Improvement Association. Alabama. Civil Rights. Desegregation. King, Martin Luther, Jr. Parks, Rosa. 1955-57. *1095*
Moody, William Henry. House of Representatives. Navies. Political Leadership. Supreme Court. 1895-1910. *689*
—. Judges. Politics. Supreme Court. 1878-1910. *874*
Moral overstrain. Constitutional law. Racism. Rhetoric. 1776-1960's. *86*
Morale. Brainwashing. Communism. Korean War. Prisoners of War. 1776-1955. *111*
Morality. *See also* Political Ethics.
—. Bakke, Allan. Blacks. Constitutional Law. Equality. *Regents of the University of California* v. *Allan Bakke* (US, 1978). 18c-20c. *158*
—. Constitutional law. Due process. Liberty. Natural rights. 1980. *1056*
—. Constitutional Law. Mormons. Polygamy. Religious Liberty. *Reynolds* v. *United States* (US, 1878). Supreme Court. 1862-78. *517*
Mormon Church. Suffrage. Utah. Women. 1895. *634*
Mormons. Amendments (21st). Prohibition. Utah. 1932-33. *919*
—. Business. Ethics. Theology. Watergate scandal. 1974. *1173*
—. Constitutional Law. Morality. Polygamy. Religious Liberty. *Reynolds* v. *United States* (US, 1878). Supreme Court. 1862-78. *517*
Morocco. Algeria. *Betsey* (vessel). Foreign relations. Hostages. *Polly* (vessel). Treaties. 1783-90. *320*
Morris, Gouverneur. American Revolution. Commerce. Political theory. 1774-1800. *1*
Morris, Thomas D. (review article). Historiography. Politics. 1780-1861. 1974. *29*
Morrisey v. *Brewer* (US, 1972). Due process. *Goldberg* v. *Kelly* (US, 1970). Public Administration (agencies). Supreme Court. 1969-74. *831*
Morse, Jedidiah. Christianity. Democracy. Dwight, Timothy. Federalism. Ideology. Republicanism. 1790-1800. *614*

Mueller v. *Allen* (US, 1982). Constitutional Law. Documents. Private Schools. Supreme Court. Tax deductions. 1983. *1178*

Mulattoes. Amendments (15th). Attitudes. Blacks. Discrimination. Legislation. Oregon. Whites. 1850-75. *602*

Munn v. *Illinois* (US, 1877). Courts, State. Eminent domain. Public interest. Supreme Court. 1850-77. *608*

Murder rates. Amendments (2d). Gun control. 1970's. *921*

Murphy, Frank. Judges. Supreme Court. 1940-49. *1029*

Music, Religious. Church and State. Constitutional Law. Public Schools. Supreme Court. 1950's-79. *1333*

N

NAACP. Amendments (14th). Blacks. Civil rights. Storey, Moorfield. 1845-1929. *985*

—. Blacks. Colleges and universities. Desegregation. Gaines, Lloyd L. Missouri, University of, Columbia. Supreme Court. 1936-50. *853*

—. Blacks. Democratic Party. Primaries. *Smith* v. *Allwright* (US, 1944). South. Suffrage. Supreme Court. 1890's-1944. *881*

—. Blacks. Democratic Party. Primaries. Suffrage. Supreme Court. Texas. 1927-45. *882*

—. *Brown* v. *Board of Education* (US, 1954). Civil rights. Constitutional Law. Marshall, Thurgood. Supreme Court. 1865-1954. *1136*

—. *Brown* v. *Board of Education* (US, 1954). Civil Rights. Legal and Educational Defense Fund. 1939-79. *1169*

—. *Brown* v. *Board of Education* (US, 1954). Constitutional Law. Public Schools. Segregation. Supreme Court. 1949-55. *961*

—. *Brown* v. *Board of Education* (US, 1954). Constitutional Law. School Integration. Supreme Court. 1954. *963*

—. Civil Rights Act (US, 1964). Employment. Equal opportunity. Seniority. Supreme Court. 1964-77. *880*

—. Constitutional Law. Democratic Party. Primaries (white). Texas. 1924-44. *1300*

—. Discrimination, Educational. Lawsuits. Segregation. 1979. *914*

—. Integration. Litigation. North. Public schools. 1954-73. *878*

NAACP (symposium). Affirmative action. Civil rights. *Regents of the University of California* v. *Allan Bakke* (US, 1978). 1970's. *1137*

National Association of Broadcasters. Amendments (1st). Family viewing. Federal Communications Commission. Programming, prime time. Television. 1975. *835*

—. Amendments (1st). Television. 1970's. *1196*

National Association Opposed to the Extension of Suffrage to Women. Amendments (19th). Suffrage. Women. 1919-20. *959*

National Characteristics. Constitutional Convention. Democracy. Pennsylvania (Philadelphia). Superstition. Violence. 1787. *435*

—. Federalism. Public Opinion. Social Organization. Values. 1787-1801. *359*

National Court of Appeals (proposed). Freund, Paul A. Supreme Court. 1972. *884*

National Emergencies Act (US, 1976). Congress. Constitutional Law. Executive branch. Political power. Public Policy. 1933-78. *967*

National Fast Day. Amendments. Civil War. Fundamentalism. Lincoln, Abraham. National Reform Association. 1863-1945. *513*

National Labor Relations Board. Colleges and Universities. Labor Law. Supreme Court. Teachers. Yeshiva University. 1970-80. *1347*

National Labor Relations Board v. *Gissel Packing* (US, 1969). Collective Bargaining. Labor relations. Supreme Court. 1969. *948*

National League of Cities v. *Usery* (US, 1976). Federalism. Legislation. Supreme Court. 1792-1976. *69*

National Reform Association. Amendments. Civil War. Fundamentalism. Lincoln, Abraham. National Fast Day. 1863-1945. *513*

National security. Amendments (1st, 4th). Civil Rights. Wiretaps. 1941-75. *861*

—. Articles of Confederation. Foreign Relations. 1780's. *335*

—. Civil rights. 1945-82. *1077*

—. Civil Rights. Plamondon, "Pun". Supreme Court. Surveillance. Wiretaps. 1940-72. *788*

—. Congress. Constitutional Law. Executive Power. Foreign Policy. Supreme Court. War. 1935-80. *1258*

National Socialist Party of America. Amendments (1st). American Civil Liberties Union. Collin, Frank. Demonstrations. Illinois (Skokie). Nazism. 1977. *1208*

National Socialist White People's Party. Amendments (1st). Freedom of Speech. Illinois (Skokie). Jews. Nazism. 1977. *1280*

National Woman's Party. Belmont, Alva. Equal rights amendment. Feminism. Paul, Alice. Political Participation. 1919-28. *778*

Nationalism. Amendments (13th). Ashley, James M. House of Representatives. Ohio. Political Parties. 1848-65. *560*

—. Articles of Confederation. Federalism. Government. Politics. Sectionalism. 1774-87. *327*

—. Articles of Confederation. Historiography. 1781-87. *276*

—. Articles of Confederation. Madison, James. 1780-83. *223*

—. Bill of Rights. Politics. Washington, George. 1783-93. *482*

Nationalization. Amendments (14th). Civil Rights. Constitutional Law. Supreme Court. 1873-1969. *1194*

Nation-building. Amendments (13th, 14th, 15th). Authority. Citizenship. Federal government. Freedmen. Reconstruction. 1865-70. *510*

NATO. Europe. Foreign relations. Troop reductions. USA. 1971. *866*

Natural history. Brazil. Jefferson, Thomas. Letters. Maia, Jose Joaquim da. Political Theory. Social Conditions. 1786-1819. *453*

Natural law. Civil Rights. Indian Civil Rights Act (US, 1968). Pueblo Indians. *Santa Clara Pueblo* v. *Martinez* (US, 1977). Supreme Court. Tribal government. 1939-77. *1050*

—. Hamilton, Alexander. Positivism. 1787-89. *411*

—. Locke, John. Philosophy. Supreme Court. 1775-1968. *63*

Natural Rights. Amendments (9th). Courts. 1789-1979. *197*

—. American Revolution. Manifest Destiny. 1776-1976. *38*

—. American Revolution. Political Theory. Popular Sovereignty. Separation of Powers. 18c. *324*

—. Constitutional law. Due process. Liberty. Morality. 1980. *1056*

—. Economic development. Free market. Law. Supreme Court. 1775-1920. *64*

Naval Office. Customs law. State Government. Virginia. 1776-89. *226*

Navies. House of Representatives. Moody, William Henry. Political Leadership. Supreme Court. 1895-1910. *689*

Ordinance of 1785. Educational Policy. New England. Northwest Ordinance (1787). Ohio Company. 1785-87. *386*

Ordinance of 1787. Declaration of Independence. Historiography. 1776-87. *227*

Oregon. Amendments (1st). News sources, confidential. Shield laws. 1973-74. *738*

—. Amendments (15th). Attitudes. Blacks. Discrimination. Legislation. Mulattoes. Whites. 1850-75. *602*

Organizations. Lawsuits. Lobbying. Supreme Court. Women's rights. 1869-1979. *1235*

Orgone energy. Amendments (1st). Food and Drug Administration. Reich, Wilhelm. Scientific Experiments and Research. 1939-79. *823*

Owens, Leslie Howard. Antislavery Sentiments. Constitutional Law. Slavery (review article). South. Wiecek, William M. ca 1650-1977. *56*

Ownership. *See also* Landownership.

—. Antitrust. Justice Department. Law. Mass Media. Supreme Court. 1946-76. *779*

—. Documents. *Nixon v. Administrator of General Services* (US, 1977). Presidents. Supreme Court. 1791-1981. *977*

Ozawa Takao. Citizenship. Immigration. Japan. Lawsuits. Supreme Court. 1906-22. *898*

P

Paine, Thomas. Adams, John. Amendments (1st). Jefferson, Thomas. Madison, James. Religious Liberty. 1776-89. *274*

—. American Revolution. Europe. Political Theory. 1770's-90's. *39*

—. American Revolution. Friends, Society of. Political Attitudes. 1737-77. *262*

—. Philosophy. Political Theory. Psychology. Theology. ca 1776-96. *207*

—. Political Theory. 1776-1802. *54*

—. Political Theory. Republicanism. 1776-1802. *195*

Paine, Thomas *(Common Sense)*. American Revolution. Social change. 1774-76. *249*

Paludan, Phillip S. (review article). Constitutional law. Equality. Reconstruction. 1868-80's. 1975. *580*

Panama Canal Treaty. Constitutional Law. Federal Government. Foreign Relations. House of Representatives. Property. 1978. *1174*

Pardons (refused). Amendments (5th). *Burdick v. United States* (US, 1915). New York *Tribune*. Newspapers. Supreme Court. 1913-15. *741*

Parents. Amendments (1st). Compulsory education. *Pierce v. Society of Sisters* (US, 1925). 1925. 1976. *715*

—. Authority. Children. Civil Rights. Constitutional Law. Supreme Court. 1983. *1277*

—. Civil Rights. High Schools. Students. 1982. *1361*

Parks, Rosa. Alabama. Civil Rights. Desegregation. King, Martin Luther, Jr. Montgomery Improvement Association. 1955-57. *1095*

Parliamentary supremacy. American Revolution. Declaratory Act (1766). Stamp Act (US, 1765). 1766-76. *233*

Partisan realignment. Elections. Judicial review. Supreme Court. 1800-1970. *49*

Partisanship. Conservatism. Courts, District. Federal Government. Liberalism. Political Parties. Supreme Court. 1960-76. *1060*

Patents. Law. South Africa. Supreme Court. 1790-1979. *216*

Paterson, William. Antifederalism (review article). Boyd, Steven R. O'Connor, John E. 1787-99. *375*

—. New Jersey. Politics. State Government. Supreme Court. 1745-1806. *666*

Patriotism. Constitutional law. Iredell, James. Supreme Court. 1751-99. *459*

Paul, Alice. Belmont, Alva. Equal rights amendment. Feminism. National Woman's Party. Political Participation. 1919-28. *778*

—. Constitutional Amendments (21st). Equal Rights Amendment. Suffrage. Women. 1907-72. *832*

Pearson, Drew. Anderson, Jack. Constitutional Law. Courts. Journalism. Libel. 1949-74. *1183*

—. Constitutional Law. Lawsuits. Libel. Reporters and Reporting. 1932-69. *711*

Pearson v. Dodd (US, 1965). Constitutional Law. Courts. Documents. Government. 1960's-73. *787*

Pennsylvania. Addison, Alexander. Constitutional Law. Federalists. Freedom of Speech. Sedition Act (US, 1798). 1792-98. *605*

—. Amendments (15th). Blacks. Suffrage. 1780-1900. *599*

—. Amendments (19th). Feminists. Suffrage. Women. 1837-1920. *598*

—. American Revolution. Baptists. New England. Religious liberty. Virginia. 1775-91. *292*

—. American Revolution. Conservatism. Dickinson, John. 1757-1808. *164*

—. American Revolution. Politics. 1760's-1813. *171*

—. Antifederalists. Federal government. Ratification. 1787-92. *373*

—. Articles of Confederation. Boundaries. Connecticut. Courts. 1782-83. *314*

—. Bridges. Navigation, Inland. Ohio River. *State of Pennsylvania v. The Wheeling and Belmont Bridge Company et al.* (US, 1852). Supreme Court. Virginia. West Virginia (Wheeling). 1847-56. *583*

—. Democratic-Republican Party. Federalism. Political leadership. 1783-1800. *261*

—. Democrats. Federalists. Ratification. 1787. *357*

—. Documents. Political Conventions (state). Ratification. 1787. *487*

—. Political Parties. Ratification. State Politics. 1787. *410*

—. *Prigg v. Pennsylvania* (US, 1842). Slavery. Supreme Court. ca 1842-50. *515*

Pennsylvania (Philadelphia). *Aurora*. Bache, Benjamin Franklin. Federalism. *General Advertiser*. Newspapers. Political Attitudes. 1790-98. *695*

—. Constitutional Convention. Democracy. National Characteristics. Superstition. Violence. 1787. *435*

—. Constitutional Convention. Founding Fathers. 1787. *440*

—. Constitutional Convention. Military officers, retired. Society of the Cincinnati. Washington, George. 1783-87. *473*

—. Constitutional Convention. Slavery. 1787. *495*

—. Constitutional Convention. Washington, George. 1787. *441*

—. Democratic-Republicanism. Swanwick, John. 1790-98. *508*

—. Documents. Federalism. Rush, Benjamin. 1787-90. *372*

Pennsylvania v. Mimms. Amendments (4th). Burger, Warren E. Judicial Administration. *Schneckloth v. Bustamonte*. Supreme Court. 1971-79. *1360*

Pentagon Papers. Amendments (1st). Freedom of the Press. Supreme Court. 1971. *1020*

Periodicals. Blacks. Constitutional Amendments (19th). *Crisis*. DuBois, William Edward Burghardt. Suffrage. Women. 1910-34. *1163*

—. Freedom of the press. Howard Morland. Nuclear arms. *Progressive*. Supreme Court. 1979. *1113*

Political Factions. Amendments (19th). Delaware.
Suffrage. Women. 1919-20. *885*
—. Articles of Confederation. Attitudes.
Republicanism. 1780-87. *270*
—. Jay Treaty (1794). Newspapers. Nominations
for Office. Rutledge, John. Supreme Court.
1794-95. *585*
Political Leadership. American Revolution. Foreign
policy. Historiography. Internationalism.
Liberalism. 1776-1801. *260*
—. Democratic-Republican Party. Federalism.
Pennsylvania. 1783-1800. *261*
—. Federalists. Values. Virtue. 1789-1800.
681
—. House of Representatives. Moody, William
Henry. Navies. Supreme Court. 1895-1910.
689
—. Madison, James. Political parties. Presidency.
Republicanism. 1780-1820. *74*
—. Presidency. 1787-1865. *46*
Political offices. *Federalist.* Republicanism. 1787.
443
Political Participation. Amendments (1st).
Employees. Law. Public Schools. 1867-1977.
1306
—. Amendments (24th). Blacks. Voter registration.
Voting Rights Act (US, 1965). 1964-67.
1106
—. Belmont, Alva. Equal rights amendment.
Feminism. National Woman's Party. Paul,
Alice. 1919-28. *778*
Political Parties. See also Primaries.
—. Amendments (1st). Croly, Herbert. Federal
Regulation. Law. Ritchie, Thomas. ca
1850-1980. *1285*
—. Amendments (13th). Ashley, James M. House
of Representatives. Nationalism. Ohio. 1848-65.
560
—. Antifederalists. Constitutional Convention. New
York. Whigs, Radical. 1788. *499*
—. Antifederalists. Ratification. Republican
ideology. 1789-93. *365*
—. Congress. Kentucky. Monroe, James. ca
1781-89. *240*
—. Congress. Roll-call voting. 1789-1803. *550*
—. Conservatism. Courts, District. Federal
Government. Liberalism. Partisanship. Supreme
Court. 1960-76. *1060*
—. Constitutional Amendments (12th). 1800-04.
628
—. Constitutional Law. Courts. Freedom of
association. 1960's-83. *969*
—. Democracy. Reform. 1880-1980. *1189*
—. Elections, presidential. Nominations for office.
1787-1978. *20*
—. Ideology. State Legislatures. Voting and Voting
Behavior. 1780's. *334*
—. Madison, James. Political Leadership.
Presidency. Republicanism. 1780-1820. *74*
—. Nominations for Office. Political Conventions.
Presidency. 1789-1832. *648*
—. Pennsylvania. Ratification. State Politics. 1787.
410
—. Supreme Court. 1850's. 1890's. 1930's. *686*
—. Virginia. 1782-1800. *449*
Political Parties (review articles). Banning, Lance.
Federalists. Ideology. Jeffersonians. Zvesper,
John. 1790's. 1977-78. *576*
Political philosophy. Government. Statesmanship.
1789-1829. 1900-74. *653*
Political Power. Centralization. Federalism.
1789-1979. *116*
—. Congress. Constitutional Law. Executive
branch. National Emergencies Act (US, 1976).
Public Policy. 1933-78. *967*
—. Federal Government. 1789-1976. *159*
Political Protest. Equal Rights Amendment. Public
opinion. 1970's-83. *767*

Political Reform. Amendments (1st). Curricula.
Educators. Meiklejohn, Alexander. 1898-1964.
1342
—. California. Campaign Finance. Constitutional
Law. Federal Regulation. 1976.
1346
—. Catholic Church. Constitutional Law. Ireland.
Irish Americans. O'Conor, Charles. O'Conor,
Charles Owen. Reconstruction. 1865-85.
531
—. City government. Courts. Nonpartisanship.
1970's. *1002*
—. Congress. 1970-74. *1010*
—. Conservatism. McCumber, Porter James.
McKenzie, Alexander John. North Dakota.
Republican Party. 1898-1933. *1068*
—. Constitutional Law. Realist tradition.
1890-1932. *725*
—. Elections. 1977. *1067*
—. Elections. Presidency. 1970. *825*
Political representation. Apportionment. *City of
Mobile* v. *Bolden* (US, 1980). *City of Rome* v.
United States (US, 1980). Local government.
State Government. Supreme Court. Voting
rights. 1966-80. *819*
—. Blacks. Census. Education. Racism. Revenue
sharing. 1787-1980. *82*
—. Congress. Connecticut Compromise.
Constitutional Convention. Delegates.
Quantitative Methods. Roll-call voting. 1786-87.
417
—. Constitutional Convention. Madison, James.
Virginia Plan. 1787. *414*
—. Election districts. Supreme Court. 1970-79. *852*
—. *Federalist.* 1776-87. *480*
Political scandal. Boyd, Julian. Hamilton,
Alexander. Reynolds, Maria Lewis. 1791-97.
1971. *505*
Political science. Diamond, Martin. Fisk, Winston
M. Garfinkel, Herbert. Textbooks. 1787. ca
1950-70. *52*
Political systems. American Revolution.
Conservatism. Revolution. 1776-1976. *124*
—. Apportionment. Majority rule. Supreme Court.
1965-68. *916*
—. Barlow, Joel. Federalism. History. Jefferson,
Thomas. 1790-1815. *568*
—. Confederation. Netherlands. 1783-89. *422*
—. Constitutional Convention. Founding Fathers.
1783-1980. *62*
—. Executive power. 1790-1976. *70*
—. *Federalist* No. 10. Government. Madison,
James. Representative Government. 1740-88.
285
—. Government. 1789-1972. *144*
Political Theory. 17c-1789. *272*
—. Adair, Douglass. *Federalist* No. 10. Hume,
David. Madison, James. Republicanism. Wills,
Garry. 1788. *392*
—. Alberdi, Juan Bautista. Argentina. Hamilton,
Alexander. USA. 1787-1860. *376*
—. Amendments (1st). Brown, Cynthia Stokes.
Capitalism. Foreign Relations. Meiklejohn,
Alexander (review article). 1912-55. *795*
—. Amendments (2d). Military. 1656-1791. *383*
—. American Revolution. 1776-1974. *175*
—. American Revolution. Armies. 1776-80's. *301*
—. American Revolution. Bailyn, Bernard. Berkin,
Carol. Calhoon, Robert McCluer. Great
Britain. Loyalists (review article). 1760-83. *287*
—. American Revolution. Beccaria, Marchese di.
Founding Fathers. 1764-83. *250*
—. American Revolution. Books. Emigration.
Great Britain. 1776. *221*
—. American Revolution. British North America.
Government, Resistance to. 1763-76. *300*
—. American Revolution. Commerce. Morris,
Gouverneur. 1774-1800. *1*

—. Amendments (1st). Freedom of Speech. Supreme Court. 1940-69. *1318*
—. American Revolution. Antifederalists. Federalists. Public opinion. 1787-88. *369*
—. American Revolution. Declaration of Independence. *Federalist.* Ideology. 1776-89. *341*
—. Constitutional law. Moral overstrain. Racism. 1776-1960's. *86*
—. *Federalist.* Republicanism. 1787. *503*
—. Federalist Party. Republican Party. 1789-1800. *678*
—. Garfield, James A. Lawyers. Speeches. Supreme Court. 1860-80. *683*
—. Supreme Court. 1895-1905. *597*
Rhode Island. Antifederalists. Collins, John. Hazard, Jonathan J. Ratification. 1786-90. *421*
—. Conservatism. Dorr Rebellion. Social Change. Suffrage. 1835-55. *635*
—. Constitutional Law. Dorr Rebellion. 1842-43. *529*
—. Dorr Rebellion. Election Laws. *Luther v. Borden* (US, 1849). State government. Supreme Court. 1842-49. *528*
Rhode Island v. Innis (US, 1975). Constitutional Law. Crime and Criminals. *Miranda v. Arizona* (US, 1966). Supreme Court. 1971-79. *1171*
Riddleberger, Patrick W. Castel, Albert. Johnson, Andrew (review article). Reconstruction. Sefton, James E. 1865-69. *507*
Right to know. Amendments (1st). Civil Rights. Federal Government. Freedom of the press. 1972. *1051*
Rios v. Reynolds Metals Company (US, 1972). Arbitration, Industrial. Discrimination. *Griggs v. Duke Power Company* (US, 1971). Supreme Court. 1964-73. *742*
Rist, Ray C. Civil rights. Graglia, Lino A. Harvey, James C. School Integration (review article). Supreme Court. 1964-78. *1159*
Ritchie, Thomas. Amendments (1st). Croly, Herbert. Federal Regulation. Law. Political Parties. ca 1850-1980. *1285*
Rock, John S. Blacks. Lawyers. Supreme Court. 1825-66. *520*
Rodney, Caesar. American Revolution. Germantown, Battle of. Letters. Washington, George. 1777-81. *256*
Rodriguez v. San Antonio Independent School District (US, 1973). Education, Finance. Supreme Court. Tax reform. 1973. *860*
Rodriguez-Fernandez v. Wilkinson (US, 1980). Human rights. Law Enforcement. Supreme Court. 1980. *965*
Roe v. Wade (US, 1973). Abortion. Blacks. Civil Rights. *Dred Scott v. Sandford* (US, 1857). Personhood. Supreme Court. 1857. 1973. *611*
—. Abortion. Civil Rights. Constitutional Law. Fertility. Women. 1973-82. *1145*
—. Abortion. Constitutional Law. Women. 1950's-70's. *1240*
Rogers v. Bellei (US, 1971). *Afroyim v. Rusk* (US, 1967). Expatriation. Law. Supreme Court. 1790-1973. *61*
Role theory. Douglas, William O. Jackson, Robert H. Political Attitudes. Supreme Court. 1939-68. *905*
Roll-call voting. Congress. Connecticut Compromise. Constitutional Convention. Delegates. Political representation. Quantitative Methods. 1786-87. *417*
—. Congress. Political parties. 1789-1803. *550*
Romania. 1787-1880. *511*
Roosevelt, Franklin D. Amendments (18th, 21st). Democratic Party (convention). Prohibition. Raskob, John J. 1928-33. *933*

—. Congress. New Deal. Political attitudes. Tennessee. 1933-40. *775*
Roosevelt, Theodore. Constitutional Law. Executive Power. Marshall, John. Taft, William Howard. 19c-1913. *609*
Rousseau, Jean Jacques. *Federalist* No. 10. Madison, James. 1787. *382*
Rush, Benjamin. Documents. Federalism. Pennsylvania (Philadelphia). 1787-90. *372*
—. Federalism. Jeffersonianism. Political Attitudes. Republicanism. 1776-1800. *267*
Rutledge, Edward. Amendments (10th). Congress. Debts. Hamilton, Alexander. Letters. Smith, William L. South Carolina. States. 1789-94. *454*
Rutledge, John. Jay Treaty (1794). Newspapers. Nominations for Office. Political Factions. Supreme Court. 1794-95. *585*

S

St. Clair, Arthur. Executive Branch. House of Representatives (investigations). Indian Wars. 1791-93. *541*
San Antonio Independent School District v. Rodriguez (US, 1973). Constitutional Law. Education. Supreme Court. 20c. 1973. *1355*
—. Democracy. Education. Human rights. 1787-1980. *206*
—. Discrimination, Educational. *Milliken v. Bradley* (US, 1974). Supreme Court. 1974. *896*
San Joaquín Grant. Commons. Land grants. Law. New Mexico. 1806-97. *532*
Sanford, Edward Terry. Amendments (14th). Civil rights. *Gitlow v. New York* (US, 1925). Supreme Court. ca 1890-1930. *938*
Santa Clara Pueblo v. Martinez (US, 1977). Civil Rights. Indian Civil Rights Act (US, 1968). Natural law. Pueblo Indians. Supreme Court. Tribal government. 1939-77. *1050*
Schenck v. United States (US, 1917). Amendments (1st). Espionage Act (US, 1917). Holmes, Oliver Wendell. Supreme Court. 1917. *1268*
Schneckloth v. Bustamonte. Amendments (4th). Burger, Warren E. Judicial Administration. *Pennsylvania v. Mimms.* Supreme Court. 1971-79. *1360*
Scholarship. Higher Education. Supreme Court. 1779-1976. *122*
School boards. Lawsuits. Public Schools. 1871-1976. *1281*
School desegregation. Law. *Milliken v. Bradley* (US, 1974). Supreme Court. 1960's-70's. *1177*
School Integration. Amendments. Arkansas (Hoxie). Blacks. 1954-56. *1129*
—. Amendments (14th). *Brown v. Board of Education* (US, 1954). Illinois (Chicago). South. 1954-77. *899*
—. Arkansas (Little Rock). Law. Politics. 1954-57. *827*
—. Blacks. Educational Policy. Federal Government. Law. Supreme Court. 1954-82. *1040*
—. *Brown v. Board of Education* (US, 1954). Constitutional Law. Federal Policy. Judicial Administration. 1954-77. *1350*
—. *Brown v. Board of Education* (US, 1954). Constitutional Law. NAACP. Supreme Court. 1954. *963*
—. Byrd, Harry F. Chambers, Lenoir. Editors and Editing. Supreme Court. Virginia. 1955-59. *1015*

T

—. California. Fair housing. Housing. Referendum. ca 1960-67. *1158*
—. Constitutional Convention. 1787. *415*
—. Constitutional Convention. Slave Trade Compromise. 1787. *413*
—. Federal Government. "One man, one vote". 1787-92. *400*
—. Ideology. Information access. Judges. Supreme Court. 1969-76. *1036*
—. Ideology. Political Parties. State Legislatures. 1780's. *334*
—. Ideology. Supreme Court. 1972-75. *752*
—. Judges. Social Status. Supreme Court. 1947-56. *1119*
—. Judges. Supreme Court. 1953-80. *872*
—. Judges. Supreme Court. *Williams* v. *Rhodes* (US, 1968). 1972. *856*
—. Supreme Court. 1946-67. *749*
Voting rights. Apportionment. *City of Mobile* v. *Bolden* (US, 1980). *City of Rome* v. *United States* (US, 1980). Local government. Political representation. State Government. Supreme Court. 1966-80. *819*
Voting Rights Act (US, 1965). Amendments (14th, 15th). Congress. Elections. Federal Election Campaign Act (US, 1971; amended 1974). Supreme Court. 1965-75. *801*
—. Amendments (24th). Blacks. Political participation. Voter registration. 1964-67. *1106*
—. Blacks. *South Carolina* v. *Katzenbach* (US, 1966). Suffrage. 1865-1966. *798*
Voting Rights Act (US, 1965; Section 5). Apportionment. Attorneys General. Courts. Election Laws. Intergovernmental Relations. 1965-77. *734*
Voting Rights Extension Act (US, 1970). Absentee Voting. Amendments (26th). 1960-72. *813*
Voting Rights Disputes. Apportionment. Supreme Court. 1845-1969. *1199*

W

Waite, Morrison R. Supreme Court. 1870's-80's. *587*
Walker v. *City of Birmingham* (US, 1967). Alabama (Birmingham). Amendments (1st). Desegregation. King, Martin Luther, Jr. Supreme Court. 1960-71. *1148*
—. Alabama (Birmingham). Civil Rights. King, Martin Luther, Jr. Supreme Court. 1963. 1967. *1251*
Walnut Street Presbyterian Church. Amendments (1st). Kentucky (Louisville). Property. *Watson* v. *Jones* (US, 1860). 1860-1970. *631*
War. *See also* Conscientious Objection.
—. Civil Disobedience. Constitutional Law. Federal Government. 1970. *1250*
—. Civil Rights. Lincoln, Abraham. 1861-65. *595*
—. Congress. Constitutional Law. Executive Power. Foreign Policy. National Security. Supreme Court. 1935-80. *1258*
—. Congress. Constitutional Law. Presidency. 1982. *1215*
—. Congress. Executive Power. Korean War. Vietnam War. 1776-1970. *251*
—. Constitutional Law. International Law. Presidency. 1787-20c. *189*
—. Emergency, states of. Executive power. Habeas corpus. Martial law. 1861-1944. *601*
War crimes. Citizenship. Deportation. *Fedorenko* v. *US* (US, 1981). Supreme Court. 1981. *1102*
War, declaration of. Acheson, Dean. Congress. Constitutional Law. Korean War. Truman, Harry S. 1950-64. *952*
War powers. Congress. Constitutional Law. Executive Power. Foreign Policy. Vietnam War. 1960's-72. *1271*

—. Congress. Constitutional Law. Foreign policy. Presidents. 19c-1974. *36*
—. Congress. Executive Power. Police. 1776-1960. *14*
—. Congress. Presidency. 1789-1820's. *672*
—. Congress. Presidency. 1797-1973. *208*
—. Constitutional Law. Foreign Policy. Sofaer, Abraham D. (review article). 18c-1976. *65*
—. Separation of powers. 1787-89. *464*
War Powers Resolution (1973). Congress. Constitutional Law. Executive branch. Presidency. 1973. *1109*
—. Congress. Executive Power. 1969-73. *822*
Warren, Earl. Amendments (1st). Higher Education. Students. Supreme Court. 1953-69. *1267*
—. Amendments (4th). Colleges and Universities. Students. Supreme Court. 1953-69. *1272*
—. Apportionment. Dogmatism. Pragmatism. Supreme Court. 1962. *903*
—. Archives, National. Judiciary Act (1789). Speeches. Supreme Court. 1789. 1964. *470*
—. Burger, Warren E. Civil Rights. Federalism. Supreme Court. 1953-78. *974*
—. Burger, Warren E. Civil Rights. Habeas corpus. Institutions. Supreme Court. 1954-77. *973*
—. Burger, Warren E. Civil Rights. Law Reform. Supreme Court. 1937-73. *792*
—. Burger, Warren E. Federal Policy. Funston, Richard (review article). Judicial Administration. Supreme Court. 1953-79. *1103*
—. California. Family. Governors. Judges. Law. Supreme Court. 1911-74. *1132*
—. Cardozo, Benjamin. Holmes, Oliver Wendell. Law. Supreme Court. 1953-69. *958*
—. Chief Justices. Law. Supreme Court. 1800-1965. *563*
—. Civil Rights. Legal information. Supreme Court. 1953-69. *1352*
—. Civil Rights. Supreme Court. 1953-69. *1257*
—. Law and Society. Supreme Court. 1952-68. *1114*
Warren, Earl (obituary). Chief Justices. Supreme Court. World peace through law movement. 1891-1974. *546*
Wasby, Stephen. Ball, Howard. Bickel, Alexander M. Constitutional Law (review article). Politics. Sorauf, Frank. 1975-76. *1064*
Washington, Bushrod. Justices. Supreme Court. 1798-1827. *679*
Washington, George. Adams, John. Federalism. Hamilton, Alexander. Jefferson, Thomas. 1775-90's. *239*
—. American Revolution. Bill of Rights. Constitutional Convention. Declaration of Independence. Hamilton, Alexander. Inflation. Liberty. 1607-1800. *18*
—. American Revolution. Germantown, Battle of. Letters. Rodney, Caesar. 1777-81. *256*
—. American Revolution. Leadership. Military officers. Political Theory. Whigs. 1775-83. *308*
—. American Revolution. Military Strategy. Public Policy. 1770's-90's. *88*
—. Bill of Rights. Nationalism. Politics. 1783-93. *482*
—. Constitutional Convention. Military officers, retired. Pennsylvania (Philadelphia). Society of the Cincinnati. 1783-87. *473*
—. Constitutional Convention. Pennsylvania (Philadelphia). 1787. *441*
—. Federalism. 1789-96. *424*
—. Federalists. Politics. Presidency. 1789-97. *418*
—. Veto. 1789-97. *466*
Washington (University of, Law School). Admissions Policy. Colleges and Universities. *DeFunis* v. *Odegaard* (US, 1974). Discrimination. Supreme Court. 1971-75. *1176*

AUTHOR INDEX

APPENDIX:
THE CONSTITUTION OF THE UNITED STATES

The Constitution of the United States

PREAMBLE

We the People of the United States, in Order to form a more perfect Union, establish Justice, insure domestic Tranquility, provide for the common defence, promote the general Welfare, and secure the Blessings of Liberty to ourselves and our Posterity, do ordain and establish this Constitution for the United States of America.

ARTICLE I

SECTION 1. All legislative Powers herein granted shall be vested in a Congress of the United States, which shall consist of a Senate and House of Representatives.

SECTION 2. The House of Representatives shall be composed of Members chosen every second Year by the People of the several States, and the Electors in each State shall have the Qualifications requisite for Electors of the most numerous Branch of the State Legislature.

No Person shall be a Representative who shall not have attained to the age of twenty five Years, and been seven Years a Citizen of the United States, and who shall not, when elected, be an Inhabitant of that State in which he shall be chosen.

Representatives and direct Taxes shall be apportioned among the several States which may be included within this Union, according to their respective Numbers, which shall be determined by adding to the whole Number of free Persons, including those bound to Service for a Term of Years, and excluding Indians not taxed, three fifths of all other Persons. The actual Enumeration shall be made within three Years after the first Meeting of the Congress of the United States, and within every subsequent Term of ten Years, in such Manner as they shall by Law direct. The Number of Representatives shall not exceed one for every thirty Thousand, but each State shall have at Least one Representative; and until such enumeration shall be made, the State of New Hampshire shall be entitled to chuse three, Massachusetts eight, Rhode-Island and Providence Plantations one, Connecticut five, New York six, New Jersey four, Pennsylvania eight, Delaware one, Maryland six, Virginia ten, North Carolina five, South Carolina five, and Georgia three.

When vacancies happen in the Representation from any State, the Executive Authority thereof shall issue Writs of Election to fill such Vacancies.

The House of Representatives shall chuse their Speaker and other Officers; and shall have the sole Power of Impeachment.

SECTION 3. The Senate of the United States shall be composed of two Senators from each State, chosen by the Legislature thereof, for six Years; and each Senator shall have one Vote.

Immediately after they shall be assembled in Consequence of the first Election, they shall be divided as equally as may be into three Classes. The seats of the Senators of the first Class shall be vacated at the Expiration of the second Year, of the second Class at the Expiration of the Fourth Year, and of the third Class at the Expiration of the sixth Year, so that one third may be chosen every second Year; and if Vacancies happen by Resignation, or otherwise, during the Recess of the Legislature of any State, the Executive thereof may make temporary Appointments until the next Meeting of the Legislature, which shall then fill such Vacancies.

No Person shall be a Senator who shall not have attained to the Age of thirty Years, and been nine Years a Citizen of the United States, and who shall not, when elected, be an Inhabitant of that State for which he shall be chosen.

The Vice President of the United States shall be President of the Senate, but shall have no Vote, unless they be equally divided.

The Senate shall chuse their other Officers, and also a President pro tempore, in the Absence of the Vice President, or when he shall exercise the Office of President of the United States.

The Senate shall have the sole Power to try all Impeachments. When sitting for that Purpose, they shall be on Oath or Affirmation. When the President of the United States is tried the Chief Justice shall preside: And no Person shall be convicted without the Concurrence of two thirds of the Members present.

Judgment in Cases of Impeachment shall not extend further than to removal from Office, and disqualification to hold and enjoy any Office of honor, Trust or Profit under the United States: but the Party convicted shall nevertheless be liable and subject to Indictment, Trial, Judgment and Punishment, according to Law.

SECTION 4. The Times, Places and Manner of holding Elections for Senators and Representatives, shall be prescribed in each State by the Legislature thereof; but the Congress may at any time by Law make or alter such Regulations, except as to the Places of chusing Senators.

The Congress shall assemble at least once in every Year, and such Meeting shall be on the first Monday in December unless they shall by Law appoint a different Day.

SECTION 5. Each House shall be the Judge of the Elections, Returns and Qualifications of its own Members, and a Majority of each shall constitute a Quorum to do Business; but a smaller Number may adjourn from day to day, and may be authorized to compel the Attendance of absent Members, in such Manner, and under such Penalties as each House may provide.

Each House may determine the Rules of its Proceedings, punish its Members for disorderly Behaviour, and, with the Concurrence of two thirds, expel a Member.

Each House shall keep a Journal of its Proceedings, and from time to time publish the same, excepting such Parts as may in their Judgment require Secrecy; and the Yeas and Nays of the Members of either House on any question shall, at the Desire of one fifth of those Present, be entered on the Journal.

Neither House, during the Session of Congress, shall, without the Consent of the other, adjourn for more than three days, nor to any other Place than that in which the two Houses shall be sitting.

SECTION 6. The Senators and Representatives shall receive a Compensation for their Services, to be ascertained by Law, and paid out of the Treasury of the United States. They shall in all Cases, except Treason, Felony and Breach of the Peace, be privileged from Arrest during their Attendance at the Session of their respective Houses, and in going to and returning from the same; and for any Speech or Debate in either House, they shall not be questioned in any other Place.

No Senator or Representative shall, during the Time for which he was elected, be appointed to any civil Office under the Authority of the United States, which shall have been created, or the Emoluments whereof shall have been increased during such time; and no Person holding any Office under the United States, shall be a Member of either House during his Continuance in Office.

SECTION 7. All Bills for raising Revenue shall originate in the House of Representatives; but the Senate may propose or concur with amendments as on other Bills.

Every Bill which shall have passed the House of Representatives and the Senate, shall, before it becomes a Law, be presented to the President of the United States; If he approve he shall sign it, but if not he shall return it, with his Objections to that House in which it shall have originated, who shall enter the Objections at large on their Journal, and proceed to reconsider it. If after such Reconsideration two thirds of that House shall agree to pass the Bill, it shall be sent, together with the Objections, to the other House, by which it shall likewise be reconsidered, and if approved by two thirds of that House, it shall become a Law. But in all such Cases the Votes of both Houses shall be determined by Yeas and Nays, and the Names of the Persons voting for and against the Bill shall be entered on the Journal of each House respectively. If any Bill shall not be returned by the President within ten Days (Sunday excepted) after it shall have been presented to him, the Same shall be a Law, in like Manner as if he had signed it, unless the Congress by their Adjournment prevent its Return, in which Case it shall not be a Law.

Every Order, Resolution, or Vote to which the Concurrence of the Senate and House of Representatives may be necessary (except on a question of Adjournment) shall be presented to the President of the United States; and before the Same shall take Effect, shall be approved by him, or being disapproved by him, shall be repassed by two thirds of the Senate and House of Representatives, according to the Rules and Limitations prescribed in the Case of a Bill.

SECTION 8. The Congress shall have Power To lay and collect Taxes, Duties, Imposts and Excises, to pay the Debts and provide for the common Defence and general Welfare of the United States; but all Duties, Imposts and Excises shall be uniform throughout the United States;

To borrow Money on the credit of the United States;

To regulate Commerce with foreign Nations, and among the several States, and with the Indian Tribes;

To establish an uniform Rule of Naturalization, and uniform Laws on the subject of Bankruptcies throughout the United States;

To coin Money, regulate the Value thereof, and of foreign Coin, and fix the Standard of Weights and Measures;

To provide for the Punishment of counterfeiting the Securities and current

Coin of the United States;

To establish Post Offices and post Roads;

To promote the Progress of Science and useful Arts, by securing for limited Times to Authors and Inventors the exclusive Right to their respective Writings and Discoveries;

To constitute Tribunals inferior to the supreme Court;

To define and punish Piracies and Felonies commited on the high Seas, and Offences against the Law of Nations;

To declare War, grant letters of Marque and Reprisal, and make Rules concerning Captures on Land and Water;

To raise and support Armies, but no Appropriation of Money to that Use shall be for a longer Term than two Years;

To provide and maintain a Navy;

To make Rules for the Government and Regulation of the land and naval Forces;

To provide for calling forth the Militia to execute the Laws of the Union, suppress Insurrections and repel Invasions;

To provide for organizing, arming, and disciplining the Militia, and for governing such Part of them as may be employed in the Service of the United States, reserving to the States respectively, the Appointment of the Officers, and the Authority of training the Militia according to the discipline prescribed by Congress;

To exercise exclusive Legislation in all Cases whatsoever, over such District (not exceeding ten Miles square) as may, by Cession of Particular States, and the Acceptance of Congress, become the Seat of the Government of the United States, and to exercise like Authority over all Places purchased by the Consent of the Legislature of the State in which the Same shall be, for the Erection of Forts, Magazines, Arsenals, dock-Yards, and other needful Buildings;—

And

To make all Laws which shall be necessary and proper for carrying into Execution the foregoing Powers, and all other Powers vested by this Constitution in the Government of the United States, or in any Department or Officer thereof.

SECTION 9. The Migration or Importation of such Persons as any of the States now existing shall think proper to admit, shall not be prohibited by the Congress prior to the Year one thousand eight hundred and eight, but a Tax or duty may be imposed on such Importation, not exceeding ten dollars for each Person.

The Privilege of the Writ of Habeas Corpus shall not be suspended, unless when in Cases of Rebellion or Invasion the public Safety may require it.

No Bill of Attainder or ex post facto Law shall be passed.

No capitation, or other direct, Tax shall be laid, unless in Proportion to the Census of Enumeration herein before directed to be taken.

No Tax or Duty shall be laid on Articles exported from any State.

No Preference shall be given by any Regulation of Commerce or Revenue to the Ports of one State over those of another; nor shall Vessels bound to, or from, one State, be obliged to enter, clear or pay Duties in another.

No Money shall be drawn from the Treasury, but in Consequence of Appropriations made by Law; and a regular Statement and Account of the Receipts and Expenditures of all public Money shall be published from time to time.

No Title of Nobility shall be granted by the United States: And no Person holding any Office of Profit or Trust under them, shall, without the Consent of the Congress, accept of any present, Emolument, Office, or Title, of any kind whatever, from any King, Prince, or foreign State.

SECTION 10. No State shall enter into any Treaty, Alliance, or Confederation; grant Letters of Marque and Reprisal; coin Money; emit Bills of Credit; make any Thing but gold and silver Coin a Tender in Payment of Debts; pass any Bill of Attainder, ex post facto Law, or Law impairing the Obligation of Contracts, or grant any Title of Nobility.

No State shall, without the Consent of the Congress, lay any Imposts or Duties on Imports or Exports, except what may be absolutely necessary for executing it's inspection Laws: and the net Produce of all Duties and Imposts, laid by any State on Imports or Exports, shall be for the Use of the Treasury of the United States; and all such Laws shall be subject to the Revision and Controul of the Congress.

No State shall, without the Consent of Congress, lay any Duty of Tonnage, keep Troops, or Ships of War in time of Peace, enter into any Agreement or Compact with another State, or with a foreign Power, or engage in War, unless actually invaded, or in such imminent Danger as will not admit of delay.

ARTICLE II

SECTION 1. The executive Power shall be vested in a President of the United States of America. He shall hold his Office during the Term of four Years, and together with the Vice President, chosen for the same Term, be elected, as follows.

Each State shall appoint, in such Manner as the Legislature thereof may direct, a Number of Electors, equal to the whole Number of Senators and Representatives to which the State may be entitled in the Congress: but no Senator or Representative, or Person holding an Office of Trust or Profit under the United States, shall be appointed an Elector.

The Electors shall meet in their respective States, and vote by Ballot for two Persons, of whom one at least shall not be an Inhabitant of the same State with themselves. And they shall make a List of all the Persons voted for, and of the Number of Votes for each; which List they shall sign and certify, and transmit sealed to the Seat of the Government of the United States, directed to the President of the Senate. The President of the Senate shall, in the Presence of the Senate and House of Representatives, open all the Certificates, and the Votes shall then be counted. The Person having the greatest Number of Votes shall be the President, if such Number be a Majority of the whole Number of Electors appointed; and if there be more than one who have such Majority, and have an equal Number of Votes, then the House of Representatives shall immediately chuse by Ballot one of them for President; and if no Person have a Majority, then from the five highest on the list the said House shall in like Manner chuse the President. But in chusing the President, the Votes shall be taken by States, the Representation from each State having one Vote; a quorum for this Purpose shall consist of a Member or Members from two thirds of the States, and a Majority of all the States shall be necessary to a Choice. In every Case, after the Choice of the President, the Person having the greatest Number of Votes of the Electors shall be the Vice President. But if there should remain two or more who have equal Votes, the Senate shall chuse from them by Ballot the Vice President.

The Congress may determine the Time of chusing the Electors, and the Day on which they shall give their Votes; which Day shall be the same throughout the United States.

No Person except a natural born Citizen, or a Citizen of the United States, at the time of the Adoption of this Constitution, shall be eligible to the Office of President; neither shall any Person be eligible to that Office who shall not have attained to the Age of thirty five Years, and been fourteen Years a Resident within the United States.

In Case of the Removal of the President from Office, or of his Death, Resignation, or Inability to discharge the Powers and Duties of the said Office, the Same shall devolve on the Vice President, and the Congress may by Law provide for the Case of Removal, Death, Resignation or Inability, both of the President and Vice President, declaring what Officer shall then act as President, and such Officer shall act accordingly, until the Disability be removed, or a President shall be elected.

The President shall, at stated Times, receive for his Services, a Compensation, which shall neither be encreased nor diminished during the Period for which he shall have been elected, and he shall not receive within that Period any other Emolument from the United States, or any of them.

Before he enter on the Execution of his Office, he shall take the following Oath or Affirmation—"I do solemnly swear (or affirm) that I will faithfully execute the Office of President of the United States, and will to the best of my Ability, preserve, protect and defend the Constitution of the United States."

SECTION 2. The President shall be Commander in Chief of the Army and Navy of the United States, and of the Militia of the several States, when called into the actual Service of the United States; he may require the Opinion, in writing, of the principal Officer in each of the executive Departments, upon any Subject relating to the Duties of their respective Offices, and he shall have Power to grant Reprieves and Pardons for Offenses against the United States, except in Cases of Impeachment.

He shall have Power, by and with the Advice and Consent of the Senate, to make Treaties, provided two thirds of the Senators present concur; and he shall nominate, and by and with the Advice and Consent of the Senate, shall appoint Ambassadors, other public Ministers and Consuls, Judges of the supreme Court, and all other Officers of the United States, whose Appointments are not herein otherwise provided for, and which shall be established by Law: but the Congress may by Law vest the Appointment of such inferior Officers, as they think proper, in the President alone, in the Courts of Law, or in the Heads of Departments.

The President shall have Power to fill up all Vacancies that may happen during the Recess of the Senate, by granting Commissions which shall expire at the End of their next Session.

SECTION 3. He shall from time to time give to the Congress Information of the State of the Union, and recommend to their Consideration such Measures as he shall judge necessary and expedient; he may, on extraordinary Occasions, convene both Houses, or either of them, and in Case of Disagreement between them, with Respect to the Time of Adjournment, he may adjourn them to such Time as he shall think proper; he shall receive Ambassadors and other public Ministers; he shall take Care that the Laws be faithfully executed, and shall Commission all the Officers of the United States.

SECTION 4. The President, Vice President and all Civil Officers of the United States, shall be removed from office on Impeachment for, and Conviction of, Treason, Bribery, or other high Crimes and Misdemeanors.

ARTICLE III

SECTION 1. The judicial Power of the United States, shall be vested in one supreme Court, and in such inferior Courts as the Congress may from time to time ordain and establish. The Judges, both of the supreme and inferior Courts, shall hold their Offices during good Behaviour, and shall, at stated Times, receive for their Services, a Compensation, which shall not be diminished during their Continuance in Office.

SECTION 2. The judicial Power shall extend to all Cases, in Law and Equity, arising under this Constitution, the Laws of the United States, and Treaties made, or which shall be made, under their Authority; to all Cases affecting Ambassadors, other public Ministers and Consuls;—to all Cases of admiralty and maritime Jurisdiction;—to Controversies to which the United States shall be a Party;—to Controversies between two or more States;—between a State and Citizens of another State;—between Citizens of different States;—between Citizens of the same State claiming Lands under Grants of different States, and between a State, or the Citizens thereof, and foreign States, Citizens or Subjects.

In all Cases affecting Ambassadors, other public Ministers and Consuls, and those in which a State shall be Party, the supreme Court shall have original Jurisdiction. In all the other Cases before mentioned, the supreme Court shall have appellate Jurisdiction, both as to Law and Fact, with such Exceptions, and under such Regulations as the Congress shall make.

The Trial of all Crimes, except in cases of Impeachment, shall be by Jury; and such Trial shall be held in the State where the said Crimes shall have been committed; but when not committed within any State, the Trial shall be at such Place or Places as the Congress may by Law have directed.

SECTION 3. Treason against the United States, shall consist only in levying War against them, or in adhering to their Enemies, giving them Aid and Comfort. No Person shall be convicted of Treason unless on the Testimony of two Witnesses to the same overt Act, or on Confession in open Court.

The Congress shall have Power to declare the Punishment of Treason, but no Attainder or Treason shall work Corruption of Blood, or Forfeiture except during the Life of the Person attainted.

ARTICLE IV

SECTION 1. Full Faith and Credit shall be given in each State to the public Acts, Records, and judicial Proceedings of every other State. And the Congress may by general Laws prescribe the Manner in which such Acts, Records and Proceedings shall be proved, and the Effect thereof.

SECTION 2. The Citizens of each State shall be entitled to all Privileges and Immunities of Citizens in the several States.

A Person charged in any State with Treason, Felony, or other Crime, who shall flee from Justice, and be found in another State, shall on Demand of the executive Authority of the State from which he fled, be delivered up, to be removed to the State having Jurisdiction of the Crime.

No Person held to Service or Labour in one State, under the Laws thereof, escaping into another, shall, in Consequence of any Law or Regulation therein, be discharged from such Service or Labour, but shall be delivered up on Claim of the Party to whom such Service or Labour may be due.

SECTION 3. New States may be admitted by the Congress into this Union; but no new State shall be formed or erected within the Jurisdiction of any other State; nor any State be formed by the Junction of two or more States, or

Parts of States, without the Consent of the Legislatures of the States concerned as well as of the Congress.

The Congress shall have Power to dispose of and make all needful Rules and Regulations respecting the Territory or other Property belonging to the United States; and nothing in this Constitution shall be so construed as to Prejudice any Claims of the United States, or of any particular State.

SECTION 4. The United States shall guarantee to every State in this Union a Republican Form of Government, and shall protect each of them against Invasion; and on Application of the Legislature, or of the Executive (when the Legislature cannot be convened) against domestic Violence.

ARTICLE V

The Congress, whenever two thirds of both Houses shall deem it necessary, shall propose Amendments to this Constitution, or, on the Application of the Legislatures of two thirds of the several States, shall call a Convention for proposing Amendments, which, in either Case, shall be valid to all Intents and Purposes, as Part of this Constitution, when ratified by the Legislatures of three fourths of the several States, or by Conventions in three fourths thereof, as the one or the other Mode of Ratification may be proposed by the Congress; Provided [that no Amendment which may be made prior to the Year One thousand eight hundred and eight shall in any Manner affect the first and fourth Clauses in the Ninth Section of the first Article; and] that no State, without its Consent, shall be deprived of its equal Suffrage in the Senate.

ARTICLE VI

All Debts contracted and Engagements entered into, before the Adoption of this Constitution, shall be as valid against the United States under this Constitution, as under the Confederation.

This Constitution, and the Laws of the United States which shall be made in Pursuance thereof; and all Treaties made, or which shall be made, under the Authority of the United States, shall be the supreme Law of the Land; and the Judges in every State shall be bound thereby, any Thing in the Constitution or Laws of any State to the Contrary notwithstanding.

The Senators and Representatives before mentioned, and the Members of the several State Legislatures, and all executive and judicial Officers, both of the United States and of the several States, shall be bound by Oath or Affirmation, to support this Constitution; but no religious Test shall ever be required as a Qualification to any Office or public Trust under the United States.

ARTICLE VII

The Ratification of the Conventions of nine States, shall be sufficient for the Establishment of this Constitution between the States so ratifying the Same.

AMENDMENT I

[First ten amendments ratified December 15, 1791]

Congress shall make no law respecting an establishment of religion, or prohibiting the free exercise thereof; or abridging the freedom of speech, or of the press; or the right of the people peaceably to assemble, and to petition the Government for a redress of grievances.

AMENDMENT II

A well regulated Militia, being necessary to the security of a free State, the right of the people to keep and bear Arms, shall not be infringed.

AMENDMENT III

No Soldier shall, in time of peace be quartered in any house, without the consent of the Owner, nor in time of war, but in a manner to be prescribed by law.

AMENDMENT IV

The right of the people to be secure in their persons, houses, papers, and effects, against unreasonable searches and seizures, shall not be violated, and no Warrants shall issue, but upon probable cause, supported by Oath or affirmation, and particularly describing the place to be searched, and the persons or things to be seized.

AMENDMENT V

No person shall be held to answer for a capital, or otherwise infamous crime, unless on a presentment or indictment of a Grand Jury, except in cases arising in the land or naval forces, or in the Militia, when in actual service in time of War or public danger; nor shall any person be subject for the same offence to be twice put in jeopardy of life or limb; nor shall be compelled in any criminal case to be a witness against himself, nor be deprived of life, liberty, or property, without due process of law; nor shall private property be taken for public use, without just compensation.

AMENDMENT VI

In all criminal prosecutions, the accused shall enjoy the right to a speedy and public trial, by an impartial jury of the State and district wherein the crime shall have been committed, which district shall have been previously ascertained by law, and to be informed of the nature and cause of the accusation; to be confronted with the witnesses against him; to have compulsory process for obtaining witnesses in his favor, and to have the Assistance of Counsel for his defence.

AMENDMENT VII

In Suits at common law, where the value in controversy shall exceed twenty dollars, the right of trial by jury shall be preserved, and no fact tried by a jury, shall be otherwise re-examined in any Court of the United States, than according to the rules of the common law.

AMENDMENT VIII

Excessive bail shall not be required, nor excessive fines imposed, nor cruel and unusual punishments inflicted.

AMENDMENT IX

The enumeration in the Constitution, of certain rights, shall not be construed to deny or disparage others retained by the people.

AMENDMENT X

The powers not delegated to the United States by the Constitution, nor prohibited by it to the States, are reserved to the States respectively, or to the people.

AMENDMENT XI *[Ratified February 7, 1795]*

The Judicial power of the United States shall not be construed to extend to any suit in law or equity, commenced or prosecuted against one of the United States by Citizens of another State, or by Citizens or Subjects of any Foreign State.

AMENDMENT XII *[Ratified June 15, 1804]*

The Electors shall meet in their respective states and vote by ballot for President and Vice-President, one of whom, at least, shall not be an inhabitant of the same state with themselves; they shall name in their ballots the person voted for as President, and in distinct ballots the person voted for as Vice-President, and they shall make distinct lists of all persons voted for as President, and of all persons voted for as Vice-President, and of the number of votes for each, which lists they shall sign and certify, and transmit sealed to the seat of the government of the United States, directed to the President of the Senate;—The President of the Senate shall, in the presence of the Senate and House of Representatives, open all the certificates and the votes shall then be counted;—The person having the greatest number of votes for President, shall be the President, if such number be a majority of the whole number of Electors appointed; and if no person have such majority, then from the persons having the highest numbers not exceeding three on the list of those voted for as President, the House of Representatives shall choose immediately, by ballot, the President. But in choosing the President, the votes shall be taken by states, the representation from each state having one vote; a quorum for this purpose shall consist of a member or members from two-thirds of the states, and a majority of all the states shall be necessary to a choice. And if the House of Representatives shall not choose a President whenever the right of choice shall devolve upon them, before the fourth day of March next following, then the Vice-President shall act as President, as in the case of the death or other constitutional disability of the President;—The person having the greatest number of votes as Vice-President, shall be the Vice-President, if such number be a majority of the whole number of Electors appointed, and if no person have a majority, then from the two highest numbers on the list, the Senate shall choose the Vice-President; a quorum for the purpose shall consist of two-thirds of the whole number of Senators, and a majority of the whole number shall be necessary to a choice. But no person constitutionally ineligible to the office of President shall be eligible to that of Vice-President of the United States.

AMENDMENT XIII [Ratified December 6, 1865]

Section 1. Neither slavery nor involuntary servitude, except as a punishment for crime whereof the party shall have been duly convicted, shall exist within the United States, or any place subject to their jurisdiction.

Section 2. Congress shall have power to enforce this article by appropriate legislation.

AMENDMENT XIV [Ratified July 9, 1868]

Section 1. All persons born or naturalized in the United States and subject to the jurisdiction thereof, are citizens of the United States and of the State wherein they reside. No State shall make or enforce any law which shall abridge the privileges or immunities of citizens of the United States; nor shall any State deprive any person of life, liberty, or property, without due process of law; nor deny to any person within its jurisdiction the equal protection of the laws.

Section 2. Representatives shall be apportioned among the several States according to their respective numbers, counting the whole number of persons in each State, excluding Indians not taxed. But when the right to vote at any election for the choice of electors for President and Vice President of the United States, Representatives in Congress, the Executive and Judicial officers of a State, or the members of the Legislature thereof, is denied to any of the male inhabitants of such State, being twenty-one years of age, and citizens of the United States, or in any way abridged, except for participation in rebellion, or other crime, the basis of representation therein shall be reduced in the proportion which the number of such male citizens shall bear to the whole number of male citizens twenty-one years of age in such State.

Section 3. No person shall be a Senator or Representative in Congress, or elector of President and Vice President, or hold any office, civil or military, under the United States, or under any State, who, having previously taken an oath, as a member of Congress, or as an officer of the United States, or as a member of any State legislature, or as an executive or judicial officer of any State, to support the Constitution of the United States, shall have engaged in insurrection or rebellion against the same, or given aid or comfort to the enemies thereof. But Congress may by a vote of two-thirds of each House, remove such disability.

Section 4. The validity of the public debt of the United States, authorized by law, including debts incurred for payment of pensions and bounties for services in suppressing insurrection or rebellion, shall not be questioned. But neither the United States nor any State shall assume or pay any debt or obligation incurred in aid of insurrection or rebellion against the United States, or any claim for the loss or emancipation of any slave; but all such debts, obligations and claims shall be held illegal and void.

Section 5. The Congress shall have power to enforce, by appropriate legislation, the provisions of this article.

AMENDMENT XV [Ratified February 3, 1870]

Section 1. The right of citizens of the United States to vote shall not be denied or abridged by the United States or by any State on account of race, color, or previous condition of servitude.

Section 2. The Congress shall have power to enforce this article by appropriate legislation.

AMENDMENT XVI [Ratified February 3, 1913]

The Congress shall have power to lay and collect taxes on incomes, from whatever source derived, without apportionment among the several States, and without regard to any census or enumeration.

AMENDMENT XVII [Ratified April 8, 1913]

The Senate of the United States shall be composed of two Senators from each State, elected by the people thereof, for six years; and each Senator shall have one vote. The electors in each State shall have the qualifications requisite for electors of the most numerous branch of the State legislatures.

When vacancies happen in the representation of any State in the Senate, the executive authority of such State shall issue writs of election to fill such vacancies: *Provided,* That the legislature of any State may empower the executive thereof to make temporary appointments until the people fill the vacancies by election as the legislature may direct.

This amendment shall not be so construed as to affect the election or term of any Senator chosen before it becomes valid as part of the Constitution.

AMENDMENT XVIII [Ratified January 16, 1919]

SECTION 1. After one year from the ratification of this article the manufacture, sale, or transportation of intoxicating liquors within, the importation thereof into, or the exportation thereof from the United States and all territory subject to the jurisdiction thereof for beverage purposes is hereby prohibited.

SECTION 2. The Congress and the several States shall have concurrent power to enforce this article by appropriate legislation.

SECTION 3. This article shall be inoperative unless it shall have been ratified as an amendment to the Constitution by the legislatures of the several States, as provided in the Constitution, within seven years from the date of the submission hereof to the States by the Congress.

AMENDMENT XIX [Ratified August 18, 1920]

The right of citizens of the United States to vote shall not be denied or abridged by the United States or by any State on account of sex.

Congress shall have power to enforce this article by appropriate legislation.

AMENDMENT XX [Ratified January 23, 1933]

SECTION 1. The terms of the President and Vice President shall end at noon on the 20th day of January, and the terms of Senators and Representatives at noon on the 3d day of January, of the years in which such terms would have ended if this article had not been ratified; and the terms of their successors shall then begin.

SECTION 2. The Congress shall assemble at least once in every year, and such meeting shall begin at noon on the 3d day of January, unless they shall by law appoint a different day.

SECTION 3. If, at the time fixed for the beginning of the term of the President, the President elect shall have died, the Vice President elect shall become President. If a President shall not have been chosen before the time fixed for the beginning of his term, or if the President elect shall have failed to qualify, then the Vice President elect shall act as President until a President shall have qualified; and the Congress may by law provide for the case wherein neither a President elect nor a Vice President elect shall have qualified, declaring who shall then act as President, or the manner in which one who is to act shall be selected, and such person shall act accordingly until a President or Vice President shall have qualified.

SECTION 4. The Congress may by law provide for the case of the death of any of the persons from whom the House of Representatives may choose a President whenever the right of choice shall have devolved upon them, and for the case of the death of any of the persons from whom the Senate may choose a Vice President whenever the right of choice shall have devolved upon them.

SECTION 5. Sections 1 and 2 shall take effect on the 15th day of October following the ratification of this article.

SECTION 6. This article shall be inoperative unless it shall have been ratified as an amendment to the Constitution by the legislatures of three-fourths of the several States within seven years from the date of its submission.

AMENDMENT XXI *[Ratified December 5, 1933]*

SECTION 1. The eighteenth article of amendment to the Constitution of the United States is hereby repealed.

SECTION 2. The transportation or importation into any State, Territory or possession of the United States for delivery or use therein of intoxicating liquors, in violation of the laws thereof, is hereby prohibited.

SECTION 3. This article shall be inoperative unless it shall have been ratified as an amendment to the Constitution by conventions in the several States, as provided in the Constitution, within seven years from the date of the submission hereof to the States by the Congress.

AMENDMENT XXII *[Ratified February 27, 1951]*

SECTION 1. No person shall be elected to the office of the President more than twice, and no person who has held the office of President, or acted as President, for more than two years of a term to which some other person was elected President shall be elected to the office of the President more than once. But this Article shall not apply to any person holding the office of President when this Article was proposed by the Congress, and shall not prevent any person who may be holding the office of President, or acting as President, during the term within which this Article become operative from holding the office of President or acting as President during the remainder of such term.

SECTION 2. This Article shall be inoperative unless it shall have been ratified as an amendment to the Constitution by the legislatures of three-fourths of the several States within seven years from the date of its submission to the States by the Congress.

AMENDMENT XXIII *[Ratified March 29, 1961]*

SECTION 1. The District constituting the seat of Government of the United States shall appoint in such manner as the Congress may direct:

A number of electors of President and Vice President equal to the whole number of Senators and Representatives in Congress to which the District would be entitled if it were a State, but in no event more than the least populous State; they shall be in addition to those appointed by the States, but they shall be considered, for the purposes of the election of President and Vice President, to be electors appointed by a State; and they shall meet in the District and perform such duties as provided by the twelfth article of amendment.

SECTION 2. The Congress shall have power to enforce this article by appropriate legislation.

AMENDMENT XXIV *[Ratified January 23, 1964]*

SECTION 1. The right of citizens of the United States to vote in any primary or other election for President or Vice President, for electors for President or Vice President, or for Senator or Representative in Congress, shall not be denied or abridged by the United States or any State by reason of failure to pay any poll tax or other tax.

SECTION 2. The Congress shall have power to enforce this article by appropriate legislation.

AMENDMENT XXV *[Ratified February 10, 1967]*

SECTION 1. In case of the removal of the President from office or of his death or resignation, the Vice President shall become President.

SECTION 2. Whenever there is a vacancy in the office of the Vice President, the President shall nominate a Vice President who shall take office upon confirmation by a majority vote of both Houses of Congress.

SECTION 3. Whenever the President transmits to the President pro tempore of the Senate and the Speaker of the House of Representatives his written declaration that he is unable to discharge the powers and duties of his office, and until he transmits to them a written declaration to the contrary, such powers and duties shall be discharged by the Vice President as Acting President.

SECTION 4. Whenever the Vice President and a majority of either the principal officers of the executive departments or of such other body as Congress may by law provide, transmit to the President pro tempore of the Senate and the Speaker of the House of Representatives their written declaration that the President is unable to discharge the powers and duties of his office, the Vice President shall immediately assume the powers and duties of the office as Acting President.

Thereafter, when the President transmits to the President pro tempore of the Senate and the Speaker of the House of Representatives his written declaration that no inability exists, he shall resume the powers and duties of his office unless the Vice President and a majority of either the principal officers of the executive department or of such other body as Congress may by law provide, transmit within four days to the President pro tempore of the Senate and the Speaker of the House of Representatives their written declaration that the President is unable to discharge the powers and duties of his office. Thereupon Congress shall decide the issue, assembling within forty-eight hours for that purpose if not in session. If the Congress, within twenty-one days after receipt of the latter written declaration, or, if Congress is not in session, within twenty-one days after Congress is required to assemble, determines by two-thirds vote of both houses that the President is unable to discharge the powers and duties of his office, the Vice President shall continue to discharge the same as Acting President; otherwise, the President shall resume the powers and duties of his office.

AMENDMENT XXVI *[Ratified July 1, 1971]*

SECTION 1. The right of citizens of the United States, who are eighteen years of age or older, to vote shall not be denied or abridged by the United States or by any State on account of age.

SECTION 2. The Congress shall have power to enforce this article by appropriate legislation.